MY DARLING CLEMENTINE

'Enthusiastic reviews, by themselves, do not account for the fact that *My Darling Clementine* has been a runaway best-seller on two continents. The book's enormous popularity springs from the richness of the subject matter itself. Her dedication to her unpredictable husband through moments of heartbreak and exultation, her tact and wisdom in nurturing his genius, make this book one of the most memorable love stories of our time.'
READER'S DIGEST

'Mr. Fishman has put us in his debt by telling the world of this great lady and of her work for the world.'
Earl Attlee in the SUNDAY TIMES

'Clemmie and Winston—the mighty coalition. A fascinating biography. The book that spells success.'
DAILY EXPRESS

'A chirrupy, button-holing yet sometimes moving account of Lady Churchill's life with Sir Winston.'
OBSERVER

'A storehouse of anecdotes.'
EVENING STANDARD

'A fascinating story . . . intimate, human and often humorous . . . It is a love story deep and tender.'
BIRMINGHAM POST

'Here is history . . . No man, and certainly no woman whose heart has been stirred by Winston Churchill's oratory and deeds will want to miss this.'
SUNDAY EXPRESS

D1357468

MY DARLING CLEMENTINE

The Story of Lady Churchill

by

Jack Fishman

with an introduction by
Mrs. Eleanor Roosevelt

Revised and extended Centenary Year edition

A STAR BOOK
published by
W. H. ALLEN

A Star Book
Published in 1974
by W. H. Allen & Co. Ltd.
44, Hill Street, London, W1X 8LB

First published in Great Britain by
W. H. Allen Ltd. 1963

Copyright © 1963 by Jack Fishman

Printed in Great Britain by
Richard Clay (The Chaucer Press), Ltd., Bungay, Suffolk

ISBN 0 352 30019 1

For
LILIAN, MY WIFE
from whom I learnt to appreciate
how much any man owes to his wife

CONTENTS

AUTHOR'S PREFACE

> Marriage is the greatest earthly happiness when founded on complete sympathy:—DISRAELI

WINSTON CHURCHILL was the Statesman the whole world recognized. Clementine Churchill the diplomat few knew.

This book began on a bomb-site in the East End of London, during the Blitz days of 1940, when I was a newspaper reporter covering a tour by the Prime Minister and his wife, of bombed areas.

People who had lived through the night were cheering this man to whom they looked for leadership and hope. But it was the woman beside him—or, at least, one pace behind him—who held my attention. What kind of woman could share his life, could be his wife? The question remained unanswered a long time. I watched her on many occasions seated in the Distinguished Strangers' Gallery of the House of Commons when her husband held the floor of the Chamber below; I covered part of her own Blitz tour with Mrs. Eleanor Roosevelt.

Through the years, I constantly added notes and anecdotes to a file I kept at home marked 'Clementine'. I gathered stories and facts from people she met; people with whom she worked, and who worked for her; Ministers and their wives; Members of Parliament; relatives, friends—literally hundreds of people—known and unknown, whose paths had crossed hers. I went to many who had already written of Winston Churchill and asked them to view various events again from a different aspect—his wife's.

To persuade her to write her own story, or to write a book about her, was an ambition of mine since those early war days. Her husband is the most written about man of our times, but largely because she avoided the limelight, this was the first book ever to be written about her, and her place in the Winston Churchill legend.

It does not pretend to be her life story, and is in no sense a full biography, for to tell her story would occupy almost as many volumes as those written by her husband on his own incredible life.

Some years ago I initiated a proposal for her to write her autobiography. At first she was intrigued with the idea, then she decided to leave writing in the family to her husband and to her son Randolph.

At the time of this approach to her, I was acting on behalf of Kemsley Newspapers, of which I was an editorial executive. I even prepared a draft outline of the manner in which I thought her story could be told—based on the notes and anecdotes I had collected over the years.

The canvas of her life was so large that I suggested the story-telling be concentrated on revealing her point of view of a number of incidents in their lives. Because her life was so much bound up with his, I wanted to see historic moments through her eyes; wanted to record some of her share in them.

I decided to write this tribute to her based on my 'Clementine' file of some 600,000 words of notes. From these I chose approximately 200,000 to present the story of a unique marriage, and a woman married to the world's most unique man—a woman who could have basked in her own limelight, but chose to walk in his shadow.

The original edition of this book, published on her birthday in April 1963, closed in the year of their golden wedding. After his death, I revised and extended for the May 1966 edition. Now there is more to tell. Hitherto confidential documents and correspondence have become available, enabling me to add what could not be written before. I have been permitted to include for the first time, extracts from letters they wrote to each other when he was out of office and just a front-line soldier in France. I have also brought her story right up to date—to the centenary year of his birth.

Clementine Churchill played a bigger part in history than most realized. She had the right conception of woman's power. She knew that companionship and understanding are the strength and foundation of true marriage. She also knew that a woman's real influence is behind the scenes, and that this is especially true in the world of diplomacy and politics.

The wife of any man eminent in public affairs must, of necessity, be a somewhat shadowy figure, ever present, but never too much in the foreground. The ability to submerge her own vivid personality was one of Clementine Churchill's special talents. Whatever her personal achievements—and they were many—she contrived to remain, first and foremost, Winston Churchill's wife. She never tried to be anything else.

To make her marriage a success she had to be armed with infinite patience, for she had to live with a husband who at one could be a roaring lion, at another a lively fox terrier, and again, a brooding teddy-bear.

My sincere appreciation is due to those who helped, co-operated, and advised, and in particular to Baroness Spencer-Churchill's cousin, the Hon. Mrs. Sylvia Henley, for guiding me on a number of points in the first chapter; to the Dowager Lady Hillingdon; General Lord Ismay; Lady Limerick of the British Red Cross Society; Mrs. Doris Moss, Chairman of the Woodford Conservative Association; Gerald O'Brien of the Conservative and Unionist Central Office for giving me access to their files; Sir Tom O'Brien; General Sir Frederick Pile; the Dowager Marchioness of Reading; Walter H. Thompson, formerly Detective Inspector of Scotland Yard and Mrs. Thompson, who was a war-time secretary to both Mr. and Mrs. Churchill; Miss Ruth Walder, National General Secretary of the Y.W.C.A.; and Colonel Barlow Wheeler, Sir Winston's constituency agent.

Acknowledgement and thanks are also due to General H. H. Arnold; the Asquith family; Constance Babington Smith; the Earl of Birkenhead; Lord Beaverbrook; Bernard M. Baruch; Sarah Churchill; John Spencer Churchill; Sir Winston Churchill; General Mark Clark; John Colville; Lady Diana Cooper; General Dwight D. Eisenhower; Milton Gendel; General Sir Leslie Hollis; Lieutenant-General Sir Brian Horrocks; H. Montgomery Hyde; Major-General Sir John Kennedy; Field-Marshal Viscount Montgomery of Alamein; Elizabeth Nel; Vic Oliver; Mackenzie King; Elliot Roosevelt; Samuel I. Rosenman; Robert E. Sherwood; Dame Margot Fonteyn; Michael Wardell; Sir David Llewellyn; Sir Robert Menzies.

I have drawn on innumerable documents, diaries, and memoirs, and my indebtedness to many of these is recorded in the Bibliography.

I am also grateful to the Y.W.C.A. and the British Red

Cross Society for allowing me to use extracts from their reports and files, and for permission to quote from some of Baroness Spencer-Churchill's correspondence.

Finally, I wish to record my deepest debt of gratitude to another unique woman who assisted and advised me—the late Mrs. Eleanor Roosevelt. She was the only person I ever hoped would contribute the prologue to this book. I am glad she was able to help me tell some of the Clementine Churchill story.

JACK FISHMAN

INTRODUCTION

by Mrs. Eleanor Roosevelt

LADY CHURCHILL has always had a very keen sense of the responsibility she carried. Her husband was Prime Minister at a most crucial time in England and she knew that in the first place she must make life as easy as she could for him at home with as much attention to detail as possible, to ensure that his life would be comfortable and lightened of any burdens she could remove.

In those days we understood and admired the kind of courage and tenacity her husband was beginning to put into words that expressed the spirit of the people in Britain after Dunkirk.

My husband thought Mr. Churchill typical of John Bull, and considered him to be a man with whom he really could work. The bond between them strengthened every time they met. Their friendship grew with their respect for each other's ability.

Mrs. Churchill, as she then was, had to endure many anxieties. She had, of course, long periods of anxiety during the war when he was away; then, when she did accompany him, she had her own duties.

I remember when she was in Quebec with the Prime Minister on one occasion, and I was there with my husband. My husband and Mr. Churchill were meeting over certain questions that had to be decided, and I remember Mrs. Churchill had to do a great many things which were her responsibility and not in any way connected with his work, except that they were things people appreciated and liked her doing because they brought them closer to both her and her husband. Everything she did, whether it was addressing meetings or making a broadcast, she did remarkably well.

She was more or less propelled into public life, as I was. When this happens, you learn to develop ideas of your own as well as developing the initiative and ability to act on them.

In many cases the need for doing things will in itself develop an ability to do them. You might not have this ability naturally, but it comes because you have to do it. This is a capability that may be in any woman, although it might lie dormant for ever if you didn't have to bring it out to meet special situations. It is, I suppose, like a man who doesn't know his own courage or his own strength.

A woman, no matter what she may have in her, can fall by the wayside and fail unless she carries responsibility and is aware of her responsibility. As far as I was concerned, it was much easier than it must have been for Mrs. Churchill.

The wife of the President of the United States can, to a large extent, do whatever she wishes, really. There are certain duties—you must be a hostess—but outside of that you make your own life. But I don't think this is true of a woman in England who is married to a prominent political figure. She almost automatically must take part in the political work of her husband. She really hasn't got the separate life that a First Lady can have in the White House. Perhaps, because of this, her sacrifice is, in certain respects, all the greater, because she is willing to make the sacrifice.

But Mrs. Churchill would never have married her husband unless she was prepared to make this sacrifice and unless she really enjoyed the responsibilities demanded of her, because she would have certainly known beforehand what marrying him might entail.

As for realizing that it could also entail abuse, discredit, and almost political ruin, I think you get accustomed to that. You don't really care much about that, except as it affects the ability of your husband to do whatever his work may be. You develop a sort of philosophical point of view that, after all, these things have to be settled by history; they can't be settled by you. Therefore, you just forget about them.

As my husband used to say: 'Nobody should go into politics unless they have a hide like a rhinoceros.' Perhaps they have to pass along a little of that to their wives.

A wife must have tremendous belief in her husband to bear this kind of thing because criticism comes to anyone who lives his or her life more or less in the public eye. Much of the criticism may be unfair, but you come to accept it as one of the hazards.

Mrs. Churchill was, I am sure, able to face all the trials she had to face because she achieved an inner calm that enabled her to withstand the strain. This inner calm gave her added strength.

Self-discipline of this kind is absolutely essential. It is essential in a life in which you are liable to be constantly meeting defeats and recovering from disasters. You can face whatever has to be faced if you master your own fears and simply go on.

Mrs. Churchill has always been the perfect partner for her husband. As far as she was concerned, whatever trials had to be faced, she faced, and whatever duties were expected of her, she did.

One cannot live in a political atmosphere without absorbing some of it. You learn to appreciate what is important to your husband; you learn to appreciate many things. You find that good timing is always essential, and you consequently have to choose to say things at what you consider to be the right moment, even though the reaction to what you have to say may be unfavourable and uncomfortable at first.

Lady Churchill has always been very much an individual in her own right. It is a brave thing to have the courage to be an individual. It is also often a lonely thing. But it is better than not being an individual, which is to be nobody at all.

She certainly did not agree with her husband on every issue. Two people must differ at times, on method if not on principle. But whatever differences she might have had with her husband on political matters, she would never air any such differences in public.

My husband never asked me to refrain from speaking my own mind on any issue, and I am sure it has always been the same with Sir Winston and his wife.

A man and woman who are both anxious to discover the truth in a political situation may, through study and argument, influence each other, but the ultimate decision must always remain with the individual.

Some people say that a wife can ruin a husband if she does not give him stability in the home. It would of course be very hard to ruin a man of the stature of Winston Churchill, very hard. But you could make it more difficult for him to do his work; there is no question about that.

His wife organized her time to first and foremost suit his needs. This planning of time—although never so rigid as to be inflexible—must have contributed greatly to the smooth running of his home and daily life. But then meeting the needs of others is what makes life worth living—especially, perhaps, for a woman.

A man may have to turn at times to someone in moments of great emotional stress. If he turns to his wife, and she happens to be the wrong wife for him, she would not be a constructive force in his life—she could, in fact, be destructive. On the other hand, the right wife can give a man something that helps him, and makes his life.

Mind you, I think my husband would have led his life and done the same things exactly whether I had been there or not. I made it easier. I took certain things off his shoulders, but he would have done it just the same. And I think Sir Winston would have, but life can be made easier and pleasanter, and that is important. A home can be made a haven—or a hell. That happens.

But Lady Churchill is warm, unselfish, full of understanding and real human sympathy, and a very delightful person.

A wonderful person, she always gives the impression of being so welcoming to everybody and so happy to be with any of her husband's friends and any of the people who came to meet him. She carries her responsibilities in a very extraordinary way.

She has always made the effort to establish an understanding relationship with people in any and every walk of life.

Her capacity to entertain and meet the great and the simple, the distinguished and the unknown with equal charm, graciousness, and hospitality, made a tremendous contribution to her husband's success.

Whenever we were together we never seemed to have enough time, there were always things to be done, and we went and did them.

The deep and obviously sincere affection which both of them had for my husband and I, we reciprocated. I think the war would have been harder to win without the friendship of our two husbands.

16

When Mr. Churchill was not re-elected after the war, it was a great shock, both to him and his wife, as well as to us all. I thought he would be elected at this time. I know he didn't expect defeat. He had repeatedly said that he would like to stay in office until the men had come back and been rehoused and restarted again. I know my husband felt that Mr. Churchill would be elected the first time, although he did not expect him to be elected more than once after the war. At least I don't think he went beyond that.

My husband often said he felt sure Mr. Churchill would retire from office after the war, but definitely expected him to have his say about the policies to be laid down for the future.

When he was voted out of office, I think to most of us in the United States, and to me personally, it seemed a rather cruel thing to have done, but we didn't try to contact them at that moment—somehow you don't feel that either a man or a woman want to be sympathized with in a situation of that kind. You just accept what the people have done and that's all there is to it. You just accept it, that's all. It's part of the life of a political person. Sometimes he loses, even though his defeat may seem like ingratitude, but ingratitude is exactly what a person in public life very often does get.

Lady Churchill undoubtedly fulfilled, I think in a very ideal way, all the things that a man in public office could possibly ask or want. She built the right kind of atmosphere around him—an atmosphere that enabled him to work at his best.

A man in public office must be sure his wife and family are ready to accept a mode of life which is unlike any other.

I sometimes wonder whether people realize the price the wife and family of a man in public life have to pay.

In my own autobiography I said that there was little or no personal compensation for the members of the family of such a man. There is, of course, pride in the man's achievement and gratitude if he is able to help his countrymen and the world.

Love is usually selfish; but when sufficiently disciplined, a family may be glad that a man has the opportunity to fulfil his heart's desire, and they will work with him in every way they can to help him achieve his objectives. But something of the personal relationship must be lost.

17

It is the price paid for a life spent almost entirely in public service.

Mr. John Winant, who was, during the war, the United States Ambassador in London, once wrote to my husband that he hoped some future historian would recognize and record Mrs. Churchill's service to Britain. I am therefore glad to have been able to assist with this book by telling anything I know, and I am delighted that such a tribute to this great woman has been written at last.

As I saw more of Mrs. Churchill over the years, my admiration and affection for her grew. She has had no easy role to play in life, but she has played it with dignity and charm.

Eleanor Roosevelt

1

YOUNG MAN IN A HURRY

'MISS CLEMENTINE HOZIER—Mr. Winston Churchill.'

It was as simple as that—the beginning of their love story, their historic marriage partnership.

The introduction took place at a dinner party at the London home of Clementine's great-aunt, Lady St. Helier, in the spring of 1908.

Winston, one of the most eligible bachelors in Britain—hated, loved, unpredictable, tempestuous—hadn't given marriage a thought; he was too busy with his political career and was already feeling his strength, saying:

'Sometimes I think I could carry the world on my shoulders.'

And he was already President of the Board of Trade, and a member of the Cabinet.

Miss Clementine Hozier, aged twenty-three, came from an aristocratic family, but she was poor. She was one of the four children of ex-cavalry officer Colonel Sir Henry Hozier, who became a Secretary of Lloyds. Sir Henry was twenty-five years older than his wife. The marriage broke up, and Blanche Hozier, daughter of the fifth Earl of Airlie (tenth but for the attainder), was left to care for their children Kitty, Clementine, Nelly, and her twin brother Bill, on a modest allowance from her mother Blanche, Countess of Airlie.

The Hozier children had a tough childhood with a nurse who spurred them to housework with a cut of the cane on their bare legs. Apart from occasional visits to Cortachy Castle, the Forfarshire home of the Airlies, Lady Blanche and her children lived in lodgings in London and Seaford.

Blanche Hozier struggled to keep up appearances on her very limited income. Clementine helped finances by teaching French privately. The family moved to France when she was thirteen, and there she learned her excellent French during the years they resided inexpensively in the obscurity of Dieppe. It was in Dieppe that her eldest sister, Kitty, died of typhoid at the age of seventeen.

The family returned to England and to the small house at Berkhamsted in which they had lived before. In April 1900, when Clementine was fifteen, her mother enrolled her at the Berkhamsted School for Girls. In answer to the application form query 'Has she been a pupil at a school before, and if so, where?' Blanche Hozier wrote:

'For three months at the Convent Les Soeurs de la Providence of Rouen, at Dieppe.'

Said one of her school colleagues: 'Clementine Hozier and her sister used to show us how to play cricket when we were in the first form.'

Clementine, with her already excellent mastery of French, became Mademoiselle Kroon's star pupil. Mlle. Kroon was, of course, the school's French mistress, and her humour, her great love of flowers, and her sparkling personality, had a deep influence on Clementine. She, and her classmates, remembered the Mademoiselle's lessons with vividness—it was no use thinking of other things, they recalled. If the mind wandered in the slightest degree one would hear: 'Now, you fat bolster, wake up and translate the next passage.' Sometimes a pupil was 'pudding' or 'boiled owl'. Clementine loved Mlle. Kroon, and did her proud by winning a silver medal for French.

The Hoziers moved back to London to live in a little rented house at 51 Abingdon Villas, Kensington. Clementine shared a room with her sister and supplemented her dress allowance of £30 a year with the money she continued to earn from giving lessons.

She came out at a ball given by Lady Stanley of Alderley for her daughter Sylvia, who was Clementine's cousin.

Intelligent, independent, liberal-minded like her grandmother, the Dowager Countess of Airlie, and passionately interested in politics, she was a lovely girl who had no intention of conforming to the accepted customs of the times of being 'suitably married off'. *She* was going to do the choosing.

It was her great-aunt, Lady St. Helier, known in those days as 'Lady Santa Claus' because of her kind heart and reputation for never refusing to help anyone—tall, gracious, Lady St. Helier—the finest hostess in society, who was giving the party at her London home at 52 Portland Place, the night that Winston Churchill met Clementine Hozier.

'Lady Santa Claus' had herself been left £250,000 by her famous husband who had been a Judge of the Probate and Divorce Court. In her role as a fairy godmother, she had taken a small house in the slums of Shoreditch from which she could work to help the poor. She was elected to the London County Council, and the L.C.C. suburb of St. Helier perpetuates her name. She was to play fairy godmother to the young Churchill and her great-niece.

While independent Clementine had been saying 'No' to many of London's eligible bachelors, Winston had been successfully fighting a defensive action against society mothers with matrimonially inclined daughters.

A girl of placid features, and steady, clear, grey eyes, Clementine looked radiantly lovely that night in her white satin princess dress. The dress had been a gift from her grandmother.

The society magazine *The Bystander* described Clementine in a 1908 issue as having 'Lovely brown hair and most delicately aquiline features, fine grey eyes, and a delightful poise of the head. Her shoulders and neck have something of the grace and distinction and soft strength of early Grecian art; she is divinely tall.'

Also speaking of the reigning beauties of the era, Lady Cynthia Asquith described her as:

'Classical, statuesque; yet full of animation. A queen she should have been; her superbly sculptured features would have looked so splendid on a coin. "There's a face that will last", said everyone. How right they were!'

Winston arrived at the dinner party late, as usual. For more than six society seasons he had been the matchmaking mama's despair. Not that he was oblivious of the charms of beautiful young ladies; he was just too busy. 'You see,' he would explain, 'we Churchills are apt to damp off after forty.'

It must have been Fate that sent young Winston, who disliked social functions, to that party.

Eyes turned to watch his entrance, not that he was a handsome figure of a man—he wasn't. But the atmosphere of his personality, his very presence was electric. His blazing red hair, and his equally blazing blue eyes, compelled attention.

His head was crowned by wisps of ginger hair that protruded sideways. Even in those days his face was thrust forward as if to defy enemies, and his lips pouted. Although young, he already walked with a slight stoop and would pace the room with restless explosive energy, talking all the time.

Everyone in the room knew of the young Mr. Churchill. Born at Blenheim Palace, he had crossed the floor of the House of Commons in 1905 to join the Liberals and win his first Ministerial post as Under-Secretary for the Colonies.

To the Tories he was a renegade and a traitor. He had achieved fantastic political success at an incredibly early age. Even his father, who was considered precociously successful in Parliament, did not attain a Ministerial post until he was thirty-six.

But Winston was a young man in a hurry.

'Some men change their party for the sake of their principles; others their principles for the sake of their party,' he said in answer to his critics.

Winston had little time for women, but they were eagerly willing to devote plenty of time to him for not only was he a target of the husband hunters, but he was also a target of the Suffragettes. Suffragettes just wouldn't leave him alone and seemed to make a particular bee-line for the bachelor Cabinet Minister, continually barracking and attacking him at meetings.

'Get away, woman!' he once roared at one young Suffragette in Dundee who followed him about constantly ringing a deafening dinner-bell.

'It's no use your being cross,' she replied, and went right on ringing the bell as close to Winston as possible.

Added Winston: 'I won't attempt to compete with a young and pretty lady in a high state of excitement.'

Suffragettes bombarded him with rotten fruit, eggs, coal, and stones. One of them slashed at him with a riding whip which he managed to take away from her.

And then what did he do? He fell in love with a girl who was a Suffragette at heart and passionately believed in 'Votes for Women'.

Winston and his friend Edward Marsh had devised a pastime for soirées. They would often stand together within sight of the ballroom entrance, watching the ladies arrive, and, using the classic line 'Was this the face that launched a thousand ships?' as their theme, would assess the beauty of each young thing as she appeared.

'Two hundred ships, or perhaps two-hundred-and-fifty?' one of them might hazard, studying the latest piece of feminity to grace the scene.

'By no means,' the other might reply—'A sampan, or small gun-boat at most. . . .'

They unanimously agreed that among the rare few worthy of the full thousand score were Lady Diana Manners, and Miss Clementine Hozier.

It was love at second sight for Winston. They had met only once before. Now, talking to her at Lady St. Helier's, he recognized in the vivacious girl ten years his junior, a spirit equal to his own. He admired her gaiety, her conversation, her independence—so he continued to listen.

Said her Aunt Mabell, Countess of Airlie: 'I think that subconsciously I had expected Clementine to make a romantic marriage. She was a lovely girl; I always kept in mind the picture of her one evening when she was staying with us at Cortachy [Cortachy Castle] and came down to dinner in a white satin dress which she had made herself. It was very simply cut, and her only jewellery was a little string of pearls, but her beauty needed no adornment. She looked like a lily.

'After that I did not see her for a year or more. I heard that she had many admirers, but her own heart was not touched.'

When it came to the opposite sex, Winston and Clementine were both hard to please.

There was only one other woman who might have become Mrs. Churchill had she given Winston half the chance. In his youth he had a 'crush' on actress Ethel Barrymore, who was then the toast of London.

'I sent a note to Winston asking him to send me a ticket for the gallery at the House of Commons. He sent one by his secretary, Sir Edward Marsh, and he and Winston and I had tea together in Winston's rooms,' recalled Miss Barrymore.

Enchanted by her beauty and dignity, he sent her almost nonstop gifts of flowers, and went almost every night to Claridge's Hotel for supper, knowing she always went there too after her performance at the theatre. But he was just one of her army of hopeful admirers and didn't get very far.

Years later when Winston was passing through Washington and she was appearing in one of the city's theatres, she received a box of flowers from him accompanied by a note reminding her how much he had always admired her.

Strangely, Clementine had much in common with Ethel Barrymore's looks and character, and they met in later years from time to time.

Visiting New York, when he was twenty-six years old, Winston 'met everybody, but would sit in the midst of the most delightful people absorbed in his own thoughts. He would not admire the women he was expected to admire,' so said the noted Mr. George Smalley, describing the visit.

Continued Mr. Smalley: 'They must have not only beauty and intelligence, but the particular kind of beauty and intelligence which appealed to him; if otherwise, he knew how to be silent without meaning to be rude ... it was useless to remonstrate with him. He answered: "She is beautiful to you, but not to me."'

With Clementine it was different. It was very difficult in those days for girls to find work, yet somehow she managed to keep bolstering the family's housekeeping money with her French lessons, as well as reading to an elderly lady for so much an hour. Winston respected her for it.

He also admired her all the more because, although he loved flattery and revelled in success, here was a girl who didn't simper, didn't pander to him.

For the first time in his life, after the ladies—in accordance with custom—had withdrawn from the dinner table, friends observed that Winston was plainly anxious to leave the port-and-men-only conversations on topics of the times, to rejoin the ladies as speedily as possible.

Years later, asked whether at that first meeting she considered Winston handsome, Clementine answered tactfully:

'I thought he was very interesting.'

At the same party an admiral was also attracted to the beautiful Miss Hozier; Winston counter-attacked by sidetracking the admiral and out-manoeuvring him.

There were other campaigns on Winston's mind at the

time—he was busy preparing for a by-election at Dundee, but once he had decided that this was the girl for him, he lost no time. He became a regular caller at the Hoziers' Kensington home, courting Clementine, and he made sure everyone knew it.

Lady Blanche Hozier was impressed with the eloquent young man who was so nervous in her presence and yet so distinguished a politician with a reputation as a firebrand. His mother-in-law-to-be knew Winston much better than he realized. She had known his mother for many years, and was aware that Lord Randolph Churchill had fallen madly in love at first sight with the dark, lovely, intelligent American, Jennie Jerome; Lord Randolph courted, won, and married Jennie against the wishes of both his and her parents. Lady Blanche recognized the tremendous influence of Jennie Jerome on Winston's life.

'My mother,' he wrote in later years, 'made a brilliant impression upon my childhood's life. She shone for me like the evening star, I loved her dearly but at a distance. She always seemed to me a fairy princess.'

Those who knew Winston said he owed a lot to his American grandfather, Colonel Jerome, who in his seventies went to a circus and got so annoyed at the boasting of the professional strong man that he accepted a challenge to wrestle. The colonel threw his man all right, but strained his inside doing it and subsequently died from the effects.

Whirlwind courtships ran in the Churchill family. Winston's father boasted that when he met nineteen-year-old Jennie Jerome, he proposed and was accepted all in three days.

Of their courtship, Clementine said: 'He was of a temper that gallops till it falls.'

Lady Blanche saw that Winston was also an incurable romantic and that the woman in his life could make or break it.

Knowing her daughter, she recognized that, although a natural rebel, her disciplined modesty, her discretion, her gift of devotion, plus sense of duty, would make her the right woman for Winston.

Lady Blanche was certain that in spite of Clementine possessing a distinct personality of her own, her sense of dignity would never allow her temperament to create domestic turmoil that would intrude into her husband's public or private life.

Even in those days, when Winston wanted something, he usually got it, and he wanted Clementine.

He asked his cousin, the Duke of Marlborough, to invite Blanche Hozier and her daughter Clementine to Blenheim Palace.

'A female friend, amiable, clever, and devoted, is a possession more valuable than parks or palaces; and without such a Muse few men can succeed, and none can be happy.'

Those were the words of Benjamin Disraeli, and young Winston Churchill was certain that his success and happiness were bound up with Clementine Hozier.

One day in August he strolled with Clementine from the front entrance of historic Blenheim Palace, where he had been born, towards Diana's temple—the stone pavilion set among the yew trees by the lake he loved so much.

Within the temple a bas-relief shows Hippolytus offering a wreath of flowers to Diana. The first line of the inscription, which is in Greek and English, reads:

'To thee bright Goddess, these flowers I bring....'

It was there he proposed and she accepted.

Said Clementine: 'Now I have got you, the trouble will be to keep you.'

To which Winston replied: 'You will find that no trouble at all, my dear.'

His mother, who had known Clementine from a baby, was delighted with the match. Her son was affectionate, emotional, home-loving. She was sure Clementine was the wife he needed.

An excited Blanche Hozier wrote to a friend from Blenheim Palace with the news of the engagement, saying:

'Clementine is to marry Winston Churchill. Yesterday he came to London to ask my consent, and we all three came on here. He is so like Lord Randolph, he has some of his faults, and all his qualities.

'He is gentle and tender, and affectionate to those he loves, much hated by those who have not come under his personal charm.'

Her mother also wrote to her sister-in-law:

'I do not know which of the two is the more in love. I think that to know him is to like him. His brilliant brain the world knows, but he is so charming and affectionate in his own home life.'

A few days later Clementine, answering her Aunt Mabell's letter of congratulations, wrote:

Dearest Aunt Mabell,
Thank you very much for your letter. It gave me a great deal of pleasure.
I cannot describe my happiness to you. I can hardly believe it is true. I have been engaged nine days now. I cared very much for him when he asked me to marry him, but every day since has been more heavenly. The only crumpled rose-leaf is the scrimmage getting ready in time. September 12th has now been settled for our wedding. We shall have only seventeen days away as Winston has to be back in London on October 3rd.

Said Clementine's Aunt Mabell:
'My mother-in-law had the final word....
'"Winston is his father over again, with the American driving force added," she wrote in a letter to me. "His mother and he are devoted to one another, and I think a good son makes a good husband. Clementine is wise. She will follow him and, I hope, say little."'

Clementine certainly did follow Winston loyally and devotedly, but not in the role of a meek, mild, submissive wife, with opinions she was afraid to voice.

When society heard of the engagement, sceptics said it would never work. 'No one can live with Winston Churchill without upheavals,' they predicted.

'Clementine is a girl who likes her own way, and Winston will never give in to anyone,' they added.

To which Clementine replied: 'Being married to him couldn't be easy, but I think it would be tremendously stimulating.'

Clementine found her mother-in-law-to-be an incredible, delightful compound of worldliness and eternal childhood. She was loyal, warm-hearted, witty, sincere, and courageously pugnacious. Clementine saw in Lady Randolph the pattern of the kind of woman she herself became. In many ways she was to become like a mother to Winston, and he could see his mother in her.

27

The Hoziers' modest Kensington home was a little too modest for the kind of wedding reception expected of a Churchill, so once again 'Lady Santa Claus'—Lady St. Helier—stepped into the picture.

Clementine and her mother were invited to move into the St. Helier home in Portland Place on 8 September—four days before the wedding. This was to be the home from which she would leave to be married in St. Margaret's, Westminster.

There had already been one wedding in the family a few weeks earlier when Winston's cavalry officer brother Jack had married Lady Gwendeline Bertie, who became the mother of Clarissa—later to become the wife of Lord Avon —Anthony Eden.

Winston held a stag dinner at his house in Bolton Street. Guests included the Chancellor of the Exchequer, Mr. Lloyd George, and the Bishop of St. Asaph.

Clementine also entertained a small party of close friends to tea at 52 Portland Place, and in the evening dined with her mother, Lady St. Helier, and other relatives and friends.

But even as some of the guests departed from the two parties, they were saying 'It will never work out.' They were echoing the talk of London society.

Lord Rosebery forecast: 'The union will last about six months, with luck,' and concluded: 'their marriage will fail because Winston is not the marrying kind.'

Know-alls said: 'He hasn't any money, and neither has she,' and in society, in those days, it was the accepted 'thing' to marry for money.

They reckoned without the wisdom, self-restraint, and modesty of Clementine, and they reckoned without her masterly discretion which always watched, guided, and even, on occasions, restrained her turbulent versatile husband.

'Something Old' was supplied by Winston's mother—lace to trim the bride's cuffs and neckline. The bridal gown was ready, so were the dresses of the five bridesmaids. London was excited at the prospect of the occasion—it was to be one of the most brilliant weddings of the year.

Now that he had found his Clementine, Winston couldn't wait. A month after he proposed, they married. It was like a royal wedding. Extra mounted as well as foot police were there to control the crowds of thousands spread from St. Margaret's to Whitehall and Parliament Square. It was a Saturday, and half London seemed to have turned up to cheer. People had waited hours all along the miles of wedding route. At twenty minutes to two, Winston with his best man, Lord Hugh Cecil, arrived at the church, having left Bolton Street at half past one, and driven by way of Piccadilly and Whitehall. As they stepped from their motor-car to enter the church, the crowd gave a welcoming roar. A smiling Winston walked into the body of the church from the vestry, bowed to relatives seated in the front pew, then leaned over and shook hands with the Duchess of Marlborough.

At two minutes past two Winston looked at his watch. The bride was late. So was Mr. Lloyd George, who arrived at this moment and took the seat next to the best man. Winston, Lord Hugh Cecil, and Mr. Lloyd George were the only occupants of the front bench.

Lady Blanche Hozier, dressed in purple, her hair decorated with some soft, white material, and the wrists of her gown trimmed with white fur, drove in a brougham with Clementine and her twenty-year-old brother William, a Royal Naval lieutenant, from Portland Place to arrive at four minutes past two.

Sixteen hundred guests were waiting at the church. The packed congregation included most of the eminent personalities of the day. Mr. Joynson-Hicks, M.P., and his wife were among the first to arrive. 'Jix', as he was later known when he was the Home Secretary, had only recently beaten Winston in a Manchester by-election. Others present included the Duke of Marlborough, the Marchioness of Blandford, the Duke and Duchess of Sutherland, Mrs. Beerbohm Tree, and many Members of Parliament.

The bride, when she entered, took the congregation's breath away. Sparkling, yet serene. She walked down the aisle on her brother's arm, the organ boomed, and many stood on the pews to get an extra good look at her.

The church was decorated with palms and chrysanthemums and arum lilies. The chancel and altar were wrapped in white flowers, chrysanthemums and camellias in a setting of green. The bride, a picture of white in her satin princess gown and veil of Brussels net, carried a bouquet of

29

white lilies and myrtle and a prayer book bound in white kid.

On her head was a simple coronet of orange blossoms.

Nelly, the bride's sister, led the bridesmaids. With her was the Hon. Venetia Stanley, daughter of Lady Stanley of Alderley, cousin of the bride; Miss Clare Frewen (later Clare Sheridan, distinguished author and sculptor), cousin of the bridegroom; Miss Horatia Seymour, daughter of the late Sir Horace Seymour; and Miss Madeline Whyte, daughter of Lady Whyte, cousin of the bride. Winston had given each of the bridesmaids a necklace of platinum with pendants of diamonds and a sapphire.

The bride's only jewellery was a pair of diamond ear-rings—a gift from the groom.

The organist finished the Wagnerian wedding music, the choir sang the hymn 'Lead us, Heavenly Father', and the bride's procession moved to the chancel.

Some weeks earlier Winston had had a political dispute with the Bishop of St. Asaph over education, but the Bishop was nevertheless at St. Margaret's to conduct the marriage service. The headmaster of Harrow in the days when young Churchill was one of the school's worst scholars, Bishop Welldon, at that time Dean of Manchester, was present to give the address to his former pupil.

The clergy came down to the chancel and, as his bride approached, Winston put out his hand and shook hers warmly.

The ceremony began.

In his address Bishop Welldon uttered prophetic words: 'The sun shines on your union today.

'Allow me to remind you how much you may be to each other in the coming days, in the sunny hours and in the sombre hours.

'There must be in a statesman's life many times when he depends on the love, insight, penetrating sympathy, and devotion of his wife.

'The influence which the wives of our statesmen have exercised for good on their husbands' lives is an unwritten chapter of English history too sacred perhaps to be written in full.

'May your lives prove a blessing, each to the other, and both to the world.'

They were wed, and the signing of the register was witnessed by 'Jennie Cornwallis West', Winston's mother, 'D. Lloyd George', and William Hozier. The groom signed himself as Winston Leonard Spencer Churchill. His father was described on the register as 'Sometime Secretary for India, Chancellor of Exchequer'.

Commented Lady Blanche Hozier's poet friend, Wilfrid Blunt: 'It is a good marriage for both of them, for Clementine is pretty, clever and altogether charming, while Winston is what the world knows him, and a good fellow to boot.'

Of the wedding he said: 'It was quite a popular demonstration. Lord Hugh Cecil, Winston's best man, and the great crowd of relations, not only the church full, but all Victoria Street, though that may have partly been for the Eucharistic Congress.... At St. Margaret's I arrived late when all the seats were taken, but Blanche Hozier found me one in the family pew.

'The bride was pale, as was the bridegroom. He has gained in appearance since I saw him last, and has a powerful if ugly face.

'Winston's responses were clearly made in a pleasant voice, Clementine's inaudible.'

First to congratulate Mr. and Mrs. Winston Churchill was the Chancellor of the Exchequer, Lord Redesdale, his mother, and the Dowager Countess of Airlie, who were among those present in the vestry.

Even the Suffragettes, who had fought and barracked Winston all over the country, called a truce for the wedding day, although in case of any demonstrations, plain-clothes police officers occupied seats in various parts of St. Margaret's during the ceremony. They had received warnings that several militant Suffragettes intended to interrupt the service.

The Suffragettes were there all right—cheering with the rest of the crowds.

As the bride and groom left the church, the police couldn't hold back the crowd's enthusiasm and hundreds broke through, surrounding the motor-car to get a clearer view.

Winston and Clementine bowed and waved to the six-deep throngs on the pavements along their return route up Whitehall and Regent Street to Lady St. Helier's where the reception was to be held.

'Good old Winnie!' delighted thousands shouted, and many ran alongside the car to wave personal greetings.

Recalling the day Clare Sheridan said: 'The outstanding thing I remember is the crowd lining the streets from St. Margaret's to the reception in Portland Place. It was as deep as it would have been for the King and Queen.

'As we drove past, they shouted "good old Winnie!" and "God bless Winnie!"

'Clementine looked absolutely radiant, with a wonderful smile. She looked so beautiful that people were stunned. Winston looked very handsome too.

'We bridesmaids wore amber satin dresses and carried cream roses. We also wore large hats of stretched black satin with a row of waxen white camellias.'

And Clare Sheridan's brother, Oswald Frewen, wrote in his diary:

'Got a pew pretty near the front and despite a large pillar saw the ceremony pretty well. Afterwards went to 52 Portland Place and attended the extremely crowded reception.... At Clare's suggestion we strewed the petals of the roses from the bridesmaids' bouquets over the Bride and Bridegroom and their path instead of the usual rice....'

At 52 Portland Place champagne flowed, guests gossiped, presents lined the tables, Dukes and Duchesses were there in their dozens as well as Counts and Countesses, Lords and Ladies, the even more famous plain 'Misters' such as Mr. Austen Chamberlain, Mr. Balfour, Mr. Rufus Isaacs, and, of course, Mr. Lloyd George.

Wedding gifts included a gold-mounted walking-stick engraved with the Marlborough arms, sent by King Edward VII; from Lloyd George had come a silver fruit basket; Edward Grey sent a bound set of Marlborough's dispatches, while other Cabinet colleagues gave such varied books as novels—Mr. Asquith sent ten volumes of Jane Austen—and *Conversations with the Duke of Wellington*.

There were travelling clocks, silver trays, gold, silver, and jewellery for the bride from the Rothschild family and from Lord Northcliffe, who also gave Winston a walking-stick. Lady Blanche Hozier gave her daughter diamonds and sapphires, and also presented her new son-in-law with three glass perfume bottles.

There were also gifts from the Royal Family, and from admirers. Antique silver candlesticks, in fact twenty-five candlesticks in all among the gifts. A Bible came from the deputy Lord Mayor of Manchester; ten cigarette cases; eight salts and twenty-one inkstands. Joseph Chamberlain sent two silver decanter stands. Almost no great name was absent from the wedding gift list. King Edward's malacca cane gift had a massive gold knob, richly chased and engraved 'WLSC'.

But the most important present of all was recorded as: 'Bridegroom to Bride; fine ruby and diamond cluster necklace, with ruby and diamond drop, pair of diamond cluster ear-rings.'

The wedding cake with its ornamentation stood nearly five feet high and weighed over a hundredweight.

The newly wed Churchills didn't stay long at their own wedding reception. Early in the afternoon they left to spend the first part of their honeymoon at Blenheim Palace, where Winston had proposed.

Clementine's going-away outfit was a smart grey costume, and Winston wore the wedding suit which the 'Tailor's Bible'—the *Tailor and Cutter*—described as 'one of the greatest failures we have seen, making the wearer look like a glorified coachman'. Winston's taste in clothes never improved with the years either, in spite of his wife's efforts.

The honeymooners drove to Paddington Station where a special reserved coach awaited them. It was uncoupled at Oxford and switched to Woodstock, where they were received by another great crowd who had been standing for hours to catch a glimpse of them.

They later left Blenheim to spend a week of their honeymoon at Bareno on Lake Maggiore, in Italy, and then travelled to Austria to stay with Baron de Forest, one of Winston's friends, on his estates in Moravia.

Sir Edward Carson—later Lord Carson of Duncairn—wrote in a letter to a friend: '... I suppose you did not come to town for Winston's wedding. I never saw anything so much advertised—nearly as much as "Eno's Fruit Salts!"...'

And so the story began. As Winston himself later wrote:

33

It was in 1908 that I met the young lady of dazzling beauty who consented to be my wife.

On her mother's side she was one of the Airlies whose country seat is so close to Dundee.

Her father, who was dead, Colonel Sir Henry Hozier, had been a prominent member of Lloyds, and had written a valuable account of the Austro-Prussian War of 1866.

We had a wonderful wedding at St. Margaret's, with enormous crowds in the streets and everybody gave us presents without the slightest regard to politics.

Theirs was a complete love match. His 'Clemmie', as he called her from almost their moment of meeting, was his ideal. Even his youthful thoughts were of a woman like her.

In his only novel, which he wrote at the age of twenty-three, his hero, Savrola, fell in love with a woman named Lucile.

Describing Lucile, Winston wrote: 'her perfect features, her vivacity of expression which is the greatest of woman's charms, her tall figure ... instinct with grace'. It described his mother, and it described Clementine.

2

THE VOICE OF THE PEOPLE

THE honeymoon was over, and they set up home at 33 Eccleston Square, Westminster. Winston held almost nightly discussions with friends in his study on the first floor, and Clementine began to experience her first sampling of a husband who enjoyed staying up half the night working or talking.

From the earliest days of their marriage, people made it abundantly plain to Clementine that they considered him a 'noisy, shameless, truculent and pushing person'.

She alone recognized that no assessment of his character could be further from the truth. She knew another Winston Churchill—one of the most sensitive of aspiring politicians, who only by the exercise of remarkable courage had mastered a terrible nervousness.

Ambition drove Winston; but it was courage—his own and his wife's—which carried him through to final triumph.

An impediment of speech, which would have deterred lesser men even from attempting to enter public life, made his words almost unintelligible in moments of stress. Winston never allowed that to stop him.

When he rehearsed his speeches with Clementine she noticed his vocal difficulties were most apparent during his opening sentences. The painful effort of mastering his utterance would make his normally pale cheeks flush angrily. Directly he had managed to establish sympathy with his audience his speech became almost clear and the fiery patches in his cheeks disappeared.

In those days, only Clementine knew that the accent of brutality in his speech was the mark, not of a truculent nature but of a highly strung temperament fighting its own sensibilities for the mastery of its own mind. Winston was fighting himself more often than his enemies.

At times, when Clementine's was the one loyalty on which he could really count, he had to fight desperately with body and mind to keep his place in the political firing-line. Impossible as it may be to credit, it is nevertheless true that the man who was, in later years, to become the greatest human driving machine of the century would frequently return home to his wife physically weak from the simple strain and effort of public speaking. He was exhausted by a tongue which refused to give the standard of eloquence he desired to the torrent of thoughts flooding from his brilliant mind.

Clementine mothered him like a child. In their early years together, one of their closest friends was saying: 'But for the devotion of his wife I think he could not have held his place so long.'

The simile of mothering is not so exaggerated as it might seem. Though middle-aged, with shoulders bowed and thinning hair, Winston retained in large measure the roundness, freshness, and playfulness of youth. He might have left the playground only the day before, having been a terror to his school-fellows and a problem to his masters. His pouting, petulant lips, suddenly expanding in a broad smile which bordered on a grin, heightened the impression.

To make himself a great Parliamentary speaker and platform orator was the most difficult task Winston Churchill ever set himself.

When he first attempted to address the House of Commons his vocal handicap with its intrusive sibilance was daunting to himself and an embarrassment to his audience. He was often reduced to an agonizing stammer, and at times there was a fierce, silent struggle to voice the first syllable of a word. He was wrestling with a similar impediment to that which, years later, King George VI was to face so bravely. Sometimes his diction was so hampered that listeners suspected that he had a cleft palate.

Often he would look to Clementine, seated in the gallery of the Chamber, for silent, smiling encouragement as he fought to make his points with clarity and effect. He took heart from her, in his determination to overcome his dreadful handicap, as she helplessly watched one or two sadistically cruel young Members mercilessly mocking his affliction on the very floor of the House.

The young Winston, who found every speech an ordeal and trial of his strength, loved the English tongue and had decided views concerning its use. His creed was: 'Short words are best, and old words the best of all.' He despised the kind of officialese which described the poor as 'The lower-income group' and homes as 'accommodation units'. His insistence that every sentence should be well turned and balanced, as well as his overwhelming desire to overcome his handicap, led him not only to rehearse his speeches but always to bring a full manuscript to the House and read from it. His rehearsals were reserved exclusively for an audience of one. Clementine alone listened to him and helped him in the privacy of their home. And with her understanding and aid, the emotion and eloquence which were locked within his heart began to flow.

She would share his mood as, with tears running down his cheeks, he would declaim from a newly written speech some passage dwelling on an incident of pathos or disaster. She would laugh appreciatively at his touches of wit or nod in endorsement of his carefully prepared debating points.

Like an actor performing at a dress rehearsal, he would seek advance acclaim and criticism from Clementine, taking careful note of her shrewdly constructive comments. If she told him 'I would not say that, Winston', he would remove the offending phrase or passage, recognizing the wisdom of her caution.

Clementine told him frankly that many of his early speeches were too impetuous, over-elaborate, and frequently harsh and strident. Gradually he curbed and softened faults, and injected the understanding tolerance which was to make his outstanding speeches models of good temper as well as of grand elocution.

He was no longer diffident of showing his emotions, of revealing that sympathy with suffering and misfortune was part of his natural make-up. With her influence his genius lightened and mellowed.

True, his judgement and temperament continued to lead him astray at times, but he had the wisdom to learn from mistakes. Fortified by his wife's unwavering support and belief in his destiny, he never lost courage, never lost faith in himself.

In the first days of his Parliamentary career he liked long words and revelled in producing unusual ones with which to puzzle Members, but he seemed to lack spontaneous humour. Constant practice with Clementine strengthened his confidence and developed the ability to fight impromptu verbal duels with crisp wit, biting sarcasm, and great originality of argument.

Social reformers Sidney and Beatrice Webb were among the first guests invited to the newly wed Churchills' home.

Beatrice Webb recorded: 'We lunched with Winston Churchill and his bride—a charming lady, well bred and pretty, and earnest withal—but not rich, by no means a good match, which is to Winston's credit.

'Winston had made a really eloquent speech on the unemployed the night before. He is brilliantly able—more than a phrase-monger, I think.

'Lloyd George is a clever fellow, but has less intellect than Winston and not such an attractive personality.'

Before lunching with the Churchills, the supercilious Mrs. Webb's judgement of Winston was harsher:

'Restless—almost intolerably so, egotistical, bumptious, shallow-minded, and reactionary, but with a certain personal magnetism, great pluck and some originality ... more of the American speculator than the English aristocrat ... bound to be unpopular ... but his pluck, courage, resourcefulness and great tradition may carry him far unless he knocks himself to pieces like his father. . . .'

Those who came to dine with Winston and Clementine— though they may have been prejudiced against the ambitious young man before—left with warmer feelings and a greater respect for both, having been charmed by Clementine and given an impressive display of Winston's agile mind.

With Clementine as his most constructive critic and private audience of one for rehearsals, he became a heckler of unrivalled talent, and usually proved most formidable when apparently off-guard.

There was the time when a Member, in mid-speech, noticed that Winston, on the Opposition front bench, was shaking his head forcefully.

'I see my Right Hon. friend shaking his head,' cried the M.P. 'I wish to remind him that I am only expressing my own opinion.'

'And I wish to remind the speaker that I am only shaking my own head,' Winston replied.

Clementine admitted to friends: 'Being married to him

couldn't be easy.' It certainly couldn't be, and wasn't. Careless in personal matters, brooding, sleeping by day, working through the night, uplifted by success, desolate in failure, Winston was, to put it mildly, a handful for any girl, but she handled him gently, tactfully. She nourished him with calmness, constancy, and content. She could humour him magically, make him laugh when he wanted to cry.

In return, his tenderness towards her was wonderful. Theirs was an ideal match.

Clementine's favourite saying to about-to-get-married friends was: 'You must have four children—one for mother, one for father, one for accidents, and one for increase.'

A few months after their marriage she told Winston she was expecting their first child.

He fussed, and treated her like a piece of fragile porcelain, and Clementine laughed.

In 1909 their daughter Diana was born.

Lloyd George asked him: 'Is she a pretty child?'

Winston beamed. 'The prettiest child ever seen.'

'Like her mother, I suppose,' remarked Lloyd George.

'No,' Winston answered solemnly. 'She is the image of me.'

Even in the House of Commons he could never resist the opportunity of being the proud father.

Their domestic happiness was plain for all to see, and many who had previously disapproved of the match began to feel that, after all, it might prove to be a good marriage. Miss Stanley—Aunt Maud, as she used to be called—was one who changed her mind about Winston. She had been most upset and brought to tears on hearing that her ward, Clementine, had become engaged to the young Mr. Churchill. A year later, she was saying: 'Oh, we all like him so much; he is such a good husband.'

In the happiness of his home, and with the faith of his wife, Winston's confidence as a politician and orator flourished.

Recognizing that the written word is not necessarily the same as the spoken word, he was never content merely to read speeches after dictating them. First, he would voice the draft aloud; then, when satisfied, send it to Clementine, and she would either make her remarks on a separate piece of paper or go to his study to discuss and listen to his personal phrasings of passages which she felt seemed to need further expansion or clarification.

He tried to imagine, days or even weeks beforehand, the sort of conditions and situations which could arise in the House when particular issues were debated.

'Guided by this light I prepared and wrote out my arguments with the greatest care, and then learnt them so thoroughly by heart that I knew them backwards and forwards, as well for instance as one knows the Lord's Prayer, and could, within limits, vary the sequence not only of the arguments but of the sentences themselves,' Winston confessed.

'Not many people guessed how little spontaneity of conception, fullness of knowledge, or flow of language there was behind this fairly imposing façade,' he added.

Curiously, Winston continued to display a certain diffidence about the effectiveness of his oratory. A friend said: 'He worried about people going to sleep during his speeches and kept saying, as he worked: 'Now I had better drop in a joke to wake them up.' Time after time, as he was coming off a platform after a public meeting, I watched him turn to the chairman or his wife and say: 'Well, what did you think of that? Was it all right? Was it what was wanted?' He seemed to like somebody around to reassure him.

'A few words from Clementine on anything that he did or said seemed to give him a very special lift—and he loved those lifts.'

The dedication of her own powers to the well-being of the man she loved, so that he might realize to the full the strength and brilliance of his talents—that became her contribution to his greatness. He could easily have been spoiled by adoration, but by standing up to him, by refusing to be overwhelmed, she made sure that despite his genius he kept both feet firmly on the ground.

From the earliest days of their marriage, when to be a political hostess meant more than it does today, Clementine devoted herself to being her husband's wife, and to being a skilled and charming hostess who could put the most difficult guest at ease. Her consideration and patience would balance his frequent impatience; her outward calm would make up for his turbulence.

From the beginning of their partnership she had to learn to live with danger, because he loved danger. He loved a battle and sniffed brimstone at the slightest provocation.

'Politics,' he once told her, 'are almost as exciting as war and quite as dangerous, although in war you can be killed only once but in politics many times.'

Clementine had to contend with a husband like no other; always something of an unknown quantity, something of an enigma, possessed with reckless courage, incredible industry, daring flights of imagination, a dazzling inability to limit himself to the dogmas of party, and a martyr to excitement.

She had to live with a man to whom life was a perpetual drama in which he was the hero and his enemies the villains. Politics, to him, were also drama. The gods might hurl him into the wings for a time, but before long he would be back in the centre of the stage.

Winston's tempestuous life evolved amid three impregnable family relationships: first with his mother, secondly with his wife, and thirdly with his daughter; and of these three influences unquestionably Clementine was immeasurably the greatest.

From the beginning, Winston always considered Clementine's opinions long and carefully, and often followed her advice. Though she would never reveal in public if she was at variance with him on any subject, at home she never hesitated to disagree if she felt he was in the wrong.

With Winston a political and social outsider during many of the early years of their marriage, life was difficult for Clementine; but she treated difficulties merely as a challenge, never doubting he would achieve to the full his latent greatness. Meanwhile, through the years, she often mothered him like a precocious, unruly child.

To any other woman Winston would have been an impossible husband, but was always able to turn to 'Clemmie' to lean on her without hesitation, without fear, in the secure knowledge that she would support his spirit and give him strength to go on.

Safe in her love, he rose to greater heights than he could ever have achieved without her. When he was just a voice, to whom few wanted to listen, she fortified him with her belief that one day he would be heard.

41

Although at the beginning of their marriage they moved in exclusive social circles, and although he was a distinguished politician, they were poor by the financial standards of the day. Winston had little money. He had to work hard as a journalist and author to pay the household bills. He has always had to earn his living. But, in the happiness of his home, he was able to say: 'I had no idea that ordinary life could be so interesting.'

No marriage continues through the years without crises, and the Churchills had more than their share of them.

Clementine has a genius of her own, for none but a genius could cope with Winston's temperament, his changes of mood, and his way of life. Sometimes, in the small hours of the morning, he would restlessly ask her to talk to him or even to sit down and play bezique with him. Clementine became the safety valve for his explosive mind. No wonder that his book *My Early Life* ends with the words: '... until September, 1908, when I married and lived happily ever afterwards.'

In fact, their wedding bells did not ring in an era of unalloyed happiness. Trouble was waiting for both bride and groom.

Winston in his role of President of the Board of Trade launched attacks on the House of Lords, was called a traitor to his class, and both he and Clementine were ostracized by many of their acquaintances. Because he was such a radical, he was politically the most hated man in the country.

Less bitter opponents were saying: 'If he ever does rise to the leadership of the Party, he won't lead it successfully or for long. The function of a leader is to lead public opinion. Winston follows it—often a little late. Very often he does not know his own mind.'

As Home Secretary in 1910, soon after their marriage, he was absorbed in his Home Office work, and although realizing that prison reform was no vote-winner at elections, visited prisons, introduced changes, and conceived at least one new reform a week. In the interests of his work Clementine took him to hear what John Galsworthy had to say in his new play *Justice*. The play affected him very much and spurred him still more to achieve penal reforms.

One evening he returned home to inform his wife that

prayers had been offered on his behalf in the Home Office. It transpired that General Booth had called personally at the Home Office to discuss with him the views of the Salvation Army. To strengthen his argument the white-bearded, fiery-eyed General had knelt and prayed loudly for the conversion of the Home Secretary.

There were renewed hostilities, too, on another flank. The Suffragettes had sworn a vendetta against Winston which was to continue until universal suffrage was finally granted. Sylvia Pankhurst had announced that 'in Winston Churchill, the Liberal Government will receive the weight of the women's opposition'. Wherever Winston went, the women were also sure to go.

His romance with Clementine had temporarily softened the hearts of the most militant crusaders, but the wedding truce was over, and he was once more howled down at meetings.

Clementine made it plain to Winston that she agreed with the Suffragettes; and she showed her sympathy by being present at every prosecution of their leaders. But though, even in later years, Winston still had qualms about the entry of women into public life, he always permitted his wife to be mistress of her own thoughts. Indeed, throughout a lifetime spent in trying to change people's opinions, he never used his will to compel Clementine to his own point of view.

He was, in a rather tepid manner, a Suffragist, but whatever interest he had in the question of equal rights for women was fostered by Clementine's keenness on the principle. She tried enthusiastically to win him over to the cause of women's suffrage, but the campaign waged against him by the Suffragettes and their leader, Miss Sylvia Pankhurst, muffled his ears to all her persuasive efforts.

Some of their friends maintained that, in his heart, Winston was not as antagonistic towards the Suffragist cause as he outwardly appeared, and there is at least one incident to support that view.

William Beveridge (later Lord Beveridge), who conceived the scheme of employment exchanges which Winston backed and brought into being, went to Winston for help in the middle of the election campaign in 1910 when he was being asked to address meetings all over the country. He walked into Winston's bedroom one morning with a list of the first women divisional officers to be appointed to the labour exchanges.

Winston, who had suffered constantly at the hands of militant Suffragettes demanding equal status for men and women, looked at the list of females now seeking to take equal administrative responsibility beside the male employment officers. He looked at the list hard and long, then announced: 'Let there be women!' and signed the order approving the appointments.

Two years after his marriage Winston was still a target for the Suffragettes. Diana, their first child, had to be specially guarded in her pram because of the fear that the Suffragettes might kidnap her.

Clementine was with him when three women climbed on to the roof of a hall and throughout his address barracked and shouted demands for votes through a ventilator. Clementine, seated on the platform, waved gaily to the demonstrators while Winston spoke.

Few women who have married a genius have succeeded in staying happy for long. When such a marriage does succeed credit is due not to the genius but to his wife.

Clementine had chosen as her partner for life a restless, ambitious man for whom trouble was an almost constant acquaintance. She set herself to provide the emotional security, the roots, without which his career, his very existence, must have foundered.

She sustained him simply by being in love with him. She gave him children, a family, a home, a haven from the turbulent world in which he normally walked.

Before their love began he was a man with a chip on his shoulder, thrusting, undisciplined, and frequently rude. Her gentle influence changed him. Bitterness left his voice; confidence grew; his ability shone more brilliantly; his oratory improved.

She went with him everywhere, applauding triumphs, helping him to smile through misfortunes.

Although to see a wife and mother on an election platform was an almost unheard-of thing in those days, she joined him in public because she knew he needed her to do so. In the days before 1914 they set something of a precedent by travelling together to inspect battleships.

44

In return for her love, Winston proudly showed his devotion to his Clemmie in public. He continued to do so throughout his life.

With her at his side his stature grew. To their home at 33 Eccleston Square the famous came. The young Mrs. Churchill was a success as a political hostess.

Lloyd George was always completely at home with his friends the Churchills. Winston and the Welsh Wizard made a wonderful partnership for dinner-table conversation.

'I am all for the social order,' Winston said once.

Lloyd George, looking over his glass of champagne, replied: 'No! I am against it.'

And Winston, wrinkling his nose as he did when he knew he was going to be impertinent, retorted: 'You are not against the social order, but only against those parts of it which get in your way.'

Lord Esher, confidant of King Edward VII, was another who went to dine with them in their first home. He noted afterwards:

'He has a charming double room on the first floor, all books. A splendid library.

'It was a birthday dinner. Only six people. But he had a birthday cake with thirty-five candles. And crackers. He sat all the evening with a paper cap from a cracker on his head. A queer sight, if all the thousands who go to his meetings could have seen him.

'He and she sit on the same sofa, and he holds her hand. I never saw two people more in love.

'If he goes out of office, he has not a penny. He would have to earn his living, but he says it is well worth it if you live with someone you love. He would loathe it, but he is ready to live in a lodging—just two rooms—with her and the baby!

'They have a cook now, two maids, and a man. She ran down to the kitchen before dinner to see that it was all right. And an excellent dinner it was!'

Winston had played an influential part in the settlement after the Boer War. South Africa's peace offering to the Crown was the Cullinan Diamond. The Boers knew that it was largely owing to Winston that the gift had been accepted, so they sent him as a souvenir a replica of the stone.

Delighted, Winston gave it to Clementine to keep, and every now and again he would proudly ask her to produce it for inspection by his guests.

One day his cousin, Lady Lilian Grenfell, came to lunch. Winston asked Clementine to send for the replica stone. Meanwhile the conversation turned to other topics.

Eventually the butler presented himself at Lady Lilian's elbow, bearing the stone on a salver—a shapeless mass looking like a not very well-strained jelly which had escaped from its mould.

Lady Lilian eyed it with distaste, and said coldly: 'No, thank you.'

Although Winston was so unpopular with many of his political colleagues, Clementine knew that those who worked with him respected him. Sir Edward Troup, Permanent Secretary to the Home Office in 1909, confessed to her: 'There is no period of my time in the Home Office of which I have pleasanter recollections than the eighteen months when Mr. Churchill was my chief. Once a week, or perhaps oftener, he came down to the office, bringing with him some adventurous and impossible project; but in half an hour's discussion something was evolved which was still adventurous but no longer impossible.'

The trials and stresses of politics demand a hostess, a loyal comrade, an unshakable supporter, ruling over a home in which politics can be forgotten. Clementine provided Winston with such a setting—a home to which the world's indebtedness is even greater than her husband's.

Her own assessment of values in the domestic sphere is practical, down-to-earth.

She was once asked: 'Who is the most important person in your home?'

'The cook, of course,' she replied.

Attending a speech day at St. John's School, Leatherhead, she told the parents and students why she had once had to refuse a job in that capacity.

She said that an old boy of St. John's, the late Sir Leonard Woolley, had asked her to join one of his archaeological expeditions and do the cooking. She had been tempted to accept, but when Winston heard of the proposal he told her firmly: 'If you are going to cook for anybody, you can cook for me!'

46

Two years after their marriage the Churchills were entertaining guests and the conversation had turned to a weighty discussion of Home Rule and the nationalization of railways when Clementine entered the room with baby Diana in her arms. Immediately, politics forgotten, Winston was down on the floor playing with the baby.

At the age of thirty-five he was sharing with Lloyd George the leadership of the progressive Liberals, he was already the Secretary of State for Home Affairs, he had a baby daughter, and he had his Clemmie.

3

MEN MUST FIGHT

WINSTON was transferred from the Home Office to the Admiralty. To put the Fleet 'into a state of instant and constant readiness for war in case we are attacked by Germany'—the Prime Minister instructed him.

During the years between 1911 and 1915 in which, as First Lord of the Admiralty, he was reorganizing the Navy, he was so determined to gain an understanding of his Ministerial task that he left Clementine and his family to spend more than eight months afloat.

In those months he visited almost every ship in home waters and in the Mediterranean, meeting all the captains, commanders, and crews, and hearing all kinds of things which no official files could have taught him about his job. Throughout his journeys he slept aboard the Admiralty yacht *Enchantress*—the same vessel on which he and Clementine, in the spring of 1913, sailed on holiday with the Prime Minister, Mrs. Asquith, her stepdaughter Violet, and two other friends. They went sightseeing by gondola in Venice; sailed to the historic palace of Spoleto; and drank beer under giant plane-trees at Ragusa.

Now holidays and pleasures were far from his thoughts, and he had made the *Enchantress* his office afloat and left his family while he learnt his job.

While he was preoccupied with the Admiralty, including the formation of a revolutionary Naval Staff, both he and Clementine encountered ever-increasing bitterness in the political and social worlds. They found themselves unwelcome in many more homes into which they had formerly been enthusiastically received. Once, after an attack on her friend Mrs. Asquith, Clementine packed her bags and left Blenheim in protest. But their friend, poet Wilfrid Blunt, remained sympathetic and hospitable. They stayed at his Sussex home one week-end in October 1912, and it turned out to be a memorable party.

Winston started a political argument with another guest,

George Wyndham, which went on from tea-time, through dinner, until midnight.

'It was a fine night,' said Blunt, 'and we dined in the bungalow, dressed in gorgeous Oriental garments; Clementine in a suit of embroidered silk purchased last year in Smyrna, Winston in one of my Baghdad robes. George in a blue dressing gown, and I in my Bedouin robes. . . .'

Noting the change in Winston since his marriage, he added: 'Winston was very brilliant ... he kept his head, and played with George's wild rushes like a skilled fencer with a greatly superior fence. He is certainly an astonishing young man and has gained immensely within the last two years in character and intellectual grip.'

Clementine had to accustom herself from the first to Winston's extraordinary capacity for work. When he became First Lord of the Admiralty, Edward Marsh, writing to a friend, said: 'He stays till at least 8 every day. Even Sundays are no longer my own. We have made a new commandment: "The seventh day is the Sabbath of the First Lord; on it thou shalt do all manner of work." '

Also noting the improvement in Winston brought about by Clementine's influence, Marsh wrote: 'He is becoming the idol of the Tory party. The sailors seem to like him very much. He has completely changed his character in some ways and has come out with a brand-new set of perfect manners. . . .'

The late Sir Edward Marsh, for years Winston's private secretary, was to become a dear friend to whom he and Clementine would turn in many moments of crisis. Eddie, as they called him, was a great foil for Winston's love of argument, and he also made a great tennis partner for Clementine.

Winston had asked for Edward Marsh as private secretary when taking up his appointment as Under-Secretary for the Colonies in 1905. Marsh was not sure whether he would enjoy the honour and sought the opinion of Lady Lytton, who knew the Churchills well. Her sole comment was: 'The first time you meet Winston you see all his faults, and the rest of your life you spend in discovering his virtues.'

Eddie Marsh took the job.

He was optimistic in his assessment of his chief as a

potential 'idol of the Tory party', however. At the outbreak of the First World War, Winston was still battling vicious unpopularity. The warmth of his home and family was almost the only comfort for him anywhere.

Clementine was in the gallery of the House of Commons when his former Conservative Party colleagues screamed 'Traitor!' at him and when one overwrought Member threw a large book across the Chamber at his head. She walked with him into a city of hate when they went to Belfast, where he had undertaken to address a public meeting of the Ulster Liberal Association on 8 February 1912.

Threats of violence and a rough reception had been so serious that Winston had been compelled to write to Lord Londonderry, warning him . . .

'The very grave and direct responsibility which will fall upon you if serious rioting occurs in Belfast on the occasion of my visit makes me sure that you will not seek lightly to widen the grounds of the quarrel. For my own part, I only care about one essential thing. It is my duty to keep my promise to the Ulster Liberal Association and to assert our right of free speech and public meeting. . . .'

Determined to take no chances, the Government in Belfast drafted strong military reinforcements to the area. Five infantry regiments, a cavalry squadron, and a detachment of Royal Engineers were already in the city, and had marched through it to their barracks watched by great crowds.

Clementine had decided to accompany Winston, and no threats of violence or riots could make her change her mind. She left with him for Belfast, and their party also included a secretary and two Liberal M.P.s.

Of their reception, former Northern Ireland M.P., H. Montgomery Hyde, says:

'Hostile onlookers hissing and booing lined the route as they drove from the station in Belfast to the Grand Central Hotel, but no attempt was made to interfere with their progress. But on leaving the hotel in the early afternoon for the Celtic football ground, a more ominous incident occurred.

'Royal Avenue, through which they had to drive, was now densely packed with people. As the car moved slowly along, men thrust their heads in, shaking their fists and muttering fearful imprecations. At one moment, two of the car's wheels left the ground, but whether this arose from a deliberate attempt to overturn the vehicle or merely from the involuntary pressure of the throng against its side is not clear.

'There is no doubt, however, that it was the most critical moment of this critical visit. It was said afterwards by many who witnessed the scene that, had it not been for the fact that Mrs. Churchill was also a passenger, the car might have been smashed and the Minister seriously if not fatally injured, before the police and military could have got through to his assistance. As things turned out, Mr. Churchill, who has never been lacking in courage, did not flinch, and no harm befell him. And his wife displayed equal courage.'

Winston addressed the meeting of several thousand Nationalists at the football ground in heavy rain. Later, as they stepped up the gangway of their departure ship at Larne quayside, dockers pelted them with rotten fish.

Back in London, Clementine admitted to their friend, Lord Riddell: 'I was not afraid of being killed, but feared I might be disfigured for life by the glass of the motor being broken or by some other means.'

She said Winston wasn't nervous and that the opposition and threats seemed to 'ginger him up'.

Lord Riddell recorded in his diary: 'The Suffragettes gave them more trouble than the anti-Home Rulers, as they disturbed their sleep both on the boat and on the train. Winston threatened to smash the face of one of the male tormentors who forced his way into their compartment on the train.'

In the summer of 1912 Clementine suffered her first serious illness—an illness that almost crippled her for life and might have, in consequence, altered the course of Winston's life and of history.

For months medical treatment made no headway and her condition deteriorated. Winston could hardly bear to leave her a moment.

One day a bed-ridden Clementine said to him:

'I am a poor wrecked ship. You must take me in hand as if I were one of your battleships. Think my case carefully over, and decide what is to be done.'

Winston did. He called in another doctor, who changed

the treatment. The crisis passed, and she was cured.

On 22 October 1912 Lord Riddell wrote in his diary:

'Lunched with Mr. and Mrs. Churchill. The latter seems to have completely recovered from her serious illness. She said she had steadily got worse and feared she would become a permanent invalid.... Winston is charming in his home life and Mrs. W. a most attractive person, full of charm and vivacity. Little Diana, their daughter, is clever, pretty, and intelligent.'

A few weeks later Lord Riddell reciprocated their luncheon invitation, and, talking of friendship, Winston remarked: 'I don't readily take to people. I have few friends, but those I have are very dear to me.'

During the meal Winston explained some of Disraeli's policies to Clementine. Noted Lord Riddell:

'It was pleasing to see the satisfaction Winston took in furnishing the information and the evident delight of his wife in the trouble he was taking....'

Clementine told their host that on a previous evening she and Winston had been involved in yet another clash with the Suffragettes, who attacked them, this time at a theatre. Lord Riddell noted: 'Mrs. Cornwallis-West, who was with them, went for the Suffragettes and told them they ought to be forcibly fed with common sense!'

By the summer of 1914 war with Germany was an imminent certainty, but Clementine was determined the children should have a holiday, and that Winston should take a short, badly needed break with them from his Admiralty duties.

She took Diana, Randolph, and baby Sarah down to Overstrand, near Cromer in Norfolk, where they were joined by Winston's brother Jack, his wife, and their children John George Churchill and baby Pebin (Henry Winston). The families had rented two cottages. Clementine had chosen Pear Tree Cottage, while the other Churchills were at the opposite end of the lawn in a little place called Beehive Cottage.

Winston came down and things immediately got organized with the issue of buckets and spades, and plans marked out on the sands for the construction of giant fortresses.

'More sand for the outer defences!' Winston, with trousers rolled up to the knees, would cry, flourishing his cigar. A wonderful time was had by all until buckets and spades had to be packed away. The call now was for rifles and artillery.

On 4 August 1914 Germany had invaded Belgium, and Britain had sent an ultimatum to Berlin. In their living quarters above the Admiralty, Winston and Clementine sat waiting. Through the open windows they could hear the excited crowd gathered outside Buckingham Palace singing 'God Save the King'.

The chimes of Big Ben began to boom the hour. It was eleven o'clock. Britain's ultimatum to the Kaiser had expired.

Winston dispatched his 'war telegram' to all the ships of His Majesty's Navy. Then he left his wife and children and walked to Downing Street to inform the Cabinet.

When Clementine evacuated Diana, Randolph, and Sarah, with children from other branches of the Churchill family, to an old farmhouse, she remained to share with Winston whatever was to come.

She was to walk with him proudly when, after the war, his enemies never tired of shouting the names of Antwerp and Gallipoli, which they had adopted as convenient terms of abuse. In fact, those strokes of military strategy had been sound in conception.

Had Winston's plan to make Antwerp a sea-supplied threat to the rear of the German armies been followed with decisive action, the right flank of the enemy forces would have been affected fatally.

The idea of forcing the Dardanelles by a combined sea and land attack was a conception of genius, and few doubt now that if it had been carried through it would have removed the menace of Turkey and Bulgaria, given us a direct link with Russia, and certainly shortened the war.

Had the Dardanelles expedition been sent sufficient reinforcements by Lord Kitchener, Constantinople would have been taken, Russia saved, and the collapse of Austria precipitated.

Antwerp and the Dardanelles were bungled by Military Command. Winston had conceived the strategical enterprises; others had failed to support them, but he was made to take the responsibility. It is the author of the play, not the actor, who has to bear the stigma of failure.

On hearing the news that he was to be dropped from the Admiralty, Clementine angrily wrote to the Prime Minister, Mr. H. H. Asquith:

My dear Mr. Asquith,

For nearly four years Winston has worked to master every detail of naval science. There is no man in this country who possesses equal knowledge capacity & vigour. If he goes, the injury to Admiralty business will not be reparable for many months—if indeed it is ever made good during the war.

Why do you part with Winston? Unless indeed you have lost confidence in his work and ability?

But I know that cannot be the reason. Is not the reason expediency—'to restore public confidence'. I suggest to you that public confidence will be restored in Germany by Winston's downfall.

There is no general desire here for a change, but it certainly is being fostered by the press who have apparently made up their minds. I trust they are not making up yours for you.

All you have to do is to stand by Winston and the Board of the Admiralty and Sir Arthur Wilson. (Admiral of the Fleet).

If you throw Winston overboard you will be committing an act of weakness and your Coalition Government will not be as formidable a War machine as the present Government.

Winston may in your eyes & those with whom he has to work, have faults, but he has the supreme quality which I venture to say very few of your present or future Cabinet possess; the power, the imagination, the deadliness to fight Germany.

If you send him to another place he will no longer be fighting. If you waste this valuable war material you will be doing an injury to this country.

Yours sincerely
Clementine S. Churchill

Winston, who craved always to be engaged on some momentous enterprise in which he believed, with the faith of positive fanaticism that he alone among his countrymen could guide the forces of triumph, was out of office, devoid of power. He was forced to resign his office of First Lord of the Admiralty in May 1915, although he remained a member of the Cabinet and War Council.

He was to write: 'I have never in my life suffered anything that compared in pain with my removal from the Admiralty.

'At this juncture I was sure that if I had been left at my post I could have carried through the great naval and amphibious operation I had launched, and for which I take full responsibility.

'I had as a Cabinet Minister to watch for six hateful months the great enterprise slowly and shamefully muddled and cast away by half measures and three-quarter measures all taken just too late.'

Clementine had watched him ceaselessly striving to win the war, fighting a lone hand, pushing and buffeting his way in all directions, struggling for a way to victory, tearing up miles of red tape, treading on corns, standing on no ceremony which delayed results while men were dying on the battlefields. Critics began to call him the 'amateur Commander-in-Chief of Navy'.

It was no wonder that many considered him a 'troublesome fellow', and made no secret of their preference for a nice, quiet, respectable war with Germany.

So they got him out.

His friend Edwin Montagu, then Financial Secretary to the Treasury, wrote to Clementine:

26 May 1915   *Treasury Chambers*
                                         Whitehall
My dear Mrs. Winston,
  My heart bled to see you so unhappy and I came back from your house to write a line in the hope of atoning for my lack of capacity to express myself verbally.
  It is a hard time and it is true that Winston has suffered a blow to prestige, reputation, and happiness which counts above all. All that is not worth arguing.
  But it is also indisputably true that Winston is far too great to be more than pulled up for a period. His

courage is enormous, his genius understood even by his enemies, and I am as confident that he will rise again as I am that the sun will rise tomorrow, yes, and in a far shorter time than you think possible. He will begin to be missed before he is well out of the Admiralty and he will be soon busy adding fresh lustre to the marvellous accumulation he has obtained in so wonderfully short a life.

The reaction in his favour among those who were the hardest critics is already beginning, and he will gain new friends every day by his humility under undeserved rebuffs and by the courage with which you and he are facing all that is happening.

Be as miserable as you must about the present; have no misgivings as to the future; I have none, Winston I am sure has none, and I know that in your heart and amid your gloom you have undaunted confidence in the man you love.

And the infinite kindness which you and Winston have always shown me gives me the proud right and ability to share your unhappiness and the joyful prospect of sharing in your triumph.

Yours ever to command
Edwin S. Montagu

The day he wrote this letter, Edwin Montagu confided to a friend:

'I went to see poor Mrs. Winston. She was so sweet but so miserable and crying all the time. I was very inarticulate, but how I feel for her and him.'

The following day, Lady Cynthia Asquith went to lunch with Winston, whom she called the 'setting sun' Minister. As soon as she arrived at the Admiralty, she made a point of seeing Clementine alone first.

'I always knew it would happen from the day Fisher (Admiral of the Fleet Lord Fisher) was appointed,' Clementine told her.

'After ten years in the Cabinet, and five years in the most important office, he is still by ten years the youngest member and the best they've got!' she added furiously.

Lady Cynthia tried to console her, but a dejected yet defiant Clementine was unconsolable.

Commented Cynthia Asquith afterwards: 'She looks very sad, poor thing, and Winston also looks unhappy, but is very dignified and un-bitter. I have never liked him so much.'

On a wintry evening, before a roaring fire on the hearth of the sitting-room in their home, he was crouched in his large arm-chair, and Clementine could see that neither the fire nor the arm-chair with its cushioned ease gave him comfort. His heavy brows scowled and his eyes flashed suddenly in anger.

'I have nothing to do,' he complained. 'How terrible it would be to get resigned to a state like this.'

His restless, energetic spirit was suffering the wretchedness, the boredom of idleness, and maddened by the knowledge that, for the present, it must be unemployed.

'I can do nothing,' he said. 'None of us can do anything —without power.'

Speaking of this period, Winston's great friend, General Lord Ismay, who in the Second World War became his Chief of Staff at the Ministry of Defence, said:

'He had conceived the Dardanelles operation, which, if he had been properly supported, would have shortened the war by two years. But he was not supported—he was dismissed—after having been acclaimed as the greatest War Minister since Pitt. He had been denied any further employment by the hatred of the Tories, and he felt his life was broken. That experience had the most tremendous impact on him, an impact that people never realized, and I am sure that the memory of it was at the back of his mind throughout the Second World War.

'I think it must have been, above all, the belief of his wife in him that was his rock during that terrible time, because I cannot imagine what other comfort he could have had. He had to have something and someone to preserve his sanity, because there was no immediate work to be done as he had refused minor office in the Government; there was the Dardanelles—his wonderful conception—he saw that being thrown away; and he was waiting to go to France to take his turn in the battle line. For a man of his dynamic energy, there had to be solace, and someone to support him in those awful moments.'

This man who could see the play of life and the clash of

material forces vividly, imaginatively; who could leap at his conclusions with an assurance which swept away all doubt; who could burst into battle with a conviction so clear, so burning, that all opposition was stampeded—this man was now discarded, weary, desolate.

Only Clementine's belief in him never wavered. He knew it, and was grateful.

'The change from the intense executive activities of each day's work at the Admiralty to the narrowly measured duties of a Councillor left me gasping,' he said.

'I had great anxiety and no means of relieving it; I had vehement convictions and small power to give effect to them. I had long hours of utterly unwanted leisure in which to contemplate the unfolding of the war.'

It was at that time, on a Sunday afternoon, at Hoe Farm, in Surrey, where the family had been spending part of the summer, that Clementine said: 'Are these toys any good to you? They amuse some people,' and handed him one of the children's paint-boxes.

Characteristically, in a flash, he felt a compelling urge to paint. A buried talent was seeking an outlet. Winston Churchill, the artist, began.

Immediately after breakfast next morning he bought a paint-box, easel, and canvas. The revelation which they brought him prompted him to say: 'It will be a sad pity to shut off or scramble along through one's playtime with golf and bridge, pottering, loitering, shifting from one heel to the other, wondering what on earth to do—as perhaps is the fate of some unhappy beings—when all the while, if you only knew, there is close at hand a wonderful new world of thought and craft, a sunlit garden gleaming with light and colour of which you have the key in your waistcoat pocket.'

Painting, however, was not enough to satisfy his turbulent soul. He was by temperament and training a soldier, and nothing less than the spur and exhilaration of danger could rout the devils which plagued him.

Winston left his desk to go and fight at the front. His mother, Lady Randolph, was grief-stricken and anxious, but Clementine's farewell to him was calm and assured. Her conviction then that a great destiny awaited her husband was as unshakable as it remained throughout the years of his stormy career.

On the night before Winston was due to depart for France and the front line, Lord Beaverbrook went to his home.

'The whole household was upside-down while the soldier-statesman was buckling on his sword,' he recorded. 'Downstairs his dear friend and secretary Edward Marsh was in tears; upstairs his mother was in despair at the idea of her brilliant son being relegated to the trenches; and Clementine—she seemed to be the only person calm and collected—was confident that Winston would return to her and to the great destiny she was so certain awaited him.'

During November 1915, from somewhere in France with the British Expeditionary Force, he wrote to Clementine:

> *I must try to win my way as a good & sincere soldier*
> *... I see that the Army is willing to receive me back as*
> *'the prodigal son' ... I did not know what release from*
> *care meant. It is a blessed peace. How I ever could*
> *have wasted so many months in impotent misery,*
> *which might have been spent in war, I cannot tell ...*
>
> *Here I am in the line. The conditions of life though*
> *hard are not unhealthy, & there is certainly nothing to*
> *complain about in them—except for cold feet. I want*
> *you to get me the following things and send them* with
> the utmost speed *to GHQ.*
>
> *1. A warm brown leather waistcoat.*
> *2. A pair of trench wading boots. Brown leather*
> *bottom, & water proof canvas tops coming right up to*
> *the thigh.*
> *3. A periscope (most important).*
> *4. A sheepskin sleeping bag; that will either carry*
> *kit, or let me sleep in it.*
>
> *In addition*
> *Please send me*
>
> *5. 2 pairs of Khaki trousers.*
> *6. 1 pair of my brown buttoned boots.*
> *7. Three small face towels.*
> *Voila tout!*
> *Your little pillow is a boon & a pet ...*

Filth & rubbish everywhere, graves built into the defences & scattered about promiscuously, feet & clothing breaking through the soil, water & muck on all sides; and about this scene in the dazzling moonlight troops of enormous bats creep & glide, to the unceasing accompaniment of rifle & machine guns & the venomous whining & whirring of the bullets which pass over head. Amid these surroundings, aided by wet & cold, & every minor discomfort, I have found happiness & content such as I have not known for many months...

Will you send now regularly once a week a small box of food to supplement the rations. Send me also lots of love & many kisses...

Do you realize what a very important person a Major is? 99 people out of every 100 in this great army have to touch their hats to me. With this inspiring reflection let me sign myself

Your loving & devoted husband
W.

(Winston and Clementine used abbreviations for many words in all their letters to each other, but for clarity, I have avoided them in these extracts from their correspondence.)

One morning, a telegram arrived ordering Winston to report immediately to the Corps Commander. He was furious at having to leave the trenches when they were under bombardment, but, of course, obeyed. Fifteen minutes later, the dugout in which he had been living was blown up by a shell.

He wrote home:

When I saw the ruin I was not so angry with the General after all.

Now see from this how vain it is to worry about things. It is all chance and our wayward footsteps are best planted without too much calculation. One must yield oneself simply & naturally to the mood of the game and trust in God which is another way of saying the same thing...

I love your letters and it is a delightful thought to

*me that you are at home with your 3 kittens thinking
of me & feeling that I am doing right. I do not feel the
least revolt at the turn of events ... Show complete
confidence in our fortunes. Hold your head very high.
You always do. Above all don't be worried about me.
If my destiny has not already been accomplished I
shall be guarded surely. If it has been there is nothing
that Randolph will need to be ashamed of in what I
have done for the country ...*

Throughout his years in Ministerial office, he often
showed Clementine highly confidential papers and reports,
even though disclosure of such documents was strictly
against regulations. But he wanted to share his thoughts on
them with her and keep her fully in the picture because he
so greatly valued the opinions and advice she offered at
times. In one of his letters from France he referred to certain secret papers, then warned:

*Please lock up all these papers after reading them, &
never say you have seen them.*

On another occasion he added:

*The enclosed will tell you what is known officially.
It is a good summary. You must not fail to burn it at
once.*

While he was in the trenches, she was his most important
link with London and the centre of Government. He relied
on her to keep him informed and asked:

*Don't fail to keep the threads in your fingers ... All
you tell me, all I read and hear fills me with indigna-
tion & contempt towards Asquith & Kitchener. These
are the real miscreants. LG (Lloyd George) is only an
understudy. I am sure their doom is sealed ...*

In all his letters, he referred to Clementine as 'the Cat';
the children as her 'kittens', and even in those early days of
his career, his partiality to showmanship was already in
evidence. He asked her to send him a special steel helmet.

In December 1915, on receiving a parcel from her, he replied:

> *My Darling, the most divine & glorious sleeping bag has arrived, & I spent last night in it in one long purr. Also food boxes are now flowing steadily; & I get daily evidence of the Cat's untiring zeal on my behalf. The periscope was the exact type I wanted. How clever of you to hit it off. My steel helmet is the cause of much envy. I look most martial in it—like a Cromwellian. I always intend to wear it under fire—but chiefly for the appearance.*
>
> *My dearest one—I have your little photograph up here now—and kiss it each night before I go to bed.*
>
> *Love to the children & all other near & dear*
>
> *Always your devoted*
> W.

The Prime Minister stopped him becoming a Brigadier-General and commanding his own Brigade. Winston, who had already been told he was being promoted, and then suddenly informed the decision had been reversed by Asquith personally, was bitterly disappointed. He wrote home:

> *Believe me I am superior to anything that can happen to me out here. My conviction that the greatest of my work is still to be done is strong within me: & I ride reposefully along the gale ... I feel a great assurance of my power: & now—naked—nothing can assail me ...*

Then Clementine received letters from him filled with resentment at the loss of command of his own Brigade, but, as she was about to reply, yet another letter arrived from France:

> *Darling, I want you to burn those two letters I sent you yesterday. I was depressed & my thought was not organized.*
>
> *It is now quite clear & good again & I see plainly the steps to take. You will do this to please me. Everyone*

has his hours of reaction; & there is no reason why
written record should remain . . .

Clementine burned the two letters.
At Christmas 1915 he wrote:

> *Do not be lonely or low-spirited. Everything will
> come out right in the end: and we shall look back
> upon these days with satisfaction—even pride . . .
> These letters are for you* alone *but you may read to or
> copy out for Mamma & others anything not purely for
> us two . . .*

On January 1st, 1916, he sent her new year wishes and
added:

> *I cannot help feeling the lack of scope for my
> thought & will power. I see so much ought to be done,
> that could easily be done, that will never be done: & I
> can't help longing for the power to give those wide
> directions which occupied my Admiralty days. There
> seems such want of drive & fresh thought in the mili-
> tary world. As for the Navy—it has dozed off . . .*
> *My Darling, what should I do if I had not you to
> write to when I am despondent?*
> *You cannot write to me too often or too long—my
> dearest & sweetest. The beauty & strength of your
> character & the sagacity of your judgement are more
> realized by me every day. I ought to have followed
> your counsels in my days of prosperity. Only some-
> times they are too negative. I should have made noth-
> ing if I had not made mistakes . . .*

He wrote to her daily, and in his January 1916 letters
said:

> *I do not ever show anything but a smiling face to the
> military world: a proper complete detachment & con-
> tentment. But so it is a relief to write one's heart out to
> you . . .*
> *What should I find to hold on to without you? All
> my great political estate seems to have vanished away*

—all my friends are mute—all my own moyens *are in abeyance. But there is the Kat with her kittens, supplied I trust adequately with cream & occasional mice. That is all my world in England ...*

Clementine begged of him to keep notes on his experiences and thoughts. She appreciated that they could become historic documents. She wrote:

I do hope Darling that even if you do not write actually for the press at the moment, you are writing for the future. Everything will have an enormous interest & a great value that you write on any topic & how much more so on the experiences through which you are now passing, experiences common to so many ordinary persons who cannot express themselves, unique to a man who has been in the positions you have held ... Please *every day make some notes & send them to me to lock up ...*

He answered that he was finding it difficult to write anything for print in France because, he felt, he had almost lost the art of writing while he was at the Admiralty. But, he added, he was gradually regaining it through writing letters home.

She sent him constant reports on the domestic political scene and informed him she was keeping fully in touch with many of his old colleagues in Parliament. He advised: 'It is important to be there & not be there at the same time. Persevere, the DCM (Distinguished Conduct Medal) is yours.'

In March 1916, he came home on leave, savoured the taste once more of politics, and, on his return to battle front wrote:

I am sure my true war station is in the House of Commons. There I can help the movement of events. I cannot tell you how much I love & honour you and how sweet & steadfast you have been through all my hesitations & perplexity ...

I was so grieved to think of you tired & lonely on the pier as my destroyer swept off into a choppy sea ...

Don't we live in a strange world—full of wonderful pictures & intricate affairs. Across the troubled waters one can only steer by compass—not to do anything that is not honourable & manly, & subject to that, use my vital force to the utmost to win the war—there is the test I am going to try my decision by . . .

During his leave, pressures built up for him to quit the Army and return to Parliament—to lead the Opposition. Clementine wrote to him afterwards sending a full account of a meeting she had arranged with the Attorney General, Sir Edward Carson. She told Winston that Carson had expressed grave doubts about the wisdom of making too precipitate a return to Parliament, and ended her letter:

Now I feel helpless & can only wait & pray. God bless you & keep you & guide & inspire you my Darling & bring you peace of heart . . .

Winston answered that he was still considering his course, although he was impressed with Carson's misgivings. Nevertheless, he was certain that it was right for him to come home, though he was not as yet clear as to when and on what grounds. He advised her not to use arguments or take up an attitude in conflict with his general intention, and to do nothing to discourage friends who wished for his return. On the contrary, he asked her to labour, as opportunity served, to create favourable circumstances. The sole question, he said, was whether he could help to a victorious peace more in the House of Commons than at the battle front.

She repeatedly cautioned against risking his political future by too hurried a return to Parliament, stressing that with patience, and waiting for the right and good opportunity, the future would be all his.

He told her how much he treasured and counted on her aid and counsel, and then, in March 1916, made up his mind to return reassuring her:

I am absolutely sure it is the right thing to do—& all these fears of taunts & criticisms should be treated as if they were enemy shells—they should not deter from

65

any action which is necessary in the general interest. Have confidence & do not easily lend yourself to the estimate formed by those who will never be satisfied till the breath is out of my body. All this dawdling is wrong. Manoeuvring for position is only a minor part of war; a strong army and a good cause & plenty of ammunition drives ahead all right ... I am prepared to follow my instinct ...

Frankly I do not think any really responsible or influential body of MPs are likely to take the responsibility of inviting me to return, without knowing what I mean to do or say. And on the other hand if I wait for a Ministerial crisis, will it not look as if I had come back like a sultan hastening to an unbidden feast ... Nothing could I think deprive me of my hold on the public attention. Even a controversy about whether I should or should not have come home would only increase the interest in what I said, and the need for justice and Parliamentary expression is so great & widely felt & so real & so recurring that everything will come right. Therefore, if, as I expect, it will not be possible to get the barbed wire cut beforehand, I shall nevertheless try to make my way through it ...

A weary, lonely Clementine replied:

These grave public anxieties are very wearing. When I next see you I hope there will be a little time for us both alone. We are still young, but Time flies, stealing love away, and leaving only friendship which is very peaceful but not very stimulating or warming ...

Winston replied:

Oh my darling, do not write of friendship to me—I love you more each month that passes & feel the need of you & all your beauty. My precious charming Clemmie—I too feel sometimes the longing for rest & peace. So much effort, so many years of ceaseless fighting & worry, so much excitement & now this rough fierce life here under the hammer of Thor, makes my older mind turn—for the first time I think to other things than

66

action ... But would it not be delicious to go for a few weeks to some lovely spot in Italy or Spain & just paint & wander about together in bright warm sunlight far from the clash of arms or bray of Parliaments? We know each other so well now & could play better than we ever could ...

Sometimes also I think I would not mind stopping living very much—I am so devoured by egoism that I would like to have another soul in another world & meet you in another setting, & pay you all the love & honour of the great romances ...

In April 1916, still striving to restrain his impatience, she wrote:

If you come back before the call you may blunt yourself. People will always try to deny you power if they think you are looking for it. To gain a share of war direction you are contemplating a terrible risk, the risk of life-long disappointment & bitterness ... For once only I pray be patient. It will come if you wait. Don't tear off the unripe fruit which is maturing though slowly, or check its growth by the frost of a premature return ...

At last, when she, and others felt the moment was right, he returned.

He might have stayed in the trenches; might have been killed in the trenches, but for Clementine and friends in Parliament pressing him to return to Westminster—'Your abilities are needed more in England where they will do the most good, than in the trenches where their scope is limited,' letters to him pleaded.

Finally, he was persuaded that he hadn't the right to remain at the front, and his decision to return was strengthened by information he received in messages from home.

He came back, but it was some time before he was restored to Ministerial power—old prejudices against him still kept him from public office.

'My life is finished,' he said. 'I am banished from the scene of action.' Clementine was as optimistic as he was pessimistic.

On 17 July 1917 Lloyd George, Prime Minister again, felt himself strong enough, in spite of great Tory opposition, to bring Winston back into the Government. He appointed him Minister of Munitions.

The family's house in Cromwell Road became, almost overnight, Winston's second war headquarters, with only the remotest resemblance to a home. Prime Minister Lloyd George and other Cabinet Ministers came and went at all hours; official dispatch boxes piled up in the hall and on the stairs, and as soon as one lot of the boxes was cleared another pile appeared. Telephones, and secretaries pounding typewriters were everywhere, and Clementine and the domestic staff had their work cut out keeping the children out of the way.

Winston didn't help much either, when, one morning, on discovering the children building a crane with a construction set they had been given, he suggested that they make a bridge instead. On finding there were not enough parts for this project, he sent a secretary on a mission to buy additional construction sets, and the dining-room was transformed into a workshop.

Clementine's complaints about girders on the sideboard, and nuts and bolts all over the carpet, got her nowhere. The result was the total occupation of the dining-room by a bridge some fifteen feet long and eight feet high, stretching from wall to wall. Finally, yielding to protests about the loss of the dining-room, he transferred the bridge to the hall, where visitors, including Cabinet Ministers, had to stoop under the raised centre section of the bridge to get through the door.

During the remainder of the war, Winston directed the supply of arms to the Forces; but trouble still had a way of finding him—though perhaps it was the other way round.

With Clementine and their friend Edward Marsh, he visited a munitions factory outside London. Shortly after they had begun their return journey, an automobile carrying a convalescent out for her first airing hit their car broadside, turning it completely over.

Eddie Marsh recalled: 'There was I, with Clemmie sitting on me in what struck me at the time as a remarkably becoming attitude. I felt inclined to ask her, as a man in one of Gilbert's plays asks the lady who has fainted in his arms by arrangement: "Is that comfortable?" hoping that she would reply, as the lady does in the play: "It is luxurious!"

'We were neither of us frightened till Winston began banging on the glass over our heads. "Don't do that," we said irritably—but he explained that he wanted to get us out before the car caught fire (which it didn't), so we forgave him.'

On the morning of 11 November 1918 Winston and Edward Marsh were looking through a window of the Admiralty at the figure of Lord Nelson in Trafalgar Square when, once again, Big Ben chimed eleven o'clock. Armistice had been signed. The war was over, and the church bells throughout London joined in the general thanksgiving.

As they rang out jubilantly, Clementine, radiant, excited, ran in to share the moment with her husband. Together they left the building and drove through the cheering thousands in Whitehall to see the Prime Minister. Some of the more enthusiastic celebrants clambered on to the car and stood, yelling, on the running-boards.

Winston had been one of Prime Minister Lloyd George's war-winning team, but the fighting was over, and with its ending Clementine joined her husband in the political shadows. The public's gratitude, adoration, and limelight seemed to be reserved exclusively for their war leader, David Lloyd George.

At the beginning of 1919 Winston was Secretary of State for War, dealing with the great problems of demobilization.

The situation in Russia was also, at this time, a frequent topic in the Churchill home. One afternoon a guest—newly arrived from eastern Europe—joined them for lunch. It was Lieutenant-General Sir Adrian Carton de Wiart. He had returned with a first-hand report of the offensive launched against the Bolsheviks by Denikin—commander of the White Russian troops. Denikin was advancing so fast that it looked as if he would reach Moscow.

Whenever Clementine was present at discussions with military or political colleagues or informants, her role was mainly that of the good listener. But if her own shrewd assessment of a conversation differed from Winston's, she gave her opinions. Its clear grasp immediately commanded respect, and often obviously influenced him.

General de Wiart's luncheon with them to discuss the Russian revolution provided an example of this. Of the meeting, the General says:

'I returned home to report, and Mr. Churchill, who was then at the War Office, asked me to lunch. Mrs. Churchill and Jack Scott, his secretary, were the only other people at the lunch. It was the first time I had met Mr. Churchill. I was immensely flattered by the idea of discussing with so great a man what was at that moment an important situation.

'Mr. Churchill wished me to get the Poles to join in Denikin's offensive, but I repeated Pilsudski's warning (Poland's Chief of State, General Pilsudski, had told him that Denikin would fail and soon be pushed back to the Black Sea).

'I remember Mrs. Churchill saying: "You had much better listen to General de Wiart."'

Winston did listen, and within weeks Pilsudski was proved a good prophet, and the White Russian forces were back in the Black Sea.

In January 1921 Winston was appointed Colonial Secretary, with the Middle East as his chief concern.

Throughout the changes Clementine was constantly at his side, confident and smiling whatever her inward thoughts might have been. It was a time when Winston was in need of every ounce of her comfort and support, for politically he was in eclipse. Indeed it was already being said that he was 'growing old and was a politician with a past and no future'.

That was something she would never believe.

4

ARREST WINSTON!

THE fortunes of politics played havoc with their early married life.

Few who honour the name of Winston S. Churchill realize how intensely that same name was once hated and despised. While Winston jutted his chin more determinedly in defiance of his enemies, Clementine displayed her pride in him for all to see as she endured with him the catcalls and jeers of rowdy political meetings; and lived with her family virtually as social outcasts.

For more years than most people care to remember, Winston and Clementine walked together through their public and private lives, almost friendless.

She was the only person who saw the two faces of Winston Churchill. The public one was for all to see: the other turned only to her for consolation and the strength to continue.

How many women who envy Clementine Churchill her place in history would have envied her in the days when the cries were: 'Arrest Winston!'—'Try him for treason!'?

Claiming that he had made war on the Soviet Republic without the approval of the electors, the Scottish Independent Labour Party, with the approval of other Socialist circles, demanded in August 1920:

'The arrest and impeachment of Winston Churchill,' and the Newport, Monmouthshire, branch of the National Union of Ex-Servicemen passed the following resolution:

'That this meeting of Ex-Servicemen calls upon the Prime Minister to immediately bring to trial Mr. Winston Churchill on the charge of high treason, as much as he secretly gave help by way of British troops to Admiral Koltchak, an adventurer, without explaining the truth of the whole gamble to the country.'

Winston absolutely denied the accuracy of the statements contained in the allegations made against him, but the mobs continued to yell for his blood.

Clementine listened to them demanding again his political destruction, when, as Chancellor of the Exchequer in 1928, his policies raised the cry once again—'Churchill must go!' from hundreds of M.P.s and influential men outside the House of Commons.

They accused him of being 'the evil influence in the Cabinet which had intimidated the Prime Minister and his other colleagues', they labelled him a 'dangerous and distrusted political renegade'. They shouted 'Will the greatest limpet that has ever clung to the Treasury bench renounce his last political refuge?' The cries of the mob and his opponents couldn't waver his wife's supreme faith in him.

He thought he had done well at the Colonial Office. He had achieved settlement of Middle East problems in 1921; brought into being the Irish Treaty of 1922; his speeches were winning greater than ever Parliamentary acclaim and he seemed about to reap a reward in public opinion and public popularity. Then, inexplicably, at that point his career went into a decline.

The resignation, in 1922, of Lloyd George's great First World War Coalition Government brought Winston's first General Election disaster and Clementine's first public trial of strength.

Three days before the opening of the campaign in Dundee, Winston went down with appendicitis.

The operation, performed only just in time, made active electioneering impossible for him.

'My wife and a few friends had to keep the battle going as well as they could,' said Winston. 'The tide flowed fierce and strong against us.

'Meetings were everywhere interrupted and disorderly, not through the efforts of individuals, but far worse—from general discontent and ill will.'

At four previous elections he had easily held the Dundee seat, but by 1922 post-war reaction and disillusion were rampant.

In his election memorandum Winston declared: 'I stand as a Liberal and a Free Trader,' but Dundee wasn't convinced that he really was a Liberal, for, in the four years since the end of the First World War, he had publicly advocated the idea of a Centre Party to be composed of moderates from both Conservatives and Liberals.

With political fortunes going against him, illness denied

him the opportunity of defending his policies and actions.

As he lay bed-ridden in a nursing home, the entire weight of the election campaign fell on Clementine.

She arrived in Dundee with her little daughter Diana, and opened the campaign for his re-election by addressing two meetings the first evening—one at which she faced a rowdy threatening crowd in the Larch Street Hall, the other preaching to the converted at a ladies' meeting in the club rooms at the Liberal and Unionist Association's headquarters.

Just before she arrived at the Larch Street meeting a quantity of 'electric snuff' was released by trouble-makers in the crowded and stuffy hall. The meeting was off to a rough start, and efforts to retain order met no success.

Windows were hurriedly flung wide to clear the atmosphere.

Clementine's entry was greeted by hoots and some subdued cheers.

She bowed to the audience and smilingly took her seat on the platform.

A fresh supply of snuff was released by someone and the platform party were among its first victims. Clementine was overwhelmed by an almost uncontrollable bout of sneezing.

She rose to speak, and, finally mastering the urge to sneeze, said: 'I'm glad to see that you are all alive and kicking in Dundee.'

She was immediately interrupted by about a dozen hecklers, and there was temporary pandemonium again.

She stood, calmly waiting for the noise to quieten. When order had been restored, she added: 'I only wish that my husband had not been prevented by his illness——'

A voice interrupted: 'Oh! Is he ill?'

'He has been very ill,' answered Clementine. 'If he had not been very much better I would not be here tonight. I hope he will be here before the end of the week. I don't think it is very sporty of you to ask such a question. My husband has had the great honour of representing this great city for fourteen years.'

(Voice: 'Fourteen years too long.')

'He is much handicapped by not being able to be present at this election,' Clementine continued, 'but I feel a great deal of confidence in that the great majority of the men and women of Dundee will not take advantage of that fact; and I should not be a bit surprised if he got a much bigger majority at this election than ever before.'

There were groans and hisses; and a voice yelled: 'Don't be daft!'

'And any rate, I would not like to see that the voters who came out for him all these years should let him down when he is ill,' she went on.

A barrage of incoherent questions followed, to which Clementine, raising her voice, replied, her words ringing through the hall: 'Do you think this is a good advertisement of the proceedings of an open meeting?'

She gave as good, and better, than she got, and finally departed the undoubted victor.

Two nights later, at a gathering of almost 4,000 people in Caird Hall, Dundee, she faced and handled pandemonium created by a section of the meeting.

The hall had filled hours before, and a queue stretched on and on round to the Green Market.

Clementine rose to address the meeting, but, before she could speak, some women near the front of the gallery, two of whom were carrying babies in their arms, proclaimed themselves to be Communists, and started to shout almost incoherent arguments at the top of their voices. They screamed and waved their fists at her, and Clementine just stood there, waiting for the storm to subside. She began again:

'A great many people,' she said, 'throughout the country —and I am told some of them live in Dundee—think and say that the unemployment in the country——'

'What about a bob a week for a baby?' interrupted a woman from the gallery. Hissing started.

'I am rather inexperienced, and unless the lady is quieter my speech will take much too long,' countered Clementine.

'A great many people, I say, think that the prevailing unemployment and distress is caused by the shortcomings and wrongdoing of the late Government——'

Barrackers chorused their agreement.

'—and, as my husband was a member of that much-abused Government, and he is the only member of the Government that you here in Dundee can get at, some of you say, "It is all Churchill's fault—let's put him out."'

('Hear! Hear!')

'That is what some people say; now *I* have a chance, and I want to tell you what *I* think.

'I want you to consider whether this unemployment and distress is really the fault of the late Government or is rather, in great measure, caused by those men who profess to lead the working men and women of the country, but who very often give them very bad advice?'

Her voice, at this point, was drowned by shouts, boos, and hissing.

Once more she waited for the outburst to die a little, and then proceeded to review the industrial situation since the 1918 election.

'Until then,' she said, 'Labour was represented in the Cabinet. But, in the autumn of that year, Labour withdrew its Ministers and went into Opposition. Shortly after the election, a threat of a coal strike clouded the industrial world, and before this strike there was the great railway strike in 1919 which greatly hindered the revival of trade and threw many out of work. Now it is known that the railway men secured nothing by the strike that they could not have had by negotiation.

'The good sense of the railway men and transport workers prevented a disastrous general strike, but for three months idleness in the mines lost fifty million tons of output and thirty millions in wages, while unemployment was increased enormously.'

An interrupter screamed: 'What about Mesopotamia? Your husband was responsible for all the millions spent there.'

'Most of the millions there were spent *before* my husband took over control,' emphasized Clementine.

The gallery howled her down. She waited patiently with a smile until the hall was reasonably quiet again.

'The latest evidence of this unhelpful attitude,' she went on, 'was seen in the reluctance to co-operate with the Cabinet to produce measures and schemes to cope with unemployment.'

Applause and jeers greeted this.

'Now, the late Government, so abused and despised, had stood between the community and all these threats. By constant work, impartial attitude and fairness, and yet by its

75

alertness, it had guided the ship of State safely so far through all those dangerous shores and quicksands.'

Cheers and protests.

Disregarding a query from a woman heckler in the gallery, asking: 'Does your bairn live on a shilling a day?' Clementine said she could not believe the citizens of Dundee would vote for the Socialists, or for Mr. Pilkington, who was simply splitting the Liberal vote.

A woman cried: 'Your supporters should be ashamed to support you, the way you are keeping down the working classes.'

'*You*, my dear lady, need not support me,' replied Clementine.

Communists in the hall started to sing 'The Red Flag', and there was pandemonium again.

The following morning the local *Dundee Advertiser* headlined the meeting—'Mrs. Churchill Again in a Storm', and the *Glasgow Herald* declared: 'Although she has not by any means encountered smooth water, Mrs. Churchill has proved herself a "bonny fechter" on behalf of her husband. Facing an enormous audience in the Caird Hall, she got the best hearing of all the speakers, mainly as the result of admirable tact and determination in handling the obstreperous interrupters, who were Communists. . . .'

At yet another meeting, Clementine faced, for the first time, the cry: 'Your husband is a warmonger!'

Defiantly she stood up to defend him: 'He's not a warmonger!' she cried.

Then she asked the packed hall:

'Will you trust my husband once more?'

'Never again!' 'He is incapable!' shouted people from the audience.

'This is the first time in my life,' said Clementine, 'that I have heard my husband described as incapable.' The meeting ended.

Two days before polling day, Winston arrived to join the battle.

He had to be assisted from the train and practically carried to his room up the stairs of his hotel. He nevertheless insisted that he would address an important meeting himself.

'If you are going to speak,' said Clementine, 'you must sit

down—you are not fit enough to stand for an hour.'

He promised to follow her advice.

The hall at which he was to speak was besieged long before the time advertised for the commencement of the meeting.

Ten thousand people clamoured for admission to the hall which could only accommodate 5,000, with the majority standing.

The doors opened, and the rush for admission was such that the police had to draw their batons.

Winston entered by a back door, leaning heavily on his stick and gripping Clementine's arm. As soon as the crowd saw them, they were received with cheers, hissing, and booing, and the demonstration continued for some time.

The meeting's chairman announced that the candidate would remain seated during his speech because of his still weak post-operative condition. The unsympathetic, hostile crowd shouted: 'Stand up, Winston!'

'You'll be at the bottom of the poll!' shouted one interrupter.

'If I am to be at the bottom, you might let me have my last dying fling,' cried Winston.

'I won't go on any longer than you wish me to,' he said, and strove hard to catch some of the insults and questions hurled at him from all parts of the hall. It was hopeless. Finally, provoked to the limit, Winston forgot he was an invalid. Shaking his fist, he angrily cried: 'If about a hundred young men and women choose to spoil the whole meeting, and about a hundred of these young reptiles choose to deny to democracy, to the mass of the people, the power to conduct a great assembly, the fault, the blame, is with them, and the punishment will be administered to them by the electorate.'

Winston tried to continue the meeting. Then, rising from his chair, and leaning heavily on his stick, he surveyed the hall, and, with the colour mounting in his face, lifting his voice above the boos and shouting, he announced:

'Ladies and gentlemen!—I thank you most sincerely for the attentive hearing you have given me, and I think you have indicated in a most effective manner the devotion of the Socialist Party to free speech. It has been shown very clearly that a handful of rowdies can break up a great meet-

77

ing, and prevent ten times their number from transacting their public business. But, ladies and gentlemen, we will not submit to the bullying tyranny of the featherheads. We will not submit to be ruled by the mob.'

He resumed his seat amid renewed cheers and boos. A few moments later he rose, waved, and bowed repeatedly to all parts of the hall. Then, turning from his chair and leaning once more on Clementine's arm, they left. The meeting had lasted thirty-five minutes.

On polling day Winston and Clementine were at the count, moving from table to table watching the assortment of ballot papers grow. The mountains in favour of both his opponents were clearly dwarfing the comparatively insignificant accumulation of voting papers supporting him.

The result was soon obvious.

Clementine, who had worked ceaselessly and tirelessly throughout the campaign, stood beside him at the bottom of the steps leading to the platform from which the result, and his defeat, was declared.

They did not go on to the platform.

The post-war Coalition Government collapsed.

Winston was now not only out of office for the first time since 1900, he was out of Parliament as well.

To jeers and boos, Clementine took his arm and they stepped into a taxi and drove to their hotel. There was nothing left to do but go home.

Commenting on his defeat, the *Observer* wrote at the time: 'Dundee was more than a bombshell. It was like an electoral landmine exploding with shattering din and fantastic sequel. The circumstances were such that Mr. Churchill, on personal grounds, has, we believe, the generous sympathy of the country.

'Stricken by illness at the beginning of the struggle, late in the field, not fully restored even then, yet assailed by Communist rowdyism, he was cruelly handicapped. The burden of the task fell on his devoted wife, but, in the dour circumstances of Dundee, the odds were too great.'

On their return to London, Winston went to Buckingham Palace to hand back the seals of his office. He emerged again, no longer a Minister of the Crown, but the words 'Right Honourable' were prefixed to his name to denote his membership of the Privy Council.

'I am without an office, without a seat, without a Party, and without an appendix,' said Winston to Clementine, and added:

'If Dundee doesn't want me, I'll have to try somewhere else.'

He was exhausted, and still suffering from the after-effects of his illness. Clementine decided on convalescence: 'We're going to Cannes,' she announced.

As he climbed slowly back to health, Winston confessed he was 'getting used to sitting in arm-chairs in front of the fire and going to sleep'. He didn't fool Clementine.

Every afternoon he would put up his easel on the beach or at some countryside beauty spot, and paint, with Clementine sitting close by. They rarely spoke as he painted, but he liked her there.

Soon he settled down to work and writing the first volume of his *World Crisis*.

Although he was no longer in any way connected with the Government, threatening letters still reached him from Ireland, and, in consequence, both he and Clementine continued to live under constant guard.

He daily grew stronger, and she observed his growing impatience at being out of things. The time had come to return to London.

Suddenly, Parliament was dissolved, and together they stepped back into the political arena, to battle for Winston's election as a Liberal Free Trader at Leicester.

His opponents used the publication of his book, *The World Crisis*, as ammunition in the campaign, reviving the accusation of his responsibility for the 'Dardanelles disaster', in spite of the expedition having been triumphantly vindicated at a meeting of senior naval and army officers.

Winston counter-attacked his accusers: 'The Dardanelles might have saved millions of lives. Don't imagine that I run away from the Dardanelles. I glory in it.'

Clementine also hit back on his behalf. At an election meeting in Leicester she flayed critics and rallied supporters with:

'Perhaps your Free Trade swords have grown rusty with lying by for so long, but you must get them out and polish them up and fight for this really great cause.

'My husband has been described as unfit to represent the

79

working class in Parliament,' she declared. 'Someone has got to speak up about him, and who, if not his wife?

'There was a man at one of his meetings who said my husband was not fit to speak for the working classes. Well, I am not a politician, but I must say my blood boiled when I heard that.'

And, listing some of his efforts on behalf of the working classes, she said:

'With the single exception of Mr. Lloyd George, my husband has been responsible for the passing of more legislation for the benefit of the working classes than any other living statesman.

'When he was at the Board of Trade in 1909, he framed the Sweated Industries Act; he was responsible in a large measure for the system of Labour Exchanges, and also for the Coal Mines Regulation Act, designed to make the mines as safe as possible for the miners to carry on their work. Then there was the Shop Hours Act.

'I mention these things,' said Clementine, 'because it always vexes me when I hear people saying that Mr. Churchill is fitted principally to take part in wars.

'A great many people think he is essentially military. I know him very well, and I know that he is not that at all; in fact, one of his greatest talents is the talent of peace making.'

With her as his chief election aide again, Winston fought the battle of votes.

Arriving at a great mass meeting in Essex, a brick smashed through the window of their car, narrowly missing injuring them both. Violent crowds did everything but rush them on the platform, and Winston described it as 'the worst crowd I have ever seen in England in twenty-five years of public life.'

He failed to gain the Leicester seat too.

Both of them were now under constant fire. He was out of favour and Clementine felt the sting of social unpopularity.

One morning, as they were driving past the Houses of Parliament, Winston turned to her and said: 'It's difficult, after one has been nearly a quarter of a century in that place, to know that one has no longer any right there.'

'The opportunity will come,' she answered.

5

THE CHANCELLOR'S LADY

THEY waited impatiently for another chance. It came. The Abbey Division of Westminster faced a by-election.

Winston, who had been a Conservative, then a Liberal, decided to contest the division as a 'Constitutionalist and Anti-Socialist candidate'.

The constituency, which includes the Houses of Parliament, the seat of the Government, Buckingham Palace, all London's principal clubs and theatres, with areas varying from St. James's Street and the Strand to Soho, Pimlico, and Covent Garden, is one of the strangest and most remarkable in the world.

The poorest and the richest are there.

In this novel constituency they campaigned and won all manner of support—dukes, jockeys, prize-fighters, actors, actresses, business men, and restaurateurs.

Clementine persuaded the chorus girls at Daly's Theatre in Leicester Square to sit up all night, after the shows were over, addressing envelopes and dispatching election leaflets.

'It was,' said Winston, 'incomparably, the most exciting, stirring, sensational election I have ever fought.'

It certainly was.

Even in the very cosmopolitan Abbey Division, the two of them faced, and met, nonstop trouble.

Travelling from one meeting, the driver of their car took a wrong turning, and found himself in a cul-de-sac. A large crowd closed in. A man jumped from the crowd on to the running-board of the car, and the fight started.

Winston's personal detective sent several attackers sprawling. The mob eventually gave way, and the attackers' ringleaders were chased down the street.

Back in the car, Brendan Bracken, later M.P. for North Paddington and one of the Churchills' closest friends, was found to have been stabbed in the thigh during the scrap!

Clementine, working from a luxurious house in Lord North Street filled with priceless Gainsborough paintings, organized and led an army of canvassers ranging from peeresses and beautiful society girls to theatre chorus girls.

Eve of polling day a great car procession, with Winston and Clementine in the leading vehicle, wound its way through every street in the constituency until the small hours of the morning, sounding their horns, whirring rattles, and shouting 'Vote for Churchill!'

The vote count was held at Caxton Hall.

As the last packet was being carried to the table, some-one shouted: 'You're in, Winston, by a hundred!'

Clementine embraced Winston excitedly and kissed him, and onlookers cheered. Churchill was back in politics.

His opponent's officials went across to the returning officer and demanded a recount.

The result—his opponent was declared by a small major-ity!

Now it was the turn of Winston's agent to demand a recount, and the final answer was reached:

Winston had been beaten by forty-three votes! He was out again.

Clementine had helped wage a tremendous fight, but they had lost. This time there was no deep bitterness—it had been a fair battle and they had got close to victory.

Neither of them was downcast. Both were convinced their political fortunes were about to change. They hadn't long to wait. Parliament was dissolved again.

The autumn 1924 election, which became known as 'the Red Letter Election', brought a red-letter day for the Chur-chills.

Winston was invited to stand at Epping in Essex. He was returned with a majority of 10,000.

Said Winston: 'It makes me earnestly hope that I have now found a resting place amid the glades of Epping which will last me as long as I am concerned with mundane affairs.'

A few days after the election the new Prime Minister—Stanley Baldwin—sent for him.

Winston walked out of No. 10 Downing Street, and moved with Clementine and the children into No. 11, next door—he had been appointed Chancellor of the Exchequer. The tide had turned in their favour again.

A happy, smiling Winston, accompanied by Clementine,

their son Randolph, and daughter Diana, stepped out of No. 11 on 28 April 1925 for a great day—the presentation by the new Chancellor of the Exchequer of his first Budget.

As the family appeared in Downing Street, waiting crowds cheered, and Winston, gripping the little traditional red dispatch box containing the Budget secrets, promenaded with his family down Whitehall to the Houses of Parliament.

People stopped, buses stopped, cars stopped—everything stopped for the Churchills and the little Budget box that day.

Clementine took her seat in the gallery to witness the scene in the crowded Chamber of the House. Showman Winston put on a great performance. In the middle of a sentence he broke off, filled a glass before him with what was unmistakably not water, and, raising it, announced with a grin and a typical Churchillian touch: 'It is imperative that I should fortify the revenue, and this I shall now, with the permission of the Commons, proceed to do.'

With that pronouncement, he looked up, raised the glass to Clementine in the gallery, and drank a toast to her. Her laugh echoed through the Chamber above all others.

As wife of the Chancellor of the Exchequer, and hostess of No. 11 Downing Street, Clementine found new scope for her own remarkable personality.

It is said that the devoted wife of an outstanding public man is liable to be a somewhat shadowy figure, for it is in the nature of the role she has chosen that she should be ever present but never too much in the foreground.

More than one Minister's wife has sought to gain the reputation of being a power behind the throne, a buttress for her husband's brilliance.

Clementine decided to be neither, but instead a little of both. The art of not being overshadowed, yet never stealing the limelight, became one of her special achievements.

Her self-appointed task was to bring a sense of normality into the home life of her abnormal husband.

Her reputation as a hostess had already been established. Now, as the Chancellor's Lady, she was in her element and at her best.

She introduced personal touches into historic No. 11, bringing a new warmth to the usually formal, cold rooms of the house. She made it a home.

She also made it a social centre. Winston loved to entertain, and whoever the guests, and whatever the subjects for discussion, he liked Clementine to be at the head of the table facing him. Her subtle role and influence was obvious to everyone who dined or lunched with them.

She was ever ready to take over when one of his moods threatened to turn table talk at a meal into disaster. She could melt conversational ice with the warmth of a smile.

That Winston worshipped her was plain to everyone. Millions idolized him. She gave him someone to idolize. She is the only person who ever knew how to really handle him, but it was never by any attempt at domination.

He had his life—she had to make her own. To a large degree, she had to learn to lead a separate existence. Wrapped in his own world, Winston could, though in the same house, leave her very lonely for a great deal of the time. Their temperaments, completely different—their marriage would never have worked had it been otherwise—found a clear appreciation of each other's role in their home and public life.

Above everything else, she considered his creature comforts. Comforts which to others are luxury, but which to Winston were the breath of his existence, leaving his thoughts unfettered. She organized their home, letting the staff carry out her orders in their own way; but always personally watching over his foibles and wishes.

She fashioned a rule for living for both of them—a pattern for making the best use of time, allotting specific activities to specific hours each day. She found it necessary to plan in advance whatever needed doing, though, at the same time, wisely allowing sufficient flexibility for the unexpected.

She believed implicitly in this plan for daily living and made her daily schedule pivot around her husband, her work, and her family. She would start each day knowing what she wanted to accomplish with it, beginning with instructions to secretaries and staff to ensure everyone knew exactly what duties were expected of them and knew what part they were required to play in the day.

Without this basic routine, the machinery that ran the Churchill homes through the years could never have contended with the countless unpredictable things that happened within their walls.

Like Winston, she also believed in relaxation as a vital necessity to good health, and that the best relaxation is change. To conserve energy, she found it essential to live sensibly, regulate living and habits, and keep a careful balance between activity and relaxation. She implicitly followed this code of living herself, and did her utmost to see that, as far as possible, Winston followed it too.

Without question, it is this pattern for living that carried Clementine and Winston so successfully through the immense turmoil of their lives.

The public vision of her has always been of a controlled, calm person. In fact, by nature, she is excitable, vivacious, bubbling. But she managed to achieve an inner calm, enabling her to work undisturbed by everything around her, and to concentrate on matters in hand.

The willpower that gave her the strength to stay outwardly and inwardly calm became, perhaps, her greatest asset, although at times this disciplined rein on herself has temporarily broken, but it would be incredible and inhuman if it had not. In the main, she succeeded in maintaining a peace within herself in spite of all the tensions and crises around her.

Without this control she could never have withstood the terrifying wear and tear on her nervous system. With all the strains and stresses with which she has had to contend, it is miraculous that her outbursts of irritation and impatience have been so comparatively few.

And, like Winston, her powers of concentration are remarkable. When she is talking to you, you are conscious that during those moments it is you and only you receiving her undivided attention with no distracting impression that she is thinking of the next person while speaking to you.

Even in those early days she attached tremendous importance to general care of health and to conserving energy, and her stamina and energy for a woman of her responsibilities was remarkable.

Her tennis was of tournament class, and one of her favourite tennis opponents was Sir Edward Marsh, who for years was Winston's secretary, and who became Sarah's godfather. Eddie Marsh was one of their closest and dearest friends throughout his life.

When Edward Marsh became seriously ill, Clementine nursed him back to health at Chartwell. He wrote in his diary:

'With Clemmie and Winston. If only there were a God I could thank for those who love me.'

When later he was stricken with pneumonia, a letter arrived from Chartwell. It read:

> *My Dear Eddie,*
>
> *I was much concerned to read in a press cutting which coupled our names of your illness. . . . Randolph tells me that you are recovering all right, but that you had to have two nurses. I am indeed sorry for this calamity and wish I had known about it before.*
>
> *We shall be down here a great deal now and if you like come and pay a visit, pray let us know. You could rest comfortably here. Clemmie says you must come. Just—vegetate—as I do.*
>
> *Love from*
> *W.*

Eddie Marsh accepted the invitation to convalesce again at Chartwell.

Both at their Chartwell home and at No. 11 Downing Street, Clementine made an outstanding success of her duties. She made a personal impact on the social and political scene. But, on one occasion, the Chancellor's Lady put the Chancellor on an embarrassing spot.

She had gone with a number of her friends on a visit to Paris—a shopping spree for, among other things, some new dresses.

On her return, Winston went to Victoria Station to meet her. She arrived with just some hand baggage which was put into the car. Her heavy baggage had been registered and sent ahead to London.

On reaching Downing Street she asked Winston whether he was using the car; if not, she wanted to send the maid and another member of the staff to the station to collect the registered baggage. Winston wasn't going out again, so off went the two messengers.

When they had located the baggage, a Customs officer

asked whether they contained anything to declare.

'I have no idea what is inside them,' answered the maid, 'so perhaps you had better open them yourself and see.'

The Customs officer was about to do so when he noted the labels, the name on them, and that they were addressed to Downing Street.

'Never mind,' he said, changing his intention of examining the cases, and, chalking clearance markings on them, passed them through unopened.

The following week the friends who had journeyed with Clementine to Paris came to lunch. During their conversations, one of them asked Clementine how much duty she had paid on the new dresses she had brought back from Paris.

'I didn't pay any at all,' she answered.

Overhearing this, Winston inquired why not. She explained what had happened when her maid had gone to collect the baggage from the station and about the obliging Customs officer.

She had thought no more of the incident at the time.

Winston immediately requested the bills for the dresses. When she had found them, he instructed his secretary to telephone the Customs and Excise and ask for an officer to come round to No. 11 the following day. The officer duly arrived, examined the bills and the dresses, did a swift calculation of duty due, and the Chancellor of the Exchequer's wife paid up.

She was upset at first at her forgetful oversight in not dealing with the duty liability from the outset, knowing how particular Winston always was about payment of duty on anything he, or any of the family, purchased abroad. It had been a slip on her part in all the excitement of her home-coming. A few days later they both laughed about it all, and her unintentional smuggling episode became a family joke.

As the months and years passed at No. 11 Downing Street, Winston's popularity and following increased. He presented five Budgets to Parliament, but Clementine sensed an increasing resentment and fear of his aggressive personality among many who purported to be their closest friends and political colleagues.

Newspapers started to turn on him viciously. 'His life is

one long speech,' declared one newspaper.

Clementine listened to his critics saying:

'At what age does a politician cease to be a promising young man and become a middle-aged disappointment? At what period are we obliged to confess that the mischances and indiscretions have accumulated to such a total, that failure has become a habit with him?

'Mr. Winston Churchill has been before the country for some 25 years and has now reached the respectable age of 50 or so. Despite much personal charm and a very creditable amount of industry, it is not unfair to say that, having regard to the time at his disposal, he has mismanaged more public business than anyone else of whom we have any recollection.'

The cold wind of change was beginning to blow against them again.

In 1929 Baldwin's Government went to the country. Clementine went down to Woodford for the fight. Accompanied by Diana and Mary, she mounted the gaily decorated motor wagon being used as a platform, and explained to a mass meeting in the market-place at Epping:

'My husband is away at Liverpool speaking to two big meetings so I am at home keeping shop for him.'

She then invited the Irish M.P., Sir Robert Lynn, to talk. In the course of his speech there were several interruptions, and one man called out, 'What is Winston—Constitutionalist, Conservative, or What?'

Clementine asked to be allowed to answer the question.

'My husband, in his later years, returned to his old Party. His father was Lord Randolph Churchill, who endeavoured to start a Party which he called "Tory-Democrat", so it was natural that his son should join the Tory Party.

'Some twenty-five years ago, however, he left that party on the question of Protection and joined the Liberals. He remained with them until 1924, when Mr. Asquith put the Socialists into office. He then sought election as an Independent at Westminster, and although that was a strong Tory stronghold, he was only defeated by a few votes.

'He was asked by the Epping Conservatives to represent them as a Constitutionalist, and did so. Now, however, he was assured that the Party did not include Protection in their programme, and he was a Conservative. He had always been a Free Trader, and always would remain so.'

Another interrupter called out: 'What about his previous defeats?'

Never lost for a quick answer, Clementine replied: 'It is no disgrace to be defeated.'

She asked the crowd to give three cheers for Winston, and they did.

Later, adding his words to hers in answer to the cries of 'Turncoat!' Winston himself replied.

'A policy is pursued up to a certain point; it becomes evident at last that it can be carried no further.

'New facts arise which clearly render it obsolete; new difficulties, which make it impracticable. A new and possibly the opposite solution presents itself with overwhelming force. To abandon the old policy is often necessarily to adopt the new.

'It sometimes happens that the same men, the same Government, the same Party have to execute this volte-face. It may be their duty to do so because it is the sole manner of discharging their responsibilities, or because they are the only combination strong enough to do what is needed in the new circumstance.

'In such a case the inconsistency is not merely verbal, but actual, and ought to be boldly avowed.

'Few men avoid such changes in their lives, and few public men have been able to conceal them. Usually youth is for freedom and reform, maturity for judicious compromise, and old age for stability and repose.'

He was re-elected, and the Conservatives weren't. Once more, the Socialists emerged as the largest Party, and resumed power with Liberal support, but Winston's popularity was now at its lowest ebb in years.

A story told by Lord Baden Powell, father of the Boy Scout movement, reminded Clementine of Winston's ability to bounce right back at a moment of apparent defeat.

He recalled days in India when Winston led the polo team of his regiment to victory in a great polo tournament, scoring two goals with a dislocated arm strapped to his side.

Said Lord Baden Powell: 'Winston delivered one of the finest orations ever pronounced on polo at the dinner that followed the victory. He had, until then, made one short speech in public.

'After this, someone moved—"that this be enough of Winston".

'The motion was carried—naturally enough—with one dissent—and they put young Winston under an upturned sofa to be kept there for the rest of the evening, and the fattest subaltern in the regiment sat on top of the sofa and him.

'After a few minutes, Winston wriggled out from under the sofa's arms, and, grinning up at the company, spoke prophetic words:

' "It's no use sitting on me—I'm indiarubber!" '

Nervous of Winston's personality and bounce, Baldwin swore he would never include him in any future Government he might form, and Baldwin kept his word.

Winston and Clementine went back into the wilderness.

A friend inquired: 'Don't you think No. 10 Downing Street would be a lovely place to live?'

'No, I don't,' replied Winston. 'I've lived next door to it long enough to know.'

6

LIVING WITH DANGER

FROM the early days of their marriage, whenever the call and demands of work took Winston overseas, Clementine insisted on going with him if it was possible. She knew he liked to share his official life with her too, and valued her opinions and comments.

So in March 1921, when he departed on a Middle East tour, he was accompanied by Sir Hugh Trenchard (later Lord Trenchard), Sir Archibald Sinclair—his Parliamentary Private Secretary—and Clementine.

At that time Winston was combining the joint offices of Air Minister and Colonial Secretary. The visit to Egypt was to decide whether an increase in air installations there would relieve some of the pressure on army garrisons in the area, and he also hoped to simplify policing of the Suez Canal zone by the introduction of an improved air patrol system.

Clementine was under no illusions about the trip—it would be no picnic, no Cook's Tour. She was well aware that Russell Pasha, head of the Egyptian Police, had warned: 'Churchill is in the greatest danger; trust no one, black or white throughout your journey.' As far as she was concerned, the warning was all the more reason for being at his side.

Winston and his official party travelled overland via Paris to Marseilles. In those days the Paris–Lyons–Marseilles Express was one of the worst and most uncomfortable rail journeys in Europe. She didn't like the journey, but knew Winston was enjoying it, and that was good enough for her.

Before boarding ship for Alexandria, Winston felt like indulging in a little painting. Immediately after lunching on bouillabaisse, the two of them set out by car along the Marseille coastline to a spot overlooking the town. Up went the famous Churchill portable painting table, and he continued to paint the beautiful view almost until sailing time, with

Clementine keeping him company.

A tremendous crowd of Egyptians and Arabs watched the ship dock at Alexandria. As the Churchills and ther party walked down the gangway, the noisy dockside seemed abnormally silent. Suddenly the silence was shattered, and as Winston and Clementine walked towards the waiting Air Force car, police, using long thin canes, drove shouting, threatening demonstrators back until the cars moved off.

In defiance of the hostility around them, they insisted on riding in the back of an open touring car. With Sir Archibald Sinclair, they drove through the streets along which Egyptian nationalists, voicing their opposition to Britain, yelled insults and threats.

The Egyptians stared at the impeccably dressed Englishwoman seated at the side of her husband in the car, who, in spite of the menacing crowds, showed no fear—unafraid for herself and unafraid of anyone. Courage is a quality she and Winston had in common.

On reaching the hotel in Alexandria and tidying up in their rooms, they went down to lunch. After they had eaten, Winston, who didn't believe in wasting time, started his tour of inspection at a large R.A.F. camp outside the city. Serious complaints had reached Whitehall of conditions in a number of camps, and he was going to see for himself. Clementine was particularly insistent on inspecting the married quarters. The officer in charge didn't seem too happy at her interest, but, acting as her husband's aide on the one subject on which she was the foremost expert in the party, she looked everywhere, at everything, examining bedrooms, kitchens, not missing a thing. Any point deserving attention she pointed out to Winston, who, in turn, dictated a note to his personal secretary for future action.

Outside the aerodrome, demonstrators marched about screaming 'A bas Churchill!' and 'Iskut (shut up), Churchill!' Native police breaking up a 'Down with Churchill!' demonstration were stoned and forced to take flight.

Reinforcements arrived and fired on the crowd. At first it was believed that three people had been killed, but casualties turned out to be nine rioters injured with bullet wounds, and twenty police injured by stones.

When the party returned to Alexandria, the men held a

dinner conference. Clementine, exhausted from the long day in the heat, preferred to retire to her room. As she lay resting on the bed, she became conscious of someone moving about the adjoining room. It was supposed to be unoccupied.

The room next to their suite had been reserved for the storage of boxes containing official documents.

She realized it would be useless rushing downstairs to summon assistance—the intruder could be gone by the time they returned—and so could important papers. There was only one thing to do, and she did it,

She opened the door of her room and yelled.

'Quick! Quick!' she shouted. 'There's someone in the next room!'

Her cries for help were answered by their personal detective. He rushed to the room, but the door was locked. The intruder could still be heard rummaging about inside.

The detective stepped back and charged the door. It didn't give. He ran back and charged again. This time it smashed open to expose an Arab disappearing through the window. Before the detective could draw his revolver, the man had vanished somewhere on the roof.

Clementine and the detective checked the contents of the room and were relieved to find that the seals of all the boxes were still unbroken.

The incident was over by the time Winston, hearing of the disturbance, hurried to Clementine. It was agreed that the detective should sleep in the room with the boxes to prevent any further attempt, and a bed was put in there for him.

It was decided to maintain absolute secrecy for their departure from Alexandria. Arrangements were made for them not to leave from the station but to join the train at a point along the line.

They slipped away from the hotel by car early one morning and took a roundabout route along obscure thoroughfares, heading for the rendezvous.

The King's personal train was to take them out of Alexandria. It was garishly painted pure white, and that included the locomotive itself. There was bunting around the boiler door, and flags waving from the cowcatcher.

Despite all attempts at secrecy, Egyptian nationalists still managed to discover the route, and, as they boarded the train, angry mobs appeared on both sides of the line, screaming abuse and hurling stones at the carriage windows.

One large stone shattered the window beside Clementine, and glass splintered all over her. Miraculously, she was unhurt. Her reaction was calmly and meticulously to brush the pieces of glass from her clothes.

More stones hurtled through the broken window. Throughout the attack, Winston, unperturbed, sat smoking a cigar. The perspiration on their faces was due to the heat of the day, not the heat of the mob.

Clementine snapped on a fan in the royal compartment and began to read while Winston busied himself with a dispatch box of papers. As the train slowly approached a crossing, more stones were flung at the windows by Egyptians beside the railway track. Some tried to jump the train and cling to the doors. Window after window was smashed, glass splinters were everywhere. Clementine stopped reading—she wasn't scared, she was annoyed. Attendants in red uniforms started to sweep up the glass, the train went on, and she went back to her book. This woman who could charm anyone could also freeze to a block of ice with a look that would make an Arab intruder shiver in the noonday sun.

The remainder of the journey was uneventful until, about five miles outside Cairo, the train suddenly, and unexpectedly, slowed to a halt. Beside the railway line stood a number of open cars. Two British staff officers appeared at the carriage door and informed them that tremendous crowds were awaiting their arrival in Cairo. What kind of 'welcome' the crowds were anxious to give, the two officers didn't make clear. It was therefore decided that the Churchills and their party would leave the train and proceed by car to the city. It was just as well. When the train steamed into Cairo station, mobs broke through police cordons to storm it. Winston and Clementine's entry into Cairo that day could have been their final exit.

When they reached Cairo's Semiramis Hotel, General Allenby, conqueror of Damascus, and Russell Pasha, Chief of the Egyptian Police and greatest enemy of international drug smugglers, were waiting. Both emphasized the seriousness of the threats to their lives. Following the stoning of the train at Alexandria, there was no question of their warnings being taken lightly. Nevertheless, they decided that the next day, they would, for the first time, act like typical tourists and treat themselves to a visit to the Pyramids.

Two of the guides asked them to sponsor a race between four natives to the top of a main pyramid and back. Clementine was appointed starter and judge and, at her signal, the four natives commenced to scale the pyramid like monkeys. They climbed at an incredible rate, and she presented the winner with a money prize.

Another commercially minded native then offered the hot and weary visitors some 'freshly brewed' English tea. Only Sir Archibald Sinclair drank the tea. The following morning, he went down with typhoid—almost certainly caused by the tea—and the inspection tour continued without him.

The following morning, Colonel T. E. Lawrence—'Lawrence of Arabia'—joined them for a visit to Sakkara, site of the famous excavations, which was a two-and-a-half-hour camel ride across the desert from the Pyramids.

Lawrence was introduced to her, and she studied this strange man about whom she had heard so much from Winston—this man who had been of such tremendous help to the Allied cause during the First World War, and had by his leadership and personal magnetism prevented Arab forces from joining Germany.

She saw before her a shy, slight, awkward, untidy little man, whom she swiftly put at ease.

She penetrated his reserve, and they were soon laughing and talking animatedly together.

She was deeply impressed with the sincerity with which he talked about his adopted people, the Arabs.

Lawrence made no attempt to hide from her the risks of the visit to both her and Winston, and warned that their lives would be in jeopardy every moment in Egypt.

'The Egyptians are convinced that Mr. Churchill's visit is to interfere with their internal affairs. They are bitterly resentful of British policy,' he told her.

Their arrival at the Pyramids was greeted by a magnificent turn out of local sheiks mounted on Arab horses. There were also a number of camels belonging to the Egyptian Camel Corps. Clementine mounted the wooden saddle on a large bony camel that had been decorated for the occasion with a vivid purple shawl. Winston mounted his animal and was like a schoolboy revelling in the novelty.

At a command, the camels swayed to their feet and, accompanied by the escort of Arabian sheiks and their stallions, the party galloped off.

It is hard for any novice camel rider not to look ridiculous first time out, but somehow Clementine contrived to look in command of everything on her camel.

Once you mount a camel you go where the camel goes. A cord runs from the saddle to the camel's right nostril but pulling it sometimes only brings a dirty look from the camel—and nothing else.

She looked at Winston incongruously astride his camel and noticed he was slipping to one side of the saddle and was anxiously looking for something to hold on to. There wasn't anything.

Suddenly, the cavalcade came to an abrupt halt—Winston had fallen off! There was complete confusion. Sheiks dismounted and rushed to him.

The girths of his beast obviously hadn't been tightened enough, so the saddle had slid round, toppling him off into the sand.

The Arabs begged him to continue the journey on one of their horses. He wouldn't. They also offered Clementine a horse. She politely refused, equally determined to continue by camel.

Said Winston defiantly: 'I started on a camel, and I'll finish on a camel.'

As he remounted the kneeling animal, Colonel Lawrence, convulsed with laughter, exclaimed: 'You know what happened, Winston, when that camel of yours knew you were going to ride on its back and they were putting on the saddle and tightening the girth, he blew himself up with pride, but when he got out in the desert and found you were the same as any other man, pride went before the fall. He just decided to get rid of you as speedily as possible, so he let out the air, the saddle girth loosened, and off you came.'

And off they went.

Going out there were seven in the Churchill party. Coming back there were only five. Throughout the two-and-a-half-hour rocking, swaying, bumping, camel journey, Clementine never once complained, determined to stick it out with the rest of the novices. But when it was time to return to Cairo, she didn't mount her camel again—she went back by car.

For days she didn't stop chiding Winston on how easily the mighty are fallen and how simple it was for an Air Minister to be brought down to earth.

Back in Cairo, a procession of students awaited their arrival.

The students marched up and down outside the Semiramis Hotel crying to heaven to bring down a curse on the heads of the Churchills. The students were about again when Clementine and Winston set out for the Abdin Palace to call on King Fuad of Egypt.

As the car reached the palace gates, crowds screamed hatred. Then the mob broke loose. Students engulfed the car, clambering on the running-boards. Two of the guards in the car hit out at shrieking attackers, and palace officials rushed out to give added protection. The car eventually managed to pass through the gateway.

For their departure, they took a different route back to the hotel, and even then only just escaped violent mobs.

The Churchills decided to go to the Holy City accompanied by Colonel Lawrence, and Sir Herbert Samuel, who was then British High Commissioner for Palestine.

Sir Herbert Samuel had come to Cairo to warn the Churchills of a plot to murder them with a bomb or shoot them somewhere along the route from Cairo to Jerusalem.

As Clementine packed for the trip to Jerusalem, Winston received a message from London. An Italian General named Badoglio was preparing a troop movement into Libya for his chief—dictator Mussolini. The Italians were moving into Africa. Winston stood alone for a moment on the balcony of their suite and looked across the wilderness of North Africa. He stepped back into the room and said to Clementine: 'If Badoglio is on his way, we'll have to come back here some day.'

On the way to the Holy Land, the train stopped at Gaza, and they took the opportunity to tour the city, and to visit various local institutions, including a pottery factory. As the party emerged from one building, they found it impossible to pass through the enormous crowd outside which, by now, was obviously unfriendly. Straining to force a passage, mounted police rode their horses straight at the crowd, but people just seized the horses' bridles and pushed them back. The mob moved forward and was about to swamp the party when Colonel Lawrence held up his hand. His voice rang out. He spoke only a few words, and miraculously, the great crowd parted like the Red Sea, allowing the party to return to the train.

Clementine had become accustomed to living with danger. She never showed fear, nor did she ever conspicuously try to stop Winston from taking risks. Instead, quietly, she would see that every possible precaution was taken for his safety, and would constantly try to introduce additional safeguards with the aid of members of their staff. She was fully conscious of the numerous attempts on his life, and these attempts also frequently endangered her life.

On their return from the East, they continued to live with danger, for soon afterwards came a new threat—this time from the Sinn Feiners—the Irish underground organization then engaged in a campaign of murder and outrage.

Winston was in the House of Commons when the news came of the assassination of Sir Henry Wilson by Irish gunmen. If Sir Henry had been shot, Clementine realized only too well that Winston, as Secretary of State for the Colonies, and therefore the man responsible for the conduct of Irish affairs, could be the next target.

They were living at the time in Sussex Square, Paddington, London. During the weeks following Sir Henry Wilson's murder, their home was guarded like a fortress, and she was aware that the danger was not only to him, but also to herself and her children, for the stop-at-nothing Sinn Feiners might decide to use the kidnapping of one of them as a weapon against Winston.

She daily watched her home searched from top to bottom for bomb plants. A Rolls-Royce car completely armoured with half-inch steel plates and weighing some two-and-a-half tons was placed at their disposal, and two Special Branch men—expert shots—were detailed to shadow the Rolls in a motor-cycle and sidecar.

Each night, before going to bed, she saw detectives check their house, room by room—they were taking no chances of a gunman slipping through their guard. The Rolls took Winston to Whitehall by a different route every day, as a precaution against possible ambush.

Clementine learned the necessity of the safeguards when Winston arrived home one evening to tell her of a 'near miss'. That morning, the armoured Rolls had been driving through Hyde Park by way of the Bayswater Road, when he had spotted two men standing back, almost in some bushes, by the side of the road. One of them appeared to signal to another man standing by a tree about one hundred yards or so ahead. Traffic had slowed the car and Winston and his detective guard were both on the alert. 'You saw them—if they want to have a go, let's have a go at them.' The detective wouldn't let him have his way, and ordered the chauffeur: 'No stopping—get your foot down and get going!'

The driver steered the car into the middle of the road where it could be screened by other vehicles.

Another safety touch in their home was the addition of a steel plate fitted into the back of Winston's favourite bedroom chair. Clementine added a feminine touch by decoratively covering the plate with attractive tapestry cloth. Every night Winston would place a fully loaded ·45 Colt on this chair. 'If they come, Clemmie,' he said, 'they will receive a warm welcome, and not obtain a walkover.'

But even as Sinn Feiners threatened the safety of his wife, children, and self, he worked on for peace for Ireland, and, with typical strategy, arranged a secret meeting between Sir James Craig, then leader of Unionist Northern Ireland, and Michael Collins, leader of the Sinn Feiners, upon whose head the British Government had placed a 'dead-or-alive' price.

Even before their marriage, Clementine had heard that Winston not only lived with danger, but invited it.

'Winston told me that his first escape from death or serious injury occurred when he was a child of four,' she once said. 'He was in Ireland at the time, and one day he was out with his nurse riding a pet donkey when a procession approached. The donkey took fright and started kicking, flinging Winston off and giving him concussion of the brain. He described the incident as his first introduction to Irish politics.

'He was also only eighteen when, while on holiday with his aunt Lady Wimborne at Bournemouth, and playing a game with his younger brother and cousin, he jumped from a bridge crossing the chine, crashed thirty feet to the ground, and regained consciousness three days later. It was three months before he could crawl from his bed.'

It was never a shock for Clementine to hear of his miraculous escapes. She grew accustomed to the 'surprises'.

In 1912 he received his first flying lesson at Eastchurch. The following day, Winston's instructor crashed in the plane in which they had been flying together, and the pilot was killed. A few weeks later, Winston insisted on making a flight in a new type of seaplane. He was delighted with the test result—the new machine had behaved perfectly, but when he returned home there was a message waiting for him saying it had dived into the sea a few hours after he had left taking three men to their death.

Another plane in which he was taking off suddenly turned somersault, struck the ground, and left him hanging head downwards fastened to his seat by his belt. The plane was smashed, but all he suffered was cuts and bruises.

From their first days together, she knew the man she had married was the kind who might be killed at any moment.

She never let him know by anything she said, that she was unduly worried.

Winston would simply say: 'Under sufficient stress—starvation, terror, warlike passion, or even cold intellectual frenzy—the modern man we know so well will do the most terrible deeds, and the modern woman will back him up.'

Clementine shared his brand of fatalism.

7

DEAD OR ALIVE

'WINSTON CHURCHILL will not be permitted to leave the United States alive.'

That was the information received by the State Department in Washington when the Churchills arrived in the United States, in February 1932, on a lecture tour.

This was no empty threat. The India Office in London had received confirmation of a plot to assassinate Winston in America. He didn't believe in hiding its seriousness from Clementine, nor could it in any way be hidden from her, for Washington had assigned Secret Service agents to reinforce the police in protecting them throughout their stay. Winston told Clementine that an Indian terrorist society with headquarters at San Francisco, and members in almost every city in the U.S.A., had ordered his assassination because he had bitterly opposed the Indian White Paper, urging that Indians were not, as yet fit to govern themselves.

Washington even circulated descriptions of Indians considered likely to cause trouble and be directly involved in the threat.

New York gave the Churchills a typical big city welcome. Waiting for them on the quayside when their ship docked were several cars and motor-cyclist policemen to supply a howling-siren escort through the streets all the way to the Waldorf Astoria hotel.

The State Department's Chief Special Agent, Mr. R. C. Bannaman, was one of the first to greet them. He told them: 'The repeated threats made on your life are believed to come from Hindus, chiefly those in California associated with the Chard Party which is composed of reckless Indians favouring direct action to obtain Indian independence. The threatening letters we received state that Mr. Churchill has incurred this party's enmity by his speeches on India and his pronounced views on the Indian question.'

Secret Service shadowers followed them everywhere, aware the terrorists might switch their attention to Mrs.

Churchill as a reprisal for her husband's political stand on India. This possibility was not shielded from her.

Special bodyguards were posted at every railway station with instructions that no East Indian be admitted to lecture halls in which the Churchills were to appear. Plain clothes detectives were also positioned among audiences.

First real sign of trouble from the Indian secret societies came at Detroit. As Winston and Clementine entered a lecture hall, Indian 'students' paraded outside with placards attacking his policies. But it wasn't until they reached Chicago that a dangerous incident occurred.

The lecture had, as always, been an outstanding success. As they left the platform, they both started to speak to members of the audience crowding round them. A group of admirers stood chatting to them in the forecourt of the building when a well-dressed Indian, walking with one hand in his pocket, came through the glass swing doors, and headed straight for the Churchills.

One of the watchful detectives spotted him, pulled a gun, and pointed it straight at the Indian. The man stopped, spun on his heels, and went crashing through the swing doors into the arms of more waiting detectives.

Seeing his colleague held, another Indian waiting outside started to run down the street chased by two more detectives. While all this was happening Winston and Clementine continued being sociable with the group of admirers.

Although Indian extremists didn't manage to injure Winston or Clementine during that visit to America, a New York taxi cab driver nearly rewrote the Churchill story. It happened on the night of 13 December 1931. They had just finished dinner and decided to retire early when the telephone rang. It was an old friend, Bernard Baruch, who was head of the War Industries Board during the two years that Winston was Minister of Munitions. The acquaintanceship, begun through official cables, developed on a personal basis.

It was about 9.30 p.m. when Bernard Baruch telephoned to invite them round to his home to meet some mutual friends. Clementine decided to make an early night of it, and Winston descended the thirty-nine storeys to street level alone.

About 10.45 p.m., the phone rang again in their suite. It

102

was a doctor from New York's Lennox Hill hospital, calling to inform Clementine that Winston had been knocked down by a cab and been taken to the hospital. With her daughter Diana, she rushed to him. He was swathed in bandages in a private room. The injuries were obviously extensive. She asked to see Dr. Otto Pickhardt and Dr. Foster Kennedy, who had attended him, to learn the nature of his injuries.

Dr. Pickhardt told her: 'After a prolonged X-ray examination to determine the full extent of the internal injuries and especially whether there was any danger of pleural haemorrhage ensuing from injuries to the membranes of the lungs and thorax, he is resting comfortably after sustaining severe shock and concussion without loss of consciousness.

'There are many large bruises on the right arm, chest, and leg together with wounds to the tissues of the forehead and nose which have been stitched.

'I am afraid he will be unable to do active work for several weeks.'

For some time Clementine sat by the bedside holding Winston's hand and speaking to him reassuringly, but his eyes remained shut. Finally they flickered open and she smiled at him. Behind her stood Bernard Baruch. Then Winston spoke:

'Tell me, Baruch, when all is said and done, what is the number of your house?'

'1055.'

'How near was I to it when I was smashed up?'

'Not within ten blocks.' (Half a mile.)

And Winston began to explain what had happened. The accident occurred as a result of his having momentarily forgotten the difference between the British and the American rule of the road. On his way from the Waldorf Astoria to the Baruch home, he realized he'd forgotten the exact number of the house. Peering out of the cab scanning the houses as they sped past, he decided to walk across the road and inquire at a likely-looking house.

He explained to Clemmie: 'In England we frequently cross roads along which fast traffic is moving from both directions. I did not think the task I set myself either difficult or rash. But at this moment habit played me a deadly trick. I got out of the cab somewhere about the middle of the road and told the driver to wait. Then I instinctively turned my eyes to the left.

'Suddenly upon my right I was aware of something utterly unexpected. I turned my head sharply. Right upon me, scarcely its own length away, was what seemed a long dark car rushing forward at full speed. I thought quickly: I am going to be run down and probably killed. Then came the blow. I felt it on my forehead and across the thighs. But besides the blow there was an impact, a shock, a concussion indescribably violent. I do not understand why I was not broken like an eggshell or squashed like a gooseberry. I certainly must be very tough or very lucky or both. I did not lose consciousness for an instant.

'Then a constable bent over me and asked my name. "Winston Churchill," I replied and I thought it lawful and prudent to add, "The Right Honourable Winston Churchill from England!" "What is your age?" asked the officer. "Fifty-seven," I replied, and at the same moment the odd thought obtruded itself upon my mind. How very old to be knocked down in the street by a car. I shall have a very poor chance of getting over it.

'When the constable proceeded to demand particulars of the accident my mind and speech apparatus worked apparently without hitch and I said "I am entirely to blame: it is all my own fault."

'Another constable came with the question "Do you make any charge against any person?" To which I replied, "I exonerate everyone." '

On arrival at hospital Winston asked to be allowed to telephone the Waldorf Astoria so that he could tell Clemmie himself that whatever had happened he was going to get well. He was informed: 'She is already on the way here.'

Clementine spent the night at his bedside. Not until the following evening when the doctors assured her that he was completely out of danger and that there were no complications, did she return to the hotel, cheerful though exhausted by the long strain.

The news broke in Britain and telephones never stopped ringing with condolences and inquiries. Randolph phoned his mother regularly from London to ask after his father's progress. Then, the following evening, pleurisy developed as a result of the blow to Winston's chest, and there was serious anxiety over his condition. Once more Clementine remained by his bed. At last, Randolph received a cable. It said simply: 'Doing splendidly.' Winston was on the mend again.

Among the cables Clementine opened at the Waldorf Astoria was one from their friend 'The Prof'—Professor Lindemann (later Lord Cherwell), Winston's scientific and economic adviser. Professor Lindemann, putting the accident into mathematical perspective, cabled:

Just received wire delighted good news stop Collision equivalent falling thirty feet on to pavement equal six thousand foot pounds energy equivalent stopping ten pound brick dropped six hundred feet or two charges buck shot point blank range stop Shock presumably proportional rate energy transferred stop Rate inversely proportional thickness cushion surrounding skeleton and give of frame stop If assume average one inch your body transferred during impact at rate eight thousand horse-power stop Congratulations on preparing suitable cushion and skill in taking bump Greetings to all Lindemann Hotel Continental Nice

Only for one other person did she divert attention from her husband during those anxious days and that was for Mario Constansino, driver of the car that had knocked him down. Each day conscience-stricken Mario called at the hospital asking anxiously after the condition of the patient. Hearing this, Clementine invited Mario to call at her hotel. A nervous Mario was ushered into the suite at the Waldorf Astoria.

Always the perfect hostess, Clementine quickly put him at ease and offered him tea.

'I wish to assure you that my husband entirely blames himself for the accident,' she told Mario. 'I understand that you are unemployed. Did the publicity surrounding the accident hinder your efforts to find work?' she asked.

'It hasn't helped,' he replied.

'Would you accept a cheque from us?' she asked tactfully, but Mario declined. 'Well, in that case,' she added, 'would you like to see my husband?' Mario was delighted with the suggestion, and with her promise to make an appointment for him as soon as it was permissible.

A week later, the doctors told her that the patient's steady recovery made it possible for him to leave although his condition still necessitated complete rest and he would be unable to resume his lecture tour as yet. So, 'battered but not shattered', as he described himself, Winston left Lennox Hill accompanied by two nurses, to spend Christmas Day at the hotel quietly with Clementine and Diana, but before he did so, Clementine kept her promise to Mario. He was invited to Winston's hospital room where the Churchills entertained him to tea and reassured him again that he was blameless.

For half an hour the car driver, the victim, and the victim's wife, chatted.

'I never want to drive a car again,' said Mario. Winston and Clementine tried to persuade him not to give up the pleasure of motoring, and then, as he was about to leave, she picked up a book from the bedside cabinet and said, 'We thought you might like this as a memento of the occasion.' It was an autographed copy of the latest Churchill book—*The Unknown War*.

Ethel Barrymore came to see him at the hotel as soon as he came out of the hospital, and discussing fate and his lucky escape he said, 'You know, Ethel, I have a terrible past.' Ethel and Clementine both roared at this.

'I think he was thinking about the time he left the Conservative Party and for a few years was a Liberal,' commented Miss Barrymore—'he was always chiding himself like that, more or less humorously.'

While Winston recuperated in his hotel room, an unexpected offer of a 'tonic' arrived one afternoon with a ring at the door of his suite.

Clementine opened the door to a young man who presented a card. The well-spoken, well-dressed man, it seemed, disagreed with the restrictions of Prohibition then in force in the United States, preventing Mr. Churchill from enjoying the pleasure and benefit of a glass of whisky. He therefore offered to supply any quantity of liquor of whatever quality or vintage required, explaining that regular supplies were 'fished out of the sea'.

Clementine diplomatically and graciously declined the bootlegger's offer, at the same time expressing her appreciation of the thought. Nevertheless, the following day a number of 'sample' bottles of vintage champagne and genuine Scotch were delivered 'With compliments and good wishes'. The straw round the champagne bottles was, in fact, seawater stained.

8

NIGHTS AT THE ROUND TABLE

At Chartwell, Clementine entertained guests from all over the world. Most didn't just come to enjoy the social pleasures of their home—they were part of Winston's personal intelligence service. With their aid, he created an information service on affairs in other countries as good at least as those of the Foreign Office itself, and often better.

Winston used luncheons and dinners to help widen his general knowledge, to debate subjects of topical controversy, and to sharpen his intellect on the strop of the opinions of others.

After the meal was over, rather than retire to the drawing-room, Winston, as a rule, preferred to remain, and continue talking with his elbows on the table.

He used guests as a sounding board, gathering more actual knowledge from them than he could gain from a file of official reports.

'What do people say?' was the question that most frequently launched after-dinner conversation at Chartwell.

Those fortunate enough to be asked to lunch or dine with the Churchills found the experience memorable for many reasons—and not only because of the importance of their host. Their hostess, and her influence on the proceedings, was equally impressive.

Listen to a dinner guest's description of his reception at Chartwell:

'There were few more flattering experiences than to be one of Clementine Churchill's guests at Chartwell.

'She had the quality of being able to get the best out of anyone.

'On arrival at Chartwell, you passed the beautiful garden setting of the semi-circular drive, entered the great door, and then were shown into the high-ceilinged drawing-room, with its long spacious windows, and dominating portrait of Winston.

'Waiting to greet you was the tall, elegant, silver-haired

woman with a smile that immediately made you welcome. Her clothes were impeccable. You always remember her elegance, but never the details of what she wore—which is the hallmark of a well-dressed woman.

'Her voice is soft, and unaffected, her conversation simple, direct. You were not made to feel gratified at being allowed to "mingle with the mighty".

'Clementine would offer a glass of sherry and you would find yourself from the start more relaxed than you ever dreamed you could be. You barely noticed that because of the non-appearance of your host, the meal was late—you were too flattered by the genuine interest being shown by your hostess in your nervous small talk.'

Guests considered her a felicitous hostess, ever watchful of the husband opposite her at the head of the table, ever prepared to stimulate conversation when he became moody. Apparently shy, she was in fact always in control of the situation, and could steer the table talk from holidays abroad to Russian scientific progress, the ambitions of Mao Tse-Tung, and back to some new recipe she had been trying.

She has the kind of grace which makes people say: 'She seems to get lovelier each year.' She radiates a charm that makes young people say: 'I hope I may look as attractive as I grow older.' Tall and slim, she moves easily and lightly. Her large grey eyes shine beneath strongly marked thick eyebrows which are never plucked. She has a classic profile, which her daughter Sarah has inherited. In her younger days she wore her hair parted in the middle, but now she prefers a modern style, with curls high on her forehead. Somehow, years did not submerge her youth and beauty.

Hers was a gracious well-ordered family life geared to the comfort and peace of mind of the man she married.

Finally, late as usual, Winston would arrive, with his poodle Rufus at his heels. He was happiest at meals when the company included Rufus on his left and Mickey, the tom cat, on his right.

Immediately all were seated, a maid brought a small mat and a plate of dog food. The mat was laid beside Winston's chair and the bowl handed to him. Rufus was then led into the room and Winston gave him his meal. Thereafter, the little dog sat quietly at his master's feet.

Apart from the Continental delicacies which Clementine delighted in trying out from time to time, the Chartwell table offered, in the main, straightforward English food: meat, game, or poultry.

At first Winston might take over the conversation, but he was just as apt to fall into sudden, complete silence, devoting all his attention to his plate and becoming apparently unaware of everyone and everything.

Instantly, Clementine carried the ball, adroitly keeping the conversation flowing.

She always liked round tables because she considered them best for conversation as everyone can see everyone and nobody is left out.

Through the long course of their marriage she acted as hostess to the world's most eminent men and women, and no guest who ever sat at her table can ever remember anything going wrong.

There were times, however, when Clementine had to change the conversation very swiftly to avert disaster.

Mrs. Leo Amery, wife of the ex-Secretary of State for India, was at dinner with Winston when Sir Stafford Cripps, his colleague in the Government of the day, was sitting opposite to him. Cripps was a strict vegetarian.

Winston, thoroughly enjoying himself, tucking into turkey and asparagus with hot butter sauce, suddenly leaned over to Mrs. Amery, glanced mischievously at Cripps, who had refused every savoury dish, and said: 'I am glad I am not a herbivore. I eat what I like, I drink what I like, I do what I like....' Then, after one of his emphatic pauses, he concluded: '... and *he's* the one to have a red nose!'

At another dinner when a well-known personage, a man of the highest rectitude and towering stature, was a guest, his moral sentiments and general air of gloom made a marked impression.

When at last he left the table, Winston glowered at Clementine and the other survivors, and demanded: 'Who will relieve me of this Wuthering Height?'

Winston's moods were unpredictable.

Clementine, on the other hand, was always the diplomat. No matter what happened in her home, she remained self-disciplined and seldom lost her dignified composure. She appreciated that when her husband 'came home from the office' he might be bringing with him the problems of the future of civilization, and that sometimes when he was late for dinner it was because he was trying to combat the evil ambitions of dictators. So, serenely, she made sure that he had a good meal.

Because he was notoriously unpunctual, she was always on time. He was known for the informality of his attire. She always dressed perfectly.

Winston always entertained extensively, and liked to have Clementine at the head of the table facing him. If conversation seemed to be foundering, she had the knack of ending a long-drawn-out discussion with a sparkling remark.

To achieve her superb meals, she spent half an hour every morning with the cook, discussing the day's menus. Usually they comprised hors-d'oeuvres, soup, fresh trout or sole, roast sirloin of beef or plump pheasants, fruit, sweets and cheese, and sometimes one of the new savouries she had copied experimentally from some publication.

Looking after a genius and bringing up a family was a full-time job, but Clementine is a woman who loves her home.

She loves flowers, particularly roses, and floral decorations are a feature of her dining-room. The centrepiece of the dining-table is always arranged at low level, so that guests are not hidden from each other and conversation impeded.

Every morning, after her interview with the cook, she personally supervises the seating plans for luncheon and dinner. Her skill at placing neighbours at table is unerring, though it was no mean feat to juggle with Cabinet Ministers, Service chiefs, top-ranking civil servants, trade union leaders, and perhaps, visiting foreign potentates. To facilitate the trick, she prefers whenever possible to seat company at a round table.

It is a tragedy that there was no latter-day Boswell to record in full the fascinating and often dramatic exchanges across the Churchill table, for it was often at luncheon and dinner that Winston was most self-revealing, and Clementine her most skilful.

Ten years before the Second World War, at Chartwell, she arranged a small, intimate luncheon party of young

111

people at which the table talk became almost a duel between a youth of 19 and Winston, and an elder guest interjecting an occasional word.

It began when the elder man said: 'Your memories, Mr. Churchill, are a romance of adventure and achievement which modern young people will feel they cannot afford to miss. Now, if you had your life to live over again, with all the experience and knowledge of the years you now possess, would you do the same things?'

Winston: 'Probably, but I should try to waste less time than I did in my early days. I wasted time until I was twenty-two. It was only then that I got the desire for learning.'

Youth: 'Would you go in for politics?'

Winston: 'Politics are greatly changed. They are no longer so interesting. There are not the same prizes. Our politicians are not the brilliantly dominating men they were. They are not given the same position by the public. The world is not the same ... yet if I lived again, I suppose I should do as I did before; but I should make a different set of mistakes and miss a different set of chances.'

Youth: 'What *were* your mistakes and missed chances?'

Winston: 'I did not acquire a love of learning until I was twenty-two. My effective education was almost entirely technical. Afterwards I wished I had gone to Oxford.'

Youth: 'Would you *care* to live your life again?'

Winston: 'Not from the beginning, anyhow. I would like to start at twenty. Thence to twenty-five are the best years. The whole world is then before you. I would not like to have my schooldays over again. I never enjoyed school. No doubt it was my fault. I was not good either at work or play. I did not like routine.'

Youth: 'And you wish you had been at a university?'

Winston: 'Yes; but I think a boy in the main must choose his own path.'

Elder guest: 'Should not the parents have some say in the matter?'

Clementine: 'In these days it often makes no difference if they try. Modern young people will do as they like. The only time parents really control children is before they are born. After that their nature unfolds remorselessly, petal by petal.'

Youth (to Winston): 'Have you enjoyed your life?'

Winston: 'Yes, indeed, since my schooldays. I have mostly done what I most wanted.'

Youth: 'That's all very well. We can't all do that. You had advantages.'

Winston (throwing some salt over his left shoulder): 'I had a name, I had a little money and no possessions. I had to find my own opportunities.'

Elder guest: 'You had qualities of push and go which are not given to all young men, you know.'

Winston: 'Except for my name, all the rest I had to work for, to fight for. When I was twenty-two, with my small Army pay not covering expenses, I realized that I was handicapped and unable to live my life as I wanted to. I wanted learning, and I wanted freedom.

'I realized that there was no freedom without a little money. I had to earn money to get independence. So I set to work. I wrote. I studied. I lectured. I won my freedom. I can hardly remember a day when I have found nothing interesting to do. I am always employed on something.'

Youth: 'Now what about politics?'

Winston: 'I was troubled about the state of things in this country. The people have the power; they are responsible. Are they paying enough attention to the job they have demanded and undertaken? Are things thrashed out as they ought to be and as they used to be?'

Youth: 'You would not advise young men to go in for politics, then?'

Winston: 'I did not say that; but the attraction and glamour of Parliament are much less than they used to be. Everywhere democracies and their leaders are shirking facts; hoping to solve problems and pay off perils with well-meant platitudes.'

Youth: 'Do you ever regret that you didn't give your life to literature?'

Winston: 'Why should I regret that?'

Youth: 'Do you not think a great pen might do a greater life-work than an eloquent voice and a political genius?'

Winston: 'That's an old subject of debate. Perhaps what you say is true, though I am not prepared to admit that I have either the one faculty or the other in any high degree. If I were to pronounce one way or the other, I should say I

113

was much more at home with a pen than on the platform. To speak in public takes a great deal out of me. I never excelled as a platform speaker.'

That was the luncheon table self-assessment of the man whose immortal war-time speeches were to save Britain and ensure the freedom of the civilized world.

But Clementine also had to learn to contend with a man who frequently at dinner parties would pretend to be deaf so that he could concentrate on his food. (It was then that she took over the conversation.) She saw that he got his favourite foods; he preferred meat to fish.

His breakfasts had to be plain and simple. He liked bacon and eggs, kidney. Sometimes chicken. And always coffee.

He had a weakness for liver, cut thick and very lightly done. Whenever they went to a restaurant, he always said exactly how he wanted his food cooked, and heaven help them if they didn't follow his instructions.

Winston always liked clear soup. One evening, in error, he was served with thick soup, and their guests with clear soup.

'What is this white creamy looking stuff?' he growled, and the offending plate was hastily removed.

Clementine is very fond of French cooking, knows all about it, and likes the right dishes with the right sauces and condiments. Such refinements were wasted on Winston.

He liked plain, solid English fare: a good steak and kidney pudding or a steak and chips.

Her thrifty, strict upbringing was the ideal grounding in housekeeping for one who liked his meals solidly Victorian while proclaiming that, domestically at least, 'I very much enjoy the luxury of indecision.' The food served at the Churchill tables was always excellent, not because Clementine spent a great deal of money on it but because she took great pains to see that it was infinitely varied and always of the very best quality.

However much he underestimated his own talents on the platform, Winston often expressed at the table his strong views on how a speech should be made. Said General Eisenhower: 'At dinner one evening, he jumped on me and gave me unshirted hell for speaking from memory and not following the text of a prepared speech. It was at a ceremony and I had been given a speech of 125 words, which I memorized.

' "Never trust your memory in anything like that, with people following every word you say," warned Winston.'

It was Clementine who passed on to 'Ike' at dinner the counsel of the greatest orator of our times. She said: 'Winston is a great believer in the use of spectacles. You should wear spectacles—big, round ones which you can take off and shake in their faces. And if you have notes, don't try to hide them. Shake those in their faces, too.'

Winston gave similar advice to Lord Halifax, British Ambassador to the United States during the war years.

'Do you speak from notes?' he asked.

Lord Halifax said that he did.

'That's quite all right,' said Winston, 'but never try to pretend to your audience that you are not using them. If you do that, you get into a sort of competitive game of hide-and-seek in which you're bound to lose. If you are perfectly open about it, you can keep them waiting as long as you like while you find your place in your notes, and put on your glasses to read them, and they won't mind at all.'

Winston's slight difficulty with the letter 's', far from marring his conversation, seemed to add a special kind of emphasis from time to time. His Parliamentary and broadcast utterances were deliberately spoken. His table talk, though generally faster, was nevertheless unhurried and broken from time to time with telling effect.

Often his vehemence would practically exhaust guests by its overwhelming power, and it was left to Clementine to bring calm back to the conversation.

One day at table, somebody remarked that nothing was worse than war. Winston, almost rising out of his chair, thundered: 'Dishonour is worse than war! Slavery is worse than war!'

Field-Marshal Montgomery sparked him off another way. They were lunching just before the end of the war when Monty, dressed in his famous beret and pullover, remarked: 'Now that it's nearly all over I suppose you will be spending the evening of your days quietly.'

'*Evening?*' roared Winston. Then, more softly: 'And you, I suppose, will be getting into uniform.'

Another occasion Monty said to Winston: 'I don't drink,

I don't smoke, I don't lie in bed, and I am fit.'

'Ah!' said Winston. 'Well, I do drink, I do smoke, and I do lie in bed—and *I'm* fit!'

Winston and Clementine often openly revealed their enchantment with each other at the dinner table when he smiled at her and she returned his gentle look. When he was inclined to be a little short with guests who bored him with idle chatter, Clementine moved in with an extraordinary range of knowledge and personal understanding of each guest present. She made it a practice to discover beforehand the interests of all her guests. Even if she were not interested in the subjects involved, she would consider her guests by swotting them up in advance.

She could never have been the complete companion to Winston without having a brilliant mind and striking personality of her own. She is a wonderful chatelaine, though not an outstanding cook, being better at training cooks than at preparing meals herself.

Her warm smile gives a hint of humour. A witty and charming conversationalist, she has the knack of seeming to take you into her confidence with her smile, just as Winston enjoyed jolting you into activity with his words. Her knowledge of affairs, political and domestic, is tremendous.

Reminiscences were always a feature of his table talk, and Clementine, a perfect listener, never ceased to enjoy his re-telling of some vivid incident in his career. Even though she may have heard the story in some form before, such was his magic and mastery of words that she ever showed her obvious pleasure. And indeed, to listen to him relating one of his countless exploits, as he pared an apple at the dining-table, was an unforgettable experience.

To some luncheon guests he told the story of the destroyer which had dropped a depth charge, but instead of finding a submarine they saw bits of an old wreck come to the surface.

'And would you believe it?' he concluded. 'There was a door bobbing around with my initials on it!'

Clementine's luncheon and dinner parties often proved the turning point of men's careers.

Instead of summoning Ministers and possible Ministers to Number 10, Winston preferred whenever possible to invite those involved in Government shuffles to Chequers or

Chartwell. That is how a new stage in the political career of Mr. Harold Macmillan was reached when he and his wife were invited for the week-end to Chequers.

Canada's Mr. Diefenbaker went with some trepidation to dinner with the Churchills. He is a total abstainer.

'Sure enough,' he said afterwards, 'when I refused wine and asked her for a soft drink with my meal, Winston began muttering and grumbling about prohibitionists being the curse of North America.

'I protested that I was not a prohibitionist but merely a teetotaller.

'"Ah!" said Sir Winston. "That's not so bad. You believe only in doing harm to yourself."'

Dinner with the Churchills could prove an uncomfortable meal for the most distinguished of guests if, in some way, they had incurred disapproval.

On one occasion when Clementine turned the table talk to a discussion on minor vices, Winston said of drinking: 'All I can say is that I have taken more out of alcohol than alcohol has taken out of me. But we all despise a man who gets drunk.' On smoking: 'Some people say I smoke too much. I don't know. If I had not smoked so much, I might have been bad-tempered at the wrong time.'

And then, in a reminiscent mood he declared:

'But consider! How can I tell that the soothing influence of tobacco upon my nervous system may not have enabled me to comport myself with calm and courtesy in some awkward personal encounter and negotiation or carried me securely through some critical hours of waiting? How can I tell that my temper would have been as sweet or my companionship as agreeable if I had abjured from my youth the goddess Nicotine.

'Now I think of it, if I had not turned back to get the matchbox which I had left behind in my dugout in Flanders, might I not have just walked into the shell which pitched so harmlessly one hundred yards ahead?'

Clementine is as much a diplomat when she is a guest of others as when she is hostess in her own home. At a private dinner party which she attended with Winston, the guests included a foreign gentleman of considerable eminence.

When dinner was over, the hostess confided to Clementine with some embarrassment that the distinguished foreigner had been seen purloining an exquisite little silver salver. It was one of an antique set and quite irreplaceable. What was she to do?

Clementine thought for a few moments, and then spoke quietly to Winston. She told him what had happened, and suggested a plan to retrieve the salver. With an impish smile, he readily agreed to co-operate.

Under cover of his table napkin he, also, appropriated a salver. Then, sidling up to the potentate and slyly revealing the piece of silver sticking out of his pocket, he whispered: 'I've got one, as well as you; but we'll have to put them back, you know. We've been rumbled!'

He duly replaced the salver, and the potentate followed his example.

Anthony Eden was one of the Churchills' favourite guests. Clementine and Winston loved him like one of the family, and nothing pleased them more than when, in 1952, he actually became one of the family by marrying Winston's relative, Clarissa.

The Churchills were both fans of Charlie Chaplin, so Clementine invited him to lunch one day, but while his hosts wanted to hear about his work, all Charlie wanted to discuss was politics. In deference to him, Clementine let him have his way and Charlie let fly with a long soliloquy on pacifism and peace at almost any price. He obviously meant every word sincerely and achieved something few could do—he silenced Winston who was shaken by the outburst.

Winston finally recovered and tried to divert him by inquiring what role he hoped to play next.

'Jesus Christ,' Charlie replied.

There was a moment's silence, then Winston asked: 'Have you cleared the rights?'

Clementine hurriedly switched the conversation again. As he was about to leave, Charlie, sensing the children's inquisitiveness about him, asked Clementine if she happened to have a bowler hat and walking stick. She pointed to a cupboard; Charlie disappeared an instant inside it, then reappeared to everyone's delight as the beloved little character of the screen. For an encore, he brilliantly parodied other actors, including John Barrymore rehearsing 'To be or not to be' while picking his nose.

There was never a dull moment at Chartwell.

Sir John Rothenstein, then director of the Tate Gallery, was invited to Chartwell to lunch and to inspect Winston's latest painting.

'We fortified ourselves with an excellent lunch, washed down with the contents of certain receptacles which Sir Winston had immortalized in a series of paintings which he called his "bottlescapes",' Sir John said. 'Afterwards Sir Winston offered me a cigar. I put it firmly aside, declaring that every man should have at least one virtue, and mine was not smoking.

'He looked me sternly in the eye and replied: "There is no such thing as a negative virtue. If I have been of service to my fellow man, it has never been by self-repression, but always by self-expression." '

Concerning birth he said, at another dinner party: 'My mother intended that I should be born in London, but I elected otherwise. I arrived more than a month before my time, while she was staying at Blenheim.'

Clementine added smilingly: 'Winston is half American and all English.'

He nodded. 'I am directly descended, through my mother, from an officer who served in Washington's army. I have my pedigree supported by affidavits at every stage if it is challenged.'

One of the most notable features of Winston's table talk through the years was his almost uncanny gift of prophecy.

Prompted by a remark of Clementine's concerning scientific development, at a luncheon given years before the Second World War, he said:

'May there not be methods of using explosive energy incomparably more intense than anything heretofore discovered? Might not a bomb no bigger than an orange be found to possess a secret power to destroy a whole block of buildings—nay, to concentrate the force of a thousand tons of cordite and blast a township at a stroke?'

Discussing invasion, he asserted: 'The Germans could not have invaded us. They did not command the air, and that is what counted. In any case, Hitler did not know how to invade.

'I wrote a long paper on the use of landing craft for inclusion in The World Crisis (his history of the First World

War). Happily, it did not appear, otherwise the Germans might have seized on my suggestions and planned a more realistic invasion.

'Some people misguidedly wonder whether Hitler will appear in history as the equal of Napoleon.

'Hitler was a psychopath!' he added vehemently.

Introduction of international affairs into the Churchill table conversation could be relied upon to evoke a response from the host. During a discussion of the situation in Greece, someone remarked that the Greek political leader, Archbishop Damaskinos, was in the habit of securing himself from interruption by hanging a notice on his door: 'His Beatitude is at prayer.'

'I'd like to try that at Downing Street,' said Winston, 'but I'm afraid no one would believe it.'

They both showed great sympathy for the problems of young people beginning life in this uncertain modern world. Said Winston: 'We are ceaselessly disturbed or amused, or at any rate occupied, by fleeting superficial sensations. Old books are unread or undigested. The churches are empty. And the younger generation ask us: "What are we to do?"

'Still, there are some very simple things which can be said.

'Do not be frightened. Do not despair. Keep your head. The trees do not grow up to the sky. Strength will be given as it is needed, and guidance will be given to nations which deserve it. Do the right and simple thing according to your conscience and honour in your own sphere. We know quite well what that is. Search diligently but resolutely for practical solutions. Conquer or go down fighting. No one can do more.

'We ought not to be afraid of running risks. Since when have we learned that we are entitled to security in this transitory world of chance and illusion? The only way to avoid risks is never to have lived at all. Choosing a career is a risk. Marrying is a risk. Childbirth is a risk. All around the most careful man—every breath he draws, every step he takes, every mouthful he eats—are hazards that may be mortal....'

His most scathing utterances were reserved for dictators and dictatorship. Three years before the outbreak of war, when, against the general political stream, he was vehemently advocating rearmament, he said: 'We live in a country where the people own the government, and not in a country where the government owns the people.... You see these dictators on their pedestals, surrounded by the bayonets of their soldiers and the truncheons of their police ... while in their hearts there is unspoken fear. The little mouse of thought appears in the room and even the mightiest potentates are thrown into panic....'

With such trenchant, uncompromising pronouncements in mind, it is easy to understand why Clementine was delighted by and treasures a catalogue of fruit trees she received from a Hampshire nurseryman.

It lists among its offerings:

'Winston Dessert (March–May): This new introduction was originally called Winter King, but it transpired that the name was already borne by another variety, so it was appropriately renamed Winston because it will weather storm. Very thick skin. Remains firm until the end of its season. Slightly bitter. Juicy. Prolific. Upright. Fruit hangs tightly to tree after leaf-fall. Late bloomer. Wonderful keeper.'

On the subject of dinner with the Churchills, their dear friend Bernard Baruch had this to say:

'The world should be a guest at your dinner table and enjoy the treat of hearing you talk, with a bottle of wine always at hand, of military tactics in the American Civil War, of your early adventures in South Africa, of Gibbon and Macaulay, of the knaves and fools you have known. The spirit with which you could denounce them!

'There is also a quiet side to your life of which the world should know, and which is perhaps best symbolized in your gracious and beautiful wife.

'No one but you knows how enormous has been Clemmie's influence and contribution to your own career. I have sensed your respect and devotion to her in how quickly you would heed her gentle admonition:

' "Winston, I wouldn't say that!" '

9

ALONE—TOGETHER

THROUGH ups and downs, almost unprecedented even in British political life, she walked with him loyally.

During his ten years 'down', before the Second World War, she fought ceaselessly to soften the bitterness of political exile. In the jungle of politics, a politician—and his wife—are often ruthlessly clawed by their opponents if they lose the slightest foothold. Winston bore the hostility, the snubs, the sneers, that would have destroyed another man, with a fortitude strengthened by her absolute faith in his future.

Clementine knew only too well that Winston lived for the day when he could once more assume power and authority. He hated to be out of office.

They made a strange, yet perfectly matched team. Winston, the showman, from the tip of his cigar to the top of one of his many hats; playing to the gallery with his uncanny sense of theatre; bathing in the waves of affection rolling towards him from cheering crowds; loving to inspect guards of honour, and revelling in the trappings of high office.

And, as Winston added the human, humorous touch in public, Clementine balanced the picture with her charm and strong sense of dignity, as if to remind us all that the showman beside her was also a man of great importance.

During the mid-1930s it seemed he had 'missed the bus'. He was a lone wolf, champion of lost causes and forgotten loyalties.

There was nothing of which political prophets were surer than that he would never be Prime Minister. He had made too many enemies. Was still making enemies. His constant warnings of the menace of Hitlerism were dismissed by a public which preferred comfortable words. 'Let him write history,' they said. 'It is too dangerous to allow him to make it.'

She heard again the cries of people ignorant of the tragedy about to overwhelm them, calling him 'warmonger' during years when he was one of the few to see what was happening; when he was the lone voice in the desert.

She was with him when he went to the Central Hall, in Peckham, London, in 1931. The catcalls against him brought the meeting to uproar. All over the hall there were fist fights as members of the audience fought to reach the platform while he was speaking. There were running fights in the gallery; men, knocked out by the dozen, were carried outside the hall to recover.

During the singing of the National Anthem, many refused to remove their hats, so others proceeded to make them take them off by force.

Through it all Clementine listened to Winston, her attention riveted to him as he recalled: 'As a young man, I remember the great days of Queen Victoria. I was brought up in that reign and I was present at her Diamond Jubilee.

'As a young man I saw her carriage surrounded by scores of kings and princes. We were a great nation then and headed the world. We were the world's iron masters, its cotton spinners, shippers, and bankers. We had the sovereignty of the seas and of the land. We were envied and honoured by all. We were rich and peaceful, swelling in our own habitation. I would like to see some of those glories return. I would like to see this native land of ours resume its rightful place among the nations of the world.

'Today is Trafalgar Day. I would remind you what Pitt said: "England has saved herself by her exertions and she will save the world by her example!"'

Through the years Winston and Clementine faced the wrath of those who labelled his policies as 'personal glorification and ambition', or those who, when he stopped attacking, accused him of 'soft pedalling criticism to win a Cabinet job by his silence'.

Her friend, Margot Asquith, Countess of Oxford and Asquith—long an admirer of Winston—said she considered he would be well advised to give up politics entirely.

'He is the greatest political historian that we have had since Macaulay, and it is regrettable that he should waste a moment of his time on politics, as his lack of conviction will always prevent him from being either a good leader or a good follower,' asserted Margot Asquith.

'There are some that you cannot change; you must either swallow them whole, or leave them alone. It is no use your saying you could wish this or that were different, so as to counteract certain deficiencies ... you must make up your mind to take them or leave them. You can do something with talent, but nothing with genius, and Winston Churchill has a touch of—what we all recognize but never can define —genius.'

Clementine refused to agree with well-meaning Margot Asquith's assessment of Winston as an unsuitable leader, or as a politician without a future.

Whichever line he chose, it seemed he could do no right. Two years before the last war when the Government stood firm against rearmament, he attacked it on that issue. When Britain finally rearmed, he was abused for no longer criticizing the Government.

One Sunday morning in 1937 Clementine read in a newspaper, and marked for Winston's attention, the following passage. It said:

'Will Mr. Churchill be in the new Cabinet? He should be.'

Winston persisted in drawing attention to the smell under people's noses even if they preferred to consider that it wasn't there.

Ignoring popular feeling, he continued to cry 'Danger!'

'I urge the Government to tell the British people exactly what is going on. Let them know the truth. ...'

When news of Hitler's 'blood purge' was telephoned to them one afternoon at Chartwell, he said to her: 'The Dark Ages have come again. Germany has gone back to barbarism.'

Bernard Baruch was one of the few permitted to share with Clementine the Winston he kept well hidden in those days from the public.

'The years between the wars were bleak ones for him,' recalls Mr. Baruch, who, whenever he visited their home during that period, was recruited as an ally by Clementine to help boost Winston's morale.

'Once, as we walked through his garden, he unburdened himself to me,' said Mr. Baruch. 'His public career seemed at an end, and he wondered whether he ought not to enter some business. I tried to hearten him by pointing out that, although he might be denied political leadership for a time, he could achieve greatness with his pen. And I told him that I was sure England could not and would not go on ignoring him.

'Fortunately for her and the world, England did not when the great trial began.'

Sometimes they managed to ease the tension by inviting friends, completely unconnected with politics, to stay with them. Noticing in the newspapers that Winston's bachelor days' 'flame', Ethel Barrymore, had come to London to appear in a play, Clementine couldn't resist inviting her down to Chartwell. She liked Ethel—and, of course, knew Winston did too, and they had enjoyed her company at lunch the previous time she had been in London.

'I motored down to see the Churchills at Chartwell and spent the night,' said Miss Barrymore. 'Winston and Clementine showed me about the place, and I remember him waving his hand at the grounds and the house and saying: "Ethel, all this is out of my pen!"'

'He was out of power then, a voice crying unheeded, and prophesying with what was proved to be uncanny accuracy, the consequence of giving way before Hitler's increasing belligerency.'

The social ostracism they bore during those years hurt, but, wherever she went, Clementine walked, head high, certain that her husband was right and everyone else was wrong.

Her courage was equal to his. She had shown great courage in marrying him at all, as he was, even when they met, classed as an 'unpredictable, egotistical buccaneer of Edwardian politics and a traitor to his class'.

At meetings, when his enemies threw bricks, rotten eggs, or even spat at him, she faced them fearlessly with him.

Through the years when his hopes and aspirations floundered, she cherished and fostered them; and when he was desolate, cast aside, she comforted him.

Whatever his mood or fortune, Winston felt secure and strengthened in the knowledge that his Clementine would remain steadfast.

He was restless with a restlessness inflamed by his sense of imminent catastrophe.

Neville Chamberlain was nervous of this restlessness.

They were advised that because Mr. Chamberlain had such a high opinion of Winston's ability, it was his intention to offer him a Cabinet post as soon as he had found his feet as Leader of the Party. The call never came.

Discussing why the Cabinet avoided recruiting Winston to its ranks, Sir Archibald Sinclair, one of their closest friends, told Clementine:

'He's too big for them and they cannot contain him. You cannot stop a soft tooth with a gold filling.'

As 1938 passed, Clementine, their family, and home, lived in the constant shadow of his fears for the security of the country.

Even treasured moments with her in the gardens of Chartwell were somehow unrelaxed.

He lashed himself, trying to escape the terrible frustration by sounding warnings in weekly contributions to the Press, and in his speeches to Parliament. He was obsessed with the danger to this country, to the world, to his wife, and his family.

To guests who came to their home, both of them talked of little else, for nothing else mattered. To them, they constantly expressed the fear that England would refuse to show her hand until it was not only too late to avoid war, but too late to win a war.

For years he had been stumping in and out of meetings all over the country, warning how alarmingly Britain's armament programme lagged behind other nations, and demanding a national effort to close the gap.

Clementine, seated on the platform with him, listened to the thousands boo, hiss, and hurl insults at his advice.

Wherever he went to wage his one-man war for peace—to public meetings or to the House of Commons—Clementine accompanied him, listening as he cried out:

'I predict that the day will come when at some point or other, on some issue or other, you will have to make a stand, and I pray God that when that day comes you may not find that through an unwise policy we are left to make that stand alone.'

And, as she looked down from the gallery of the House on 24 March 1938, two weeks after the German invasion of Austria, she watched him, an almost lonely figure in the packed chamber, say, with his head thrust forward:

'For five years I have talked to this House on these matters—not with very great success. I have watched this famous island descending incontinently, fecklessly, the stairway which leads to a dark gulf. It is a fine broad stairway at the beginning, but after a bit the carpet ends. A little farther on there are only flagstones, and a little farther on still these break beneath your feet. . . .'

When he resumed his seat, there was complete silence for a moment, as though everyone there was wrestling with fears he had stirred within them, struggling to dismiss the warning words from their thoughts as if they had never heard them.

The Chamber came to life again, and many of the members who had crowded the benches took their leave.

At Chartwell, Clementine began to entertain international journalists, travellers for British and commercial and financial houses—all came with information for Winston—they were part of his preparation for the war he now felt was inevitable.

Clementine handled the new pattern of visitors with her customary charm and diplomacy. Winston relied on her to create the right atmosphere for all the informal but vital discussions which took place week after week at Chartwell.

'It was of great value to me, and it may be thought also to the country, that I should have the means of conducting searching and precise discussions for so many years in this very small circle,' said Winston. 'On my side, however, I gathered and contributed a great deal of information from foreign sources.'

But the world wanted to listen even less to Winston's words when, delirious with relief, it welcomed the black-coated umbrella-in-hand figure of Neville Chamberlain back from Munich with his 'Peace in our time' paper promise from Hitler. Winston cried:

'One pound was demanded at the pistol point. When it was given two pounds was demanded; finally the dictators consented to take one pound seventeen and sixpence and the rest in promise of goodwill for the future.'

Late on the night of 20 February 1938 a telephone message reached them at Chartwell. It brought news of the sequel to Chamberlain's forgiving Hitler his invasion of Austria, and offering the hand of friendship to Mussolini.

The appeasement gesture had compelled the resignation of their great personal friend, Anthony Eden.

Winston was overwhelmed with despair. Here was he, an outcast, an outsider without the power of office. Their friend, Anthony Eden, was their one ally on the inside, thinking and feeling much as they did. Now he was gone.

Clementine, suppressing her own fearful depression at the news, tried, in some measure, to console Winston.

He confessed . . .

'My heart sank, and for a while dark waters of despair overwhelmed me. In a long life I have had many ups and downs. During all the war soon to come and in its darkest times I never had any trouble in sleeping. In the crisis of 1940, when so much responsibility lay upon me, and also at many very anxious, awkward moments in the following five years, I could always flop into bed and go to sleep after the day's work was done—subject of course to any emergency call. I slept sound and awoke refreshed, and had no feelings except appetite to grapple with whatever the morning's boxes might bring. But now on this night of 20 February 1938, and on this occasion only, sleep deserted me. From midnight till dawn I lay in my bed consumed by emotions of sorrow and fear. There seemed one strong young figure standing up against long, dismal, drawling tides of drift and surrender, of wrong measurements and feeble impulses. My conduct of affairs would have been different from his in various ways; but he seemed to me at this moment to embody the life-hope of the British nation, the grand old British race that had done so much for men, and had yet some more to give. Now he was gone. I watched the daylight slowly creep in through the windows and saw before me in mental gaze the vision of Death.'

And then Hitler's marching armies goose-stepped into Czechoslovakia, ripping off the blinkers from the eyes of the freedom-loving peoples of the world.

They turned to the only voice that had been unafraid to say in the past what the future would be. Jeers turned to cheers.

It was plain for Clementine, and everyone else, to see how, in the House of Commons, his arrival was marked more closely than anyone else—and that included the Prime Minister.

Clementine read letter after letter vindicating Winston as, with almost every post, people wrote to Chartwell asking:

'How much longer is Parliament and the country going to allow your energy to operate in a vacuum?'

'Your undoubted gifts and proper grasp of the situation in Europe today make it imperative for the safety of this country and all that it stands for that you be given an important post in the cabinet without delay, preferably that of Minister of Defence, with full control over the defence forces of the nation,' declared another letter writer.

The gathering storm had brought the increasing realization that Winston had been right. To reinforce the balance of power, he sought alliance with Russia—'... but how improvidently foolish we should be when dangers are so great, to put needless barriers in the way of the general associations of the great Russian mass with resistance to an act of Nazi aggression.'

A group of the younger Tories were already in almost open revolt, denouncing Chamberlain's weakness towards Germany, and looking to Winston as their leader.

'It's all very well for those young fellows,' he said to his wife, 'but it's Chamberlain who has to press the button. It is a terrible thing at a time like this when you are the one man who has to decide whether to press the button or not.'

In the second week of August, the French invited him to visit the 'impregnable Maginot Line'.

On returning home he admitted to Clementine that he had been compelled to cancel the visit he had intended to make to the Duke of Windsor in the south of France, because of a warning from a leading French statesman that his life was in danger.

'The Germans believe I am one of their formidable enemies.

'They will not stop short of assassination.'

He believed in her being aware of danger if she was expected to face it.

As he looked through the windows of their home at the beautiful and peaceful gardens beyond, he sat wrapped in thought, then said slowly, and sorrowfully:

'Before the harvest is gathered in—we shall be at war.'

They moved constantly between Chartwell and their London flat in Morpeth Mansions, near Westminster Cathedral.

M.P.s said they had chosen the Morpeth Mansions apartment because it was so near Parliament, which meant that if he heard the division bells ring he could cover the distance to the division lobby in time to record his vote.

Clementine joined ambassadors and peers in the Distinguished Strangers' Gallery of the House on the evening of Friday, 1 September.

Germany had attacked Poland at dawn that morning. The mobilization of all our forces had been ordered.

Few had listened to him during their years in the political wilderness. All listened when the moment came. More than anyone, Clementine knew his whole life had been a preparation for that moment.

All eyes were on Winston, sitting in his accustomed seat, his face clearly lined with grief. The debate was brief. He said nothing; not even to members who crowded around him as he left.

The following day was even worse. It was the first time in years that the House had sat on a Saturday. The atmosphere was almost unbearable. Clementine smiled at no one, not even the familiar faces of dear friends. She had come from Parliament Square where she had stood among the strained tense faces of people in the streets, watching the almost endless stream of buses loaded with children heading for the distant open countryside.

Children were leaving the city. Evacuation had begun.

Seated in the gallery of the Commons that day, Clementine's eyes were for the silent figure in the corner of the Front Bench below the gangway. For years he had usually had something to say, but most of those around him had been unwilling to listen. Now they waited for his words, but there were none.

Clementine watched him as he sat brooding, overcome by the disaster he had foreseen for so long, until he stood up, and walked slowly and silently out.

Later that afternoon Winston returned to Morpeth Mansions and told her that he had just come from No. 10 Downing Street. The Prime Minister had sent for him. He told her Chamberlain, seeing no hope of averting war with Germany, intended to form a small War Cabinet of Ministers without departments, to conduct it, and had invited him to become a member of the War Cabinet. He said he had agreed to the proposal without comment, and had discussed men and measures at length with the Prime Minister.

After midnight he sat down at his desk and wrote to Mr. Chamberlain:

'Aren't we a very old team? I make out that the six you mentioned to me yesterday aggregate 386 years or an average of over 64! Only one year short of the old age pension! If however you added Sinclair (49) and Eden (42) the average comes down to $57\frac{1}{2}$.'

After commenting on the Labour Party having indicated their unwillingness to share in a National Coalition Cabinet, and his expectation that an announcement would be made of a joint declaration of war by Britain and France that afternoon, he ended the note with: 'I remain here at your disposal.'

But no reply came the next day from Mr. Chamberlain. Last-minute efforts were being made to preserve peace.

Clementine received an unusual group of callers at their flat opposite Westminster Cathedral. They were men of prominence from all parties.

United in the face of tragedy, they had come to the home of the husband and wife many of them had scorned as outcasts for years, to express their deep anxiety lest Britain should fail in its obligations to invaded Poland.

At nine o'clock on that Sunday morning of 3 September 1939 Hitler was presented with the ultimatum that, unless his army was withdrawn from Poland forthwith, a state of war would exist between Britain and Germany, as from eleven o'clock that morning.

Winston and Clementine listened together to the voice of broken-hearted Neville Chamberlain informing the nation in that momentous broadcast that we were at war with Germany. Their friend, Brendan Bracken, who later became Minister of Information, was with them.

Winston interrupted dressing to listen to the broadcast. As soon as it ended, he resumed dressing. Minutes later, the first air-raid warning of the war sounded.

Winston paused, collar half on, then, turning to Brendan Bracken dryly and grudgingly commented: 'You know,

131

Brendan, you've *got* to hand it to Hitler. The war's been on only a few minutes and here's an air raid already!' Clementine walked into the room and also remarked on the German's promptitude and precision.

Winston stalked to the entrance of the flats and stood outside in the street staring up into the sky. Clementine hurried after him to persuade him to go to an air-raid shelter. He refused. She reminded him that it was his place to set an example to others. Back he went into the flat, and, grabbing a bottle of brandy, set off with her and members of their staff, down the street to a basement shelter which had been prepared for such an emergency.

Clementine talked to him, others talked, but Winston moved around the shelter like a caged animal, hearing no one.

Immediately the 'All Clear' sounded he was off back down the street and up to the roof at Morpeth Mansions where he stood scanning the cloudless sky for aircraft. Clementine stood beside him, saying nothing.

As they gazed over the roofs and spires of London, above them were thirty or forty anti-aircraft barrage balloons. Both gave the Government a good mark for this evident sign of preparation.

Winston described the scene in the shelter that day: 'Our shelter was 100 yards down the street and consisted merely of an open basement, not even sand-bagged, in which the tenants of half a dozen flats were already assembled. Everyone was cheerful and jocular, as is the English manner when about to encounter the unknown.

'As I gazed from the doorway along the empty street and at the crowded room below, my imagination drew pictures of ruin and carnage, and vast explosions shaking the ground; of buildings clattering down in dust and rubble, of fire brigades and ambulances scurrying through the smoke, beneath the drone of hostile aeroplanes. For had we not all been taught how terrible air raids would be?

'After about ten minutes had passed, the wailing broke out again. I was myself not sure that this was not a reiteration of the previous warning, but a man came running along the street shouting "All clear", and we dispersed to our dwellings and went about our business.'

Winston's 'business' was to hurry to the House of Commons which met at noon.

The Prime Minister spoke: Winston spoke, but it was no 'I told you so' speech.

It was the first Sunday Parliamentary sitting of the decade. In the streets outside, men were queueing at recruiting offices; lorry-loads of soldiers and arms were speeding by; people were already looking at each other with that 'all in it together' feeling which was to become a national spirit.

Clementine listened in the Commons' Chamber to Chamberlain's formal announcement of the commencement of war, then watched Winston rise to pay tribute, without bitterness and with typical generosity, to those who had fought for peace.

'In this solemn hour,' he said, 'it is a consolation to recall and to dwell upon our repeated efforts for peace. All have been ill-starred, but all have been faithful and sincere ... outside, the storms of war may blow and the land may be lashed with the fury of the gales, but in our hearts, this Sunday morning, there is peace. Our hands may be active, but our consciences are at rest....'

Afterwards they joined Sarah and their son-in-law Vic Oliver for lunch at the Olivers' apartment in Westminster. Diana and Duncan Sandys and Randolph Churchill were also there. At the end of the meal they opened a bottle of champagne. Winston stood up, raised his glass, and proposed a toast:

'Victory,' he said.

'No one would listen to my warnings, but now that war is here, we shall have to forget the past. Britain shall never yield to her enemies.'

Everyone present then signed their names on a sheet of paper dated 3 September 1939.

'I shall join my regiment,' said Randolph. Duncan Sandys announced he would be doing the same. Diana and Sarah discussed what war contributions they could make.

Then the phone rang. Winston was wanted on the phone.

'I'll take it in the bedroom,' he said. There was something in the way he said it, as if he felt this was a moment to be alone.

Clementine and the family remained seated and silent round the dining-table.

All instinctively felt that this was no ordinary telephone call.

Each moment of Winston's absence increased the tension, then the door opened.

He stood there with the fingers of both hands spread on his waistcoat, looking at his family with tears in his eyes.

No one spoke until Clementine said quietly: 'Tell me.'

Looking straight at her, and no one else, he said: 'They have given me a job again—I am First Lord of the Admiralty.'

Everyone excitedly congratulated him—everyone but Clementine.

She just sat looking at him.

He spoke again: 'It's a wonderful feeling to know that the country needs you. I don't care any more what they said about me—now I can show them what I can do.'

'What will you do?' asked Sarah.

'What am I going to do? I'm going to sleep,' he answered.

It was time for his regular afternoon nap, and nothing and no one would prevent him having it.

He retired to the bedroom, leaving the family to discuss the war and the future.

An hour-and-a-half later he was back, refreshed.

'Well, good-bye,' he said.

'Where are you going?' asked Diana.

'To the Admiralty,' he replied. 'The *Bremen* is on the high seas, and we're going to get her.' And, with that, Winston kissed Clementine and went to war.

10

ROOMS IN WHITEHALL

SHE didn't see him again until almost lunch-time the following day.

The night had brought memories to both of them of a quarter of a century before when he had walked out of the Admiralty after being removed from his post as First Lord. They had shared so much since then—triumphs, tragedies, and political oblivion.

As they lunched alone, Winston told her how, when he had walked back into the Admiralty office he had quit in pain and sorrow so long ago, he had observed that the self-same wooden map-case he had fixed to the wall behind his chair in 1911 was still there.

It was a staff officer's duty to mark daily the movements and disposition of the German fleet on the wall chart, and it was Winston's rule to check the chart as soon as he entered the room each morning.

'To inculcate in myself and those working with me a sense of ever present danger,' he explained.

But, apart from memories that had crowded back, he brought Clementine other news.

The night war was declared the Germans had torpedoed and sunk without warning the liner *Athenia*, two hundred miles west of the Hebrides. There were 1,400 passengers on board. Miraculously most of them and the crew had been saved.

After lunch he was due to resume his place on the Treasury bench, and Clementine rode with him once more to the House.

He was not, as yet, Prime Minister, but was unquestionably the man to whom everyone turned as he entered the Chamber.

He rose to speak, looked up, as always, at Clementine in the gallery, and was given an ovation the like of which had rarely been heard before. The applause was long and loud, and a sincere tribute to the new Minister.

Winston seemed unfamiliar in his new seat in the House. Instead of resting his notes on a dispatch box, he held them in his hand like a back bencher.

He announced the news of the sinking of the *Athenia*.

This first great naval disaster of the war developed an unusual twist when the Germans, on learning that there had been 311 American citizens aboard, immediately broadcast to the world that the sinking was the work of Winston Churchill!

The telephone rang in their apartment as they were finishing dinner, and Winston was asked to take the call. When he came back into the room, he said: 'Do you know who that was? The President of the United States. It is remarkable to think of being rung up in this little flat in Victoria by the President himself in the midst of a great war.' The President had wanted a question answered concerning the *Athenia* incident. Excusing himself to their two guests, Winston added: 'This is very important and I must go and see the Prime Minister at once.'

Within two days Winston had reintroduced the convoy system to protect our merchant fleets and our supplies. By then, Clementine and Mary had moved some of their personal possessions into the small apartment at the top of the great Admiralty building in Whitehall—into rooms originally designed to house the servants of the First Lord.

Knowing Winston would live with his job twenty-four hours a day, there was only one way for her to take care of him—she had to live with the Admiralty too. Even their apartment in Morpeth Mansions—only at the other end of Whitehall—was too far away for him.

Clementine furnished the small rooms as best she could, bringing in some of the furniture from their London flat and from Chartwell. Converting the small Admiralty apartment into some kind of home was no easy achievement with Winston cramming all the telephones and gadgets in creation into the rooms.

There was no peace in the world, and certainly no peace for anyone in that tiny apartment, with Winston's standing order that in the event of anything important happening, day or night, he was to be told whatever the hour.

His gaudy dressing-gown, striped pyjamas, and slippers, and cigar in mouth, became a familiar awe-inspiring sight in the Admiralty corridors.

As soon as he walked through the door of the Admiralty, he wanted to see the kind of Navy he had been given, and immediately began unannounced visits to all the largest naval bases, beginning with Chatham docks. Clementine accompanied him throughout the tour.

They travelled to Thurso in Scotland, and on arrival there embarked in a destroyer for Scapa Flow, the Navy's main base.

While making for Scapa, a radio signal came through— the great warship *Courageous* had been lost with six hundred dead.

A few days later they went to the naval installations at Portsmouth and Plymouth.

Winston, furious with the lack of defences at Scapa Flow, had ordered the immediate reorganization of the base. Before it could be done, the battleship *Royal Oak* was sunk by a U-boat which penetrated Scapa's defences.

To Clementine and to his staff Winston muttered: 'If only they had taken notice of me a few years ago, this would not have happened.'

His resolve even more determined, they continued the tours as he sought information, trying to repair the neglect of years.

Once again, accompanied by Clementine, he set out to see still more for himself, as well as let others see him.

He wanted to know what was being done in the shipyards; in the factories; on the aerodromes; in the army camps; and wanted everyone to see he cared. Popularity was a new thing for him; it was also a novelty for Clementine. She was always there, just beyond the glare of the spotlight in which he now walked.

He inspired encouragement with his bulldog determination and cheerfulness in adversity, and she modestly contributed her share too. The serenity with which she shared responsibilities with him made women feel that she truly understood their fears and anxieties for their husbands, sons, and brothers.

Wherever the already famous square hat, walking-stick, and cigar went, confidence and a smile followed. The jutting jaw and hunched shoulders were here, there, and everywhere, and, most of the time, two steps behind him, walked the tall erect woman with the laughing eyes, sincerely enjoying meeting people and obviously proud of her husband's new-found popularity. They were a team, a husband and wife working together for victory.

Every week or so she managed to persuade him to spend a week-end at Chartwell, but soon week-ends became as arduous as the weeks. He wouldn't let up a moment and worked a 120-hour week, struggling to remedy deficiencies in naval strength.

He was able to announce that in the first two weeks of the war a tenth of Germany's submarines had been destroyed. They sowed magnetic mines; we found the answer. They intensified the U-boat war; we hunted them day and night. 'I will not say without mercy, because God forbid that we should ever part company with that, at any rate with zeal and not altogether without relish!' said Winston.

After the B.B.C.'s nine o'clock news broadcast on Sunday, 1 October 1939, Winston went to the microphone. Clementine and Mary listened in one of the little rooms above the Admiralty. It was the first of the broadcasts which were to become Britain's greatest 'secret weapon'—infusing the entire nation with the will to win, with the spirit of victory.

Hitler, said Winston, had decided when the war was to begin—'It began when *he* wanted it, and it will end only when *we* are convinced that he has had enough!'

Clementine had discussed the first draft of the speech with him, and they had both agreed that this was no time for long words requiring exploration in dictionaries. They felt instinctively that for a man to be a true leader of the people, he must speak with the voice of the people, and must make his appeal in plain, direct language.

'This was their finest hour' rang through the world and into history as 'their noblest occasion' could never have done.

From that time on, as far as Winston was concerned, dictionaries were for others. Simple words were all he needed for his broadcasts.

The peoples of the free world are still free because, when words were all we had to fight with, Winston chose the right ones. The good humour, the fight of the people, found their expression in him. Men and women were proud to be sharing part of a lifetime with this man—this score of human beings in one—who will rank in history books with Alexander the Great, with Julius Caesar, Napoleon and Cromwell, Nelson and Lincoln. They put their trust and lives in the hands of a man who, his friends said, 'did his honest and cheerful best to kill himself in the public service'.

The drafts of all his speeches were shown to Clementine for comment—comments that were often noted when he revised and polished the scripts until they shone with the literary perfection he demanded of himself.

Clementine's practical sense enabled her to see aspects of a speech that he had sometimes overlooked in his enthusiasm. She had learnt much of the politician's art from him, but understood more than he had taught her.

She could often sway him on points of detail, or where personalities were concerned. Her shrewdness, her authority, and deep understanding of him, helped fashion many of his words as well as the architecture of his life.

Both she and Winston could speak from the heart, speak with the voice and words of the people.

Many of his greatest speeches were dictated from his bed. Because of his complete absorption in what he was doing, Clementine was compelled to introduce her own fire safety measures as Winston had the unfortunate habit of sometimes forgetfully throwing a lighted cigar by mistake into the waste-paper basket beside the bed instead of into his basket-style ash-tray. As a result, she issued a standing order for a syphon of soda water to be kept handy in the bedroom to deal with the occasional fires he started.

Six weeks after his first great war-time broadcast, he went to the microphone again. While not underrating the dangers, his voice injected confidence into the millions listening. Hitler was 'that evil man over there', and Ribbentrop 'that prodigious contortionist'. We laughed as Winston had meant us to laugh, and the laughter he provoked brought hope.

The range and depth of his knowledge, his almost magical sensitivity to the mood of the man in the street, astonished admirers and opponents alike. Part of the secret was an eagerness to hear the opinions of ordinary people with whom either he or Clementine came into contact. Enveloped as he was in his work, he mainly relied on her to keep a close watch for him on the pulse and temperature of public trends and opinions. She was his liaison with the domestic scene.

During the winter of that year the Churchills became friendly with the Chamberlains, and Mr. and Mrs. Neville Chamberlain came to dine with them in their crammed apartment above Admiralty House. Clementine and Winston had never met the Chamberlains in such intimate social circumstances before.

There were just the four of them present. It was quite an event, because it was really the only friendly social conversation they had ever shared with the Chamberlains in all the twenty years they had known them, and it was to become an outstanding occasion in other ways too.

During dinner the war went on and things happened. With the soup an officer came up from the WAR ROOM below to report that a U-boat had been sunk. With the sweet he came again and reported that a second U-boat had been sunk; and just before the ladies left the dining-room he came a third time to report that yet another U-boat had been sunk.

Nothing like this had ever happened before in a single day, and it was more than a year before such a record was equalled.

As the ladies left them, Mrs. Chamberlain, with a naïve and charming glance, said to Winston: 'Did you arrange all this on purpose?'

Said Winston: 'I assured her that if she would come again we would produce a similar result.'

There were few rays of hope that winter. Winston rarely left his office so it was fortunate that they had set up their little home in the Admiralty itself, otherwise he would have snatched no moments of relaxation.

Clementine tried to introduce as much comfort as possible to ease his endless hours of strain. She devoted particular attention to the room in which he had to spend most of his time—his office.

Two arm-chairs were drawn up side by side in front of the cheerful coal fire burning in the grate.

Winston would read his papers sitting in one of them. Clementine had all the chairs in the room upholstered in red leather, except the one at his desk which was very plain, with no upholstery whatever, and a wooden curved back like half a barrel. It looked strangely small for such a big man.

She arranged his desk not square and straight in the room, but sideways, thereby making it impossible for him to overlook the deceptively distracting peaceful scene in the park below.

Constantly, on a table at the side of the desk, stood glasses on a tray, a syphon of soda water, and a metal box looking like a gas-mask container, but actually a tin of biscuits.

The only personal possession introduced into the office was the chart presented to him when he was Minister of Munitions in the First World War. The chart is a graph of gun production, and along the top of it is a row of black lions in silhouette. The first lion is lying down, the next, as the graph rises, sits on its haunches, and as the graph reaches its greatest heights, the lion stands on its legs.

His only brief relaxation each day was the time spent with Clementine at luncheon or dinner.

Every night the ritual was the same. Before going to bed, he would walk into the Operations Room to take a final account of the day's information.

It was in this Operations Room that he sat tensely through the hours as the *Exeter, Ajax*, and the New Zealand navy's *Achilles* hunted the German pocket battleship, the *Graf Spee*, and it was in this same room twenty-five years before that he had sat as Von Spee, the famous German naval commander, was gunned to death in the battle of the Falkland Islands.

Suddenly, news that lifted everyone's hearts reached the room. Unable to contain his excitement, he rushed upstairs to tell Clementine.

The 'little ships'—*Exeter, Achilles*, and *Ajax*—had located the *Graf Spee*, which had been roaming the North and South Atlantic, sinking merchant ships on a terrifying scale.

Engaging the *Graf Spee*, the three little cruisers hurt her, slowed her up, and chased her into Montevideo harbour. Our warships were badly knocked about too, but stayed right outside the harbour, waiting for the chance to finish

141

off the *Graf Spee*. The rest is history—the *Graf Spee* scuttled herself, and the world echoed with the victory.

Soon afterwards, H.M.S. *Cossack* attacked the German prison ship *Altmark* in Norwegian waters, freeing 299 British prisoners. Winston, master psychologist as well as master strategist, seized the opportunity to give the nation the tonic it needed.

He saw that these two great victories at sea could be turned into victories for home-front morale, and ordered a welcome-home luncheon to be given at London's ancient Guildhall at which the City would honour the men of the *Ajax* and *Exeter* on their return.

Weeks later the little ships arrived home to a fantastic reception. Clementine and Winston were among the thousands standing on the quayside at Plymouth when the ships sailed into port to a deafening greeting from ships' sirens and cheering crowds. London's turn to honour the crews of the *Exeter* and *Ajax* followed. They came to the city and marched from Waterloo Station to Horseguards Parade, where His Majesty King George VI, Winston, the entire Cabinet, and a host of other dignitaries awaited them.

Clementine watched the proceedings from the window of Winston's room in the Admiralty in the company of her personal guest for the occasion—Her Majesty the Queen.

The two little warships' crews lined up, and Winston presented them to His Majesty, who decorated a number of them. The watching, boisterous thousands hushed as the widow of Marine Wilfred A. Russell, of the *Exeter*, walked up to His Majesty to receive her husband's posthumous award of the Medal for Conspicuous Gallantry. Immediately following the ceremony, the Queen and Clementine joined the King and Winston on the saluting base to honour the crews' march past.

When the march had ended, the four left the saluting base and moved to a quiet corner of the parade ground where relatives of those who had lost their lives in the Battle of the River Plate action were waiting. The King and Queen and Winston and Clementine spoke to each of them.

This special enclosure on the Horseguards Parade, which had been reserved for those who had lost sons or husbands in the battle, was Clementine's personal idea. She never forgot the little things that mattered so much, so she arranged for all the bereaved relatives to be comfortably seated to witness the great ceremony from a vantage-point close to Admiralty House, and also arranged for coffee and other refreshments to be served to them.

Winston and Clementine drove to the Guildhall for the great luncheon of honour. Winston was in form. The end of the *Graf Spee*, he said, 'has warmed the cockles of our hearts'. And the cry of the *Cossack*'s boarding party—'The Navy's here!'—when its crew boarded the *Altmark* to free the prisoners battened down below the hatches, Winston put in the same historic proud place as Nelson's signal at the Battle of Trafalgar.

After the luncheon Winston and Clementine had to wait a few moments outside for their car. They were suddenly surrounded by hundreds of sailors who poured out of the Guildhall. Some shook him by the hand, others slapped him on the back, and some of the little too hearty slaps made Winston wince once or twice. They were moved by the warmth of their greeting, and as he and Clementine entered the car, he was near to tears.

As the appetite of the fighting services for men and munitions grew, it was to Clementine that he turned for expert advice.

His years as the special target of the Suffragette movement had made him a little cautious when it came to the role of women in war. He had his own natural prejudices to overcome.

To him, the idea of women entering the line of battle, and fighting in war, was revolting.

'The whole civilization of the Western world is based upon the traditions of chivalry which have come down from medieval times and still exert a potent force,' he maintained.

'It has become a matter of instinct among the most valiant races that women and children should be spared.'

Although later in the war his own daughters were to enter the Forces, the chivalrous cavalier in him made him shirk from advocating extensive use of women in war, although he admitted that the immunity of women from violence was taken so much for granted that few appreciated to what extent the protective cloak around them had already been discarded.

143

Although admitting that the prejudice against women fighting goes further than the roots of our civilization, extending to the earliest beginnings of mankind, he added:

'Everyone will applaud a woman who defended her children against wolves; and when human beings fall to the level of wolves in their pitiless ferocity, the distinction between the sexes perishes with all other human traits.'

Clementine was certain that if the picture was put clearly before them, the women of Britain would flock to reinforce fighting units by taking over administrative duties; helping to operate anti-aircraft batteries; and staffing armaments factories despite the knowledge that these factories were certain targets for the *Luftwaffe*. There were many things that women could do, apart from killing, which could add to the fighting power of our army, navy, and air force, and Clementine assured Winston that if the call was made, the women of Britain would answer it.

Winston sat down and wrote a speech—for women only.

When he had completed the draft, Clementine read it through and suggested several alterations. He followed her advice. It was one subject on which she was the undoubted expert in the family.

She was with him on 27 January 1940 in Manchester's great Free Trade Hall when he stood up and walked to the front of the platform to address the packed gathering. The audience was almost entirely of women.

He spoke to them sympathetically, directly. He had come to the centre of Industrial Britain to ask for a million women workers to help the war effort.

It was a startling beginning. It was, in fact, the opening of something much more—it was also the beginning of a radical social change.

The only reserve of female labour in the country was among wives of men already in the Services or the war factories. They would have to create a new pattern for living, to free themselves as much as possible from the ties of family and homes, and devote these hours of freedom to the war.

With passion and fire he called: 'Come then, let us to the task, to the battle, to the toil—each to our art; each to our station. Fill the armies, rule the air, pour out the munitions, strangle the U-boats, sweep the mines, plough the land, build the ships, guard the streets, succour the wounded, up-lift the downcast, honour the brave.

'Let us go forward together in all parts of the Empire, in all parts of the island. There is not a week nor a day, nor an hour to lose.'

For the first time in his life, Winston—a man's man—managed to appeal to the women, and win them to his side as a powerful ally.

The historic speech inspired by his wife's 'Woman's sense' brought him the million women workers he asked for—and millions more to the Services and factories.

The United States Ambassador, Mr. John G. Winant, considered there was no greater evidence of Britain's unity of purpose than the response of the women.

He recalled hearing Winston complain that the R.A.F. required seventy men on the ground to keep a plane in the air. This conversation took place at the Churchills' dining-table.

'I was present when the Prime Minister while talking of the anti-aircraft services criticized the number of soldiers assigned per gun,' said Ambassador Winant.

Winston appreciated that each pair of hands assigned to a gun was necessary for its intricate manipulation, but other branches of the Army were dangerously short of manpower, so he sent for General Sir Frederick Pile, the chief of the Anti-Aircraft Command.

Sir Frederick recalled the luncheon meeting that followed:

'The Prime Minister, Mrs. Churchill, one or two others concerned with the direction of the war, and myself, were present, when Mr. Churchill looked at me and said, "General, I have grave news for you."

'I said I was very sorry to hear that.

' "You are just getting your new weapons and new equipment, and now I want a lot of men from you," said Winston.

'Well, sir, that's all right,' I said.

' "You're very cheerful about it," he replied.

'I'll replace them with women,' I answered.

' "If you can do that it's as good as a first-class victory—to gain forty thousand men," he said. "If you can get these women as replacements, I'll get Mary to join you as one of them."

'Mrs. Churchill said, "That is an excellent suggestion." Mary wasn't with us at the time, but both her parents were thrilled with the thought, and Mary, who started out as a Private, turned out to be one of my biggest assets. She's a good girl.

'Some doubted whether women would make efficient substitutes for men on the gun sites. Everyone present at this meeting was shattered with the idea, and I remember one Minister remarking: "This is a most revolutionary proposal and I cannot believe anybody in England will accept it."

' "I don't see why not," said Mrs. Churchill. "If women can do all that they are doing in fire-fighting and everything else, I don't see why they shouldn't man guns."

'I pointed out that we would be only asking them, at the moment, to man technical equipment.

' "They will probably do it a great deal better than men because they have so much more of a light touch and your equipment needs deft but delicate handling," Mrs. Churchill added.

'In point of fact, it turned out to be so, and the best batteries in the flying-bomb blitz were those operated by women—they shot down, on the average, far more than the men. The whole thing depended on the delicate balance of the instruments, and men were more heavy-handed than women at this particular job.

'Winston completely agreed with his wife that using women on the anti-aircraft guns was a magnificent idea. She was always behind him, and had a tremendous influence on him. For example, when he was difficult with us at times— and that was often—she would say: "Now, Winston, that's all right, the subject can be let rest for the moment. We are going to have luncheon." He used to get worked up and stamp round the room, but this didn't deter her one little bit.

'She bossed him—but in the most delightful way—with great affection and with the deepest understanding of his nature. I was always amazed that this great man could be led along like a sheep by her whenever she thought it necessary. This was partially because of his great admiration for her, and also because he had such a justifiably high regard for her intellect and judgement. She has a first-class brain. Everything she did was, above all, for his good.'

Winston continued to push himself beyond all normal limits, and Clementine became increasingly concerned as to how long he could maintain the frightening pace. Her attempts to make him take greater care of his health suddenly received support from an unexpected quarter. A letter arrived from Buckingham Palace. It was a personal message for Winston.

After congratulating him on his direction of the Navy, His Majesty added: 'I also beg of you to take care of yourself and get as much rest as you possibly can in these critical days.'

While disillusioned peace-maker Neville Chamberlain made his war progress pronouncements in tones that sank the hearts of men and women, Winston's words of hope and defiance said what everyone wanted said and raised them up again.

It was a very happy day when Winston could tell Clementine that yet another ship had been launched. With each fresh addition to naval strength, his personal strength and spirit seemed renewed. In March 1940, at Barrow-in-Furness, he gave her the honour of launching an aircraft-carrier.

On their return to Downing Street from the launching, he handed a news bulletin to her. It stated that Ley, leader of the Nazi Labour Front, in a broadcast from Rotterdam, had announced that he was planning cruises for German workers to spend their holidays at the most popular sea-side resorts on the south coast of England! The cruises were scheduled for the late summer of that year—an indication of the confidence of Hitler and his generals in their plan to invade Britain during the summer of 1940.

'Do you think the Nazis can get aboard this island?' she asked.

'No, he answered. 'But they'll make a mighty try. At least I would if I were Hitler.' Then, opening his coat and revealing his revolver in its holster, he added: 'If they do try, I'll get a few before they take me,' and they both laughed.

The following month he brought her further news—this time of a change in his Cabinet job. Chamberlain had appointed him chief of a committee of Service Ministers whose duty it was to guide the War Cabinet in the general conduct of the war.

From then on not a moment of their lives was lived apart from war and thoughts of war. Winston was completely loyal to Neville Chamberlain, but Chamberlain was unable to give the people the inspired leadership they needed.

Suddenly, Hitler invaded Norway and Denmark. Winston ordered the Fleet into action and a British Expeditionary Force was sent to help the Norwegians. Without adequate air cover, it had no chance.

Allegations that the Norway campaign had been mishandled were followed by demands for a debate in the House of Commons. M.P.s were bitter and angry. The full force of their wrath came down on Mr. Chamberlain. When, on the second day of the debate, Winston attempted to accept responsibility, his effort was waved aside.

Winston wound up the debate for the Government fighting for Chamberlain and denouncing Socialists who had also rejected rearmament.

As the hands of the clock moved to ten, when the vote would be taken, neither Clementine nor anyone else could hear him above the angry shouts from the Socialists' benches.

As Neville Chamberlain left Parliament that night, knowing his Premiership was virtually at an end, a new crisis arose across the Channel in Holland.

Chamberlain strove vainly to save his régime by inviting the Socialists to join his Cabinet. In the middle of the negotiations, Hitler began the invasion of Holland, Belgium, and Luxembourg, and the British Expeditionary Force in France faced its Dunkirk.

'I would have answered that we would be lucky if we safely got away twenty or thirty thousand,' he told her. 'It is now ninety thousand, and more landing every hour.'

In four momentous days of Dunkirk, the 215,000 British and 120,000 French were rescued.

On the afternoon of 10 May 1940, in the ninth month of the war he had foreseen and striven to forestall, Winston received a message at the Admiralty. It had come from Buckingham Palace.

He went straight upstairs to Clementine in the rooms

above his office to tell her the King had sent for him.

Now he was about to achieve his life's ambition. He was the one man all parties—and the people—were ready to follow.

He left Clementine and the Admiralty building, looking tense and strained. His hour had come, but what an hour!

As he stepped from the car on returning to the Admiralty, one of his staff, congratulating him, said: 'I only wish that the position had come your way in better times for you have taken on an enormous task.'

Winston replied gravely: 'God alone knows how great it is. All I hope is that it is not too late. I am very much afraid it is. We can only do our best.'

With that, he climbed the stairs to his private apartment, and to his wife—Prime Minister of Great Britain.

The night of 10 May 1940 was also her hour. After seeing his advice neglected for so long, he had at last been called upon to try and save his country from the consequences which neglect of his warnings had entailed. His call to office coincided with one of the worst military disasters in modern history, and she realized that had it not been for this catastrophe he might never have reached the Premiership.

On the night he became Prime Minister, he wrote: 'As I went to bed at 3 a.m. I was conscious of a profound sense of relief. At last I had the authority to give directions over the whole scene. I felt as if I were walking with Destiny and that all my past life had been but a preparation for this hour and for this trial.'

To the Parliament that had unanimously chosen him as its leader, Winston, in his inaugural address, spoke his undying: 'I have nothing to offer but blood, toil, tears, and sweat.'

Then, in words every man and woman would understand, he cried: 'You ask, what is our policy? I will say: it is to wage war, by sea, land, and air, with all our might and with all the strength that God can give us. You ask, what is our aim? I can answer in one word: victory—victory at all costs, victory in spite of all terror, victory, however long and hard the road may be; for without victory, there is no survival.'

The words rang through the Chamber, reflecting the

spirit within the people, and turning it into a verbal flag he waved for all to see.

In a congratulatory speech their lifelong personal friend, Liberal leader Sir Archibald Sinclair, declared that everyone was delighted he had replaced Mr. Chamberlain.

Although what Winston murmured was an aside made as he remained in his seat, Clementine and many M.P.s present clearly heard him say: 'He's a finer man than I could ever be.'

Winston was sixty-six. He had waited for supreme Ministerial power through years of drift, dishonour, and disaster. Now he had achieved this power at a critical hour, but knowing his nature, she felt it was, perhaps, fortunate that the hour was critical. He excelled in moments of crisis; he would use the imminence of danger to close the ranks which had begun to gape.

She knew power came to him not as a load but as a release.

The terrible burden he was about to bear on his broad shoulders was to be her burden too.

BLITZ

WINSTON was flying back and forth across the Channel for emergency meetings, desperately trying to save what he could from disaster, striving to breathe strength into gasping France.

He arranged to go there for yet another conference. Flying weather was bad, and the Air Staff, concerned at the danger, pressed him to abandon the flight. He refused.

'They came to me to see if I could help,' said General Lord Ismay, Winston's Chief of Staff at the Ministry of Defence. 'They said, "The Prime Minister's going to France —have you heard?" and I said, "Yes, I'm going with him." They warned me that flying conditions were very bad, but I replied that they were pretty rough, but not as bad as all that. They insisted that it was too risky for the Prime Minister to go, but I disagreed and said I thought he ought to go, so off they went to Clemmie to tell her that Winston shouldn't go to France, and to ask her to persuade him not to risk the weather.

'She listened, and then asked: "Are the Air Force flying today?"

'They answered: "Oh, yes, of course—on operations."

'She replied: "Well, isn't Winston going on an operation?" And that was that.'

During one of these cross-Channel visits he went into a little French restaurant for a meal. A woman—later identified as a French duchess—stood waiting for him in the courtyard. As he emerged, she jumped at him, with a knife —determined to kill the Englishman whom she considered responsible for the downfall of France!

Winston's bodyguard caught her with a rugby tackle.

Clementine was informed of the murder attempt, but, on his return, Winston talked only of the evacuation of Forces.

And when the blitz of 1940 began in all its fury, there was no holding him—he just couldn't help it. The drone of enemy planes overhead, the screaming and crashing of bombs, and the answering thunder and flashing of anti-aircraft defences were an irresistible smell of danger to him.

Londoners were 'taking it', and Winston was determined to 'take it' with them.

He stood with Clementine in a doorway close to No. 10 Downing Street, watching the searchlights tear away the cover of darkness and the anti-aircraft barrage turn the sky into a hell.

There was an ominous whistling.

'Something is coming this way!' someone shouted.

A shattering explosion followed almost directly opposite the doorway in which they were standing, and flying shrapnel hit one of their party.

Winston's Cabinet colleagues tried their utmost to dissuade him from taking undue risks; from going off into the night, walking-stick in one hand, and electric torch in the other, 'to see for himself'.

It was Clementine who succeeded, and she achieved victory by outmanoeuvring him. But then, she knew her Winston.

She used a secret weapon—herself.

Living with Winston had taught her the value of carefully timed counter-attack. She waited.

At first, his jaw and cigar jutting defiantly forward, he was everywhere.

No sooner had the 'All Clear' sounded after the first heavy attack on London's docks than he was off to inspect the devastation personally. Fires were still raging, but when Winston stepped out of his car hundreds, who had been battered mercilessly, mobbed him, shouting: 'Good old Winnie! We thought you'd come and see us.'

When he heard this, and caught sight of the tiny paper Union Jacks planted on top of great mounds of death and desolation, he couldn't restrain his emotions, nor his tears.

'You see, he really cares; he's crying,' said one woman.

Winston, who disliked exercise, walked miles among the rubble and still smoking skeletons of buildings.

As darkness began to creep up on the day, dock authorities became anxious for Winston to leave for home. Recalls Lord Ismay, who accompanied him on that first blitz inspection tour:

'He was in one of his most obstinate moods and insisted

that he wanted to see everything. Consequently, we were still with him at the brightly lit target when the *Luftwaffe* arrived on the scene and the fireworks started.

'It was difficult to get a large car out of the area, owing to many of the streets being completely blocked by fallen houses. As we were trying to turn in a very narrow space, a shower of incendiary bombs fell just in front of us. Churchill, feigning innocence, asked what they were. I replied that they were incendiaries, and that we were evidently in the middle of the bull's eye!

'It was very late by the time we got back to No. 10 Downing Street, and Cabinet Ministers, secretaries, policemen, and orderlies were waiting in the long passage in great anxiety. Churchill strode through them, without a word, leaving me to be rebuked by all and sundry for having had the Prime Minister take such risks.

'Fatigue and fright are not conducive to patience, and I am alleged to have told the assembled company, in the language of the barrack room, that anybody who imagined they could control him on jaunts of this kind was welcome to try his hand on the next occasion.'

Clementine's 'Save-Winston-from-himself' campaign began the next day.

'When he went on yet another tour—she went along with him. This time, concerned for *her* safety, he returned home before nightfall,' said Lord Ismay. 'I was very much aware that this was her technique. Her presence made him cautious for her.'

Day after day Winston and Clementine walked together over rubble that was once homes; talking to the homeless, listening to their needs.

He became the idol of the people, and the people were lucky in their idol—they could trust him with a tyrant's power because they knew he would not use it like a tyrant. He humbly accepted the confidence they willingly reposed in him.

Cheered by families in streets in the East End of London that had been bombed to dust the previous night, he turned a tear-stained face to his wife and said: 'They greet me like a conquering hero. God knows why. They are a great people.'

They knew he was doing his best, and that his best was

the best that could be done.

He strengthened them with his brand of bombing arithmetic: 'It would take ten years,' he said, 'at the present rate, for half the houses of London to be demolished. After that, of course, progress would be much slower. . . .'

Clementine tramped with him through mud and slush to visit gun sites; joined him as he drove in a jeep through the shattered streets giving his V sign acknowledgement to the cheering people. She knew he undertook these journeys not only to instil encouragement into the people by his appearance among them, but also because their continued spirit in turn strengthened him.

They went down to the South Coast to inspect invasion defences. From Rottingdean to Shoreham, one brigade of some 3,000 men was stretched in a thin line along ten miles of densely populated coastline. These few troops would have stood little chance against well-organized invasion. Even so this was then probably one of the most strongly defended parts of Britain, and few realized how thin was the shield protecting them against Hitler's armies across the Channel. In command of these defences was Lieutenant-General Sir Brian Horrocks.

Sir Brian met Winston and Clementine when they came to see the defences and watch the Royal Ulster Rifles carry out a small exercise. Said General Sir Brian Horrocks:

'Though no one knew of his visit, he was quickly spotted and a large enthusiastic crowd soon gathered. The complete confidence shown in him was most touching, and rather frightening to us who knew that, to all intents and purposes, the military cupboard was bare. During one of these spontaneous demonstrations of affection, I found myself standing at the back behind Mrs. Churchill. There were tears in her eyes, and I heard her murmur, "Pray God, we don't let them down."'

When he stubbornly went out at night while bombs were falling, Clementine insisted on going too. She never made any fuss about it, never said, 'Look here, Winston, I don't want you to go.' She knew it would have been a terrible thing for both of them, for he would have probably done as she asked, but, for the first time, he would have been caged in, and it could have broken him.

Said Lord Ismay: 'She knew him completely, knew precisely how to handle him. She might instigate a brake on him, but any actual *decision* to brake would be his. She would work behind the scenes, talk to Cabinet colleagues and members of their personal staff to enlist help in protecting him in every possible way—in spite of himself. But I have never known her to oppose him directly in such matters. She would tell the staff the line to take—we'd get the "party" line from her to take with the Boss.'

She operated her own 'espionage' service on his movements to discover when and where there was likely to be any element of risk, and would then try to engineer herself on such visits.

To Winston, it was one thing to be outmanoeuvred, another to be denied freedom of decision, even if it was the decision to endanger his own life.

Clementine therefore concentrated on de-magnetizing, as far as possible, his attraction to danger. She tried to divert his course.

'She persuaded him to use an air-raid shelter *as an example to others*,' added Lord Ismay. 'Reluctantly, he agreed, and the disused underground station at near-by Storey's Gate was equipped as a special shelter for the regular occupants and visitors to No. 10.'

This was the shelter that became known as the 'Annexe'. Winston still preferred working above ground, and sometimes asserted his defiance. And Clementine herself did regular fire-watching duty near Downing Street.

From 7 September 1940 to 3 November, an average of two hundred German bombers attacked London every night. Time after time, Winston—and Clementine—remained at Downing Street until well after the alert had sounded and bombs were dropping. He would then step out and walk round St. James's Park before going into the Downing Street Annexe.

One night they entered the Annexe only minutes before a 1,000 lb. bomb dropped on to the pavement at the end of the street along which they had just walked.

Frequently, they would watch the bombing from the flat roof of the Annexe, and, if he saw a building ablaze close by he would often say, 'We will go over there,' and off they went.

Millions of Londoners slept in their beds and took their

chances. Others took refuge in the rapidly multiplying brick, concrete, and metal shelters, while thousands more made their way, night after night, to underground railway stations to snatch what little sleep they could on the bare concrete platforms.

Suddenly, it was decreed that underground stations should not be used for shelters. Thousands of nightly tube squatters considered the decision 'rubbish', and displayed their opinion by continuing to use the stations as air-raid cover.

One night, without Winston's knowledge, Clementine journeyed into a blitz to 'see for herself', and tour tube stations. She saw, and decided.

She hurried back to Downing Street in time for dinner with Winston. She had something to tell him.

As they ate alone, she explained where she had been and what she had seen.

'Something must be done for these people—and quickly,' she emphasized, although emphasis was no longer necessary—Winston had heard enough.

'You work something out, Clemmie,' he said.

She recruited Lord Beaverbrook as her ally, appreciating that the problem required dynamic speed and organization.

Hearing Clementine's report, Lord Beaverbrook visited tube stations, walked among the men, women, and children, huddled on the platforms without comfort yet full of spirit.

Lord Beaverbrook's report to Winston confirmed everything Clementine had said. Winston questioned the Cabinet on why the tubes couldn't be used, stressing that he favoured widespread utilization of both the underground stations and tube railway tracks themselves.

Clementine suggested it was important for fixed places to be assigned by ticket in the tube shelters, to avoid overcrowding, unfairness, and to ensure orderliness.

She also proposed the installation of bunks in which the shelter-goers could sleep.

Lord Beaverbrook, with customary speed, put Clementine's and his own ideas into effect. Two million bunks were ordered and the tube stations became London's great air-raid dormitories.

It was decided that No. 10 Downing Street was a deathtrap, and would never survive a direct hit. Two bombs brought home the point. One hit the Treasury, at the back of No. 10, splitting its walls on one side and shattering furniture with the blast.

The second bomb came closer.

Clementine had completed all the arrangements for a Downing Street dinner that evening. Three Ministers were guests.

The night blitz began.

Mrs. Landemare, the cook, and the kitchen maid continued working in the kitchen beside the twenty-five-feet high plate-glass window. Winston, acting on a premonition, went into the kitchen and telling the butler to put the dinner on the hotplate in the dining-room, ordered everyone there into shelter. He then returned to his dinner and his guests.

Within three minutes the bomb hit the house and blast devastated the kitchen. After the incident, Clementine's insistence that he take stricter raid precautions met with success for the first time.

Before the war, the railway authorities had constructed extensive underground offices below Piccadilly. They were seventy feet below the surface, and covered with strong, high buildings.

From the middle of October until the end of that year, Winston and Clementine used this when the night raids began. There, in safety, he was able to transact his conduct of the war, and sleep undisturbed.

'One felt a natural compunction at having much more safety than most other people; but so many pressed me that I let them have their way,' said Winston.

Eventually, the Annexe adjoining No. 10 Downing Street was strengthened, and they moved back.

'Here during the rest of the war my wife and I lived comfortably,' said Winston years later.

'We felt confident in this solid stone building, and only on very rare occasions went down below the armour. My wife even hung up our few pictures in her sitting-room, which I thought it better to keep bare. Her view prevailed and was justified by the splendid view of London on clear nights. They made a place for me with light overhead cover from splinters, and one could walk in the moonlight and watch the fireworks. In 1941 I used to take some of my

American visitors up there from time to time after dinner. They were always most interested.'

During the autumn and winter of that year, Winston took to making frequent night tours of anti-aircraft gun sites in action. His disregard of danger was frightening.

Clementine requested an armoured car to be put at his disposal.

'Mr. Churchill won't ride in it,' said his chauffeur. 'He will,' answered Clementine, 'there won't be any other car waiting for him when he goes out.'

That night, Winston stepped out of No. 10, saw the new car, and said:

'What's this for?'

'Well, sir,' answered his bodyguard, Detective Inspector Thompson, 'you're going round the gun sites, the bombs are coming down, and what with all the firing and shrapnel, we've got to keep you reasonably safe from bits of metal in the air.'

'I won't ride in it,' answered Winston determinedly. 'I'll ride in the police car.'

'I'm sorry, it's not available,' he was informed. Clementine had taken the precaution of making certain no other car would be available.

Winston was furious. Without a word, he got into the armoured car and was driven off.

As they travelled on, shrapnel peppered the car and smashed the bonnet; bombs rained down narrowly missing the car, which eventually reached Richmond Park.

'Winston watched the gun crews in action,' said General Sir Frederick Pile, 'and as he was about to leave he strode up to one of my staff car drivers and asked:

' "Is this car armoured?'

' "No sir," came the reply.

' "Sure?" queried Winston.

' "Yes sir," answered the driver.

'Winston immediately commandeered one of my ordinary staff cars, and left his armoured car behind.

'He said the armoured car was "very uncomfortable" and he didn't want it. He didn't see why he should travel around in an "iron box". He was furious.'

As he was about to enter the car, a strange thing occurred. The nearside door was opened for him—he always sat on the nearside. For no apparent reason, he stopped, turned, opened the door on the other side himself, got in, and sat there instead.

He had never done this before. The car moved off, and proceeded to travel along the Kingston by-pass at about 60 m.p.h. The raid on London was still on.

Suddenly a bomb fell close to the car. The explosion lifted it on to two wheels, and as it was about to somersault over, it righted itself again and sped on.

'That was a near one,' joked Winston, 'it must have been my beef on this side that pulled it down.'

Although he didn't mention this escape to Clementine, she heard about it anyway and decided on a new course of action.

Questioning him on the incident, she asked:

'Why did you get in on that side?'

'I don't know, I don't know,' Winston answered at first. Then he said, 'Of course I know. Something said to me "Stop!" before I reached the car door held open for me. It then appeared to me that I was told I was meant to open the door on the other side and get in and sit there—and that's what I did.'

Clementine's renewed counter-offensive worked. She again used his fear for her safety as a weapon. As he was about to leave on his next gun site tour, she appeared in coat and head-scarf, dressed to join him. He protested. Ignoring his protests, she simply got into the car with him. 'Let's go and see Mary,' she said, and off the car went to the anti-aircraft unit of which their daughter Mary was a member of the battery crew.

'She was always visiting anti-aircraft batteries by day and night, and she went to the searchlight units too,' said General Sir Frederick Pile. 'Her visits were worth a guinea a minute to me as a morale booster—she was fabulous. She would shake hands with almost everyone, and especially all the girls. Her tours of batteries were not limited to the London area—she went all over the country, including isolated sites in remote places.

'At each site she always inquired about the girls' comfort, would go into their huts, inspect their beds, their equipment, the kitchens, and their food, to make sure that they were all that they should be. She was very hot on this kind

159

of thing.

'She travelled down to the South Coast anti-aircraft batteries, and would go there with Winston not only to see the batteries in action, but also to be sure of getting him home early, otherwise the man would have stayed there till all hours.

'When she went to bombed areas, she had a remarkable effect on people—she managed to transfer to them a feeling of calmness and confidence.

'I was at Downing Street the morning after one of their blitz area visits, when Clementine brought in a little posy of flowers for Winston. She said, "These have just come from one of the women we saw yesterday in the East End to thank you for your visit." He slumped down on to the table, buried his face in his hands, and wept.

'She would often say to me, "We've got to look after the Prime Minister. He's being rather naughty about something or other; see that he wraps up; see that he goes in the right car"—in other words the armoured car. I frequently switched cars on him when he went into bad territory, and he always grumbled. He used to take a lot from me. He used to say, "I won't do that!" and then after about five minutes he'd do it.

'Returning from one trip he said, "I'm very cold—my feet are cold."

'I said, "There's only one thing to do, you must take your shoes off and wrap your feet in a rug." He refused. I said, "I've done this many times, and it's a good way of getting your feet warm. Wrap 'em up—take your shoes off." So he reluctantly said "All right," then after a few minutes added, "You were right, my feet are warm."

'The rugs were always in our cars—provided by Clementine. She always made certain he had all the comfort and protection that could be provided, and it was up to us to see that he used it. She manoeuvred him into the safest car; made sure he had a warm coat, scarf, and anything else that might be necessary.

'She and Winston's assistant, Tommy Thompson, were a strong team. Between the two of them, they endeavoured to achieve the best possible job of looking after him. Tommy didn't necessarily go on the various journeys—as a rule, she accompanied him most of the time, but he was a terrible man for ringing up at ten o'clock at night and saying, "I'm coming!—bombs are dropping on the West End and I'm going down to have a look."

'I used to say, "All right sir, if you want to." I went to meet him right away, and Clementine was usually with him, although he sometimes managed to slip off by himself unexpectedly. He couldn't resist danger and she knew this, which is why she used his fear for her safety as a weapon.'

Clementine made many blitz tours without Winston—and often without his knowledge. 'She came with me on a number of occasions round the First Aid Posts,' said Lady Limerick of the British Red Cross Society. 'Particularly at a time when the raids were bad, it was a tremendous boost to people's morale that the Prime Minister's wife should turn up informally and unannounced.

'One night when we were due to make a tour, I went to dinner first at Downing Street. A raid was on, and the Prime Minister wasn't at all pleased that she was going out in the middle of it, but, of course, nothing would daunt her. He wouldn't go so far as to ask her not to go, but he asked her—"Promise you will be careful, and go in the shrapnel-proof car." She laughed because he scorned the use of this car for himself. I said to him: "We shall do our best to look after her, needless to say, and not keep her up too late," but of course, by the time we got back it was in the early hours of the morning. He was in the Cabinet Room when we returned, and didn't even know what time we came in.

'He was so preoccupied with all his responsibilities, that he really was unaware of the incredible extent of the work she was doing. She was clever because she always managed to be there when he wanted her. There were the occasions when he knew she was going out, and that was that, but normally he would go to his room, she would go about her varied jobs, but be there to give him dinner at the right time, and being completely absorbed in his own affairs, he probably thought she was almost always there.

'By operating her own intelligence service, and being a very efficient woman, she organized her life in such a way that she was available when he wanted her, and was still able to carry out the many duties she had undertaken. She obtained estimates from the various members of his staff of how long he might be engaged on individual matters during a day, and would then plan her time-table accordingly to give the impression that she was a wife-at-home most of the time.'

There were always steel helmets in their car, but Winston refused to wear one, so she refused too.

Visiting Battle of Britain Fighter Command airfields with her, or anti-aircraft batteries, he took every precaution for her safety, achieving her purpose of making him look after himself.

Nevertheless, on occasions, he still managed to get his own way in some directions.

One night during a heavy bombing she informed his personal guard: 'Inspector, I have asked Mr. Churchill to come downstairs to bed in the shelter. He has promised to come down—will you see that he does?'

The guard replied, 'I will do my best, Madam.'

At about 2.30 a.m. Winston walked along the corridor and announced he was going downstairs to bed. There was a grin on his face.

Soon afterwards, the bell in his guard's room jangled, summoning him to the Prime Minister's room. Winston was standing beside his bed in his dressing-gown. Smiling, he said: 'Pick up my clothes, I have kept my promise. I have been down here to bed; now I'm going upstairs to sleep.'

Winston found it hard to resist going up into St. James's Park in the middle of the night to watch air raids. Clementine, assisted by members of the staff, persisted with all kinds of tactics to make these dangerous outings more difficult for him.

One short-lived strategy she instituted was the 'boots manoeuvre'.

She instructed Winston's valet, Ives, to hide the Prime Minister's boots at night.

In the middle of a raid, Ives was summoned. He found Winston sitting on the edge of his bed in his bare feet.

'My boots!' he demanded.

Remembering his instruction, Ives said the boots were being repaired.

Winston stood up, looked at Ives long, hard, and silently for a moment, then stretching out his hand, demanded again—'My boots!'

And he added, 'I will have you know, that as a child, my nursemaid could never prevent me from taking a walk in the park when I wanted to do so. And, as a man, Adolf Hitler certainly won't.'

Ives had no alternative—he brought the boots.

It was from the Annexe, with the bombs crashing down outside as he spoke, that Winston made one of his most memorable broadcasts on 21 October 1940. It was spoken in French, and echoed hope throughout France.

That Winston managed to make this broadcast so great, in a language he speaks notoriously badly, was due in no small measure to the coaching in pronunciation Clementine gave him before the broadcast.

To this day, many Frenchmen can recite the last words of that moving message.

'Good night then: sleep to gather strength for the morning. For the morning will come. Brightly will it shine on the brave and true, kindly upon all who suffer for the cause, glorious upon the tombs of heroes. Thus will shine the dawn. Vive la France! Long live also the forward march of the common people in all the lands towards their just and true inheritance, and towards the broader and fuller age.'

And then the blitz moved to the Provinces—to Glasgow, Coventry, Birmingham, Bristol, Southampton, Liverpool, Plymouth, Devonport, Sheffield, Manchester, Leeds. Winston, with Clementine by his side, went where the bombs went, touring more than sixty different towns, and aerodromes hit by the enemy. Wherever they travelled, they spoke to everyone they could.

During the blitz days of 1941, President Roosevelt, anxious for a first-hand report on the effects of bombing, requested his newly appointed Ambassador in London, Mr. John G. Winant, to tour some of the worst hit areas. Winston offered a personally conducted tour.

In April of that year, Mr. Winant, accompanied by the President's special emissary, Mr. Averell Harriman, joined Winston and Clementine. They left London by train for Swansea.

There, they talked to dock workers in the bomb-torn districts; journeyed on by car to a secret weapons establishment, and from there, to Bristol by train.

The train was halted just outside Bristol. The worst raid

the city had ever suffered was on.

Wave after wave of *Luftwaffe* bombers droned over, guns were firing, and bombs splattering down.

'I was with them on that journey,' recalled Lord Ismay, 'and our train wasn't allowed to enter the city because of the raid. We were moved into a siding and stayed there. Winston wasn't pleased about this, but there was no alternative, so we remained in the railway siding all night.

'When we finally arrived at Bristol station in the early hours, and were guided to our hotel by the city's Chief Constable, the first thing both Winston and Clementine wanted was a bath.'

Bombs had interrupted the hotel's hot water supply.

Undaunted, the hotel manager was determined to give service to his distinguished guests.

'I'll see what I can do,' he announced optimistically, and disappeared.

There followed an amazing sight. The entire hotel staff, and they numbered very few as most were away in the Services, joined with all the guests at the hotel to form a human plumbing system. They had heard of the request for a bath and were going to see that Winston got one.

Kettle after kettle of hot water was boiled, and jug after jug relayed by hand upstairs from the basement to the second floor bath which had been prepared. Every link in the human plumbing chain was laughing and so were the recipients of the water at the other end. Always the considerate husband, Winston shared half the bath water with Clementine.

Refreshed, they began their tour of the blitzed city. In the early hours of the morning, few people were about. The devastation was terrible and widespread. The city was still on fire and delayed action bombs kept going off at intervals. Damaged water mains had flooded many streets but, in spite of it all, in half-demolished houses, people were cooking breakfast wherever a stove still functioned.

As Clementine and Winston stood on a pile of rubble that, until the previous night, had been someone's home, an elderly woman came towards them. The Chief Constable introduced her, and they started asking about the bombing. She began to answer, then suddenly said: 'Oh, I can't spend any more time talking, I've got to go and clear up my house.' Her home had been smashed. Off she went, and Clementine and Winston followed her. The house was in a terrible mess, and before she left the city, Clementine personally arranged for clothing and other help to be sent to the old woman.

'I saw the most amazing thing, that morning, that I have ever seen in my life,' said Lord Ismay. 'We went to one of the Rest Centres where they were taking people who had been bombed out, and there was an old woman who was the picture of misery and dejection. She'd been bombed, had lost everything, and was sitting down pouring her soul into her handkerchief. Suddenly, she looked up, saw Winston, and her whole face lit up. She waved her handkerchief and cried—"Hooray! Hooray! Hooray!"—and the way she looked at him was the nearest thing to blasphemy that I have ever witnessed—that one man could have such an effect. It was the most moving thing I'd ever seen.

'It affected both him and Clementine terribly. Tears were pouring down his face. He was fortunate that he could release emotion. If he hadn't been able to do so; if tears had been so difficult for him as they are for some men, he would have been in agony.

'But it was incredible the way in which this old woman's hopelessness turned into ecstasy—as if she had seen a vision. Clemmie was as shaken as I was by this incident and the look on that woman's face made me think of the Bible—it was like—to touch the hem of His garment ... I felt, somehow, translated into another world.

'Both Winston and Clemmie were remarkable on these blitz tours. They had a word for everyone. There's no doubt that people regarded her as an angel of mercy. She has this almost magical gift—this great calming effect on others.'

During that visit, acting as Chancellor of Bristol University, Winston conferred the honorary degree of Doctor of Law on Mr. J. G. Winant, on Doctor J. B. Conant, President of Harvard University, in his absence, and on Mr. Menzies, the Prime Minister of Australia.

Many of the buildings of the University were still smouldering.

When the tour reached Coventry, Winston needed all of Clementine's consolation and strength. They walked through the havoc; amid the torn walls of the great cathedral; and the smashed ruins of the giant factories, and the homes of the people of the city.

Harry Hopkins, Roosevelt's special emissary, who had also seen some of the devastation elsewhere, visited them at Downing Street, and they could never recall, without visible emotion, the words he uttered in Glasgow before his departure, when he said:

'I suppose you wish to know what I am going to say to President Roosevelt on my return. Well, I'm going to quote you one verse from that Book of Books in the truth of which my own Scottish mother was brought up: "Whither thou goest, I will go, and where thou lodgest, I will lodge; thy people shall be my people, and thy God my God."' And then he added softly, 'Even to the end.'

Every day hundreds of pitying letters poured into Downing Street from the United States and other countries. While appreciating their well-intentioned sympathy, Clementine asked:

'Why are they sorry for us?'

She went alone on an official visit to the city of Nottingham.

There she voiced what was in the heart of every woman when she said:

'As the war grows in intensity and horror, we women more and more look back to the simple, happy joys of the past—family life now sadly broken up, absent friends, and the limitations of leisure. But we also project our eyes to the future, when, by the fortitude and courage of our people, those blessings of peace will be ours once more.'

Her favourite true blitz story was the incident related to her by Lady Reading, founder and head of the Women's Voluntary Services.

Clementine considered Stella Reading—'One British woman who would be qualified to serve in the Cabinet.'

Lady Reading's blitz story was of the woman in the city of Bath, who was brought into a Rest Centre after a raid. She had a black eye, was bruised and shaken, though not seriously hurt. Writing up the details of her injuries for official files, a Rest Centre assistant, in the course of asking the usual questions said: 'Are you married?'

'Yes,' answered the woman.

'Where is your husband?'

'In Libya, the bloody coward!'

On the morning of 11 May 1941, Clementine stood with Winston in the ruins of the House of Commons, which the *Luftwaffe* had bombed to dust during the night.

Winston gripped his walking-stick tightly as he looked round the shattered Chamber that for years had been the centre of his life.

No one in the Prime Minister's party spoke a word. The pain of the moment was too much for him. As they moved through the desolation the tears ran down his cheeks.

He looked at the splintered remnants of the historic members' benches, then stared up at the gallery where Clementine had so often watched him, encouraged him, as he had delivered his speeches during the years in the political wilderness, and in his years as leader. Then, turning to her, he said: 'This Chamber must be rebuilt—just as it was! Meanwhile, we shall not miss a single day's debate through this.'

After their blitzed cities' tour together, Mr. Winant sent his report to President Roosevelt. It included a special tribute to Clementine.

Mr. Winant wrote:

'On these trips the most marked determination and enthusiasm were among the middle-aged women who showed great appreciation of Mrs. Churchill coming. If the future breeds historians of understanding, the service to Great Britain by the Queen and Mrs. Churchill will be given the full measure they deserve.

'Mrs. Churchill is a wonderful person and the look that flashed between her and these mothers of England was something far deeper and more significant than the casual newspaper accounts of social interchange. I often thought of Mrs. Roosevelt.

'It is very difficult for a man to interpret these emotions. However interested a man may be I had a feeling that in this task he was about as useful as a husband at childbirth.'

12

THE LADY FROM WASHINGTON

It was Christmas 1941, and Winston for the first time in years was not spending the day at home. Clementine switched on the radio and, with her family, was reunited with her husband thousands of miles away.

The focal point of Christmas in the United States is the lighting by the President at the White House of the great Christmas-tree set up at the far end of the grounds. Touching a switch, the President floods it with multi-coloured electric lights. This time, it was an extra special occasion, for the White House was entertaining a very distinguished guest. More than 40,000 people had come to watch the tree ceremony and millions on both sides of the Atlantic were listening by their radios, but none more intently than Clementine and her family.

The great gun at Fort Meyner boomed as President and Prime Minister walked out on to the south portico of the White House and stood side by side. Then Mr. Roosevelt pressed the button that switched on the lights all over the great tree.

Introducing his 'associate and old friend', the President, speaking briefly, said Mr. Churchill and the British people had 'pointed the way in courage and sacrifice for the sake of little children'. Then Winston delivered the message he had written in his bedroom that morning with thoughts of his wife, children, and grandchildren, 3,000 miles away, uppermost in his mind.

'I spend this anniversary and festival far from my country, far from my family, yet I cannot truthfully say that I feel far from home,' he said.

'Whether it be the ties of blood on my mother's side, or the friendships I have developed here over many years of active life, or the commanding sentiment of comradeship in the common cause of great peoples who speak the same language, who kneel at the altars and, to a very large extent, pursue the same ideals, I cannot feel myself a stranger here in the centre and at the summit of the United States. I feel a sense of unity and fraternal association which added to the kindliness of your welcome, convinces me that I have a right to sit at your fireside and share your Christmas joys.

'It is a strange Christmas Eve. Almost the whole world is locked in deadly struggle and, with the most terrible weapons that science can devise, the nations advance upon each other. Ill would it be for us at this Christmastide if we were not sure that no greed for the land or wealth of any other people, no vulgar ambition, no morbid lust for material gain at the expense of others, had led us to the field. Here, in the midst of war, raging and roaring over all the lands and seas, creeping nearer to our hearths and homes, here, amid all the tumult, we have tonight the peace of the Spirit in each cottage home and in every generous heart. Therefore we may cast aside for this night at least the cares and dangers which beset us, and make for the children an evening of happiness in a world of storms. Here, then, for one night only, each home throughout the English-speaking world should be a brightly lighted island of happiness and peace.

'Let the children have their night of fun and laughter. Let the gifts of Father Chrstmas delight their play. Let us grown-ups share to the full in their unstinted pleasures before we turn again to the stern task and the formidable years that lie before us, resolved that, by our sacrifice and daring, these same children shall not be robbed of their inheritance or denied their right to live in a free and decent world.

'And so, in God's mercy, a Happy Christmas to you all.'

As the simple straight-from-the-heart message ended, a marine band led the crowd in carol singing, and a voice, so familiar to the Churchill household, could be heard joining in lustily above the voices of the crowd. Clementine and her family smiled at each other.

'God Save the King' and 'The Star Spangled Banner' ended the gathering. The White House gates were unlocked, and the thousands who had witnessed the great ceremony streamed out. They had celebrated, on the most fitting day, the birth of unity between two branches of the English-speaking race, and had listened to the voice of a friend, speaking for countless men and women the hopes of the whole democratic world.

The following morning the telephone rang at Chequers. It was Winston calling from the White House to wish his wife and family a Merry Christmas, and to tell her that he had been to church with the President and found peace in the simple service and in the enjoyment of singing the hymns. He had listened to Mr. Roosevelt reading Dickens' *Christmas Carol* to his family, and shared their turkey and plum pudding dinner. Each member of the Churchill family in turn went to the telephone to wish their father a 'Merry Christmas'.

Clementine opened a cablegram from the White House on 25 December. It read:

> *To Mrs. Churchill:*
> *Our very warm Christmas Greetings. It is a joy to have Winston with us. He seems very well and I want you to know how grateful I am to you for letting him come.*
>
> > *Franklin D. Roosevelt*

Winston and President Roosevelt were for ever chiding each other and swapping nonsense rhymes—it made a break, now and again, from more serious affairs. The President loved to tease Winston but a wide-eyed, innocent Winston got one back on him at lunch one day at the White House when Mrs. Roosevelt asked what Clementine was doing in the war.

Winston acted as if he had never heard of the fantastically active public life Eleanor Roosevelt led with her constant travels away from Washington; her visits to depressed areas; her public speaking; and her activities on behalf of the under-privileged everywhere.

In answer to her question about his wife's war work, Winston spoke of Clementine and the wives of his Ministers, praising to the skies the fact that—as he claimed—none of them engaged in any public activities or appearances. 'They just stay at home,' he said. His unstinted vocal admiration for wives who never undertook any public duties or social work shook everyone present, although no one made any comment at the time. What is more, he had them believing everything he had said on the subject, and it was talked about, by those present, for months.

'That Christmas was the first time Mr. Churchill had been to the White House,' recalled Mrs. Eleanor Roosevelt. 'His wife took the precaution of advising us in advance, through the British Embassy, of his various likes and dislikes. The information was most useful.

'My husband and Mr. Churchill got on extremely well because they liked so many of the same things. They both had a love for the navy; both liked certain kinds of literature, and, aside from work they had to do together, in which they were very sympathetic to each other, they really had a great many things in common.

'Their actual daily routines were completely different. My husband's was conditioned by the way his office had to work and the way other people had to work with him. Mr. Churchill, on the other hand, could plan his day the way he wanted to plan it and because he was a guest. He didn't have an office that had to be visited and kept running.

'That was something we had to get accustomed to. Mr. Churchill's hours and my husband's hours were a little different, to say the least, and by the time Mr. Churchill left, my husband was usually exhausted. Mr. Churchill was always ready, having had a good long afternoon nap, to work until all hours of the night, while my husband never had periods of freedom in the afternoon.'

Except for a brief trip to Canada, Winston remained with the Roosevelts until 14 January. The grand strategy of the war was designed during that visit; far-reaching military and production programmes developed; and the Declaration of the United Nations drafted and signed.

Winston hated to be away from home at Christmas. Later in the war, he was compelled to make the sacrifice again, when, as his family were enjoying their Christmas-tree—a present from President Roosevelt—he decided the situation in Athens urgently required his personal presence.

Within an hour an aeroplane was standing by at Northolt Airport and, after being gently reproached by Clementine for deserting the family gathering, he drove to Northolt and left in a Skymaster.

Wherever either of them travelled, and whatever the pressures of duty, there was always a moment for a thought, or a note for each other.

In the middle of a dinner party during the Teheran Conference at which Stalin chain-smoked and drank an estimated quart of spirits, a telegram arrived from London for Winston. It was birthday greetings from Clementine. For his Yalta Conference stay, he was housed in a villa that was an incredible mixture of Scottish castle and Moorish palace, with enormous log fires in most of the rooms. Describing it to Clementine, he said:

'We could not have found a worse place in the world ... it is good for typhus and deadly on lice, which thrive in those parts....'

Clementine had the opportunity of returning Eleanor Roosevelt's hospitality to Winston when the First Lady arrived from Washington for her first look at Blitz Britain.

'When Mr. Churchill came to the White House, he spoke of the time when my husband would visit Britain,' recalled Mrs. Roosevelt, 'but one felt that he had in mind a visit to celebrate a victory. I do not think it occurred to him that there was any reason why I should go during the war. He assumed, I think, that I would go in my proper capacity as wife when my husband went.

'It was Queen Elizabeth who thought of the idea of inviting me to see the work women were doing in the war, as well as using the opportunity to say "hello" to some of the United States' Servicemen and women stationed in England.

'It was felt that as the President could not come himself. I could be his "eyes", and, with my coast-to-coast syndicated newspaper column, also be the "eyes" of the American people.'

From the White House on 19 October 1942 came the following cable:

F.D.R. to Winston S. Churchill
Dear Winston:
   I confide my Missus to the care of you and Mrs. Churchill. I know our better halves will hit it off beautifully....

As ever.

Queen Elizabeth, Clementine, and Lady Reading—head of the Women's Voluntary Services—played hostess in turn to Mrs. Roosevelt.

With her secretary, Malvina Thompson, she stayed at Buckingham Palace, and, on the night of her arrival, Winston and Clementine joined General Smuts and his son Captain Jacobus Smuts, Sir Piers Legh, Lord and Lady Louis Mountbatten, America's Ambassador, John Winant, Mrs. Roosevelt's son Elliot, and Countess Spencer, at a welcome dinner at the Palace. In the morning, Mrs. Roosevelt, who had travelled under the code name of 'Rover', started out—anxious to see everything possible.

'The trip to Britain seemed to offer me the chance of doing something useful, and Mrs. Churchill very kindly elected herself my personal guide during a large part of the visit,' continued Mrs. Roosevelt.

'On our first journey we visited a maternity hospital as well as branches of the women's military services, including training establishments. We were touring a munitions factory when the air-raid warning sounded. I looked at Mrs. Churchill wondering what would happen. But the factory girls went right on working, doing what they were doing, and paying no attention whatsoever to the planes overhead.

'We talked to the girls in the anti-aircraft guns' crews, helping to load the guns; we talked to the air transport auxiliary women pilots who were ferrying new planes to R.A.F. stations or shot-up aircraft to repair shops, and we visited factories in which women did every kind of war work.'

With the King and Queen she had her first real look at the devastation. Their first stop was St. Paul's Cathedral, partly because their Majesties wanted to give the fire watchers who had saved the Cathedral the satisfaction of a visit from them, and partly to enable Mrs. Roosevelt to stand on the steps of the Cathedral and see what warfare could do to the heart of a city.

Clementine took her down to the bomb-torn East End of London and thousands cheered.

'I wanted to see as many blitzed areas as possible, and go among the people, and Mrs. Churchill helped me do just that,' said Mrs. Roosevelt.

'We talked with people like the old couple who still slept nightly in an underground shelter in London, though they could easily have been evacuated to a country area. They

173

told us they had lived so long in the shelter that, while they liked to go out in the daytime and sit in their old home— even though there was not enough of it left so that they could sleep there—they preferred to return to the shelter at night rather than move away.

'We visited Red Cross clubs of all kinds and went to American and British Service camps.

'During my first week-end in England, I got to know Mrs. Churchill more closely when I stayed with them at Chequers, where I watched Mr. Churchill playing on the floor with his grandson.'

Mrs. Roosevelt's shrewd comment on her hostess was: 'One felt that, being in public life, she had to assume a role and that the role had become a part of her. One wondered what she was like underneath.'

Clementine arranged for Winston's special train to be put at Mrs. Roosevelt's disposal for a general tour of the country.

'Our days,' said Mrs. Roosevelt, 'usually began at eight o'clock and ended at midnight, but I was so interested that, at the time, I did not even realize how weary I was gradually becoming.

'We lunched with some of the women who were daily feeding the dock workers and saw women from many different backgrounds working side by side just as their men were fighting side by side. We saw how distinctions and values were fast changing.

'One woman told us "the hardest thing is to keep at your job when you know the bombs are falling near your home and you don't know whether you will find your home and family still there at the end of your day's or night's work!'

'My schedule included, among other things, inspecting 26 camps in 19 days. I had been warned that we would never make it, but we did.

'I particularly remember going to Dover with her and one of the Women's Institutes on the way. She was really very wonderful.'

In front-line Dover, which had endured constant shellings from the German long-range guns at Calais, they went everywhere—there were no half measures with Mrs. Roosevelt, she was determined not to miss a thing. Clementine, herself a dynamo of vitality, found it rough going, keeping up with the tall, long-striding Eleanor. She found herself for ever running after her.

Whirlwind Eleanor achieved what no one had ever managed to do before—left Clementine breathless—so breathless in fact, that finally, from the strenuous effort of trying to keep up with her guest, an exhausted Clementine helplessly and hopelessly suddenly sat down on the street pavement to take a brief desperate rest!

Mrs. Roosevelt, until then apparently unconscious of her own strength and incredible walking pace, turned and looked with amazement at her hostess, then they both burst out laughing.

'I didn't realize I walked so fast,' said Mrs. Roosevelt, 'nor did I realize I had exhausted her to that extent.

'I am sure she wasn't as strong as I was in those days, so I think she probably was very exhausted.'

Eleanor apologized for running Clementine off her feet, but, after a short rest, the Churchill 'never-give-in' spirit reasserted itself, and the tour continued.

It was a three-week, almost non-stop whirl of Service camps, war factories, and bombed homes.

Back in London, Mrs. Roosevelt went to dinner at Downing Street. It was a small party. The guests were Brendan Bracken, the Minister of Information; Lady Denman, Head of the Women's Land Army; Lady Limerick, of the British Red Cross; Dame Rachel Crowdy, whom Eleanor Roosevelt had met in the United States; General Brooke, Chief of Staff; Henry Morgenthau, Junior, Secretary of the United States Treasury; and Mrs. Roosevelt's companion-secretary, Miss Thompson.

It was during this dinner that Eleanor learnt still more of Clementine's personality. 'She had great tact, as I discovered that night,' said Mrs. Roosevelt.

'We were discussing Loyalist Spain and this subject resulted in a difference of opinion between Mr. Churchill and myself.

'He had asked Henry Morgenthau whether the United States were sending enough to Spain and whether it was reaching there safely. When Mr. Morgenthau replied that he hoped that sufficient supplies were getting through I said that I thought it a little too late, and that we should have done something to help the Loyalists during their Civil

War.'

'I was for the Franco Government until Germany and Italy went into Spain to help Franco,' said Winston.

'I cannot see why the Loyalist Government could not have been helped,' countered Mrs. Roosevelt, to which the Prime Minister replied:

'You and I would have been the first to lose our heads if the Loyalists had won—the feeling against people like us would have spread.'

'Losing my head is unimportant,' said Eleanor.

'I don't want you to lose your head and neither do I want to lose mine,' Winston answered bitingly.

Clementine had listened silently to the argument until that point, and then, leaning across the table towards Winston she said quietly, but firmly, 'I think perhaps Mrs. Roosevelt is right.'

Winston was obviously furious. 'I have held certain beliefs for sixty years and I'm not going to change now,' he replied angrily.

'Things were getting quite difficult, so Mrs. Churchill simply decided that it had better come to an end,' Mrs. Roosevelt recalled.

'Fortunately we had nearly finished dinner, she got up, and just said to her husband:

' "I think that the time has come for us to leave you"—and we left.

'She had decided diplomatically that dinner had better be well and truly over. She was wonderul and a great tactician.

'I saw then, for the first time, how extremely well she handles him in conversations. She can give and take.'

In those brief moments Clementine clearly revealed to Mrs. Roosevelt that she was not prepared to be a rubber stamp of her husband's opinions if she disagreed with them.

Winston's anger, and the electric atmosphere, were soon dispelled as Clementine, almost effortlessly, charmed talk back to more comfortable ground.

When Eleanor arrived home on 17 November, a cable immediately went off to Downing Street:

F.D.R. to Winston S. Churchill.
Former Naval Person:
  Mrs. Roosevelt arrived safely this morning and I

*met her at airport and found her well and thrilled by
every moment of her visit. My thanks to you and Mrs.
Churchill for taking such good care of her.*

                                       Roosevelt.

Clementine became self-appointed peacemaker between
Eleanor and Winston on occasions when they got into long
arguments on how to reorganize the world.

At a luncheon discussion Eleanor insisted, with deep
conviction, 'the best way to maintain peace is to improve
the living conditions of the people in all countries'.

Winston countered: 'The best means of achieving a durable peace is an agreement between England and the
United States to prevent international war by combining
their forces. Of course, we might take Russia in, too,' he
added.

Neither would budge. Clementine changed the subject,
and the argument ended in stalemate.

On so many occasions, when Winston has ruffled people
for some reason, it is Clementine who smooths feathers
again.

On one occasion he was at the B.B.C. for a discussion
regarding a broadcast. Clementine had gone along too. The
course of the conversation was not at all to his liking, and
an annoyed Winston startled everyone present by suddenly
walking out without a word of explanation. After he had
left the room, Clementine stood up, said 'Good-bye' charm-
ingly to each person present and removed the shock from
the electric atmosphere Winston had left behind.

On 4 January 1944 a letter arrived from the White
House that had nothing to do with the war, but everything
to do with the ever-increasing affection and warmth between the Churchill and Roosevelt families. The letter
read:

*F.D.R. to Mr. and Mrs. Winston S. Churchill, in
   London.*
Dear Clemmie and Winston:
   *I find enclosed clipping on my return home. Evi-
dently, from one of the paragraphs, the Desert News of
Salt Lake City claims there is a direct link between
Clemmie and the Mormons.*

And the last sentence shows that Winston is a sixth cousin, twice removed.

All of this presents to me a most interesting study in heredity. Hitherto I had not observed any outstanding Mormon characteristics in either of you—but I shall be looking for them from now on!

I have a very high opinion of the Mormons—for they are excellent citizens. However, I shall never forget a stop which my Father and Mother made in Salt Lake City when I was a very small boy. They were walking up and down the station platform and saw two young ladies each wheeling a baby carriage with youngsters in them, each about one year old. My Father asked them if they were waiting for somebody and they replied 'Yes, we are waiting for our husband. He is the engineer of this train. Perhaps this was the origin of the Good Neighbour policy!

As ever yours,

One quiet evening during a visit by Clementine and Winston to the Roosevelts' Hyde Park home, the four of them sat enjoying each other's companionship, taking things easy awhile as old friends.

Eleanor sat knitting, and both she and Clementine burst out laughing when the President leaned over and, taking Winston's arm, remarked: 'My dear Winston, the British Empire doesn't exist any longer. It's just a figment of your imagination.'

Winston rose slowly, a puckish expression on his face, and pretending to carry a heavy load in his arms, dropped it suddenly on the President's lap. 'Do you want India?' he said, 'here it is.'

They were as one family together.

The Churchills and the Roosevelts might have their disagreements, but they made a great combination, and, after Eleanor's blitz visit to Britain, Winston wrote to her:

'Your visit has given great pleasure and comfort throughout this island and your presence and speeches have been an inspiration to the many places you have visited in your indefatigable tour. You have certainly left golden footprints behind you.' She also left a very tired Clementine.

13

MIRACLE AT MARRAKESH

'WE are told that those who hold the reins of Government carry burdens almost too heavy for human strength, and that the strains and stresses of the Premiership, if continued over a period of years, may have the gravest consequences to health.

'It is a convenient doctrine, so long as no one suggests retirement as the obvious remedy. It mutes the voice of criticism and dulls the edge of controversies. No one cares to attack a sick man, especially one who has spent himself in his country's service and whose present plight is due entirely to that fact.

'But is it true that politics must be reckoned among the dangerous occupations? Is Downing Street, in fact, only a short cut to the grave?'

That was Winston's comment some years ago on the strain of high office. Considering the overwhelming responsibilities he bore, and the fact that he did nearly all the things our mothers told us not to do, it is incredible that he lived to such an age. Downing Street would have certainly been a short cut to the grave for him but for the constant loving care of his wife.

Winston was not exactly the easiest of patients, but Clementine nursed him through appendicitis, paratyphoid, three bouts of pneumonia, and a varied assortment of other illnesses, apart from patching him up after numerous accidents all over the world. To all of which Winston said: 'Live dangerously. Take things as they come. Dread naught. All will be well.'

During the war years, Clementine fought her own Battle of Britain—the battle of her husband's health.

She had long given up attempting to persuade Winston to tune up his physical condition with regular exercises. His attitude towards over-strenuous exertion was summarized in his comment to her while watching a boat race on television.

'Many a fine healthy young man has strained his heart doing that,' he remarked.

One winter, hoping to persuade him to try a little body bending, Clementine typed out a list of P.T. movements, headed the sheet 'Exercises', and stuck it on the mirror of his dressing-table. Sticking notes on his dressing-table mirror was her method of getting him to remember anything she particularly wanted him to do.

Unfortunately, the valet altered the heading to read 'Prenatal Exercises'. The following morning, while tying his bow tie, Winston carefully studied Clementine's 'Keep Fit' suggestions. Then, calling the valet over, he inquired: 'Do I look pregnant?'

Clementine, who could be as persistent and determined as her husband, gave up trying to push home any ideas she had nursed of getting Winston to join the physical jerks brigade. He just wasn't having any.

In February 1943, the people of Britain were shocked to learn that he had contracted pneumonia. He was immediately given the new wonder drug M. & B. 693, but his life was also in danger—from himself. At first, he refused to take his condition seriously and insisted on continuing all his duties in spite of the serious deterioration in his breathing.

The doctors ordered him to stop all work and remain in bed, but this he refused to do.

To all protests he replied simply but firmly: 'I *must* do it. There is so much to be done.'

Clementine was the only one who could persuade him to take to his bed and stay there. She did this by making the only diplomatic deal possible in the circumstances. She persuaded him to continue the direction of the war from his bed. Ministers, officials, secretaries, attended his bedside in a constant stream for discussions and instructions.

In spite of a rising temperature he carried on, calling for all the State papers he would normally deal with, and dealing with them. He missed nothing. He refused to have anything shelved.

Clementine even convinced his medical advisers to be philosophical about his determination not to stop work.

'If he could not employ his phenomenally active brain, he would fret, be extremely restive, and this would not help his recovery,' she explained. And, of course, she was right.

But a worse crisis was to come the same year.

'The Prime Minister has been in bed for some days with a cold. A touch of pneumonia has now developed in the left lung. His general condition is as satisfactory as can be expected.—Signed: Moran; D. Evan Bedford (Brig.); and R. J. V. Pulvertaft (Lt.-Col.), dated 15 December.'

This, the first announcement of Winston's illness in 1943, was made in the House of Commons by Mr. Clement Attlee, the Deputy Prime Minister.

Winston, who had celebrated his sixty-ninth birthday at Teheran on 30 November, had been taken ill while still engaged in the Middle East on winding up business following the conferences with President Roosevelt, Marshal Stalin, and Marshal Chiang Kai-shek. His son, Randolph, and daughter Sarah, then a section officer in the W.A.A.F., who had accompanied her father as his A.D.C., were with him.

The weather during that fateful winter of 1943 had been treacherous in Egypt, but nevertheless, when he visited Cairo, Winston wore only a light summer suit.

Now pneumonia had struck him down for the third time in his life. Mr. Anthony Eden went to see the King at Buckingham Palace to report on the Prime Minister's health. Mr. Eden explained to His Majesty that the Middle Eastern conferences had unquestionably imposed a severe strain upon Winston. He was often at work until 3 a.m. or 4 a.m., yet always was up early and even had forgone the afternoon sleep he normally insisted on at home or wherever he went.

Doctors had advised against the Prime Minister making the journey to the Middle East by air because of the strain involved, but nevertheless the final trip from Cairo to Teheran had to be made by plane, involving the fatigue of flying at high altitudes. The Persian capital is 5,000 feet above sea-level.

For Winston this had been the most strenuous year of the war. His visit to the Middle East was the eighth major mission he had undertaken abroad during the first three years of hostilities. In the course of those missions he was estimated to have travelled approximately 60,000 miles, more than 24,000 miles of which were notched up in that fateful 1943 alone.

By the end of December he would have been absent from the country on his war journeys since the beginning of the year for about twenty weeks. The series of conferences in 1943 which led to the historic meeting of the Prime Minister, Marshal Stalin, and President Roosevelt at Teheran began with the Casablanca conference in January. Before returning from Casablanca Winston continued his journey by air to Turkey, Egypt, and Cyprus, and met our troops again in Sicily on their way to Tunisia.

In May—having recovered from his first attack of pneumonia—he went to Washington for a further conference with President Roosevelt and for the second time had the honour of being invited to address Congress. He visited North Africa again on the way back, and he was then able to congratulate British and American troops in that theatre on their final victory.

In August he again crossed the Atlantic to attend the Quebec conference and from Quebec went to Washington for further discussions with President Roosevelt. In November, he set out for the Teheran and Cairo conferences.

Hitler got wind of the Big Three meeting in Teheran and sent a planeload of Nazi assassins to kill Winston, President Roosevelt, and Stalin.

The three leaders were informed by Soviet security that a double agent had warned of a plot to kill them with a heavy mortar barrage.

Soviet fighters intercepted an unmarked German plane on the Turkish–Iranian border and shot it down when it refused to land. Soviet agents parachuted to the wreckage and discovered enough evidence to confirm the murder plan.

Winston continued to play a conspicuous part in the co-ordination of Allied war aims as well as strengthening the bonds which united them.

But he also physically exhausted himself and brought his resistance to illness dangerously low.

After the Cairo and Teheran conferences, he had planned a one-night stay in Tunis as the guest of General Eisenhower, after which he intended visiting the troops in Italy. But when he reached Tunis to be greeted by General Eisenhower, he looked ill. On arrival at the White House in Tunis, where he was to stay, he went to bed at once and slept for hours.

He had been too exhausted even to ask for his papers. It was unlike him and Lord Moran was worried. 'He is sickening for something but I do not know what,' he said, and, for safety's sake, immediately radioed for extra medical help.

Sarah stayed in the room with her father as he slept through the day. Once he opened his eyes, and instantly seeing her concern, said:

'Don't worry, it doesn't matter if I die now, the plans of victory have been laid, it is only a matter of time.' He then fell into a deep sleep again.

When he next awoke, he had a temperature and pneumonia.

Lord Moran, Winston's lifelong friend and personal physician, once told an audience of doctors: 'The time may come when you may have illness and may not be able to get a nurse. That happened to me at a place called Carthage during the war with a patient of seventy with pneumonia (Mr. Churchill), without a nurse, without a chemist's shop, without another doctor to consult.

'The first night, the detective and I shared the nurse's duties. Somehow we managed to keep awake.

'Meanwhile I received a number of telegrams from members of the Cabinet advising me what I should do and what I should not do.

'One of them went so far as to ask me: "Do you realize what will happen in England if you come back without your patient?"

'The lesson of that experience is that if you have a good nurse the rest does not matter.'

On the instructions of Lord Moran, Detective Inspector Thompson spent the first night listening to the tempo of the Prime Minister's breathing. He sat outside the bedroom door, tense and anxious. At about 3 a.m., the heavy, fast breathing suddenly stopped. Thompson crept into the room, went to the bedside, and leaned over the pillow. Mercifully, there was an almost inaudible but regular inhaling and exhaling of breath. It was a terrifying moment for Thompson. He hurried to inform Lord Moran.

A little later, in his fever, Winston said: 'I am tired out, body, soul, and spirit.'

He lay back a moment, then added: 'Yes, I am worn out, but all is planned and ready.'

Suddenly he asked: 'Where am I?'

'Tunis, sir—with General Eisenhower,' answered Thompson.

'Tunis? Carthage!' exclaimed Winston. 'In what better place could I die than here—in the ruins of Carthage?'

'Don't say that, sir!' pleaded Thompson. 'The world needs you.'

Winston sighed deeply, sank back into the pillows, and fell asleep.

Brigadier Bedford, a noted chest specialist, flew in from Cairo with three nursing sisters to assist Lord Moran. But the finest nurse of all for Winston, the one who seemed to bring about the miracle of recovery, flew into Tunis after being summoned by General Eisenhower. Winston was terribly ill, near death, and everyone at the villa waited for bulletins or whispers from the medical staff.

Then, back in London, came an announcement from No. 10 Downing Street. It simply said: 'Mrs. Churchill regrets that she will not be able to keep any engagements in the immediate future, as she has left the country in order to be with the Prime Minister during his illness and convalescence.'

'And then a wonderful thing happened,' recalls Detective Inspector H. 'Tommy' Thompson. 'Mrs. Churchill arrived. Her sudden appearance at his bedside gave the Prime Minister tremendous comfort and new strength. From that moment on, he started to come back to us.'

When she first arrived by plane Winston was much too ill even to be told. Then, when he was sufficiently conscious, the doctors permitted her to go to the bedside. She sat quietly beside him without saying a word, and held his hand. Suddenly, his eyes opened. Husband and wife smiled at each other.

'The miracle of that moment is almost impossible to describe,' said one of the Prime Minister's staff. 'The M. & B. drugs were playing their part in the fight, but Mrs. Churchill's coming there made an almost unbelievable difference to him. It was as if by holding his hand she was giving him a transfusion of her own spirit and strength.'

During the first couple of days she was there, he was still only semi-conscious, but she stayed by his bed for hours so that whenever he opened his eyes he could see she was with him when he needed her most. The very fact of her being close, of his knowing she was there, was everything to him.

Gradually the temperature began to subside and the pneumonia resolve, although an irregularity of the pulse indicated that the illness had thrown some strain on his heart. Sarah also worked tirelessly at the villa, helping her mother and helping General Eisenhower's staff in every possible way. After two anxious weeks, Winston began to recover strength so rapidly that he was able to tackle work again.

Recalling the illness in his own record of the war years, Winston said: 'I became conscious of being very tired. For instance, I noticed that I no longer dried myself after my bath, but lay on the bed wrapped in my towel till I dried naturally ... as I sat on my official boxes near the machines I certainly did feel completely worn out ... I said "I am afraid I shall have to stay with you longer than I had planned. I am completely at the end of my tether...." So here I was at this pregnant moment on the broad of my back amid the ruins of ancient Carthage....'

On returning from a Christmas Day service conducted by a British Army chaplain, Clementine told Winston a strange story. A white dove, she said, had flown into the hut in which the service was being held, and had alighted on the altar just as the Blessing was being pronounced.

'An ecclesiastical hoax!' said Winston.

Christmas Day that year was especially wonderful, for they were also able to celebrate the blessing of his recovery. Clementine and Sarah personally supervised the Christmas dinner arrangements at the villa, and Winston, tired but happy, thoroughly enjoyed it.

On Christmas morning, a small patrol vessel which had been guarding the Bay, ran up a flag signal spelling out 'Happy Christmas!' to the Prime Minister. This pleased Winston enormously, and he was very unhappy when the ship was ordered to haul down the flag to conform to security regulations.

The generals flew in and out and Winston still held the reins.

As he began to progress, Sarah sometimes took it in turns with her mother to sit beside his bed reading him *Pride and Prejudice*, for Winston always enjoyed Jane Austen.

Clementine and Lord Moran insisted on a thorough convalescence in a warm climate, and Clementine suggested that Winston's beloved Marrakesh would be ideal.

Winston had first fallen in love with the rose-red nine-hundred-year-old city, scented with orange and lemon groves, in 1936, when he went there with a small family party and found Lloyd George had had the same idea.

Before beginning his convalescence, the Prime Minister decided to issue a personal message from No. 10 Downing Street to reassure the people that he was progressing well.

The statement said: 'Now that I am leaving the place where I have been staying for an "unknown destination" after more than a fortnight's illness, I wish to express my deep gratitude to all who have sent me kind messages or otherwise helped me. I had planned to visit the Italian front as soon as the conference were over, but on 11 December I felt so tired out that I had to ask General Eisenhower for a few days rest before proceeding. This was accorded me in a most generous manner.

'The next day came the fever, and the day after, when the photographs showed that there was a shadow on one of my lungs, I found that everything had been foreseen by Lord Moran.

'Excellent nurses and the highest medical authorities in the Mediterranean arrived from all quarters as if by magic. This admirable M. & B., from which I did not suffer any inconvenience, was used at the earliest possible moment, and after a week's fever the intruders were repulsed.

'I hope all our battles will be equally well conducted. I feel a good deal better than at any time since leaving England, though of course a few weeks in the sunshine are needed to restore my physical strength.

'The M. & B.—which I may also call Moran and Bedford —did the work most effectively.

'I have not at any time had to relinquish my part in the direction of affairs, and there has not been the slightest delay in giving the decisions that were required from me.

'I am now able to transact business fully. I have a highly efficient nuclear staff, and I am in full daily correspondence with London, though I shall be resting for a few weeks, provided, of course, that we do not have any setbacks.

'I thought that some of those who have been so kind as to inquire or express themselves in friendly terms about me would like to have this personal note from me which they will please take as conveying my sincere thanks.'

Actually, although on the mend, the Prime Minister was still far from well, and Clementine was determined he should be fully recovered before returning to Whitehall. Before leaving Tunis for Marrakesh special arrangements were made for the flight, including strict limits on the altitude and the inclusion of an R.A.F. doctor, equipped with oxygen apparatus, in the party.

The plane flew at about 7,000 feet and was deliberately making a detour to avoid the Atlas Mountains. Winston, behaving momentarily like his old self, insisted on cutting out the detour and taking the more direct route over the mountains. The doctors were against the idea, but an insistent Winston was always difficult to oppose, and he had his way.

Slowly the plane climbed, and at every additional 1,000 feet Winston permitted the doctors to check his pulse and breathing. On being told he was responding well, he cried with delight: 'Of course I'm all right!'

The one person in that plane who did not try to dissuade him from having his way was Clementine. She would not attempt to dissuade him in such matters. She knew him too well. She knew that even *she* should not stop him. It had got to be done. She understood better than anyone else that Winston *had* to defy danger for his own satisfaction. In certain things she would never openly oppose him. She knew that to do so would be to strangle the very spirit of adventure that had made the man what he was.

He obediently took all the pills that Lord Moran dished out, although he added drily to Clementine: 'When ill himself, this doctor of mine refuses his own drugs with a sad air of inside knowledge.'

On arrival at Marrakesh, Winston was exhausted but happy. When ordered to go straight to bed by Clementine he went like a good boy and remained there for several days.

When she had flown out to Tunis, Clementine, in preparation for her husband's convalescence, had brought him something she knew he would want—his easel, canvases, and paints. Now, amid the splendour of Marrakesh, in the shadow of the beautiful blue mountains, he could relax and enjoy his beloved hobby.

When Winston heard that a wonderful view could be had from the top of a high tower which formed part of the house in which they were staying, he insisted on being carried up to the top of it. A chair was improvised with jutting poles, and two of the staff manoeuvred him up the winding stairs to the tower. He stayed only for a few minutes, and was heard to say: 'I am too weak to paint, but I am still strong enough to wage war.'

However, it was not long before he was busy with his brushes. Clementine left him to paint alone for hours, knowing how engrossed he became. Sometimes she would take the opportunity, while he was happily engaged in his tower, to slip into Marrakesh and wander around the quaint stalls of the bazaar. On her return Winston would be waiting to show her his painting. She was not slow to criticize, often saying: 'Look, Winston, don't you think it ought to be ...' He would usually agree with her.

With each day, and the rest and the sun and his Clemmie, he became more his old self. Lord Beaverbrook had flown out to be with him during his convalescence, and the presence of his old friend was an added tonic.

When General Eisenhower came to see him at Marrakesh, doctors were continually taking Winston's temperature, 'and', said Ike, 'whenever they approached him to remove the thermometer from his mouth, Mr. Churchill had got there first and announced his own temperature'.

'I always do that,' said Winston. 'I believe these doctors are trying to keep me in bed.'

Sometimes Clementine amused Winston after dinner by playing bezique with him, but more often a fairly fierce game of poker would start.

'Usually,' said General Sir Leslie Hollis, who was one of Winston's closest war-time aides, 'I managed to avoid being drawn into these poker games by pressure of work, but one night Beaverbrook pressed me to join. With great misgivings I did so.

'I drew the most terrible hands and lost what was, for me, a very considerable sum of money—something like a month's pay. To the others, of course, such a sum was nothing at all.

'In due course Winston totted up the score and, before I had time to calculate, myself, exactly how much I was down, he said: "You needn't worry, Hollis. It's all divided by 240!"

'I'm sure that Churchill did this division sum purely for my benefit, and one of the nicest features of his kindness was the casual way in which he did it.'

The days were warm and sunny, the nights cool, clear, and bright with brilliant stars. Together, Winston and Clementine shared again the breath-taking beauty of Marrakesh which they had loved so much before the war.

The Moroccan-styled villa in which they were staying belonged to a wealthy American woman and had every modern convenience and luxury. The furnishings of red, green, and gold particularly appealed to Winston's taste for flamboyant colours. He loved it there. As he grew stronger, Clemmie and he would take walks together, enjoying the glorious views of the Mediterranean and the snow-capped Atlas Mountains.

To this exotic setting came General Montgomery and General Bedell Smith, President Benes of Czechoslovakia, General Georges, General Sir Henry Maitland-Wilson, General Alexander, Lady Diana and Mr. Duff Cooper (later Viscount Norwich), and Mr. Harold Macmillan.

General Montgomery came on the evening of 31 December to see Winston and be given his first sight of Overlord—the code name of the invasion plan for Normandy.

As it was New Year's Eve, Clementine had arranged a dinner for the Prime Minister, his guests, and his staff.

Monty had first got to know Winston and Clementine in the summer of 1940 at his divisional headquarters on the south coast, near Brighton. Monty had taken them to Lancing College, occupied at the time by the Royal Ulster Rifles, and showed a counter-attack on a small airfield which was assumed to have been captured by the Germans. They then worked their way along the coast, finishing up in

189

Brighton in the evening when Winston suggested that Monty have dinner with them at the Royal Albion Hotel.

It was at this meal that, on being asked by Winston what he would drink, Monty replied—'Water', adding that he neither drank nor smoked yet was 100 per cent fit. To which Winston said in a flash that he drank and smoked and was 200 per cent fit.

But it was at Marrakesh that Monty's deep friendship with both Winston and Clementine really began. On New Year's Day, 1944, Clementine invited him to join in one of her famous picnic lunches. As they drove along in the car Winston and Monty continued to discuss Overlord.

Said Lord Montgomery: 'We had a quiet refreshing day in the sunshine and the warmth of the Moroccan country-side in winter, and much stimulating conversation. I got to know the Prime Minister and Mrs. Churchill well during that short visit to Marrakesh, and it was the beginning of a friendship which developed into my becoming a close friend of them both.'

Repeatedly, when discussing the Overlord plan, Winston would say to Clementine and to his generals: 'We must take care that the tides do not run red with the blood of American and British youth, or the beaches be choked with their bodies.'

He expressed this fear many times, and it was unlike Winston to repeat himself so much. Clementine appreciated that the reason uppermost in his mind were his painful memories of the tragic Gallipoli campaign of the First World War of which he had been the principal exponent.

Winston had never changed his views on the Mediterranean of being the 'soft underbelly' of Europe.

He had also frequently made it plain to Clementine that the second consideration dominating his thoughts on invasion across the English Channel was his concern for the political future of the Balkans and the threat to them from Moscow.

The villa was well organized. Clemmie saw to that. Apart from domestic staff, there were six cypher girls, a map room with a naval officer always on duty, and an army of secretaries.

Every two days Clementine organized a picnic to one of the countless beauty spots in the district; and almost everybody would go and relax—surrounded by a protective guard of military police. Clemmie delighted in finding a new and delectable spot for each picnic. Good surroundings, good food, good company, were the best medicines for Winston. There was, of course, ample food for everyone, but on one occasion her plans went wrong—for the best of reasons.

They were enjoying cold chicken when an Alsatian dog, lean and starved beyond description, hovered watchfully and hungrily near by. Half crawling, the dog advanced and then withdrew, always gaining a little but ever cautious.

The sight of the dog distracted everyone from the food. Winston threw the dog a leg of chicken which was devoured ravenously. Winston stopped eating, his whole attention concentrated on the dog.

He threw more and more chicken to the starving dog until the well-laden basket was suddenly empty. There was no more chicken left for the host or the guests. But at least the dog was happier. Gaining confidence, he at last came nearer and nearer and finally nestled in Winston's arms.

Solemnly he addressed the Alsatian: 'Dog,' he said, 'little did you think when you awoke this morning that you would meet a man called Winston Churchill and enjoy the best meal of your life.'

In January 1944 Winston invited General de Gaulle to visit him at Marrakesh. Mr. Harold Macmillan, who was then Resident Minister with the Allied Headquarters in North-West Africa, and Mr. Duff Cooper, who was British Representative to the French Committee of Liberation, were seriously concerned about the invitation because of the Prime Minister's open hostility to de Gaulle and great suspicion of him.

Eventually Duff Cooper arrived in preparation for the visit, and after discussion with Winston he was even more troubled about the reception de Gaulle might receive. He confided his fears to Clemmie.

The following day Duff Cooper and his wife joined Winston and Clemmie on one of their picnics. Lady Diana, who as Lady Diana Manners was famous as the ravishingly beautiful Madonna in Max Reinhardt's play *The Miracle*, has her own recollection of that day.

'Lady Churchill, Sarah, and I were sent off earlier—willing pioneers—to find a site which must have a vale and rock and gushing stream,' she recalled. 'These we found in a lesser Grand Canyon, where, far below over olive-treed pitch, the water rushed over high, round boulders.

'The day was charming. Natives passed Biblically with their donkeys. Motors rolled up with the guests and staff. Winston, flanked by two massive detectives, was wearing the same costume in which we had left him sitting in the Persian Garden—a ten-gallon hat on his head (as a protection from the snow-chilled Atlean breezes) and, over his boiler suit, a dilapidated Chinese dragon dressing-gown, its loose gold thread hardly holding the escaping cotton padding. Army trucks followed, loaded with food, wine, cushions, and cooks.

'A Moroccan leather chair—the only chair—was brought for Winston and a hard leather cushion put on his lap to balance his tray. The rest of us sat on the spring-green grass, crushing the flowers without a name, as we grabbed for the pigeon, olive-stuffed pastilla, nectar from the Hoggah, and brandy for heroes—listening spellbound to the "Life and Soul" as his conversation bounded from fancy to fancy, from polished prose to soldiers' slang.

'He ate like a healthy young man and drank like one, with "Lord Moran orders me another glass of brandy" (no come-back from Lord Moran!).

'The picnic was dispersing happily and I was pursuing fly-away paper for the usual aesthetic reasons when, always apprehensive, I saw to my horror that Winston was determined to follow the young and energetic adventuring down the steep trail that zigzagged down the canyon.

'I swallowed my cry of "Lord Moran, how can you allow your patient ... after such a meal and that glut of brandy! Oh, wife! Oh, daughter! Stop him!' They knew better than to try.

'Clemmie said nothing, but watched him with me like a lenient mother who does not wish to spoil her child's fun nor yet his daring.

'Nothing to do then but watch breathlessly from the brink. The path was single-file narrow. The detectives followed meekly. Down safely, he ordered the detectives to pull him up on to one of the great boulders. Again he survived the effort. How was he ever to climb up again?

'I abated the agony of watching by devising a safe return. It would have to be in the nature of an inverted parachute. The army trucks yielded no rope or hope. Nothing to be found but the long, long strip of picnic tablecloth—too white, too dirty-linen-in-public, but it was better than a straw, and I stumbled down the trail and was rewarded by Winston's immediate welcome of my device.

'He leaned back against his vast unwound cummerbund as the detectives, one at each end, dragged him slowly upwards while he discoursed on the tenderness of women, their flair for improvisation and the value of linen.'

Returning from the picnic Duff Cooper rode with Clemmie, and his wife rode with Winston. Clementine's quiet, generally unrecognized influence over Winston is revealed by Duff Cooper's own personal record.

'During that return drive,' he said, 'Clemmie told me she had given Winston a Caudle curtain lecture that morning on the importance of not quarrelling with de Gaulle. He had grumbled at the time, but she thought it would bear fruit.'

It almost did not bear fruit, for de Gaulle at first said he would not come, and Winston exploded. He was furious again about de Gaulle, and all Clementine's work appeared to be undone. Winston suggested sending de Gaulle a note saying he was sorry but he would not be able to see him after all, even if he were able to come. Duff Cooper persuaded him from this course and Winston compromised by saying he would agree to receive de Gaulle only on a purely personal basis to 'talk about the weather, and the beauty of the place, and then say good-bye'.

De Gaulle finally came. And Clementine repeated her 'don't quarrel' warning to Winston.

Winston, nevertheless, was in a bad mood when the French leader arrived and was not very welcoming. At lunch Clemmie sat next to the General and excelled herself in steering the table conversation in an amusing way. Winston, under her barrage of charm, gradually thawed and, by the time the luncheon was over, had invited de Gaulle to sit next to him. The following day he took the salute with de Gaulle at a review of troops. They stood together, acknowledging the cries of 'Vive Churchill!' and 'Vive de Gaulle!' and afterwards Clemmie invited everyone to join in another of her wonderful picnics. It was a great success. Winston was smiling. De Gaulle was smiling. And Clementine wore the biggest smile of all.

On the evening of the momentous picnic, just before dinner, Lady Diana Duff Cooper and Clementine were talking and thinking of post-war days. Lady Diana said that instead of a grateful country building Winston another Blenheim Palace, they should give him an endowed manor-house, with acres for a farm and gardens to build and paint in.

Very calmly Clementine said: 'I never think of after the war. You see, I think Winston will die when it is over.'

It was a curiously calm and sad conversation. She seemed quite certain and quite resigned to his not surviving long into the peace.

'You see, he is seventy and I am sixty and we're putting all we have into this war, and it will take all we have,' she said. It was one of those rare moments when Clementine opened up her heart and shared her deepest thoughts—thoughts that she probably would not have shared even with her husband.

At last came the day when Clementine and Lord Moran considered Winston sufficiently fit to return home. The weeks of patient care had brought their reward.

After a brief flight to Gibraltar the remainder of the journey was completed in the battleship *King George V*. Winston took over the Admiral's cabin on the bridge and, with Clementine, walked each day about the bridge and deck. But their most cherished memory of this voyage was Winston's tours of the great ship. The Prime Minister ascending the narrow steep gangways, with a sergeant of the Royal Marines using his shoulder to heave the great man's backside up the ladders, made an unforgettable sight. Clementine's peals of laughter were only drowned by Winston's own roars of amusement at this regular occurrence.

At Paddington Station all members of the War Cabinet and other Ministers plus three Chiefs of Staff were there to welcome them home. Winston's arrival had been kept secret, but a crowd soon gathered about the platform and the station approaches, and the cheers were tremendous and heart-warming.

There were cheers again when, within a few hours, Winston entered the House of Commons, completely recovered, for all to see, from his illness. A beaming Winston looked up at his wife seated in the gallery. The eyes of hundreds of M.P.s joined his own to gaze at the slender, smiling woman above them. And from those thankful M.P.s came a new roar of cheering—a grateful tribute to the lady of No. 10 who had brought their leader back to them.

During the months before D-Day, Winston was again struggling to overcome the after effects of pneumonia. Field-Marshal Alanbrooke noted in his diary: 'I began to feel that the stupendous burden that he had been carrying so vailiantly throughout the war was gradually crushing him. I am afraid he is losing ground rapidly, he seems quite incapable for a few minutes on end, and keeps wandering continuously ... he has probably done more for this country than any other human being has ever done; his reputation has reached its climax. It would be a tragedy to blemish such a past during an inevitable decline which has set in. I am filled with apprehension as to where he may lead us.'

Field-Marshal Smuts, also fearful of Winston's health, warned Clementine that he considered Winston worked too hard and exhausted himself, and that if he maintained his terrible pace, he was doubtful whether he would stay the course.

Lord Moran, Winston's personal physician, also sounded a warning, particularly against his expressed intention of journeying to Bermuda for a combined Chiefs of Staff meeting. Lord Moran informed Clementine that he was even putting the warning in writing to the Prime Minister, telling him there were three good reasons why he should not go:

1. That he might become a permanent invalid if he did.
2. Owing to his very recent bout of pneumonia he was quite likely to get another if he exposed himself to the hardships and fatigues of a journey.
3. The strain of the long journey was liable to bring on a heart attack.

Clementine, with Lord Moran's support, managed to persuade Winston to postpone the trip.

On the morning of 24 August 1949, at Lord Beaverbrook's villa La Capponcina, at Cap d'Ail, in Winston's own words, 'The dagger struck.'

It was well past midnight, and Winston was playing gin

195

rummy with a fellow guest at the villa, Brigadier Michael Wardell. At about 2 a.m., Winston complained of cramp in his right hand, but went on playing.

At the end of the game he said he felt 'peculiar' and was going to bed. He totalled the score, and wrote on a slip of paper, 'I O Mike £1.'

As they walked upstairs to the bedrooms, Winston paused momentarily, and said to Brigadier Wardell: 'The dagger is pointing at me. I pray it may not strike. I want so much to be spared at least to fight the election. I must lead the Conservatives back to victory.

'I know I am worth a million votes to them,' and, as he reached the door of his room, he added: 'Perhaps two million!'

During that night, he was taken ill. Lord Beaverbrook was told and called the local doctor. He also telephoned his son, Max Aitken, in London, to ask Lord Moran to fly out at once.

The diagnosis was clear. Winston had suffered a stroke.

Somehow, news that he had been taken ill leaked to newspapers. Reporters gathered outside the gates of the villa. Lord Beaverbrook decided it was best to mislead them.

A bulletin was issued stating: 'Mr. Churchill contracted a chill while bathing. Lord Moran was sent for and he says that Mr. Churchill is much better this morning, but that he will require a few days of rest and quiet.'.

Clementine was also immediately informed, and advised by Lord Beaverbrook of the necessity for strict secrecy to avoid arousing the wide-spread anxiety that any sudden flurry of family arrivals at the villa would undoubtedly instigate.

It was left to her to explain the situation to the rest of the family, and request them, too, to maintain absolute secrecy.

Ill as he was, the patient still kept a strong hand on his own affairs. He dictated a note to a secretary declaring:
'Lord Beaverbrook—

'Please put the communiqué out as written and let us say nothing more for the present. During the day we shall see what the reactions are, and it may well be that tomorrow some statement by Mike of the kind suggested, would be very good. Today it would be premature. Signed: W. S. C.

25.8.49.'

Concerned that Press accounts of the illness should be handled with utmost diplomacy, Winston decided to direct the operation himself. He left his bed, put on a white towelling dressing-gown, and padded downstairs to personally supervise the issuing of the bulletin. He then returned to bed and called for the newspapers. 'I want to see what they have to say about my horse.' His Colonist II had won a race the previous day.

When he attempted a game of rummy, he found it difficult to hold the cards or his cigar. The effects of the stroke were plain.

'I quite lost my equilibrium,' he said. 'It is a distressing and uncomfortable situation.'

The following day the doctors told Clementine that his condition had improved considerably. He was already overcoming the temporary paralysis.

'I feel much better today,' he said. 'Quite different from yesterday. I am really very hopeful that I shall escape the consequences. The dagger struck, but this time it was not plunged in to the hilt. At least, I think not. But the warning is there, and I shall have to pay marked respect to it.'

When Brigadier Wardell commented that he appeared to be almost recovered, Winston replied:

'I'm not really. I'm a very different man to the one who was sitting playing cards with you only three nights ago. The dagger struck. I don't ever remember spending so idle a day as this. I am changed.'

Winston decided that the events of that night should remain secret to the grave. And they were.

Some six months later—on 16 February 1950—mysteriously, as if reacting to some bush telegraph message, the world's Press began to telephone its condolences. The news had apparently leaked out that the greatest statesman of the century had died that morning.

A statement was issued immediately from Chartwell. It said: 'I am informed from many quarters that a rumour has been put about that I died this morning. It is quite untrue. It is, however, a good example of the whispering campaign that has been set on foot. It would have been more artistic to keep this one for polling day.'

The signature was, of course, 'Winston S. Churchill'.

But the story of Wednesday, 24 June 1953 was no rumour.

It was only a few weeks since the Coronation. For three months, the Prime Minister had been doubling the job of the Foreign Secretary, Sir Anthony Eden, who was very ill. As always, pressures of office were heavy and, in addition, Winston had carried much of the burden of the Coronation preparations, as well as chairing the meetings of the Commonwealth premiers in London.

That 24 June, Winston and Clementine were entertaining the Italian Prime Minister De Gasperi at No. 10. Winston made a scintillating after-dinner speech, then later, as the guests were milling about, Clementine and Christopher Soames saw him suddenly slump in his chair. At first, they thought he had fainted, but he was not, in fact, unconscious, although it was obvious he was seriously ill.

Christopher Soames told only John Colville, Winston's Joint Principal Private Secretary, and while Clementine stayed by Winston's side, they somehow emptied the room of guests without anyone noticing what was wrong, and even that the host could not get up to say good-bye to the De Gasperis. Winston was paralysed.

A stroke had attacked his left side and the left side of his face. Lord Moran was sent for.

Winston's eyes were only for his wife. As at Marrakesh, her very presence and air of confidence that everything would be all right were contagious, reassuring to him, although Lord Moran had told her that he did not expect him to live over the weekend.

She knew, that very day, Anthony Eden was undergoing crucial surgery in Boston, and Eden was the obvious successor to the Premiership if anything happened to Winston. Because of this, and in spite of Winston asking that his condition be kept secret, she knew some of his closest colleagues would have to be told. The Queen's Private Secretary was also contacted and asked to tell the Queen that she might have to find a new Prime Minister on Monday morning.

Clementine took charge of the situation. 'Downing Street is no place to be ill,' she announced. 'We must get him home as quickly as possible.' She realized that his best hope of recovery lay in his home and his own surroundings at

Chartwell.

Another man might have remained unconscious for days and never recovered. But, with the care of his Clemmie and Lord Moran, Winston regained sufficient strength to leave Downing Street only forty-eight hours later for Chartwell.

Three days after the stroke an announcement was made that 'the Prime Minister has had no respite for a long time from his arduous duties and is in need of a complete rest. He has therefore been advised to abandon his journey to Bermuda and to lighten his duties for at least a month.'

The news that the Premier's complaint was a stroke remained a State secret.

President Eisenhower spoke for the world when, in a message to his old comrade in arms, he cabled:

Dear Winston,

I am deeply distressed to learn that your physician has advised you to lessen your duties at this time and that consequently you will be unable to come to Bermuda for our talk.

I look upon this only as a temporary deferment of our meeting. Your health is of great concern to all the world, and you must, therefore, bow to the advice of your physician.

Clementine ordered that notices hung on the high brick walls, giving dates when the grounds of Chartwell would be open to the public, be taken down; and she announced:

'Owing to Sir Winston Churchill's need at this time for complete rest I have, with great regret, decided that it will not be possible to open the grounds of Chartwell next Wednesday, 1 July.

'I offer my sincere apologies to the people representing local charities who were to benefit from the event and to many members of the public who will be disappointed.'

She was ensuring in every possible way complete rest for her restless genius.

But nothing was going to stop Winston carrying on at the head of world affairs as long as there was a chance to bring about a peaceful international understanding. Nothing but an irretrievable breakdown in his health could sidetrack him from that resolve.

The curative powers of his wife, his family, and his home worked wonders. His progress was astonishing. Within days, the use of his leg and arm gradually returned. Clementine helped him to exercise and move them. His speech was unaffected, and slowly, walking around the gardens hand in hand, arm in arm, with his wife, the limp with which the stroke had left him also disappeared.

Whenever the weather was fine, he would spend some of the afternoon sitting with Clementine beneath his favourite big yew-tree overlooking the lake in which his black swans (a present from Australia) swam serenely in the sun.

The news that he had fallen ill in his seventy-ninth year had startled the world. So vital a part of the present age was he, so triumphantly had he emerged through so many hazards, that everyone seemed to take it for granted that he would go on and on and on.

Only a few months previously Winston had told President Eisenhower that he did not think of retiring because 'the opportunity for the greatest service to my country still lies ahead'. His inspired intervention in world affairs had borne out his prediction. To people everywhere this greatest of living statesmen was also the chief repository of humanity's hope for peace.

But, in spite of the encouraging news from Chartwell, many politicians declared that the House of Commons had seen Winston for the last time as Prime Minister, and that he would soon retire from the Premiership.

The exact nature of his illness was still being kept an official secret.

A month later, showing no visible signs of his stroke, he reappeared with Clementine in public and drove from Chartwell to Chequers for a fortnight's stay.

The journey to Chequers was unnecessary. It was a deliberate gesture, an excuse for Winston to say to the world: 'Here I am, still alive and kicking, and back in business again.'

Here he was, indeed—wearing a light grey suit with a homburg to match, looking a cool, summery, almost debonair figure with his cigar and cane.

When the grapevine which always warns sightseers of excitements to be relished brought out the cheering crowds to welcome him back, he grinned, made the V sign, doffed his hat, waved his cigar, and, as with each familiar gesture the cheers redoubled, turned and beamed at his wife beside him.

In October of that year he faced his most important ordeal since his absence—speaking to 3,000 delegates to the great Conservative Conference at Margate.

'How's Winnie?' was the one question in everyone's mind and the one answer they were all waiting for.

'He's here!' cried Mrs. John Warde, the chairman, peering excitedly into the wings of the platform. The suspense was almost past bearing. And then Winston and his Clemmie were before them. A Winston a little slower perhaps on foot, but agile as ever in the mind.

The wrath, the firmness, all the old mannerisms, and the wit, were there.

Only indirectly did he refer to illness when, taking stock of election prospects, he declared: 'It is not a good thing always to be feeling your pulse and taking your temperature.

'You have to do it sometimes'—and he stuck out his tongue to show his familiarity with the process—'but you don't want to make a habit of it.'

His fifty-minute speech, that day, was yet another triumph for him, and for his proud, smiling wife seated behind him on the platform.

It was not until almost two years later that the truth of his 1953 illness was finally officially revealed.

In February 1958 while staying with his literary agent, Mr. Emery Reeves at Roquebrune, Cap Martin, he developed pneumonia and pleurisy again. Clementine picked flowers from the grounds of the Villa La Pausa, which stands on one of the foothills that run down from the Maritime Alps to Cap Martin, about three miles west of Monte Carlo. As soon as she took the flowers into his suite which consisted of a bedroom, a sitting-room, and a bathroom at the east, or Italian, side of the villa, as ill as he was, his first reaction was: 'I want to paint them.'

Cautioned Clementine: 'Not yet.'

'You'll see,' he said. 'I'll be out with the brushes before any of you think I will.'

Clementine read to him some of the thousands of 'Get well soon' telegrams which had arrived from all over the world.

Characteristically, within a few days, he was asking to be propped up in bed so that, with spectacles perched on the end of his nose, he could dictate a number of business letters as well as enjoy the view of the sun-splashed Mediterranean from his window.

When Winston had arrived at the villa in January for a painting holiday, Clementine had not at first been with him. Out of her watchful sight, Winston, muffled in a great-coat, was seen around sampling grilled lobster and enjoying coffee in restaurants along the coast. He was also heard ordering a liqueur to go with the coffee in his distinctive French that results in Cognac sounding as though it were a piece of machinery (Cog-nak). And now he was ill.

When Lord Moran arrived from London, he said: 'My dear Winston, they tell me you have been overdoing it again.'

'What?' Winston exploded. '*Painting flowers?*'

With the arrival of Clementine the picture rapidly changed. With a 'now-no-nonsense' air, she would bring him the medicine he had flatly refused to take. And, of course, he took it.

Within a few days, 'for being a good boy', she permitted him, as a treat, to sit in the window-seat of his bedroom and gaze out over the sunlit sea. With his ham and salad meal in bed, she allowed him a small glass of champagne, and afterwards a brandy and a cigar. It might not be an ideal choice for any ordinary convalescent, but then this was Winston Churchill.

For after dinner she had arranged a further surprise. A record player was moved into his bedroom and together they listened to an hour of Brahms and Mozart.

Three weeks later he was able, for the first time, to walk in the grounds of the villa. As they strolled slowly, enjoying the sunshine, he took an occasional rest on a little folding stool she had thoughtfully decided to carry with her. A few days later, diners at a hill-top restaurant saw him eating in public for the first time since his illness.

In the warm, sun-glossed terrace restaurant, Winston dealt with hors-d'oeuvre and asparagus, roast saddle of lamb stuffed with Provençal herbs and served with an Alsatian white wine, then ice-cream, brandy—and a big cigar.

Diners, waiters—everyone beamed, Clementine included. Winston was himself again.

It was, appropriately, St. George's Day, glorious with sunshine, when little more than a month later Winston drove from Chartwell to his second home, the House of Commons. It was more than four months since he had last been there, and Clementine joined him for the occasion. She was in her customary seat in the gallery when a fringe of Members on the floor of the Chamber parted to reveal their returning leader.

Winston, slowly, as though struggling with the infirmity of his legs, made his way to his corner seat below the Treasury bench. The packed House let itself go with great joyful cheers. From all sides he was warmed by nods and smiles. All eyes were upon him as he settled down. He looked paler and thinner, but he was back where he belonged.

For years life at Westminster had come to depend on his health. *'Winston has a cold!'* The collective heart of the House of Commons missed a beat whenever that news was announced. And when he returned, fit and well, Parliament breathed again. Even the hearing aid which Clementine and his old friend Bernard Baruch had persuaded Winston to use in the House was never regarded by M.P.s as a sign of infirmity. He used the instrument—a tiny amplifier mounted at the end of a pencil-like stick—with similar diplomatic effect to that which society ladies of bygone years achieved with their lorgnettes, flattering by very pointedly applying the instrument to his ear as if not to miss a single word being uttered. Or, on occasion, lowering it deliberately.

A division was called. That meant a march to the lobbies —but Winston marched, even though a little shakily. Another division followed, and Winston was off again, making the circuit to the division lobby and back to his seat.

On leaving the Chamber at the end of the debate, he turned at the Bar and bowed to the Speaker, making the customary solemn obeisance to the Chair. Then, with a slight pause, hand on chest, he glanced beneficently around the House, taking it all in and ending his survey at the point in the gallery where his wife sat.

From that day he never left the Chamber without this

last ritual, as if harvesting yet another memory of the place to which he has given so many memories and in which he lived his memorable lifetime.

On Winston's remarkable ability to be the victor so often over illness, his doctor, Lord Moran, commented: 'It's fifty per cent me, fifty per cent Nature, fifty per cent Sir Winston, and fifty per cent Lady Churchill.'

That adds up to two hundred per cent, but then, Sir Winston was more than just one person.

14

'LET'S GO HOME!'

'LET'S go home!'

When Winston and Clementine Churchill said that, they meant only one thing—the place which brought them their greatest years of happiness, their own special refuge during the good and the bad times; the place which, in their hearts, was their one and only home—Chartwell Manor, near Westerham in Kent.

The drive from Westerham railway station takes you past gardens filled with hawthorn, larkspur, and gigantic rhododendrons, and woods damp and earthy with ancient elms, beeches, and oaks. There is a peaceful air of remoteness about this English countryside. From Westerham the road climbs steadily upwards, overlooking the beautiful Weald of Kent. You drive up a winding country lane, make a sharp turn, and suddenly, seemingly out of nowhere, appears the Churchill home.

Its grey stone, its ivy, its apparent timelessness, make it as much a part of the landscape as the trees around it. Nothing mars its beauty. Nothing about it seems out of place. Even the flagstones before the main entrance declare their right to live in the manor by continuing into the vestibule and on into the main hall.

The Churchills lived in many houses, but had only one real home. Clementine breathed the homeliness, the comfort, and the efficiency into Chartwell, and Chartwell breathed new life into Winston. Wherever they lived, Clementine always saw that the house was run completely to Winston's satisfaction. That, of course, is what is expected of any dutiful housewife, but no housewife in the world had a husband quite like Winston or a home life quite like the Churchills had.

Clementine has a tremendous sense of normality, and this gift gave the whirlwind Winston his anchorage.

It was on Chartwell Manor that she concentrated the greatest loving care and attention because she knew that there, above all places in the world, her husband could find some measure of true contentment.

Chartwell came into their lives when, one day, while Clementine was recovering from giving birth to Mary, Winston gathered together Diana, Randolph, and Sarah, and drove them in his old Wolseley car into the Kent countryside to inspect the house he said he was thinking of buying. On reaching Chartwell, originally a small Henry VIII red brick manor house, extended somewhat haphazardly by subsequent owners, they found it wildly overgrown, untidy, and deliriously exciting.

'Do you like it?' asked Winston.

'Oh, do buy it! Do buy it!' the three of them shouted.

'Well, I'm not sure...' said Winston teasingly keeping them in suspense until they reached home and could tell their mother how much they loved the place.

Winston thought the house needed no improvement, but Clementine, the more practical of the two, had other ideas and set to work immediately organizing additions to the building as well as thinning down uncontrolled ivy and rhododendrons, and decreasing trees to give more light.

Not too happy about the tree felling, Winston muttered: 'If you go on like this, Clemmie, we had better rename the house One Tree Hill.'

An estate agent would probably describe Chartwell Manor in some such terms as these:

'Desirable Estate of 250 acres. House, standing approximately 500 ft. above sea-level, stone built, with tiled roof, and partly covered with wisteria and lemon-scented magnolia. Spacious hall, fine reception rooms, 19 bed and dressing rooms, 8 bathrooms, electric light. Company's water, central heating throughout. Stabling, 3 garages, 3 cottages, a large studio, ideal for painting, swimming pool with floodlight built by owner.'

The Manor was originally 80 acres; but after the last war Winston added to the property Chartwell Home Farm, covering about 170 acres, to develop dairy farming and extend his agricultural activities.

'I find farming a very interesting occupation,' he once declared. 'I think that if I had heard about it when I was young, I probably never should have gone into politics at all.'

Winston's literary work and a legacy from Lord Herbert Vane-Tempest, his Irish cousin, made possible the purchase of Chartwell Manor.

Lord Herbert was killed in a Welsh railway disaster on 26 January 1921. He was unmarried, and his valuable estate known as Garron Tower and the surrounding lands in County Antrim passed to Winston, his first cousin once removed, who was then Secretary of State for War. Included in the estate were fourteen houses in the village of Carnlough. When Winston and Clementine learned that some of the fishermen tenants were hard up, and several of them unemployed, they immediately made them a present of their houses, free of all rents. Since the four-roomed dwellings were all in excellent repair and had gardens attached, it was a wonderful and unexpected Christmas-box for the hard-pressed fisher folk.

Winston and Clemmie were more excited about the purchase of Chartwell Manor than anything else they had ever bought. Already they knew in their hearts that this was to be their real home. Together they walked through the grounds, planning hedges, flower beds, lawns. They would not move in with the family until the comprehensive alterations they had in mind had been completed. Winston personally supervised the structural alterations to the house, while Clementine concentrated on the interior and on the layout of the gardens.

At Chartwell, Winston threw off political care and became like a schoolboy on holiday. He loved playing handyman around the house and grounds, digging and building the bathing pool Clementine wanted, a goldfish pond, and even a tree-top house.

The heated swimming-pool's boiler-house chimney was cunningly concealed in the trunk of an old oak, and giant rhubarb leaves camouflaged the filtering equipment; a fishery was established with a special spawning section, and lorries brought colossal chunks of mountainside from Wales to add decorative new touches to the landscape.

Clementine was delighted, but her pleasure was somewhat dimmed when, as so often happened, he arrived back in the house from pools and waterfalls dripping wet. As he walked through the corridors she scurried ahead, spreading newspapers protectively on the floors.

Of the years before the Second World War, he said:

'I lived mainly at Chartwell, where I had much to amuse me. I built with my own hands a large part of two cottages and extensive garden walls, and made all kinds of rockeries and waterworks and a large swimming pool which was filtered to limpidity and could be heated to supplement our fickle sunshine.

'Thus I never had a dull or idle moment from morning to midnight, and with my happy family around, dwelt at peace within my habitation.'

'As soon as you went into Chartwell Manor, you knew she was mistress of the house; were aware she ruled the home, and that you were in an Englishwoman's castle,' said Sir Tom O'Brien. 'Her influence on the atmosphere was unmistakable, and you felt the same thing in their Hyde Park Gate home.

'Winston in his own home—in spite of the fact that he did so much of his work at home—was never the same brash, driving personality that he was in Downing Street or in the House of Commons. Oh, he was still the same fantastic force, but his wife would make it plain—you are not in Downing Street, not at a Cabinet meeting, not in Parliament—you're at home. This home discipline of hers was a good, essential thing, because without this discipline he would have burnt himself out long ago. Mind you, she is the only person in the world from whom he took discipline. It was wonderful to watch the motherly care she gave him, as well as the wifely care.'

Chartwell is still largely preserved the way it used to be. Walk through the double-leaved oak front doors of the manor-house into the austere yet friendly hall with its walls and staircase of light oak.

A small reception room is furnished with the chintz-covered pieces so characteristic of English homes. There are paintings everywhere. French windows opening on to a stone piazza take up almost one entire side of the room, and through them can be seen a broad expanse of rolling farmlands.

The sitting-room, used by the family and friends on informal occasions, is quietly furnished in pastel shades with blue predominating.

Clementine's bedroom is surprisingly sparsely furnished:

a large bed, an equally large wardrobe, a glass-topped dressing-table with stool, and little else. She liked plenty of space about her and spent much time walking about the room, carrying on a conversation or dictating letters.

Living rooms and sleeping rooms alike were littered with scribbling pads on which she made copious notes as ideas occurred to her, and which she was frequently unable to decipher afterwards. There was always a pencil and pad beside her bed, and in the morning a collection had to be made of the notes she had written and scattered about the room. This was probably the only lapse into untidiness to be discovered in her well-ordered personal life.

Her bed linen is generally white, and she likes her pillow-slip renewed first thing every morning and again during the day if she goes to bed for a rest.

Her dressing-table always displays an array of jars and bottles of cosmetics, and her bathroom offers a wide variety of bath essences; yet, though she takes great care in cleansing and preserving the skin, she uses little make-up.

She usually washes her own silvery-white hair, never tinted or dyed, and visits a hairdresser only when it needs special styling.

She pays great attention to her hands, and her nails are manicured professionally—short, with no points, and a natural or very pale varnish.

Self-discipline plays a large part in the preservation of her youthful beauty and athletic grace. She is very fond of rich French dishes, and whenever she feels she may be putting on a little excess weight she subjects herself to a strict diet: no salt, no fruit, no alcohol, little starch, and only four cups of liquid a day. During dieting days she refrains, whenever possible, from accepting outside invitations. 'It is so difficult to resist eating,' she says.

The neutral-shaded fitted carpet in the bedroom blends to perfection with furnishing in soft pastel colours to give a general impression of size and coolness. The neutral background accentuates Clementine's own vivid personality.

She loves floral-patterned curtains for her bedroom—her favourite is a water-lily design. There is a big satin-covered bed back, and windows lead on to a little terrace with a wonderful view of the gardens she tends. There is also a dressing room and bathroom adjoining the bedroom.

There were no photographs on the walls of her bedroom —she preferred to decorate them with paintings.

A trait in her nature is a preoccupation with cleanliness. When she retires to rest in the afternoon she undresses completely, puts on a nightdress and slips into bed. When she rises to dress for the evening, she puts on fresh underwear and a fresh nightdress is laid out. She will never wear a garment twice without laundering.

Because of her fastidiousness, at one time, when she used to go shopping, she would put any coins she received in change into a separate purse in her handbag. As soon as she arrived home, the coins were washed. She dislikes anything that isn't clean.

Near her bedroom, on the left of the hall, is Winston's magnificent studio. Through the wide double doors half-finished paintings could be seen resting against the walls. Palette and paints lay on a table, ready for use. The boarded floor is bare, for this was the functional, much-lived-in room of a hard-working artist, not a dilettante.

Past the studio, along a short passage, was the general office and a small office for Clementine's secretary.

Walk up the polished oak staircase, turn right, and you are in the famous Churchill study. An ancient room, once the minstrels' gallery, it retains the original, high-arched ceiling extending up to the very roof of the house. This and the room next door are all that remain of the old Attwell Manor which was begun in the days of Edward III.

From the rafters hang wrought-iron lights, and there are decorative iron standard lamps at strategic points around the room. A few pictures hang in the spaces on the walls not entirely concealed by bookshelves.

Valuable rugs give colour and warmth to the floor of the long, narrow room. Through the rug in the centre runs the clear-cut track of Winston's feet. While dictating, he paced the length of the room like a caged lion.

'It's no use getting another rug,' said Clementine in despair one day. 'If we do, he'll only wear that out, too.'

History lives all around you. Above the wide open fireplace hangs the Union Jack the Allies flew in Italy when they invaded in 1943. (In summer it was quite usual for Winston himself to light the fire at midnight if the air had turned chilly.) In one section of the bookcase is a large diorama of the beach at Arromanches with its Mulberry Harbour. The frame carries the simple title: 'D plus 100'. On the shelf below stands a small figurine of a snarling bulldog.

Books abound. A long lectern-like stand always carried open works of reference relating to whatever subject happened to be engaging Winston's pen. Reference books were scattered everywhere.

The desk, very large and usually very tidy, stands near a window. Behind it is Winston's favourite chair, a tall, carved dark oak piece with green tapestry seat and arms.

Around the fireplace are comfortable tub chairs upholstered in a white material broadly striped in red and blue.

An archway leading from the study takes you into Winston's bedroom, which is directly above that of his wife. Like the latter's, Winston's bedroom is sparsely furnished. There was little on his dressing-table but a brush and comb and a bottle of the eau-de-Cologne which he loved to use daily on his handkerchiefs.

His bedroom is typical—it is full of gadgets. The dressing-table in front of the window looks down on the magnificent Chartwell gardens. Winston wanted nothing to hinder this view, so his dressing-table appears to have no mirror until you pull a cord beside it, and a mirror rises up. Pull the cord again, and down goes the mirror.

The bedroom, at the very top of the house, is right in the roof itself, and the great bare roof beams are the ceiling.

Again there are no vivid colours. The dark furniture contrasts with pale cream walls almost covered with Winston's 'pin-ups'—dozens of family photographs—most of them in Edwardian clothes. There is a cartoon of Lord Randolph Churchill, a contemporary print of the great Duke of Marlborough, and a portrait of Winston's nurse, Mrs. Everest.

There are a desk and four-poster bed, over which hangs the famous charcoal sketch which Sargent made of Winston's beautiful mother, Jennie Jerome. Of this picture, which has been reproduced many times and in many countries, Winston said:

'There is more colour in it than there is in any number of paintings I have seen. Is there anyone except Sargent who would dare to put that heavy outline against the light side of the face? And yet how perfectly it models.'

211

His bed is now alongside the wall, and fixed to the wall above the bed is a flap table which, when opened, spread in front of him almost the length of the bed. On this rough wooden table, made by a local carpenter, he spread his newspapers for his morning reading-the-papers routine.

Through double doors in the room he stepped down into one of his greatest personal delights—his sunken bathroom.

Winston had his own special pillow on the four-poster bed. 'Once,' a member of the household staff said, 'we swopped it for another, just to see if we could get away with it—but he knew. He felt the difference immediately.'

On the first floor, too, are the dining-room with its huge dark oak beams and rafters, a kitchen, and a large drawing-room used on more formal occasions. The drawing-room, with carpet, furnishings, and porcelain all in blue, is directly over the studio. In both wings of the first floor there are rooms reserved for guests staying at Chartwell overnight. Staff bedrooms occupy the second floor.

Below ground-level, shielded by the low box hedge, is the Churchills' private cinema, a large room which can seat perhaps a hundred people comfortably.

The cinema was Winston's greatest relaxation. He had little respect for the sacred institution of the English weekend and was seldom unoccupied for a minute. Therefore the responsibility of entertaining guests rested mainly on Clementine. But every week-end at least one film was shown and everybody at Chartwell, staff included, was invited. Film companies sent advance copies of their latest productions.

Winston preferred their private cinema, and on the rare occasions when Clementine visited a public cinema, she had to go without him. However, she is never short of escorts. When she attended one charity performance, Field-Marshal Lord Montgomery accompanied her.

'They asked me to bring somebody nice, so naturally I thought of Lord Montgomery,' she said. 'He's a very old friend of ours. My husband will stay at home. We have our own cinema and he prefers that.'

One Sunday evening at Chartwell the chosen film was Sir Laurence Olivier's production of *Hamlet*. Throughout most of the performance two voices could be heard declaiming the immortal lines—Olivier's from the screen and Winston's from the audience. Immediately the film had ended, Winston hurried upstairs for a copy of the play. Throughout dinner he continued to declaim passages, but he did not need the book to prompt him. His memory was phenomenal, as Olivier discovered on another occasion.

Sir Laurence had invited the Churchills to his performance of *Richard III* at the Old Vic. And from the rise of the curtain to the final scene Winston recited Shakespeare's words, almost putting the actors off.

They afterwards joined the Oliviers for supper, and to Sir Laurence's immense surprise Clementine said that Winston also knew by heart the whole of *Henry IV* and *Henry V*.

Almost incredulously, Sir Laurence consulted Winston on his approach to certain speeches in the plays and was instantly given an interpretation.

Clementine loves the theatre, which she visits whenever she can. Sometimes Winston might be too busy to accompany her, but when she found a play which she was certain he would enjoy, she would go again with him. She delighted taking him to plays with titles such as *The Happy Marriage* or *A Woman of No Importance*. Despite his encyclopaedic knowledge of Shakespeare, he was no highbrow.

Some years ago a political friend advised them to see Richard Burton playing Coriolanus at the Old Vic. He told Winston: 'Shakespeare foresaw you. It is really the story of your life.'

Winston and Clementine took his advice and saw the play. A few days later they met their friend again, and Winston said coldly: 'I cannot see any possible parallel between the life of Coriolanus and myself.'

'But Coriolanus saved Rome, just as you saved Britain,' the friend argued, 'and when the war was over the Romans threw out Coriolanus just as the British voters rejected you.'

'Yes,' said Clementine, 'but Winston did not cross over and join the enemy.'

Between the walled rose garden of the house and an ornate shelter called the Marlborough pavilion is a vine-covered way. The pavilion is decorated with a frieze carved from slate and painted by their famous artist nephew John Spencer Churchill. It portrays the Battle of Blenheim, at which the family's great hero, the Duke of Marlborough,

213

was the victor. Inside the pavilion are busts of the Duke and Duchess, Prince Eugene of Savoy, and Queen Anne.

During the war years Chartwell was officially closed, but many times Winston and Clementine longed for a sight of their beloved though deserted house, and they would make a sudden trip with some of their staff to taste—if only for one night—the joys of their home. On one occasion when the news was bad Clementine, sensing that the moment was right, said: 'Let's go home this evening,' and Winston snatched gratefully at the momentary escape.

Together, that night, they walked in their dressing-gowns through the rooms of their home. The rhododendrons were blooming and the magnolias brave with the largest, whitest blossoms. The paths were overgrown with weeds and grass; but when, next morning, they strolled arm in arm through the scented gardens, war seemed a long way from that haven of peace. They returned later that day to Downing Street, strengthened and refreshed by the brief hours in the old grey manor-house.

Chartwell is close enough to London for guests to motor down for lunch and dinner, and at week-ends there used to be a constant stream of people coming and going. The favourite relaxation of the Churchills was good talk, and Clementine, in sole charge of the social life of the manor, arranged all invitations.

Lawrence of Arabia, known to the family as 'Mr. Shaw', often arrived unexpectedly on a motor bike on Sunday afternoons during the period he was stationed at a nearby R.A.F. unit. The Churchills liked this slight, soft-spoken man who had such a way with their children and so enjoyed becoming one of the family in his off-duty hours. Lawrence was very fond of Clementine who, like her husband, sensed the inner strength in this enigmatic person.

Said Winston: 'Despite his dislike of publicity, Lawrence has a remarkable way of backing into the limelight.'

Recalling a luncheon at Chartwell, Major-General Sir Edward Spears said:

'There is never a dull moment in the Churchill household, where wit and intelligent discussions of people and affairs combine with a background of peculiar charm into an expression of the best that English civilization in our time can produce.

'The host was happy and relaxed as he always is with his family, in spite of having just lost an argument with Mrs. Churchill on the propriety of water glasses being filled before the meal was served. Winston had held not, but I observed nevertheless that there was water in the glasses. The meal was gay; remarks, comments, sometimes caustic, never unkind or inconsiderate.'

The staff at the Manor included a cook, two housemaids, a kitchen maid, Clementine's personal maid, and Winston's valet, and there were never less than two secretaries in attendance.

In no Churchill household was it ever a case of the staff running the show. Clementine ran everything. Every morning she saw the cook, checked menus for the day, the number of guests to be catered for, and kitchen supplies. After that she visited secretaries, gave them their instructions, though she would never interfere with any secretarial duties required by her husband. It was never a case of 'I told you what to do', and leaving it at that. She followed every job right through to make sure it was done properly.

Their nephew, John Spencer Churchill, said:

'At Chartwell it never ceased to amaze me how my aunt coped with the running of the place. Her role was that of an A.D.C. Extraordinary and Super Quartermaster to the greatest of Captains-General. For Chartwell, and indeed any other house my uncle occupied, was not only a kind of military headquarters but a large factory filled with high-powered executives. To see that this factory ran smoothly with meals at odd hours for visiting experts and the relays of secretaries working through the night called for tremendously detailed organization.

'In addition to bringing up a large family she has been present to act as gracious hostess to every conceivable sort of guest. Even when not feeling well, she never allowed anyone to know it.

'The hospitality my uncle and aunt offered at table was quite out of this world.

'It was always a pleasure to arrive at about 12.30 p.m., in time to accompany my aunt on the short walk round the garden which she liked before lunch.'

A secretary who spent some years in the Churchills' service explained: 'There are two Clementines. One is the

215

great lady—a strict disciplinarian with a very real sense of her importance in the scheme of things; the other is very human. Clementine can be very strict one moment and wonderfully charming the next. She was at her most attractive when she was able to drop the responsibilities of being "the Prime Minister's Lady" and discuss things on a level with you, just like another ordinary woman talking to you.'

Though life was comfortable, there was no extravagance at Chartwell. During their early married life, when children had to be clothed and educated and appearances had to be kept up on a limited income, Clementine learned to appreciate the truth of the old adage about 'a penny saved'. She still dearly loves a bargain.

One of her war-time secretaries recalled: 'She could not be called ungenerous but she would never pay more than she thought necessary. I remember an instance of that in the very first summer I was with them.

'She had seen a linen frock of a popular make advertised in the local paper. She pointed it out to me, saying: "Look! That costs two guineas in Town, but here it costs two pounds. It's a very cheap frock, and I'm going to get it." She was delighted at the thought of being able to save two shillings.

'I remember that frock. It was of pale blue linen, and when she came back in it, it looked lovely. She used to wear it in the garden, and on her it looked like a Paris model.'

Although at Chartwell they occupied separate bedrooms, Winston and Clementine invariably shared the first routine of the day. The sleeping arrangements were essential, for Winston's bedroom was, as is well known, also, in effect, an office in which he spent hours looking at correspondence and even dictating his books. Since he slept little and customarily did not retire until the small hours, the privacy of separate bedrooms was the obvious solution.

Clementine usually rises at about seven o'clock in the morning. She believes that every woman should take great care of her appearance, and her own success in this direction is patent. She is still beautiful, looking much younger than her years. Every morning her first task is to put on white gloves, clean her face, and set her hair. After that comes breakfast, taken in bed.

At about 8.30, in the room above, Winston would awake

and have breakfast. Wearing a dressing-gown he sat propped against pillows, with his elbows resting on two large sponges. If the sponges were not in position, he ate his breakfast from a bed-table.

Husband and wife never met until lunch-time. Winston remarked once:

'My wife and I have tried two or three times in the past years to have breakfast together but we had to stop, otherwise our marriage would have been wrecked.'

Concerning his daily routine, he said: 'When one wakes up after daylight one should breakfast; five hours after that, luncheon. Six hours after luncheon, dinner. Thus one becomes independent of the sun, which otherwise meddles too much in one's affairs and upsets the routine of work.'

At about 9 a.m. both husband and wife finished eating and then came the first joint duty of the day: the ceremony of reading the newspapers. Winston would go through them first, marking items—some, of special interest, with a different coloured ink—for Clementine's attention, and she did the same for him.

As he finished each newspaper, it was taken downstairs to Clementine. The reading of the morning's Press usually occupied about one and a half hours, and they drew each other's attention to items of interest in newspapers and magazines.

At 9 a.m. the secretary reported for duty and Clementine dealt with correspondence and household affairs from her bedroom, stopping every now and then to read marked newspaper items sent to her room from upstairs.

Occasionally she went out in the morning to keep an appointment, but usually she worked at home, answering letters, and dealing with the management problems of the Churchill houses at Chartwell and in London.

Winston remained in bed until lunch-time, relaxing his body while never ceasing to exercise his brain. Beside his bed three telephones were seldom silent for more than half an hour.

At about noon came the Order of the Bath—Winston's bath. He enjoyed the pleasure as a crown to his morning's work, and loved to wallow in the steaming water, turning the taps on and off with his toes. Sometimes he would get out of the bath to make an important telephone call, then step back into the water again.

Clementine, with the aid of members of the staff, for ever devised new methods of keeping Winston to time. His unpunctuality was one of the terrors of the household. No matter what time guests were due for lunch, he was invariably late and, but for the ruses adopted by his wife, would have been later still.

Sometimes she would send word to him in the bathroom that the guests had already arrived, though they were still on their way. She altered the time of the lunch, and even instructed the staff to tell Winston that the clocks were slow or the time later than it really was.

Winston himself said: 'Unpunctuality is a vile habit,' but it was one of his worst faults.

As a young subaltern, he once kept the Prince of Wales (later Edward VII) waiting for almost an hour. When, at last, he arrived the Prince asked: 'Do you have an excuse, young man?'

'Indeed I have,' said Winston. 'I started too late.'

Asked why he missed so many trains and aeroplanes, he explained: 'I am a sporting man. I always give them a fair chance to get away.'

When he went to Washington, she had to reproach him for being late for President Roosevelt.

The President was at the railway station, waiting to greet him, but Winston wasn't ready. The President drove Clementine to the White House and then went back to the station to wait for Winston to emerge from the train.

Being late was really a quirk in Winston's character, for he was always well aware of the time. He seemed to derive some kind of pleasure from seeing how worried everyone got. But, from time to time, Clementine gave him a sharp lesson.

A member of their staff remembers one such occasion early in the Second World War, when Winston was First Lord of the Admiralty.

'The Churchill bedrooms were next door to each other on the top floor of Admiralty House,' she said. 'I was working in Winston's bedroom. He was resting in bed. Clementine was in the next room, preparing to go out for the evening.

'She kept popping her head in and saying: "Are you getting dressed yet, Winston? Are you getting dressed?

218

Look at the time." Each time, he would reply: "I'll be all right." He said it took him thirteen minutes to bath and dress, and he knew he could do it.

'She kept on until he finally said to me: "Fill my bath."

'Clementine called me into her bedroom. "Has he gone to bath?" she asked. I said that he had, and she replied: "Good! Let me know when he is fully dressed."

'In due course I reported that Winston was ready.

' "Excellent!" she said. "Now, lock my door."

'Mystified, I did so.

' "Now," said Clementine, "he can wait for me."

'She was completely dressed, hat and everything, and she proceeded to take off every stitch. Then she said: "Now he can wait until I have put all my clothes on."

'And deliberately, leisurely, she proceeded to do just that.'

Whenever a train had to be caught, Clementine invariably told Winston three times that it was time to start for the station. One day they got to Euston just in time to see the last carriage leaving the platform.

Winston turned to his wife and said indignantly: 'The train's pulling out.'

'Yes,' she said. 'I know. You were late again.'

His face suffused with righteous injury. 'But, Clementine,' he protested, '*you only told me twice!*'

Winston's resentment of any attempt at discipline in the home was something to try the patience of any wife. Once, and only once, Clementine managed to persuade him to go on a diet, only to be told seven hours later: 'Well, that's the end of *that*!'

If she had made a gramophone record, warning 'Don't drop your ash on the carpet, dear,' it would have saved the repetition of that injunction to her husband many thousands of times.

Winston liked to pad through the rooms of Chartwell in his sky-blue siren suit and shod with soft black slippers bearing his initials worked in gold. Even more, after lunch, he loved to take a walk around the beautiful grounds ablaze with flowers. Nothing pleased him more than Clementine sharing a stroll with him.

Sometimes, while Clementine, wearing slacks, blouse, and gloves, worked in the rose garden, Winston pottered about the grounds, often getting smothered in mud. In only one aspect of their mutual love of the countryside did they differ. Winston hated to see a tree damaged or destroyed. Clementine is fascinated to see one fall. Whenever a tree has to be felled, Clementine will stand watching until the job is done.

Winston loved trees: loved to see their reflection in the water; loved to see them silhouetted bare against grey winter skies; loved to paint them in all their moods. But when the afternoon's enjoyment of the grounds was over, it was time for the most rigid discipline of the day—sleep.

He would return to his bedroom, undress, and sleep for two hours. He never missed that rest no matter where he was. On an election tour a large bed would have to be provided in one of the coaches. If required to attend the House of Commons during the afternoon at question time or for an important debate, a room and bed had to be prepared for him within the precincts of the House. Even while visiting the Royal Family—if the visit overlapped Winston's rest period—Clementine would request a bedroom to be put at his disposal and the Queen always ensured this was done.

At Chartwell, when no guests were expected, he worked in bed until 6 p.m., and Clementine made sure that for his rest period, he had his 'blinkers'—black eye-pads to shut out the light.

Clementine, too, takes as much rest as possible during the afternoon. Although physically tough, she conserves her strength carefully. If there is to be a dinner party she will frequently stay in bed all day, saying: 'I must be fit for tonight.' She believes implicitly that ample rest and relaxation preserve youth and vitality.

No one could mistake her insistence on rest for laziness. Even as a woman of fifty she played tennis brilliantly, moving across the court at lightning speed. She has always been quick-thinking, quick-speaking, and quick-moving.

Clementine is an enthusiastic croquet player, with a keen eye and a steady hand. Winston did not share her enthusiasm, but summer-time guests at Chartwell usually found themselves playing a game before lunch and another after dinner.

Asked to become an Associate of the Croquet Association, Clementine accepted with delight; but it was then discovered that the new Associate's croquet did not conform to the recognized rules. For years, it seemed, she had been playing on a lawn of the wrong dimensions. On learning this, she immediately ordered the addition of a further five yards of turfing to the Chartwell lawn in readiness for the next croquet season.

Field-Marshal Montgomery, a frequent and welcome visitor to Chartwell, had as fellow-guests one week-end Mr. and Mrs. Clement Attlee. All three were keen croquet players, but none could equal the skill of Clementine, who had achieved near-championship standard. Though Winston was also good at the game, he never approached his wife's class.

At that time Winston was Prime Minister and Attlee leader of the Opposition. Montgomery had still to attain his Viscountcy.

Clementine had frequently opposed Monty at croquet and beaten him soundly; but this time he was her ally against Winston and Attlee, and the two statesmen suffered a total political defeat. Throughout the match Winston and Monty tried to undermine each other with methods of psychological warfare. There were constant volleys of banter, Winston's thrusts being largely aimed at Monty's abstinence from tobacco and alcohol. They availed nothing. Monty and Clementine completely out-generalled their foes.

She regularly organized tennis tournaments at Chartwell, but Winston seldom watched her play. His brain somehow would not allow him to do so. He might have done if it were a question of winning anything, but most of the time he had so much else to do. Working is his idea of relaxation.

One of Clementine's methods of self-expression, it must be admitted, has met with somewhat qualified enthusiasm. As a motorist she does not excel.

After one or two minor mishaps Clementine abandoned motoring as a hobby; then, at the age of seventy-two, she decided to take a refresher course to familiarize herself with a new car which had been purchased. Warned by earlier experiences, Winston insisted at first that she should not venture out unless accompanied by a skilled driver. Clementine countered by buying her own car, which she insisted on driving personally, though she had been, to all intent, 'off the road' for almost twenty years.

Winston himself was never an easy man to drive, according to those in a position to know. He did not object to speed, but the car had to proceed at an even pace. The chauffeur unlucky enough to achieve a bumpy stop or start was liable to receive a 'rocket' in true Churchillian style.

Winston clung to an ancient Austin 10, which he used to carry him around the Chartwell estate. Clementine hated the dilapidated crock, as she hated everything untidy. She arranged to sell it to a local dealer for £40, and bought a new Hillman Minx to replace it.

For once Winston opposed her, insisting: 'I want the old car back.' It cost £80 to retrieve it, for the dealer had already sold it to another customer for that sum.

Such little excitements apart, Chartwell Manor was a place of quiet contentment. Within its bounds Clementine tried to bring a little of normality into Winston's abnormal life. His overwhelming personality never at any time overwhelmed his wife. Her vivacity, her gaiety, her spirit, were ever a complete match for him.

Clementine kept abreast of everything. She was the perfect hostess, perfect companion, and the most practical person in the family.

15

A WEEK-END AT CHEQUERS

RELUCTANTLY, during the war, Winston and Clementine had virtually to abandon their beloved Chartwell Manor for Chequers, the official country retreat of the Prime Ministers of Britain. Chartwell, prominently sited on a hill, was a landmark too easily located by bombers.

Chequers Court, a large Tudor country house, stands in a sheltered hollow nearly 600 feet above sea-level, between Great Missenden and Aylesbury in Buckinghamshire. The estate, just forty miles from London, comprises 1,500 acres of mixed farmland, park, and Chiltern beechwoods.

For hundreds of years Chequers Court was in private hands, but in January 1921 its owner, Lord Lee of Fareham, bequeathed the estate to the Premier of the day and his successors in perpetuity. The days had passed, he said, when Ministers of the Crown were always gentlemen of means, but it was desirable that the Crown's chief Minister should possess a country house where he could relax and entertain distinguished visitors.

Over the entrance to Chequers are the words 'Pro Patria Omnia'—freely translated by General Eisenhower as 'All for the Fatherland', while over a gate leading to part of the gardens are the words, 'All care abandon ye who enter here'.

Mr. David Lloyd George, who accepted Chequers on behalf of the nation, was delighted with the gift, but not all his successors have been equally fond of their inheritance. Indeed, many who stayed there criticized the house as a cold and draughty edifice, half museum and half architectural fake, filled with heavy furniture of greater historical than artistic interest.

Winston was not particularly fond of Chequers, quite naturally preferring his own beloved Chartwell, where, in any case, most of his books and papers were stored. Nevertheless, since this was plainly to be their principal war-time home, Clementine determinedly set out to make the best of it.

Chequers was coldly magnificent. With its enormous hall, its cavernous fireplaces, its Rubens, Van Dycks, Turners, Constables, its historic relics—the slippers of Oliver Cromwell, the ruby ring once worn by Elizabeth I, the historic silver and plate, the four-poster beds—it was all very impressive, but never home to the Churchills. Clementine had to bend her tastes and her wishes to its traditions, but she didn't like it one little bit.

Each of the paintings in the hall is described in a catalogue reposing on the big central desk. On this desk there is also a reproduction in red, white, and blue of the Longfellow verse sent to Winston by President Roosevelt. It reads:

> *Sail on, O Ship of State!*
> *Sail on, O Union, strong and great!*
> *Humanity with all its fears,*
> *With all the hopes of future years*
> *Is hanging breathless on thy fate.*

The Friday night exit from No. 10 Downing Street became a weekly ritual, with a procession of cars carrying secretaries, telephone operators, detectives—and the Churchills—down to rural Buckinghamshire; but it was never a 'get away from it all' week-end, for there was a ceaseless shuttle service of couriers bearing red Government dispatch boxes between Whitehall and Chequers, and an almost endless stream of distinguished personages arriving not only as guests for dinner but as V.I.P.s to be consulted on matters of national and international importance.

During those allegedly 'quiet' week-ends at Chequers Clementine played hostess to Cabinet Ministers, Service chiefs, and a multitude of home and overseas visitors concerned with the conduct of the war. General Eisenhower, Mr. Mackenzie King, General de Gaulle, General Smuts, Mr. Harry Hopkins, and Mr. Averell Harriman were among those who came.

Here is a typical week-end guest-list, prepared for Clementine by Elizabeth Nel, one of Winston's secretaries:

'The Prime Minister, Mrs. Churchill, Mr. Harry Hopkins, General Marshall, Mr. Browne (private secretary), Commander Thompson—arrive Friday evening to stay week-end.

'Admiral Pound, General Brooke, Air Marshal Portal, General Ismay—to dine and sleep Friday.

'Lord Leathers, Lord Cherwell—to lunch and dine Saturday.

'Air Marshal Douglas—to dine Saturday.

'General Ney, Admiral Mountbatten, Admiral Cunningham—to dine and sleep Saturday.

'Mr. Oliver Lyttelton—to lunch and dine Sunday.

'Air Marshal Harris, General Eaker (U.S.A.)—to dine Sunday.

'Mr. Harriman, General Paget, Mr. A. V. Alexander—to dine and sleep Sunday.'

At the beginning of 1941 Harry Hopkins, President Roosevelt's personal representative, came to England to see for himself (and the President) how the fight was going. He stayed for almost three weeks, and the Churchills took immediately to the frail little man who proved himself such a great fighter for freedom. He went everywhere with Winston and spent much time at Chequers, where Clementine, realizing he was a very sick man, mothered him almost as much as she mothered her husband. She persuaded him to rest in bed during the hours when Winston was working in bed; she took special care of his diet, and made sure that he was always dressed warmly against the biting winter cold.

Chequers is an abnormally difficult house to heat, had no central heating, and architects despaired of installing modern heating because of the fear of injuring the exquisite panelling, some of which is nearly four hundred years old.

Hopkins found those week-ends at Chequers to be the worst hardship he had to endure in war-time Britain. 'It is the coldest house I have ever visited,' he told her.

'Harry hates Chequers more than the devil hates holy water,' General Eisenhower would say.

Hopkins invariably arrived there with plenty of long woollen underwear, and Clementine made sure there was always a blazing fire in his room, but, even so, he seldom removed his overcoat. His favourite haunt was the ground-floor lavatory, which, he said, was the only room with 'central heating'. He went there to read his newspapers and dispatches; but even in that room he kept his overcoat wrapped about him.

Bernard Baruch visited Chequers several times, He said: 'It was a great treat to sit at the table with Winston and to hear him hold forth—with his inimitable verve and eloquence—on a host of subjects, great and small. In one discussion the subject of German war crimes and punishment came up. There were some original and unique suggestions on what ought to be done with Hitler if he fell into our hands alive. But Winston, I recall, thought it would be much simpler if he were to perish with the evil he had created.'

Winston's constant concern for Clementine showed itself one week-end when Admiral of the Fleet Lord Fraser of North Cape and Sir Charles Portal of Bomber Command were at Chequers. Said Lord Fraser: 'It was dark when I arrived. Mrs. Churchill had gone out visiting hospitals in the neighbourhood. This was the period when the air raids were in full swing, and when by 8 p.m. his wife had still not returned, the Prime Minister was becoming more and more anxious.

' "What a stupid thing to do, to be out late like this and no one knows where she is," he said, striding up and down the room in his zip siren suit. Rather a case of the pot calling the kettle black, I thought!

'However, she arrived a few minutes later, and as a minor explosion seemed about to occur we deemed it best to retire, although everyone appeared at dinner in the best of spirits. I suppose there are few more devoted couples in the world than Sir Winston and Lady Churchill and it was easy to appreciate his anxiety.'

'I used to be at Chequers two week-ends out of three,' said General Sir Frederick Pile,' and it was really a most domestic place in spite of its constant war atmosphere. Clementine somehow still managed to make it a home. When it was time for dinner, she wouldn't have any nonsense.

'She would say to Winston's personal assistant, Tommy Thompson, "Tommy, collect the Prime Minister. He's upstairs and he'll go on working unless you collect him." Winston would sometimes come down and say he had a bit more work to do, and she would reply, "No, we're going in

to dinner, and you can talk as long as you like afterwards."
That was her attitude all the time. She made him appreciate
that he had got to live to the rules of ordinary domestic life
for his health's sake in particular, although he still often
managed to duck the rules.

'If there wasn't roast beef for Sunday lunch, then, as far
as Winston was concerned, it was a bad lunch. He would
say: "What are we having for lunch?" Once when Clementine told him, he demanded: "Why haven't we got roast
beef?" And she answered, "I suppose you haven't heard
there's a war on and you're rationed like the rest?"

'It was the only time I was there that we didn't have
roast beef. She didn't mince words. He loved his food and
adored roast beef, which had to be underdone. If it was
done too much there was hell to pay.'

Lord Ismay added: 'To keep house—to keep an establishment over the head of a man like Winston Churchill
must have been extraordinarily difficult. Great though the
honour must be to serve him—to have no fixed hours at
all—to serve a man who might sit down to dinner at half
past eight, or might sit down to dinner at half past ten was
very rough. She used to get very angry with him at times
when he tried to get away with it. He would need some
excellent excuse, which he often had. I have known us not
leave the table until past midnight.

'You may think I am suggesting he was inconsiderate.
Well of course he was—to all of us—but he was far more
inconsiderate to himself. The only thing he thought of was
the war. Whether anyone was made uncomfortable, or
whether he was made extremely uncomfortable, didn't matter a damn—all that mattered was to win the war.

'The fact that he was so very particular about what he
ate didn't make things any easier. You couldn't just give
him eggs every day or anything like that. Nevertheless she
managed to bring some kind of sense and order into his life.
Without this he would have been chaotic.'

General Sir Frederick Pile continued ... 'To most people,
a meal is a meal, but to the Churchills it was something far
more important—it was a holiday combined with talk
about the affairs of the world. Clemmie talked with him
about every conceivable subject and often greatly influenced his ideas, as she did at a time when we were not

getting on so well with President Roosevelt.

'There were many difficulties at that period, but one of the trouble spots was our having to buy the old destroyers from the United States, and it broke Winston's heart—he thought they were third rate, and said so. Nor did he like buying them with our vital currency-earning overseas investments, nor being forced to lease America a part of the Commonwealth as a base because of the destroyer deal. He felt we were being driven into a hard unfair bargain.

'The discussion at lunch ranged round the Roosevelt problem. She said simply, out of the blue: "Why don't you get Mr. Smuts to talk to Roosevelt about this?"

'Winston jumped up at once and said, "I will!"

'He put a call through immediately to Smuts in South Africa and asked him—we were still in the room at lunch—if he would talk to Roosevelt about the various points of disagreement between us. He did, and things improved.

'Although Mrs. Churchill was terribly close to so many of the various conduct-of-war problems, she was the one person sufficiently detached to see sometimes the whole picture from a quite different angle. It was genius, because Roosevelt was a man of world importance and who could talk to Roosevelt? But General Smuts was just the right stature and he was also a tremendous friend of both of them—they both admired his statesmanship.

'Discussion of the war was never silenced because she happened to be at the table with us, or anywhere else. She knew everything that was going on. There were no secrets from her. Everything didn't stop for lunch, tea, or dinner—the war was all that mattered the whole time, and if there was business on everyone's mind, it was discussed irrespective of her presence.

'She kept Chequers running, she was ringmaster and hostess, and after a meal, we were all sent off with Winston to his library, and often didn't see her again until the following day. She never came down to breakfast. She would walk in the gardens with guests, and often had her own guests staying there—as a rule, they were people such as the wives of Ministers and those connected with the extensive war services in which she was so heavily involved.

'She is a bubbling person—the sort of woman you would like to take out to dinner. If she hadn't been the Prime

Minister's wife I might have asked her. Yet although she was always so full of life, at Chequers, she had this curious placid effect—she calmed everything down. It was an incredible feat of discipline on her part.'

'She was also a very good judge of persons,' said Lord Ismay. 'She had a keenly discerning idea of who were Winston's real friends, who were his flatterers, and who were the people on whom he could really rely. I don't think that, in many respects, he was nearly as good a judge as she was. She was a very sound and astute assessor of character.

'And in regard to the point Sir Frederick Pile makes about the business and secrets of war continuing in her presence, I can assure you that Winston was very meticulous about letting her into any big item of news, directly he knew it himself.

'After the war, before he became Prime Minister again, she was staying at my home for a week, and he rang one night to tell her that the pound was going to be devalued the next day. He had been told by Attlee, and thought that Clemmie should know at once. No official announcement on the matter had been made as yet.

'Keeping her informed like this on important affairs was habit with him, and throughout the war he did exactly the same. There were no secrets from her. It was an eye-opener to me that he was so meticulous about informing her of official matters like that.

'I think the reason he always did this was because he felt they were so close to each other. It was typical of their marriage—such an ideal marriage, I suppose one of the most ideal there has ever been. Winston's attitude was always—"Clemmie will be interested—I must tell her!"'

No one ever dared question Winston's weekend routine at Chequers—except Clementine—until General Smuts turned up. Earl Mountbatten, who was present, recalls:

'The usual thing was for Winston, visiting Chiefs of Staff, members of the Cabinet and others, to gather around midnight—after one of Mrs. Churchill's superbly organized dinners and a film show—for serious decision making. Then one weekend, Smuts was there.

' "Count me out," he told Churchill. "I am not going to be party to your killing Chiefs of Staff. They have to leave early tomorrow ... you will be lying in bed smoking a cigar

... In the afternoon they will be busy ... you will be having a siesta. They should be allowed to go to bed at midnight ... I am going to bed."

'There was a stunned silence as Smuts departed. After a long pause, Winston stood up and said: "Well, Gentlemen, I suppose we shall have to go to bed".'

Everyone kept an absolutely straight face, except Clementine, who almost uncontrollably burst with laughter as Winston, looking grim, but with a tell-tale twinkle in his eyes, stomped out of the room.

There were few visitors to Chequers who were not connected in some way with official business, but from time to time Clementine would invite an unexpected guest to help Winston relax a little.

Benno Moiseiwitsch, the distinguished pianist, who had been helping her to raise money for her Aid to Russia Fund, gave a private concert in the great hall.

At Chequers, Clementine liked to change from more formal dress into blouse and slacks, while always, after dinner, Winston would don one of the fabulous, almost exotic dressing-gowns in which he delighted—as at Chartwell—and invite their guests to see a film show. Clementine chose the films, and everyone, staff included, was asked to the shows, which took place in the long gallery on the first floor.

Often, after a film show, they would go to a small table and play a game of bagatelle. At times, when Winston's attention appeared to be concentrated on the game, he would jump up from the bagatelle board and go to his study or call an immediate meeting of Ministers and chiefs of staff.

Clementine could sense when he was doing one thing while in reality concentrating on another. It was the same with his well-known curious habit of marching to music in the great hall when he would put on records of popular songs or military bands then, turning the radiogram's volume full up, march up and down the hall, with head thrust forward, hands in pockets, humming or singing the tune being played.

'If Clementine entered the room while one of Winston's record sessions was on, she would never interrupt,' said Lord Ismay. 'She would simply let him carry on marching, and singing with absolute seriousness; then, when the music stopped, if he turned to her and smiled, she knew he had come to the decision he had been trying to reach.

'With his immense powers of concentration, he did not like his train of thought to be broken until he had reached a conclusion, although he wasn't averse to the presence of someone he knew near him, or someone who could answer a question if need be, or be sent to seek information.'

The Hawtrey room, with its lovely antique furniture and beautiful paintings, was the second main room of the house. It was the one room in Chequers which they really loved, and therefore the place in which he could work best. It was there that he wrote many of his greatest war-time speeches and broadcasts, and there that he spoke to the world on those memorable Sunday nights immediately before the B.B.C.'s nine o'clock news. As he talked into the microphone, Clementine would listen in an adjoining room.

Winston hated fuss and relished danger; nevertheless, Chequers was guarded night and day by detectives, by soldiers in Bren gun carriers, and by roof spotters always on the alert in case Nazi paratroops decided to launch a direct attack on the Prime Minister's country home. The *Luftwaffe* tried many times to hit the house, and once managed to drop bombs in the grounds close by. The only precaution Winston agreed to take was to arrange for a revolver range to be installed in the grounds. There, regularly, he practised with his rifle, Colt ·45 automatic pistol, and Webley service revolver.

When, in the invasion-threatened days, there was talk by visitors who came there, of circumstances which might possibly warrant the evacuation of the King and the Government to safety in Canada, Winston emphatically refuted any such possibility.

'Every man ought to fight to the death on his own soil,' he said, 'and if they come to London, I shall take a rifle— I'm not a bad shot—I will put myself in a pillbox at the bottom of Downing Street and shoot till I've no more ammunition, and then they can damned well shoot me.'

He never shielded Clementine from harsh truths he considered she was entitled to know. After Dunkirk he told her, as he had told his Cabinet colleagues, that although he was certain we could reach some form of peace terms with

Hitler he thought the advantage would be short-lived and, in any case, he did not feel it compatible with his own conscience and honour to do this. 'We must fight on even though it would undoubtedly mean that women and children at home would suffer terribly.' His own road, he said, was clear.

Only intimate friends realized how deeply he felt the sufferings of the ordinary men and women throughout Europe who pinned their faith so blindly on his leadership.

If Clementine continued to welcome distinguished visitors from overseas, it was not because she or Winston had time for social niceties. Guests were welcome because they could reveal what other countries were thinking.

'Have you seen the people?' he would inquire urgently. 'I am nothing. But the people ... they suffer so, and never whimper. They suffer for this stupid war, this criminal war that never should have happened if we had not been so blind. This war that should have been won before we fought it, and that now must be fought through to the end.'

Clementine talked constantly of the people with whom they had spoken on the bombed rubble of London and other blitzed cities.

'All their possessions wiped out in one blast!' Clementine exclaimed.

'An Englishman's home is a fine phrase,' said Winston. 'It was never so fine a reality. No one can govern Britain again who forgets the people.

'They saved Britain, you know, a year ago, and again after the great blitzes. They deserve to win. They deserve to win gloriously. They shall!'

One Saturday, that great war-time American journalist, Quentin Reynolds, went down to Chequers to work with Harry Hopkins on a speech Hopkins was to broadcast the following day from Winston's personal microphone.

Winston was himself preparing a two-hour speech for Parliament. Mr. John Winant came down for a hurried conference. Averell Harriman and his daughter Kathleen also arrived, and there were a host of other week-end guests who were supposed to provide relaxation for Winston—whose main form of relaxation was work.

Miss Dorothy Thompson, the distinguished American political commentator, recalls that at lunch that day they all discussed the Russian front with pessimism. Winston asked her: 'Such a state! Was there ever such a state?

'We are the hope of three-fourths of the people of all the world. The people in the remote Chinese villages, on the Russian steppes, cowering in Poland, in the rabbit warrens of Paris, on the dykes of Holland, and fjords of Norway.... The disarmed and the helpless, crying silently to the Anglo-Saxon world: "Rescue us!"'

'And the price? Suffering ... our transitory lives.... Not all of us will grow old.

'Why should people work and toil and never have a full belly or secure roofs? Strike an international balance sheet on surplus commodities. Give. Share. Produce. Use ...!

'Must a Chinese peasant live for ever on rice and a scrap of fish? Why should he? Did the Dutch ever do anybody any harm? Did they govern their colonies badly? Did they neglect their people? Did they waste their wealth? Did they trample on other nations?

'There is so much to do when all this is over. A wonderful world—or a shambles and a prison.'

Miss Thompson asked him: 'How are you going to win the war?'

'First,' he replied, 'we shall see that we do not lose it.'

Harry Hopkins wanted Quentin Reynolds to help him write his speech for the B.B.C. and get it into the kind of language which the British public would understand. That is why he had been invited by Clementine to Chequers.

He said later: 'Harry was dog-tired and had a touch of the grippe; at least, that is what he told Mrs. Churchill. I am sure that it was his old ailment bothering him, but he always sloughed that off by saying casually, "Got a little cold during the trip over."

'Mrs. Churchill was very concerned about Harry's health. She knew him so well that she could tell when he was in pain by looking at him, I think. Around eleven o'clock in the evening she would start trying to persuade him to go to bed, saying: "You have a long day tomorrow, and you can have a nice talk with Winston in the morning. I've fixed your bed and put a hot water bottle in it." I am sure Harry never got such mothering in his life except, maybe, from Mrs. Roosevelt.'

Every week-end at Chequers was a week-end of history.

On the evening of Friday, 20 June 1941, as they drove down to Buckinghamshire, Winston told Clementine that he was sure Germany would attack Russia within days or even hours.

The guests at Chequers that Saturday and Sunday were the American Ambassador, Mr. John Winant and his wife, Mr. and Mrs. Anthony Eden, Lord Cranborne, Lord Beaverbrook, and Sir Stafford Cripps, British Ambassador to Russia, who had come down to tender his resignation on the grounds of ill-health. Winston had agreed to accept his resignation.

At dinner the conversation was solely of the imminent threat to the Soviets. Sir Stafford said the Russians had been warned by British Intelligence that Germany would, in all probability, attack them, but they had largely discredited the warning as 'wishful thinking' on our part.

Winston had given a standing instruction that he was never to be awakened for anything less than the invasion of England, and so a telephone message which came through from the Foreign Office on Sunday at 4 a.m. was held until he awoke at 8 a.m. It reported that Hitler had attacked Russia on a 1,500-mile front stretching from Finland to the Black Sea.

'Tell the B.B.C. that I will broadcast at nine tonight,' he said.

He asked Sir Stafford to return at once to Russia, and Sir Stafford agreed to do so. Then, leaving Clementine to look after the guests, Winston went to his room to write the now famous speech in which, while still attacking the Communist creed, he promised Russia and the Soviet people Britain's complete support.

He had decided to range Britain's strength behind Russia in spite of the Soviets' unpopularity with the public, and in the face of his advisers' warning that 'the country will not stand for it'.

'I *know* I am right, Clemmie!' he said.

Sunday, 7 December 1941 brought another fateful evening to Chequers.

Winston had been uneasy all day. When lunch was announced, he would not sit down to table. He was waiting restlessly and impatiently for the arrival of the American Ambassador, Mr. Winant, and Mr. Averell Harriman.

Clementine took her other guests in to lunch, leaving Winston pacing up and down outside the main entrance to the house. The meal had been in progress for twenty minutes when Mr. Winant arrived, to be greeted immediately with a demand to know whether he thought there would be war with Japan.

'Yes,' said Mr. Winant.

'If they declare war on you, we shall declare war on them within the hour,' Winston declared. Then he asked: 'If they declare war on us, will you declare war on them?'

Mr. Winant could not answer the question, claiming that only the President had the right to declare war, under the United States Constitution.

Winston recognized only too well that if Japan attacked Siam or British territory in the East, Britain would be forced into an Asiatic war which would leave America out. In that event Britain would be left holding the entire baby, and the result could be complete disaster for us.

'We're late, you know. Get washed, and we will go in to lunch together,' he said, dropping the subject.

The afternoon passed quietly. Clementine walked with Mr. Averell Harriman and his daughter Kathie in the grounds until, feeling not too well, she decided to go to bed for an hour or two.

As usual, she had arranged an excellent dinner. The party entered the dining-room a few minutes before nine o'clock, and as they sat down Winston asked the butler to put on the table the little portable radio set which Harry Hopkins had sent as a gift. He switched it on, there were the usual national anthems, and then the news.

The announcer read several official war bulletins, and made an announcement which seemed to refer to Japanese attacks on British vessels in the Dutch East Indies and on American shipping at Hawaii.

It was all rather vague, but Mr. Winant and Mr. Harriman wanted to know more about the references to the attacks on the American ships. As they were discussing the matter, the butler entered the room and, interrupting, said: 'It's quite true. We heard it ourselves outside. The Japs have attacked the Americans.'

For a moment there was silence around the table. Then Winston jumped to his feet and declared: 'We shall declare war on Japan.' However, appreciating in the same instant that he could hardly declare war on the strength of a radio bulletin, he went into his office and phoned President Roosevelt in Washington.

'They have attacked us at Pearl Harbor,' he told his old friend. 'We are all in the same boat now.'

Mr. Winant spoke to the President for a few minutes, and then everybody went back into the hall—as Winston later wrote: 'to adjust our thoughts to the supreme world event which had occurred, which was of so startling a nature as to make even those who were near the centre gasp'.

Often during the winter evenings at Chequers Winston and Clementine would sit together by one of the enormous coal fires and listen to their son-in-law, Vic Oliver, playing the piano. They would get him to play over and over again all Eddie Cantor's famous songs from the film *Whoopee*, and Winston would sing the words in his hoarse, off-key baritone.

One night in 1941, Winston came down from his study with set face and pained eyes.

Clementine watched him as he came into the room and then, without a word, poured a glass of port and handed it to him. It was obvious something serious had happened. Sarah and Vic Oliver were among the company, and thinking to relieve the tension, Clementine asked Vic to play something on the piano.

He was about to strike up 'Lily of Laguna', but feeling that a popular song might be inappropriate to the seriousness of the moment, he changed his mind and began to play Beethoven's *Appassionata* sonata. He had played only a few bars when Winston rose to his feet and thundered: 'Stop! Don't play that!'

It was the first time that he had ever raised his voice to his son-in-law and everybody was shocked.

'What is the matter?' Clementine asked.

'I will not have the Dead March played in my house,' answered Winston angrily.

'It's not the Dead March,' Vic protested. 'It's the *Appassionata*.'

'You can say what you like,' Winston said. 'I know it is the Dead March.'

Unwisely, perhaps, Vic tried to make his point by play-

236

ing a few bars of each melody in turn; but as soon as he struck the first notes of the sonata Winston roared again: 'Stop it! Stop it, I say! I want no Dead March, I tell you.'

Sarah rushed to the piano and asked her husband to play a popular song instead, while Clementine went across to Winston to placate him.

The following morning it was announced officially that H.M.S. *Hood* had been sunk with heavy loss of life.

The night General Arnold, Commanding General of the U.S. Army Air Forces, went to Chequers, had been preceded by quite a day. All day, Clementine had had to deal with an irrepressible Winston who just couldn't contain his excitement. The evening was to witness the R.A.F.'s first thousand-bomber raid on Germany, and Clementine couldn't make Winston relax an instant, so she finally gave up trying and concentrated on taking care of the comfort of her other guests—the American Ambassador, Mr. Winant, Air Chief Marshal Portal, General Ismay, Averell Harriman, and Admiral Towers.

'As we sat down to dinner I knew beforehand—even without the Prime Minister's jubilation—that the R.A.F. was taking off on the greatest bombardment operation ever launched,' says General Arnold. 'This was the real beginning, in the world's eyes and in Germany's eyes, of the campaign we later came to term officially "Air Offensive Europe"—the "round the clock" destruction of Germany from the air. That night all of England was a bomber base.'

At dinner, Winston asked some technical questions General Arnold couldn't answer, so he telephoned for his pilot Colonel Beebe. When the Colonel was faced with the question of going home, Winston solved it by saying:

'You stay here and spend the night.'

'But I didn't bring my pyjamas,' the Colonel answered.

Winston, six inches shorter than the Colonel, obligingly offered to lend him his. They scarcely covered him, but the Colonel slept in the Prime Minister's pyjamas that night.

'After breakfast, Admiral Towers and I both had to go to the "johnny",' continued General Arnold. 'The door was one of those cumbersome affairs with locks dating back to Elizabethan times. I had no trouble, but Admiral Towers couldn't get out. He called to me in great consternation to come and help him. Thirty-odd years before he had contributed to the invention of aviation's first safety belt, but it couldn't aid him now.

'I called the valet. He called the plumbers, the carpenters, and the chambermaids. It was Sunday, and they were all down at the pub in the village.

'A bit later, with Mrs. Churchill, I was walking in the garden when, to our surprise, we saw the feet, then the blue uniform trousers, and finally the full uniform of an American Admiral climbing out of the first floor of Chequers.

'Mrs. Churchill said, "My, what an extraordinary way to leave the house!"'

During a subsequent visit by General Arnold to Chequers, conversation somehow got round to a discussion on honeymoons.

'I told Mrs. Churchill about the ride in an ox cart my wife and I had had from the dock at Guam to the little town of Agana when we landed there on our honeymoon,' said General Arnold.

'She said, "Tell Mrs. Arnold when Winnie and I were on our honeymoon we visited Venice. I wanted to ride in a gondola; he insisted on a motor launch—said it was far more healthy; the fumes killed the germs, and so on. So we rode in a gasoline launch!"'

Clementine added: 'There is not much romance in Winnie.'

In spite of momentous news constantly breaking the quiet of Chequers at week-ends, Clementine somehow managed to maintain an atmosphere of relaxation about the place. Like any country-house hostess in peacetime, she was meticulous about her guest book. A visitor was expected to sign it every time he entered the house.

Journeying to the south coast, General Eisenhower dropped in at Chequers unexpectedly for a few minutes. After talking with the Prime Minister, he hurried out to continue his journey; but as he settled into the seat of his car he became aware of the Churchill butler standing beside the car, waiting to speak to him.

'Sir,' said the functionary, 'you have forgotten something.' And with that, he handed Clementine's famous guest book to Ike for his signature.

In the years when the *Luftwaffe* was determined to bomb Winston Churchill off the face of the earth, if that could be done, Clementine managed to instigate a precaution reserved for 'bombers' moon', nights when the moon was full and the *Luftwaffe* was in the habit of coming over in force.

She arranged for a secret 'shadow Chequers' at Ditchley Park, near Woodstock, north of Oxford. One of the loveliest of England's stately homes, built in the seventeenth century, Ditchley was owned by Mr. and Mrs. Ronald Tree, who were old friends of the Churchills. Ronald Tree was then Parliamentary Secretary to Brendan Bracken, the Minister of Information.

Ditchley Park stood close to Blenheim Palace, where Winston was born. Three of its large ground-floor rooms were reserved as offices for him, and in subsequent years —though Winston and Clementine stayed there only during the worst of the bombing nights—the house was to see its share of war history.

When, during a Ditchley week-end, a guest remarked that Winston had given the people courage, he replied: '*I* never gave them courage. I was able to focus *theirs*.'

Winston and Clementine were at Ditchley on Sunday, 11 May 1941. Suddenly the Marx Brothers' film they were watching was interrupted by an urgent telephone call. It was their friend, the Duke of Hamilton, with a message that a German, piloting his own aircraft and dressed in the uniform of a *Luftwaffe* flight-lieutenant, had baled out over Scotland. After first giving his name as Horn, the man had said that he was Rudolph Hess, Hitler's deputy Fuehrer. He claimed that he had parachuted into Britain to negotiate a 'settlement'.

Winston was not amused. He growled: 'Will you kindly instruct the Duke of Hamilton to tell that to the Marx Brothers?'

But the Marx Brothers' antics soon took a back seat in Ditchley's cinema room to the even crazier story of Hess's mission personally to 'negotiate peace with the King'.

Chequers was not entirely reserved for official guests. Miss Mary Shearburn, one of Winston's war-time secretaries, remembers with gratitude one of Clementine's thoughtful little actions.

She told me: 'My home had been broken up on the outbreak of war, so that when I developed measles in the spring of 1941 there was nowhere for me to go when I left

239

hospital.

'When I first fell ill Mrs. Churchill had tried very hard to get me into a nursing home, but as they wouldn't take infectious cases it had to be the Fulham Fever Hospital. I was taken there in an ambulance—complete with a pot plant given to me by Mrs. Churchill as I left, to cheer me up a little.

'Every single day she personally telephoned the hospital for reports on my progress.

'As soon as I was out of quarantine, knowing that my family was far away, she simply telephoned me at the hospital and said: "You are going to Chequers to convalesce." There was no discussion—she had made all the arrangements—and that is where I went.'

Miss Shearburn later married Detective Inspector Walter H. Thompson, who was Winston's personal Scotland Yard bodyguard for many years. Thompson's memories of Chequers during the war period were mainly concerned with the extraordinary security safeguards, but he also had this to say:

'The war, quite naturally, came out ahead in all Mr. Churchill's thoughts. Mrs. Churchill had to be secondary, as must be the wife of any famous public servant. I saw how little time a Prime Minister could have with his wife. Actually Winston and his beloved wife had precious little time together and I did not envy her position. If other women in Britain did, they thought more of the honour than of the price of it.

'She was of course justly proud of his achievements, and her pride in those achievements was satisfied also by witnessing and sharing the rare experience of seeing a great man fulfil his destiny. She saw it happening in their joint presence rather than recorded and engraved at the bases of monuments for the generations ahead.

'This was going on while they were alive, not just something that was guaranteed to preserve his name after he passed, and she with him, into history. She knew this, and such moments and hours as they had together or shared with small groups were the more exquisite to her for that reason.

'A man can take some comfort in the knowledge that his name and work will survive and have meaning and use long after his death. Not so a woman. She wants all of her living to take place while she is herself alive, partaking of the many courses of the banquet table which can be laden in such plenty only once. A woman, the world over, would sooner be loved while living than famous when dead. And that is how it was with Mr. and Mrs. Churchill.

'One had a magnificent sense of the indestructibility of the immediate present whenever those two appeared together, and they felt it most of all.'

Shortly after the pilotless flying-bomb raids began, Clementine and Winston were at Chequers. On the Sunday morning she told him that she wanted to pay a visit to the Hyde Park anti-aircraft battery in which their daughter Mary was serving. For some inexplicable reason she felt she must go that very day.

'I was there when she arrived in Hyde Park,' said General Sir Frederick Pile, 'and Mary's battery was in action—flying bombs were overhead. One passed over us and demolished a house close by.

'As Clementine, Mary, and I stood together, we saw a bomb dive out of the clouds and fall in the direction of Downing Street. It landed on the Guards' Chapel at Wellington Barracks, where a service was in progress, and killed or injured two hundred worshippers, largely men and women of the armed forces.'

Viscount Alanbrooke remembers another Sunday at Chequers. It was almost the eve of D-Day.

'In the morning we went to church with Clemmie and Mary,' he noted in his diary. 'After lunch did some work and after tea we went for a walk. Dinner was followed by the usual film, after which Winston sat by the fire and drank soup. He looked very old and very tired. He said Roosevelt was not very well and that he was no longer the man he had been; this, he said, also applied to himself.

'He said he could still always sleep well, eat well, and especially, drink well; but that he no longer jumped out of bed in the way he used to, and felt as if he would be quite content to spend the whole day in bed. I have never yet heard him admit that he was beginning to fail.'

One evening, soon after D-Day, Winston, Clementine, and Harold Macmillan were sitting in the drawing-room at Chequers. Winston had spent a tiring day drafting a lengthy report.

'I am an old and weary man. I feel exhausted,' he said.

'But think what Hitler and Mussolini feel like!' countered Clementine, to which he replied, 'Ah, but at least Mussolini has had the satisfaction of murdering his son-in-law.'

The thought seemed to revive him, and he was suddenly his perky self again.

It was at moments like these, when a tired, exhausted Winston felt at his lowest, that Clementine lifted him up.

When, in May 1953, Clementine arranged for Anthony Eden to go to Chequers to convalesce after his serious illness, she was, in doing this, taking advantage of a little-known clause in the Chequers Trust which the donor, Lord Lee, drew up in 1917.

Though he gave Chequers primarily for the use of Prime Ministers, he specified that certain other public leaders, beginning with the Chancellor of the Exchequer and the Foreign Secretary, should have the use of the house if the Prime Minister did not want it.

Clementine suggested to Winston that Anthony Eden should take advantage of this clause, and he agreed.

Even though the chilly, austere mansion was never a great favourite with Winston, Clementine thought that they should personally add something to Chequers in memory of the many happy and stirring times they had spent there. She suggested that they should offer a gift of beech trees to be planted in an avenue.

Winston and Clementine submitted the offer to the Chequers Trustees, and the gift was accepted.

There was always one other important occupant at Chequers—Nelson—their huge black cat, who padded around as if he owned the place, and allowed people to stroke him—sometimes.

'Nelson's the bravest cat you ever saw,' said Winston. 'Once chased a big dog right out of the Admiralty.'

The tradition of the Chequers week-ends continued after the war when Winston once more became Premier.

Mr. Adlai Stevenson arrived for lunch one Sunday, and Winston, who never missed an opportunity of stressing his family's American connexions to any visitor from the United States, declared: 'My mother was American, my ancestors were officers in Washington's army; so I am my-

242

self an English-Speaking Union.'

Then, with a broad smile for Clemmie, who was seated at the other end of the table, he went on: 'I also have some ties with Scotland which are to me of great significance, ties precious and lasting. First of all, I decided to be born on St. Andrew's Day. I commanded a Scottish battalion of the famous Twenty-first Regiment for five months in the line in France in the last war. I sat for fifteen years as the representative of "bonny Dundee", and I might be sitting for it still if the matter rested entirely with me.

'And it was to Scotland I went to find my wife.'

16

TENANTS AT THE WHITE HOUSE

WHEN Winston set off on his travels again, Clementine went too, and so did Mary. Conferences had been arranged with Mr. Roosevelt and Mr. Mackenzie King, the Canadian Minister, to plan the total defeat of the Axis powers.

It was the first great Quebec Conference, and Clementine decided to go, not only to look after Winston's health and comfort, but also to make a return visit to the United States in acknowledgement of Mrs. Roosevelt's tour in Britain.

On the night of 4 August 1943, they left London. By the morning they reached the River Clyde, where they embarked in one of the old Calais–Dover steamers to reach the *Queen Mary*.

In their party was Mary, Averell Harriman and his daughter, all the Chiefs of Staff, Winston's doctor Lord Moran, Brigadier Orde Wingate and his wife, and a host of other planners, Intelligence, and Service personnel.

Brigadier Wingate, leader of the 'Chindits'—the Long Range Penetration Groups operating behind the Japanese lines—had been unexpectedly summoned to join the party.

Clementine and Mary, returning to Downing Street for dinner after being absent all day organizing an Aid to Russia Fund flag day, found the legendary Wingate an unexpected guest. His experiences and theories about jungle fighting made such an impression on them that Winston said simply: 'You must come and tell all this to the President,' and that was the first Wingate knew of the scheduled departure that night for Quebec.

Wingate was delighted at the opportunity and honour, then remembered that he had had no chance, as yet, of even telling his wife that he was back in England. He was longing to see her, and she was staying with her parents near Aberdeen. Winston went into action—two policemen woke up Lorna Wingate; told her to pack a suitcase, and took her by car to Edinburgh, where at 5 a.m. her husband, still in his baggy tropical uniform, stepped from the Prime Minister's train to give her a wonderful unexpected home-coming surprise.

Clementine, witnessing their station platform reunion from the window of her train compartment, was so moved by their obvious joy in each other, that she spoke to Winston and suggested that Lorna Wingate's name be added to the *Queen Mary*'s passenger list. Mrs. Wingate was invited to join the journey to Quebec, and, of course, immediately accepted.

Aboard ship, there were conference rooms, information rooms—everything continuing with the same precision as in London—including a counterpart of the Prime Minister's famous map room.

The ship observed radio silence. Outgoing messages were transmitted visually to attendant destroyers, which, after putting sufficient distance between themselves and the *Queen Mary* to avoid disclosing her position, passed the messages to London.

Winston insisted on having a machine-gun mounted in the lifeboat he and his family had been allotted, determined, as he said, to resist capture in the event of the ship's being torpedoed.

Recalled Lord Ismay, Winston's Chief of Staff throughout the war, 'We sailed in the *Queen Mary* for Halifax on 5 August ... the Prime Minister was accompanied by his wife, and daughter Mary. Mrs. Churchill's presence was a great comfort. If the Prime Minister got ill, or was too naughty, she could look after him and stop him as no one else could.

'Junior Officer Mary Churchill, A.T.S., was worth her weight in gold as her father's aide de camp. What other member of his staff could march into the Prime Minister's bedroom and make him get up in time for his appointments?'

Brigadier Wingate's wife had her own individual impression of the voyage:

'Clementine was unable to use the bathroom of their suite during the voyage as it was required, from time to time, for strategic purposes,' said Mrs. Wingate. 'Throughout the voyage to Halifax, the Prime Minister had been studying for the first time the details of Overlord—the plan for the invasion of Europe—and foremost in these plans were the synthetic harbours—the Mulberry Harbour as it was later known, which was to enable our forces to be supplied across the open beaches.

'In his bathroom, Winston would be frequently seated on a stool, wearing one of his flamboyant dressing-gowns, and surrounded by Generals and Admirals. The bath would be filled, and an Admiral would make waves while a General floated little model Mulberry harbours to illustrate their ingenious efficiency. No bathroom was ever the scene of the birth of such a stupendous military operation. No wonder Clementine could not get into it.'

As the *Queen Mary* approached Halifax, Winston, Clementine, Mary, and others on the staff, went on the bridge to view the harbour and watch the pilot manage the difficult task of bringing the great vessel into port.

Mr. Mackenzie King, the Canadian Prime Minister, was waiting to welcome them at Wolfe's Cove. The main party was quartered in the beautiful Chateau Frontenac which had been completely commandeered for conference personnel—British, American, and Canadian. Winston and Clementine were housed in the Governor General's summer residence, the Citadel—a lovely picturesque building on a hill overlooking Quebec, surrounded by stone ramparts from which could be seen the St. Lawrence river hundreds of feet below.

Anthony Eden arrived by flying boat to join the conference.

One of Winston's secretaries was a Canadian girl whose mother had taken the opportunity of flying from Vancouver to see her during the conference. Clementine, who, like Winston, always found time to think of others, suggested to him that they personally pay half the mother's fare from Vancouver, and he agreed. It was thoughtfulness such as this that helped inspire devotion of staff.

One afternoon, Mr. Mackenzie King had tea and a 'very interesting conversation' alone with Clementine.

'She spoke about how much he relied upon me and spoke of how glad he was to be with me and to share days together,' said the Canadian Prime Minister. 'She told me many things about Winston. One thing was that his being out of office for a number of years and writing the *Life of Marlborough* had had a real effect upon his character. He

246

had discovered that Marlborough possessed great patience. That patience became the secret of his achievements. . . .

'Winston would ask her whether she thought he would ever be back in government again, and she had told him he might not.

'She then told me that when Neville Chamberlain took over and succeeded Baldwin, and did not invite him into the Cabinet, she said then she did not think he would be in any future Government. She told me finally it was only four days before the war actually came on that Chamberlain told him he would like to have him in the Cabinet in the event of war.

'But, she went on to say, if war had not come, he would not have been taken into the Cabinet.'

The Canadian Prime Minister gave a dinner, and in proposing a toast to Winston's health, spoke of his bringing Clementine with him to Canada, saying it helped to give Canadians an even greater feeling of being a part of a family community in the British Commonwealth.

When the conference had ended, Winston broadcast to the world from the Citadel.

It was time to leave, but Clementine insisted that before going on to Washington, Winston should snatch the opportunity of enjoying a few days' fishing in Canada. He didn't have a chance to say 'No'—she had already made arrangements with Mackenzie King, and off they went to beautiful Snow Lake, in the heart of the logging country, where they stayed in cabins heated by giant log fires.

In Washington, the President had to go to his Hyde Park home before Winston had completed his work, and he told Winston and Clementine—'Please treat the White House as your home. Invite anyone you like to any meals, and do not hesitate to summon any of my advisers with whom you wish to confer at any time. Break your journey to Halifax at Hyde Park and tell me all about it afterwards.'

The Churchills accepted his offer and became temporary tenants of the White House.

During their Washington stay, Italy was being invaded by the Allied forces and Marshal Badoglio had agreed to sign unconditional surrender terms on 3 September. Clementine was with Winston in their suite when an urgent message arrived. Winston read it and his face became very

247

grave. For some reason the agreement with Italy was not being signed. Later that day, the famous Churchill smile returned—a message from General Eisenhower came informing him that the surrender hitch had been overcome.

Also during that visit, Winston received an honorary Doctorate of Law at Harvard University.

When it was time to leave for Halifax they broke their journey at Hyde Park for a farewell get-together with the President and Mrs. Roosevelt to thank them for their hospitality. During the day they spent at Hyde Park—it was also their 35th wedding anniversary—Clementine thoroughly enjoyed a visit to the Roosevelts' museum where she saw how, along with the treasures of the Roosevelt family, gifts from ordinary people all over the country were preserved as well with the same loving care.

President Roosevelt's comment to Clementine on her husband was:

'A great fellow, if you can keep up with him.'

They were going home on H.M.S. *Renown*. When the *Renown* left Halifax, they were housed in the Admiral's quarters high above the fore deck, but the voyage was a very uncomfortable one. The roll of the ship made it virtually impossible to sit still, and everything was perpetually sliding about. Winston even found it necessary to light his cigars by candle.

'That was the trip that Mary nearly got washed overboard on the day she was celebrating her twenty-first birthday,' said Lord Ismay.

'I had been walking with her along the quarter-deck when we were told not to walk on that part of the ship because the *Renown* was about to execute a zigzag course as an anti-submarine precaution. The quarter-deck was cleared of personnel, and we were zigzagging like mad when I saw Mary out there again escorted by a young naval officer—"Schoolie"—the schoolmaster. He'd started walking with her, obviously delighted to be with this pretty girl.

'Suddenly the ship swerved violently and a wave came over. We didn't get a chance to shout a warning to them before this enormous wave swept over them and they completely disappeared.

'I was watching it, and I thought I'd have to go. We wouldn't dare face Winston again—we would have to go in

248

after her. God, I was frightened.

'It was a miracle she wasn't drowned. When the wave receded, she and "Schoolie" were left clinging to a stanchion. She was carried to safety, battered but not beaten, and after being given a brandy, was taken to her cabin and to her mother.

'Clemmie brought her round, and both of them later turned up for dinner in the Admiral's cabin. Not a word was said by anyone to Winston about Mary's escape. I don't think that Clemmie, in fact, told him until the end of the voyage.'

Mary herself later admitted to her mother that as the wave struck her, she was certain she was about to be washed overboard and drowned.

The following year, the second Quebec Conference was called, and Clementine again made a point of going, particularly because Winston had suffered another minor attack of pneumonia, this time during a trip to Italy.

On Tuesday, 5 September, they sailed once more from the Clyde in the *Queen Mary*.

Winston had told Clementine that the time had now come for the liberation of Asia, and he intended that Britain should play its full and equal part in it. He was determined that the United States would never be able to say in later years: 'We came to your help in Europe and you left us alone to finish off Japan.'

The ship was again a miniature Whitehall, with the Chiefs of Staff meeting the Prime Minister once and sometimes twice a day during the six-day voyage.

'Winston was very ill, tired, and was bad-tempered the whole way and although Clemmie did her utmost to make him comfortable during the voyage, he was irritable and continued to push himself to the limit, and over,' said Lord Ismay. 'He shouldn't have started that trip.'

While Winston spent most of the voyage working in his stateroom, Clementine occupied the days visiting American wounded on board, talking to each one individually, and bringing them the kind of warmth, conversation, and talk of home that only a mother could give.

Landing at Halifax, the party travelled by train to Quebec. *En route*, they passed through many small towns, and the news—'The Churchills are coming' had spread in advance—crowds waited to cheer them at every station. At each stop, Winston, Clementine, and Mary appeared on the platform at the back of the train to wave to the people.

At Quebec, Mr. Mackenzie King was waiting, and so were the President and Mrs. Roosevelt. The Roosevelt train had arrived at 9.45 a.m. and drawn up at a siding.

The Earl of Athlone and Princess Alice—the Governor General and his Lady—were there too. Mr. Roosevelt and his party moved down a wooden ramp and boarded their car. Meanwhile the Churchill train had drawn into the station about fifty yards from the President's.

Smiling broadly, Winston gave the V sign and shouted to the crowd: 'Victory is everywhere.'

He walked across with Clementine to shake hands with Mr. and Mrs. Roosevelt in their car. 'I'm glad to see you, Winston,' said Mr. Roosevelt. 'Eleanor is here too. Did you have a nice trip?'

'Well, we had three beautiful days,' Winston replied, 'but I was frightfully sick at times.'

Turning to Clementine the President said: 'He has lost a lot of colour and I have lost a lot of weight.'

The official cars drove along the narrow sunken roads of the Citadel grounds to the parade ground in front of the residence.

The President remained in the car, but Winston descended and, stick in hand, approached the guard of honour. As Mr. Roosevelt's car left, Winston joined Clementine, who had also left the car, and the two walked together to the Residence. He was obviously delighted to be sharing the occasion with her, and was happy, buoyant, more like his old self.

'On our first night in Quebec, we attended a dinner at the Citadel with Mr. and Mrs. Churchill,' said Mrs. Roosevelt. 'The dinner was being given by the Governor General, the Earl of Athlone, and his wife, Princess Alice.

'This was the first time I had accompanied my husband to any war conference,' said Mrs. Roosevelt. 'It came about because when my husband and Mr. Churchill were talking on the telephone making arrangements for the conference, Mr. Churchill had said:

' "I am taking Clemmie with me again."

' "In that case," said my husband, "I'll bring Eleanor." '

250

'While we were at Quebec, Mr. Churchill produced a scale model of a D-Day landing harbour and demonstrated it.

'The old Citadel was a very novel experience, and Mrs. Churchill and I enjoyed walking about the Citadel fort, and especially along the ramparts from which we could look down on the St. Lawrence river.

'The Governor General and Princess Alice took us both for a drive in the country one afternoon, and we shared a most enjoyable picnic tea.

'While our husbands were occupied with conferences, we used the time to attend various functions; speak at meetings, and both of us also made French language broadcasts to the Canadian people.'

On Sunday, 17 September, the Churchills left Quebec by train for another visit to the Roosevelts' Hyde Park home.

'They stayed with us several days,' Mrs. Roosevelt continued, 'and it was a very busy several days. My husband wanted to fish, I wanted to picnic, and we both got our way.'

Afterwards, they returned to Halifax and boarded H.M.S. *Renown* for home.

The visit was over, but Clementine's friendship with Eleanor Roosevelt remained, and grew. Whenever, in later years, she travelled to the United States, she never failed to telephone and see Eleanor Roosevelt. Likewise, Mrs. Roosevelt did the same when she came to Britain, no matter how short her visit.

They corresponded, and Clementine regularly kept Eleanor informed of Winston's health. After his stroke, she wrote Eleanor: 'He is getting stronger every day, but it has been an anxious and sad experience.'

They were two wives who had a lot in common—each had a remarkable husband.

17

THE GREAT CHRISTMAS CAKE MYSTERY

IN our nursery days we heard with horror how the wicked witch had slain Snow White with a poisoned apple. More cynically, in maturer years, we accepted those hoary devices of the thriller-writer, the doctored cake, the poisoned chocolates, and the germ-laden cigarette. But in war-time Downing Street the clichés of the 'penny dreadful' became grim reality.

From well-wishers throughout the world came parcels of eggs, fruit, cakes, sweets, butter, sugar, and a hundred scarce delicacies, together with boxes and cabinets of the cigars which Winston loved. He saw none of them. Each consignment as it arrived was subjected to the expert scrutiny of Scotland Yard detectives and usually ended in the furnaces. Most of the gifts were innocent enough, but unless the senders were known personally to Winston and Clementine their offerings were rejected. The risks were too great to be taken.

Sometimes a small hole in the cellophane wrapping of a cigar could reveal where the needle of a hypodermic syringe had been plunged into the tobacco. A minute disarrangement of the top layer in a chocolate box might indicate that the contents had been tampered with by an enemy agent or a maniac. Since many of the presents were sent anonymously it would have been a waste of time to try to trace the source. It was safer and quicker to burn everything.

Though it was painful to Mrs. Landemare, the cook at No. 10, to see good foodstuffs destroyed, she accepted the situation, and Clementine managed to vary the menus with the very welcome food parcels sent to her from New York by Bernard Baruch.

The strict security precautions gave rise to what was to become known as 'The Great Christmas Cake Mystery'.

Said Detective Thompson: 'A beautiful Christmas cake arrived by post at Downing Street. I commandeered it at once.

'One of the staff must have told Mrs. Churchill about it, for she sent for me and asked me why I had taken the cake. I told her that I was not prepared to take a chance on it.

' "Perhaps it is all right," she said hopefully.

' "How do we know, Madam?" I asked. "We don't know where it has come from."

' "Indeed I do," she said. "I have the name and address of the senders."

'I said: "Anyone wanting to get rid of Mr. Churchill would not worry about a little thing like giving a false name and address. You might trace the real sender—and again, you might not.'

' "Well," she said, still endeavouring to save the cake, "what are we going to do about it? At least we have a name and address to go on this time."

' "We'll check the senders and have the parcel traced. I haven't destroyed the cake yet."

' "Oh, good!" she said. "So long as you haven't destroyed it. It would be so nice to have for our Christmas table."

'While my investigation was going on the cake was taken down to Chequers, with strict orders from Mrs. Churchill and myself that it was not to be touched.

'In due course we received a report from the security people assigned to the job.

'Two old ladies had saved their rationed foods all through the year to make that cake for Winston. A local baker had cooked it, and it had been exhibited in his shop before being sent off. The local police told me: "You can take our word for it that the two old ladies are perfectly genuine—and so is the cake."

'Mrs. Churchill was very relieved. She had been banking on that cake. Mrs Landemare had been badgering her: "Am I to make a Christmas cake or not?" And even the Prime Minister had asked Scotland Yard: "Please try to get the mystery of the cake solved in time for Christmas."

'The parcel took quite a while to check really thoroughly, but it was worth while.

'After Christmas, two old ladies received a letter of thanks signed personally by Winston Churchill.'

A less happy ending attended the arrival of a huge cheese cake, a confection of which Clementine was particularly fond. When it had to be destroyed she was inconsolable.

Said Thompson: 'A similar situation arose when we went to America for Mr. Churchill's first meeting with President Roosevelt at the White House. Thousands of cigars were sent to him, but they were all destroyed unless we could verify the source. The signature on every label or accompanying letter had to be checked with the utmost care.'

In spite of the misleadingly modest exterior, No. 10 is a very large house. At the rear of the ground floor are the housekeeper's office, the kitchen, and a general office controlling the official and domestic activities and arrangements of the Prime Minister and his wife.

On the first floor are the dining-room and, adjoining it, a smaller room known as the breakfast-room. On this floor, too, is the magnificent drawing-room, which Clementine refurnished to her own taste and used for formal occasions and social gatherings.

The bedrooms are directly above the Cabinet room, a long rectangualr chamber almost filled by a massive table covered with green felt and surrounded by chairs. Individual blotter pads, paper, and pencils are always laid on the table before each chair.

Winston would often remain alone in the great Cabinet room, sitting in the Prime Minister's arm-chair at the head of the table long after his Ministers had gone.

'Clemmie issued express instructions that whenever he remained behind after a Cabinet meeting, he was not to be disturbed or interrupted in any way,' said Lord Ismay.

There was no warming fire for Winston's back in his other War Cabinet room in the near-by Annexe. Instead, the empty hearth contained a fire bucket which miraculously caught almost all his cigar butts when he threw them backwards over his shoulder without bothering to watch where they landed.

In the main corridor of 'the Hole in the Ground', as it was known, there was a small door bearing a wooden plaque painted: 'Prime Minister'. In the cubicle behind it, with its walls covered in maps, Winston laboured, issued orders, made broadcasts, and generally ran everyone else into the ground. Clementine had another miniature bedroom, in which Mary Churchill would sleep on a camp bed while on leave from the A.T.S.

There was no plumbing in the bedrooms. Toilet facilities were limited to a jug of water in a bowl on a table, a china soap-dish, and a mirror on a stand.

Below were more bedrooms for the men and women employed on the staff. These were so deep below ground-level that pipes for London's sewers and gas and water mains ran through the rooms and enormous rats made them their home.

Somehow, in spite of its sprawling immensity, Clementine managed to make No. 10 run smoothly and introduced the maximum comfort possible. The trouble was that official and domestic activities tended to become so inextricably involved that keeping them separated was a continuing nightmare for her and her staff.

There was a connecting passage between No. 10 and the Annexe, and on many a morning a visitor being ushered through to the private secretary's office would be confronted by the spectacle of Winston, clad only in a white bath towel, crossing from the bathroom to the bedroom. Unabashed, the Prime Minister, like a senator of ancient Rome, would greet the visitor with a stately, dignified salute which made the situation seem even more grotesque.

Clementine's Aunt Mabell came to tea one afternoon at Storey's Gate. When she arrived, tin-hatted, uniformed guards passed her upstairs to a small lobby where she was ushered through a small door and into a sitting-room beautifully furnished, with a Romney over the fireplace, a head of Clementine's mother as a girl, and some modern landscapes on the walls. The soft lighting, the atmosphere of tranquillity and elegance seemed far removed from the war, and when her Aunt made a remark to this effect, Clementine opened her eyes in surprise.

'Do you know, Aunt Mabell, what this place really is?' she asked. And suddenly her aunt realized that these peaceful rooms were directly above London's great Air Raid Precautions centre!

The *Luftwaffe* tried repeatedly to bomb No. 10.

'They know very well where our house is, and they keep trying to hit it,' said Clementine. 'They put one not very far away once. My husband says that when his time has come it will come—but it isn't due yet.'

It certainly was not. Three torpedoes were fired by a U-boat at the 35,000-ton battleship *Nelson* west of the Orkneys. All hit the ship, but none exploded.

Aboard the *Nelson* at the time was Winston Churchill.

Admiral Karl Doenitz, Commander-in-Chief of Hitler's navy, afterwards said bitterly: 'The battleship failed to blow up because of faulty torpedoes and because Churchill was aboard.'

Clementine was part of the security arrangements surrounding Winston's war-time movements. Hitler would have given almost anything to be able to kill or capture Britain's great leader, and secrecy concerning the Prime Minister's day-to-day whereabouts was imperative; so imperative that when he left the country for his first meeting with President Roosevelt, he posed with Clementine for a photograph which showed them buying a little charity flag from a smiling woman at the door of No. 10. The photograph was put in 'cold storage' for a week before being published on the real flag day. Just another security trick to mislead the enemy.

One day, during the flying bomb period of the war, Clementine told Lady Reading that she was anxious to see the manner in which the Women's Voluntary Services tackled 'incidents' during raids.

Recalled Lady Reading: 'I went to lunch with them at Downing Street, and my car picked us up afterwards with the latest news of that afternoon's attacks.

'Too often she went to see people who were expecting her, so she said to me, "Let's just go like that and let no one know we're coming." This way she would she things as they really were. It is very seldom given to the great to see a thing as it really is because nearly always a lot of dressing up is done. She wanted to see things without reception committees and all the rest. She wanted to inform herself.

'As we were about to leave, I noticed that she was wearing a lovely new pair of shoes and I said, "Don't wear those shoes, they'll get ruined, and you had to give your coupons for them." She answered that they helped her morale and they might help other people's, and she went off looking very nice, as she always does. I have never, never seen her not look as if she's just come out of a band-box.

'We went first to Paddington, where there had just been a bad bomb incident. It upset her very much. While we were

Churchill in the uniform of the 4th Hussars 1895. *Radio Times Hulton Picture Library*

RT. HON. WINSTON CHURCHILL. M.P.

IS FIANCÉE. MISS CLEMENTINE HOZIER.
Sun/Fishnan

Competing in the Ladies' Parliamentary Tournament at Ranelagh.

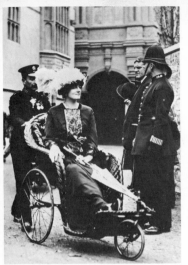

Top left: Being wheeled in a bath-chair in the summer of 1912, when suffering from the illness that almost crippled her for life. *Top right:* The Churchills climb from a pre-World War I model car. *Rosica Colin. Below:* Lady Churchill and Winston at Gladstone's memorial service (1915). *Hul*

Woodford: "If I have to go away my wife will take my place during this campaign. Other partnerships may be temporary, this coalition goes on for good." *Pictorial Press*

Mrs Churchill's wartime
bedroom in annexe of
Downing Street. *Hul*

August 19, 1941. Sir Winston and Lady Churchill arrive in London after
the sea conference with President Roosevelt. *Hul*

Left to right: Lord Woolton, Mr Geoffrey Summers, Mr Winston Churchill, Mr Anthony Eden, Mrs Winston Churchill, leaving the Grand Hotel, Llandudno, North Wales for the Conservative Party Conference closing session, 1948. *Hul*

Churchill on the eve of his seventy-fourth birthday with Old Surrey, Burston Hunt near Chartwell 1948. Mrs Churchill waves goodbye.

Top: Sir Winston leaves No. 10 for the State Opening of Parliament and his birthday presentation. Clementine leans into the car to bid him farewell (1954). *Rosica Colin. Below:* Sir Winston Churchill with Lady Churchill and Dame Margot Fonteyn enjoying a gondola ride along the Venice waterways. *United Press International*

Top: The "old boy" revisiting his school at Harrow.
Below: Final rites: The coffin of Sir Winston Churchill is carried down the steps of St Paul's Cathedral, London. *United Press International*

there, a second bomb came down, and as I thought it would be a mistake to get her killed, I suggested that we move on to the Incident Inquiry Point across the river at Battersea. We had hardly been there five minutes when a bomb fell within yards of us, so we said we'd better go down to the East End.

'We reached the East End, and within three minutes a warden yelled: "Quick!" and nearly pitched her into a brick shelter as three more flying bombs fell around us in a matter of seconds. I said: "We'd better go home now—I think it's getting too hot."

'We jumped into the car, and I had an American driver named Pauline Fenno, who was very careful about always keeping the windows half-cocked. As we drove along towards Westminster, we could hear a bomb overhead. The car in front of us stopped; four men jumped out and lay in the road, and my driver used some bad language, saying that the men were in more danger from being run over by our car than they were from being blown to bits by the bomb. At that moment the buzz bomb fell and shattered the windows of the shops all around us.

'We went on and the traffic lights ahead of us turned red, and my driver automatically stopped. We were the only car in sight. Suddenly my driver said: "Honestly what a fool I am, just because I work in England, I've stopped for this light which means nothing with a buzz bomb chasing us. What irks me," she said, "is that if we get hit, I won't even have a decent obituary. It'll just be: 'Lady Reading, Mrs. Churchill, and friend.'"

'I must say I was very glad to get Mrs. Churchill back to the Annexe on the day the flying bombs chased us. I felt a double responsibility with her because she was a rather precious person to be taken out in the middle of this lot.'

Another of Clementine's friends—Lady Hillingdon—deputy chairman of the Women's Voluntary Services, joining her on a journey to Norwich when she went to open an Anglo-American Services Club, recalls:

'When we got to Norwich, there was a civic reception with the Lord Mayor, generals, and everything else you can think of,' said Lady Hillingdon. 'In the middle of lunch, someone whispered in the Lord Mayor's ear: "The Prime Minister wants to speak to you," so out went the Lord

Mayor. He returned looking rather angry. "Can you believe it?" he said to me. "That was the Prime Minister ringing to see whether I would arrange for a sleeping car to be put on the back of the train home you are catching at four o'clock this afternoon. He was afraid Mrs. Churchill would be very tired. How can I get a sleeping car? In any case it's nothing to do with me."

'But somebody did do something, and when we walked on to the platform, with all the local dignitaries, we were shown to a first-class carriage, the door was flung open, and there were two beds laid out—one each side of the compartment. Mrs. Churchill hissed at me: "If you don't lie down when we get in this train, I'll murder you!" So we both lay down until the train left the station and then went and had tea in the dining-car.

'That shows how he used to think about her in the middle of the worst of the war. In the midst of all his problems, he phoned to see that she shouldn't overtire herself on the way back.'

Although Winston would sometimes use his influence to obtain for his wife certain extra privileges and comforts that he justifiably felt her work and responsibilities warranted, his personal integrity always prevented him from disclosing official information that might be used accidentally to his family's advantage.

Soon after clothes rationing was introduced, Clementine told a dressmaker, as she handed out her clothing coupons for a new outfit: 'I was caught like all the rest.' She added: 'The funny thing is that long ago my husband said: "You had better buy me a handkerchief or two. You never know —they might be rationed." I never bought those handkerchiefs. I thought he was joking.'

Her life in Downing Street was lonely, for she saw few friends outside the political circle. She felt it her duty to remain at home as much as possible, so that no matter what time Winston returned he would find her there. She knew that then, more than at any other time in their lives, he needed her. He could talk to her as he could talk to no one else.

Whenever he returned to the Annexe from No. 10, she was waiting to welcome him affectionately. Her greeting was not demonstrative, often no more than a comradely

258

hand on his arm, yet the effect on him was plain for all to see.

As soon as he walked into the hall he would shout at the top of his voice: 'Clemmie, darling! Clemmie, darling!' Sometimes she would hurry to the door to meet him. If she were in her room, he would go to her. The tone of his voice always told her how the day had gone, and if it had gone badly she would comfort him. Just to be charmed by her voice, to hear her say gently 'It will come out all right; you are doing your best,' gave him a tremendous spiritual lift. He talked his troubles and his heart out to her.

On the rare occasions when there were no guests, they would either eat together in the dining-room or she would have dinner in bed while he had his on a tray beside her. One such evening he returned from No. 10 distressed by some disastrous news, his eyes moist with tears. Clementine sent for a tray of food for him, and he dined in her bed-room.

The fall of Singapore rocked Winston. He felt the blow even more than the loss of France because, like everybody else, he had always considered the Far Eastern base impregnable. When friends asked what had happened there, he would shake his head and mutter: 'I really don't know.'

Clementine and members of his immediate circle did their utmost to break his depression, but nothing seemed to move it. He began to look as if he were at last feeling the strain of office. His sleep, so vital to him, was restless, disturbed. Even the famous afternoon naps no longer fully refreshed him. It was suggested that he should make a trip, the following week-end, to a Service establishment. 'You always sleep well after those trips,' he was told. 'They seem to put new life into you.' He was uninterested.

Clementine realized that a tour of inspection of some kind was the only antidote for his mood. He had to be shaken out of it before he made himself ill. She continued to stress that it was time they were seen together again, among the fighting men and women of the Services. Two weeks later they visited an Army unit, and he seemed to find himself once more. Suddenly turning to her, he said: 'We must hold on. All will come right if we have patience.'

'When the war started, Winston had to sleep during the day out of necessity, so that he could work far into the

259

night,' Clementine said, 'but he believes a man should sleep during the day, also, to be at his best during the evening when he joins his wife and friends at dinner. A good meal, with good wine, and then some brandy: that is his great moment of the day.'

Clementine had to contend with a husband whom not even his most devoted friends could call considerate, but he was demanding more from himself than from others; and following his own line that all that the human structure required was change, she was for ever trying and scheming to achieve some brief mental respite or change for him.

There were seldom more than seven or eight guests to luncheon at Downing Street. Winston usually arrived for a meal dressed in his blue siren suit, and if he were silent and brooding, Clementine would keep the conversation going until some topic ignited a spark which rekindled his attention and eloquence.

The upstairs dining-room was used only at the beginning of the war. When they decided it had become too dangerous because of the air raids, Clementine converted the low-ceilinged servants' hall below the ground floor into an alternative dining-room, which was used until the completion of the new quarters in the Annexe made a new and larger room available there.

At many of the Downing Street dinners Clementine was hostess *in absentia*. Having arranged the menu, welcomed the guests, and seen them comfortably seated at the table, she would disappear diplomatically, leaving the men together. Those were 'stag' evenings for Cabinet talk, when Winston's political associates met to discuss Parliamentary affairs and any other business which the Prime Minister wished to pursue. When the discussion had concluded, it was a question of 'Shall we join the lady?' and Clementine would be waiting to resume her duties as hostess.

Sir Tom O'Brien, M.P. and union leader, was a guest at some of those war-time 'stag' dinners.

'On various occasions, several of us on the T.U.C. General Council had to meet the Prime Minister with Ernest Bevin, who was then Minister of Labour,' recalled Sir Tom. 'We would get together for a conference, and sometimes a meal, at Downing Street, and usually Clementine would look in to see if everything was all right—especially if raids were on.

'She would often come in to indicate that it was getting late, with the watchfulness of a mother, apart from that of a wife. On one occasion she came in after dinner and virtually started to undress Winston in front of us—she started to undo his tie, loosen his collar, take off his jacket and waistcoat, give him his slippers, and generally make him comfortable.

'This was her way of encouraging him to relax, and it worked like magic. She babied this incredible man, and he loved it. They had complete understanding.

'Mind you, although she was getting him comfortable for the night—it was for the night's work, not for sleep. After people such as ourselves had departed, he would get down to his papers until the early hours.

'Even when we couldn't actually see Clementine around at Downing Street, we felt her presence in the house, and, I think, so did he. He knew there was companionship there all the time, if he needed it. He may have had little time for it in those days, but it was there, and the knowledge of it was of tremendous importance to him.

'I saw how she handled "stag" parties on an occasion after the war, when, in 1953, Marshal Tito came to London. There was an official dinner given for him at Downing Street. It was a "stag", and a distinguished crowd of about fifty guests were present at dinner. I was seated between Lord Moran—Winston's physician—and Field-Marshal Alexander. Politicians from all parties were there, as well as Montgomery, admirals, the lot.

'When we adjourned to the lounge which adjoined the great first-floor dining-room, there were several inquiries about Clementine. She was in the house, but not at the party.

'Anthony Eden came over and said to me: "Well, this is wonderful, wonderful. Where's Clementine?" He went out to look for her and to see if he could bring her in.

'We saw her coming along the corridor, past the open door. She had lunched earlier with Tito. As she went by the door, she smiled, waved, and said: "I'm not coming in."

'She knew when to stay away. She was content to smile at all of us, wave to Tito, and laughed when he waved back.

261

'She wouldn't even come in for coffee because she knew that if she did, it might deflect attention from Tito or from Winston. I have often seen quite the opposite happen with important people, where wives crashed a "stag" party. But Clementine knew her place even in her own home, and observed the same rules she set Winston.

'To handle a man like Winston required supernatural patience, and I know he recognized this.

'Clementine appreciated that, in many respects, Winston never ceased to be a boy. It was characteristic of him that, years before, when he was Home Secretary, he had absolutely refused to prohibit roller skating on the pavement. He was insistent on the right of little boys to knock down older people in their lust for speed.'

The schoolboy traits in him emerged frequently. He was vain about his feet and legs, and sent back a portrait by Bernard Hailstone to have the legs altered to his liking.

A woman from a Mayfair beauty *salon* used to visit the Annexe each week to manicure Clementine's nails. Winston often used to burst into the room, kick off his bedroom slippers, and demand: 'What do you think of my feet? *You* haven't got feet like that. Aren't they pretty?'

As a fact, his feet—like his wife's—*were* pretty.

Though the most virile of men, Winston nevertheless liked Clementine to buy eau-de-Cologne for use on his handkerchiefs. He would hold the handkerchief by one end and spray the perfume on to it with an atomizer. When his wife did the spraying for him, he was delighted.

Not all the Downing Street dinners were 'stag' affairs. One evening the chief guest was an emissary from the Vatican.

Ambassador Myron Taylor, President Roosevelt's personal representative to the Holy See, had come to London on a mission. He wanted to find a formula to prevent the bombing of Rome.

There were four people at table in the Annexe that night: Winston, Clementine, Mr. John Winant, the American Ambassador, and Mr. Taylor.

Himself an Episcopalian of Quaker descent, Myron Taylor sought a compromise between humanity and the needs of war. He argued and Winston argued; yet basically both believed in the same things, despising persecution and oppression and loving freedom.

Winston explained that with Britain fighting for her existence in the Middle East and the Allied invasion of North Africa already planned, any limitation of action might aid the enemy and completely undermine us in the Mediterranean.

While recognizing that fact, Mr. Taylor emphasized that the bombing of Rome and the destruction or damaging of the Vatican would offend Catholics throughout the world. He wanted to protect the great spiritual home of millions in its historic setting of priceless antiquity.

Winston understood the point only too well, but stressed his obligation to his forces. If Rome were removed as a possible British target, he urged, Mussolini might be tempted to strike at Alexandria or Cairo, thereby endangering the British armies at Alamein.

Neither man would give way.

'It was the most civilized conversation I have ever listened to which involved both spiritual considerations and the use of the destructive tools of war,' said John Winant.

'It was not a conflict between those two men. It had to do with man's continuing failure to establish peace and freedom through the power of love, and every time that breaks down the only answer must always be an agonizing compromise between the spiritual and the temporal. Similar conflicts arise and pass unnoticed in day-to-day life, but they are for ever highlighted by the tragedies of war.'

One evening in 1944, when the *Luftwaffe* was making a speciality of incendiary bomb raids, Clementine was presiding at a most important dinner party. Suddenly, the air-raid sirens sounded, and soon after came the 'overhead' warning signal. Winston, Clementine, and their guests were compelled to adjourn to the air-raid shelter, where they sat on chairs and stools and waited for the immediate danger to pass. Ranged round the walls of the shelter that evening were King George VI and his entire War Cabinet.

The King, a frequent visitor to No. 10 during the war, continued the dinner-table conversation and swopped jokes with Mr. Clement Attlee, Mr. Ernest Bevin, and Mr. Anthony Eden. Since Clementine saw to it that even the air-raid shelters were provided liberally with refreshments, all enjoyed the interlude.

Every now and then Winston popped his head out of the shelter, just to make sure the house was still in one piece above their heads.

Sometimes, voices that couldn't make themselves heard through official channels managed to reach Winston's ear via Clementine—provided she considered they had something worth while to say.

When Major-General Sir Edward Spears consulted Clementine as to the best means of ensuring that a matter important to her husband secured his attention, she advised him:

'Put what you have to say in writing. He often does not listen or does not hear if he is thinking of something else. But he will always consider a paper carefully and take in all its implications. He never forgets what he has seen in writing.'

Colonel the Hon. F. H. (Fred) Cripps had something important to say about the organization and management of the docks. He felt that the scheme, as it was, was unworkable, so, to ensure that his urgent criticisms didn't get pigeon-holed anywhere, he got them to the Prime Minister through the 'side' door to No. 10 Downing Street.

'I wrote my own report, after conversation with "Clemmie" Churchill,' admitted Colonel Cripps, 'and she undertook to show it to the Prime Minister.'

Clementine took a firm stand in a Downing Street 'incident' involving Clement Attlee.

John Colville, the Prime Minister's Assistant Private Secretary at the time, recalls:

'Churchill lay in bed at No. 10 Annexe, trying to throw off a cold and sunk in indignant gloom because Attlee had written to protest about the length of his monologues in the Cabinet and to complain that he was wasting his colleagues' time. Outraged by the letter, which Attlee had discreetly typed himself, Churchill sought a denial of the distasteful thesis first from Lord Beaverbrook and then from Brendan Bracken. Both said they thought Attlee was quite right. He then turned to Mrs. Churchill for consolation and support, only to be met with the reply that she admired Mr. Attlee for having the courage to put into writing what everybody else was thinking.

'Churchill spent the afternoon in a state of ill-tempered

depression. His friends, even his wife, had deserted him at time when he desperately needed support. Suddenly, he threw back his bedclothes, gave me a beaming smile and said: "Let us think no more of Hitlee or Attler: let us go and see a film." And for the rest of the weekend the sun shone.'

Clementine seldom intervened in matters of State, but at Downing Street there occurred an exception to the general rule.

The telephone in the Annexe rang one morning, and an overwrought voice at the other end of the line cried: 'Listen, Clemmie! Listen to this letter! You know how unlike Duff it is. Oh! Clemmie, what shall we do?'

The caller was Lady Diana Duff Cooper, desperate after reading a letter from her husband, who had gone to Paris on a Government mission. In it, Duff Cooper had confessed to a premonition that he would not return. The letter had been concealed in his wife's passport, obviously in the belief that it would not be discovered for some time. Lady Diana had found it quite by accident and now, frantically anxious, had telephoned the one person who might be able to help.

Clementine listened sympathetically; then she said: 'How awful! I'll tell Winston at once. He'll send out some Spitfires. Don't worry too much.'

Luftwaffe airmen may well have lain in wait to shoot down Britain's important emissary, Duff Cooper, but the escort of Spitfires sent to accompany his aircraft from Paris was sufficient to deter any such attempt. Whatever cards Destiny held in her hands that day, Lady Diana was for evermore convinced that her friend's intervention had trumped them.

There was a night during the later years of the war when Clementine might have been forced to intervene even more dramatically—and publicly—by deputizing for Winston as a broadcaster.

Millions in Britain and all over the world listened in stunned silence as, one Sunday evening, the Prime Minister came on the air. The voice was familiar, but where was the incisive phrasing, the bulldog truculence, they had been so eagerly awaiting? The broken, slurred words emanating from the loud-speaker sounded like those of a tired, bewildered old man. And in camp and saloon bar, parlour

265

and warden's post, men and women looked at each other, shocked, and declared: 'He's drunk!'

But Winston was not drunk. He was ill. It was only by super-human effort that he had faced the microphone.

Detective Inspector Thompson was there; and this is what he has to say:

'The script, as always, was ready in good time; but even before the broadcast we knew that he was not at all well. Somebody suggested: "Why not let Mrs. Churchill read it?" but the Prime Minister said: "No! They expect to hear my voice, and if they don't they'll wonder why."

'Mrs. Churchill begged him to let her read the speech in his place, but he refused. Several of his colleagues tried to persuade him, with no better success. He insisted on keeping faith with the people he led.

'When he had finished the speech, we almost carried him from the microphone and put him to bed. Mrs. Churchill sat beside him until he fell asleep.'

It is perhaps fortunate that Winston never realized the reception his gallant effort had in some quarters, for drunkenness is a sin he could neither tolerate nor forgive. He abhorred it since his Sandhurst days. Yet it is a fault of which he was sometimes accused by people who did not understand his vocal disability.

When tired, the impediment which Clementine worked so hard with him to overcome, returned. His speech became slurred, and sibilants gave him endless trouble.

Said Detective Inspector Thompson: 'In later years, as he got older, that "s" became more pronounced. When he made that broadcast in 1944, near the end of the war, a lot of people said he was drunk, and there were many arguments about it; but the plain truth was that he was very tired and he had a cold. I can remember an earlier occasion when he was very husky when he spoke. We had all kinds of cough mixture sent to us—people were recommending this one and that one—but it didn't stop the usual "drunk" yarns.'

Though the revelation may destroy a legend, in simple fact Winston neither drank nor smoked to real excess. He loved good brandy and whisky, but drank little of either. He liked a pint of champagne daily—his only health fetish —but would go for days without any other type of alcohol.

Though at receptions he was usually seen with a drink in his hand, his glass was seldom replenished. He would make one small whisky last for several hours, and often his glass contained nothing but iced soda water. Indulgence in spirits, he said, blurs thought. Although he enjoyed drink, he was never seen drunk.

During the bombing in early 1944, General Eisenhower was spending many nights in London. Concerned for his safety, Clementine suggested that he occupy one of the underground shelters in Downing Street. Winston agreed, and she arranged an apartment specially for Ike, complete with kitchen, living-room, bedroom, and secret telephone.

Alas! Ike never used nor even saw the place.

Winston's fighting instinct made him ask General Eisenhower for permission to watch the D-Day landings from one of the supporting naval vessels.

Said Ike: 'I argued that the chance of his becoming an accidental casualty was too important from the standpoint of the whole war effort, and I refused his request.

'He replied, with complete accuracy, that while I was in sole command of the operation by virtue of authority delegated to me by both Governments, such authority did not include administrative control over the British organization.

'He said: "Since this is true, it is not part of your responsibility, my dear General, to determine the exact composition of any ship's company in His Majesty's fleet. This being true," he rather slyly continued, "by shipping myself as a bona fide member of the ship's complement it would be beyond your authority to prevent my going."

'All of this I had ruefully to concede, but I forcefully pointed out that he was adding to my personal burdens in this flaunting of my instructions. Even, however, while I was acknowledging defeat in the matter, aid came from an unexpected source.'

That 'unexpected source' was a combination of Clementine, aided and abetted by King George VI and Lord Ismay.

'Winston informed the King himself of his intention to go and watch the D-Day landings,' said Lord Ismay. 'First of all he got over Admiral Ramsay who was going to command the landings. He was telling him that he wanted to go and see the landings from a destroyer when I caught them at it.

'When I went into the room, I was obviously very unpopular for coming in at that moment, and Winston said: "I am just telling the Admiral that I want to watch Overlord go in from a destroyer." I said I didn't think it was a good idea because he would be right out of touch if important decisions were needed. All I got for that was—"Keep your mouth shut and I'll take you with me."

'Well, I had no desire to go. He then told Eisenhower and the King, whose immediate reaction was—"That's a good idea—I'll come too." At that, Winston sat back on his haunches and said: "I will have to ask the Cabinet."

'He put it to the Cabinet and they decided the King couldn't go, and when Winston went back to tell him this, King George said: "Well, you can't go either."

'Winston asserted that as Minister of Defence, he had to go—it was part of his job, but the King didn't agree.

'Winston had told Clemmie, of course, but she reserved her fire as, at that moment, she could see it going in her favour and thought his scheme would be killed. When he often told her of some exploit he had in mind, if she knew perfectly well he wouldn't be able to do it, she raised no objection at first. She would bide her time and work behind the scenes to outmanoeuvre him, if she thought it necessary to stop him for his good, and for the country's good.

'Well, I went with Winston to see the invasion off and we were in a train in a siding at Southampton, about five miles from Ike's headquarters. Clemmie knew he couldn't get aboard a destroyer at Southampton—to do this he would have had to go down to the West Country, so she still held her fire.

'Our concern wasn't because we thought there was danger in his going—I didn't think there was half the risk that Winston took throughout the war flying all over the place as he did. What I was frightened of was that we couldn't tell if all the landings would succeed, and Ike might have been in the position of saying: "This is a fifty per cent British enterprise and I must have orders from the Combined Chiefs of Staff—am I to push it to the limit, or am I to pull out and have another go later?"

'Well, if we'd have had the most important man on the

British side floating about in a destroyer, things would have been very difficult. But I was certain that if Winston had persisted in going, Clemmie would have stepped in and said: "Look here, you should be staying behind in case your presence is required for important decisions."

'I always had the feeling that if I really felt a thing tremendously—as in an incident of this character—and if I couldn't stop him, I would, in the last resort, go and invoke Clemmie's help. She had far greater influence on him than anyone else could possibly have. You see, he had outlived all the great statesmen of his own generation, and there was nobody in the Cabinet, or among the Chiefs of Staff, with comparable experience, brain, or intellect. He was a giant among pygmies. There was no one who really had the right to make him listen—except Clemmie. However strong his advisers might be, I didn't feel that they carried the guns that Clemmie did to handle such a situation.

'The thing that finally killed his D-Day putting-to-sea idea was a letter we organized from the King. The letter reached him at Southampton, and gave Winston no option at all. He is a great Monarchist, and if the King came flat out, as he did, and said he was not to go, he would salute and say, "Very good, sir!"

'There was another occasion when Clemmie would have been the only person in the world to handle him, and that was when he flew to Athens after Yalta instead of coming home in the *Franconia*, as had been arranged. He was absolutely worn out. He was seventy years old. He'd had a most disappointing and discouraging conference as we had failed to get decisions on the Polish questions. He'd also had a brute of a cold, and here was the comfortable, beautifully appointed *Franconia*, with the sea most inviting, and the prospect of a voyage to Malta.

'I was very whacked, and said to him when we got on board, "Isn't it wonderful—we'll have six days rest." He said: "I'm flying to Athens." I said: "What for? It's all settled." And he replied: "I want to make sure."

'I said: "You don't want me, do you?" And he replied: "What for?" So I went back on the boat and never felt such a brute in all my life. Now if Clemmie had been there, I would have gone to her and said: "You didn't stop him, no one tried to stop him when he ruined his last Christmas to

269

go and save the situation in Athens—that was an urgent and dire necessity. But everything is all right now. Look at him—he must have a rest. We want him—we've got to save him up."

'If she'd been there, I would have gone to her, and she, and she alone, could have stopped him.'

The night of D-Day, Winston hardly left the Map Room. Clementine joined him a while before retiring. When she kissed him 'Good night', he said to her, 'Do you realize that by the time you wake up in the morning twenty thousand men may have been killed?'

Among those recommended for the Victoria Cross, the highest honour Britain can award to any of her fighting men, was the name of a sailor who had been drowned in the performance of the act for which he was cited.

When the list reached Winston, Clementine heard that the hero had left a young wife and a posthumous son, just born.

'A decoration alone will be of little value to a mother in such straits,' she said.

Winston summoned one of his secretaries, and, dictating a memorandum on the citation, said: 'Tell her that the King of England and his Prime Minister will be proud to be the godparents of the son of such a father.'

18

TO RUSSIA WITH LOVE

THE war in Europe was drawing to its close when Clementine received an invitation from the Soviet Government to visit Russia to see for herself the magnificent work achieved by her Red Cross Aid to Russia Fund.

In the summer of 1941 she had conceived the idea of a special Red Cross Fund devoted to sending medical supplies to Russia.

She knew the British people earnestly desired to help the Russian people. A variety of different appeals had been launched to raise funds for comforts and other supplies to be sent to the Soviets, but lack of knowledge of needs and conditions threatened to impair the effectiveness of their aim. A national effort was required. With the support of the British Red Cross Clementine launched the Aid to Russia Fund in October of that year. Within three months the fund had collected one million pounds. In its first year it reached well over two million, and for four years she made the Aid to Russia Fund her own special 'war baby'.

The idea originated the evening she asked Winston whether there was any immediate hope of Britain opening a second military front to relieve the terrible pressure on Russia.

She showed him a petition she had received from Servicemen's wives and mothers calling for the opening of a Second Front, and asked him to read the letter she had sent to housewife Mrs. Phyllis Dobson, of Northenden, Manchester, who had handed the petition to her.

Her reply said:

I am touched by your letter because you tell me that the women who have signed this petition begging for the opening of a Second Front are wives and mothers of men serving in H.M. Forces. This means that every one of you is prepared to accept a great sacrifice.

I can assure you that it is a great reinforcement and

encouragement to the Government to feel that the wo-
men of the country are prepared to give up, if neces-
sary, in the cause of freedom, even the lives of their
nearest and dearest.

We all long to help Russia in her agony. When we
feel impatient about a Second Front, do we not think
that we should all of us search our hearts and re-
member the years before the war, when it was impos-
sible to get anybody in the country to advocate or
work for rearmament?

The whole of Europe is now paying for these long
years of neglect, but day by day and week by week, we
are getting stronger and one day, we hope soon, we
shall be able to take powerful and effective action.

Said Winston:

My wife felt very deeply that our inability to give
Russia any military help disturbed and distressed the
nation increasingly as the months went by and the
German armies surged across the Steppes.

I told her that the Second Front was out of the ques-
tion and that all that could be done for a long time
would be the sending of supplies of all kinds on a large
scale.

Mr. Eden and I encouraged her to explore the pos-
sibility of obtaining funds by voluntary subscription
for medical aid. This had already been begun by the
British Red Cross and St. John's, and my wife was
invited by the joint organization to head the appeal for
'Aid to Russia'.

At the end of October, under Red Cross auspices, Clementine issued her first appeal. It declared:

'There is no one in this country whose heart has not been
deeply stirred by the appalling drama now going on in Russia. We are amazed at the power of the Russian defence
and at the skill with which it is conducted. We have been
moved to profound admiration for the valour, the tenacity,
and the patriotic self-sacrifice. And, above all, perhaps, we
have been shaken with horror and pity at the vast scale of
human suffering.

'Among the supplies we have already sent to Russia are

272

53 emergency operating outfits, 30 blood-transfusion sets, 70,000 surgical needles of various kinds, and 1,000,000 tablets of M. & B. 693. In addition, we have sent half a ton of phenacetin and about 7 tons of absorbent cotton wool. And this is, of course, only a beginning.

'We have declared our aim to be £1,000,000, and we have made a good start. Already the fund totals £370,000 and it is only twelve days old. Our gracious and beloved King and Queen, in sending a further £3,000 to the Red Cross last week, expressed a wish that £1,000 of their joint gift should be allocated to the Aid to Russia Fund. They have set a characteristic example.

'Much depends upon employers, and I would like to say this—wherever the employer provides the facilities to get the fund started the workers come gladly with their weekly pennies. Thus, from the King and Queen to the humblest wage-earner and cottage-dweller, we can all take part in this message of goodwill and compassion. Between the cottage and the palace, between those who can spare only pennies and a great imaginative benefactor like Lord Nuffield who can send a cheque for £50,000, there are millions of people who would like to share in this tribute to the Russian people.'

The Executive Committee of the Soviet Red Cross in a letter to Clementine said:

> The medical supplies which you are sending to us are being used to assist the sick and wounded of the Red Army as well as the civil population who have suffered so much from the treacherous invasion of the U.S.S.R. by the Hitler hordes.

Lady Limerick, who was Deputy Chairman of the Joint Committee of the Order of St. John and the British Red Cross, said: 'Mrs. Churchill did a most outstanding job for the Red Cross. Her dynamic personality overcame all obstacles and difficulties. Eleven months after her Aid to Russia Fund had been opened, it had spent about £1,850,000, and shipped 18 consignments to the Soviet, including portable X-ray units, motor X-ray units, ambulances, and articles such as 53,000 blankets; 50,000 chidren's coats; 40,000 children's breechettes, plus pullovers, scarves, mittens, gloves, stockings, balaclava helmets—a fantastic list that the Ministry of Supply officially described as "almost staggering in its proportions". All clothing sent was brand-new, and was collected and packed by the Women's Voluntary Services.

'Mrs. Churchill's tremendous enthusiasm fires people to help. She won't take "No" for an answer, and charms open many doors. She was like a Queen Bee about the place—full of industry, full of activity. Where she was also so enormously successful was that a great many organizations wanted, for various reasons, to raise money for Russia. Her drive brought cohesion to these different efforts thereby saving the enormous waste of money that would have resulted from the overlapping work as well as competition for the purchase of goods in short supply.

'Many of these organizations found they were bidding against each other in the open market for supplies, but Mrs. Churchill and her central committee cut out all this waste.

'I had close liaison with her and went frequently to Downing Street, but she regularly came to our headquarters for meetings to discuss details and policies. She was also in frequent contact with Madame Maisky, the wife of the Russian Ambassador, and this involved her in dealing with a slightly embarrassing situation because Madame Maisky used to come forward with long lists of requirements not necessarily related to the official lists from Russia.' Where she got her information from, nobody knew, but she often said we must have this, that, and the other, and on the lists from Moscow, there was no mention of these things, so Clementine had quite a job handling Madame Maisky, especially as the Soviet Ambassador had said he wanted his wife to deal with all Red Cross matters.

Clementine's shrewd diplomacy with Madame Maisky was planned like a campaign. She wouldn't go to see her unless she had previously anticipated and prepared for possible moves and counter-moves that might arise during their discussion.

On occasions she would consult Winston on her Aid to Russia work. At one time she drafted a telegram to send to Anthony Eden who was in Russia on a mission. She needed an answer on whether we could send a permanent Red Cross representative there. She showed the draft cable to

Winston to make sure it was correctly phrased for diplomatic channels. The following morning, she asked:

'Well, what about that cable—I'd like to have another look at it and re-draft it if you agree in principle.'

'It was a very good cable,' he said. 'I've sent it off.'

'To that extent, when she was doing official things, she kept him informed,' said Lady Limerick, 'but as a rule, her line was that he'd got so much on his plate and it wasn't fair to clutter him up with other problems too. She made her own decisions.

'She would walk into committee meetings with a load of ideas, throw them up in the air, and see how they landed. She wasn't unduly disturbed if many of them met with little response, but her ratio of successes was incredibly high. Her ideas were sparking-points. Basically, she worked on the same principle as Winston who also loved chucking hundreds of ideas up into the air to see what happened.

'When she wrote to Sir Stafford Cripps, who was then our Ambassador in Russia, if she proved to be unsuccessful with a proposal the first time, she would return to the attack, as she did in regard to the question of sending a Red Cross representative there. Sir Stafford Cripps was much against it at the start. Eventually someone was sent and broke the ice, to enable others to go and gather information, for she was insistent that the public in Britain should be told how their Aid to Russia money was being used, otherwise they might not continue to support the fund. She pegged away at getting this information, and eventually she went herself.'

Recalled Winston: 'For the next four years she devoted herself to this task with enthusiam and responsibility. In all nearly £8,000,000 was collected by the contributions of rich and poor alike. Many wealthy people made munificent donations, but the bulk of the money came from the weekly subscriptions of the mass of the nation.

'Thus through the powerful organization of the Red Cross and St. John, and in spite of heavy losses in the Arctic convoys, medical and surgical supplies and all kinds of comforts and special appliances found their way in an unbroken flow through the icy and deadly seas to the valiant Russian armies and people.'

Clementine would go anywhere, do anything, to raise

money for her fund. She established her own office at 10 Downing Street, and from there thousands of 'Thank You' letters went out to donors personally signed 'Clementine S. Churchill'.

Said Winston: 'The people were waiting on tiptoe to express what was in their hearts.' So when an invitation came from Marshal Stalin to visit Russia, Clementine was delighted and honoured, not only with the opportunity it offered to visit a large number of the centres of the war such as Leningrad, Rostov, Stalingrad, Sebastopol, and Odessa, but also because it would enable her personally to arrange for the equipment of two hospitals at Rostov on Don which were to stand as a lasting memorial to her great fund.

With the feeling of imminent victory everywhere, Clementine felt that at last she could leave Winston for a few weeks. Accompanied by Miss Mabel Johnson, secretary to the Aid to Russia Fund, and Miss Grace Hamblin, her own private secretary, and also Major-General J. E. T. Younger of the British Red Cross, she left for Moscow.

The instant she had gone, the restraining influence that had miraculously disciplined and kept Winston's phenomenal appetite for work within some kind of bounds disappeared too. The daily routine, so essential to the maintenance of his physical and mental health and strength, went overboard, and he seldom retired for the night before about 4 a.m. His important afternoon rest often began at 8 p.m., and dinner was usually at 9.30, and even 10, after which work continued until the early hours.

But Clementine's visit to Russia had a dual, unpublicized result. Seriously troubled at the deterioration in the relationship between Britain and the Soviet, Winston was anxious to know the pulse of the Soviet people and Government. Clementine gathered invaluable impressions on their feelings towards the Soviet's future with her Western allies. At one time he almost postponed her departure because of his concern over the deterioration of Anglo-Soviet relations.

Before leaving, Clementine, at Winston's request, had bought a gold fountain-pen which he asked her to present to Stalin as a souvenir of their meetings during the war. It was similar to his own favourite pen.

'Tell Stalin that with the gift of this pen I express the hope that he will write me many friendly messages with it,' added Winston.

They had a rough flight part of the journey, as bad weather forced their aircraft down to a dangerously low altitude over the last hundred miles.

On arrival in Moscow Clementine was met by Madame Molotov, Madame Maisky, and representatives of the People's Commissariat of Public Health. She was informed that the State guest house had been placed at the disposal of herself and her party for the duration of their stay.

Soon after their arrival she and Miss Johnson were received at the Kremlin by Stalin. He wanted to thank her personally for her untiring work on behalf of the Aid to Russia Fund.

'I wish on behalf of the Soviet Government to express my gratitude for the medical supplies and equipment which your fund has sent to my country,' said Stalin. 'We are grateful for it.'

Clementine thanked Stalin for the compliment, then presented him with her husband's fountain-pen gift.

Stalin explained that he always used a blue pencil. 'However,' said Clementine later, 'it all passed off very well.'

Mindful of Winston's particular interest in reactions in the Soviet on future Anglo-Russian friendship, Clementine was about to introduce the subject into her conversation with Stalin when he raised the issue himself by asking whether she was aware of 'difficulties' between East and West.

'I admitted that I had heard a thing or two before our meeting,' Clementine, and the Marshal earnestly remarked:

'There are difficulties and there will be difficulties but they will pass and friendship will remain.'

Clementine informed Stalin that she wished to travel at leisure and spend as much time as possible with the ordinary people of the places she was to visit.

He granted her wish by providing her with a well-equipped train in which to tour the country at a sightseeing speed of 20 m.p.h. to ensure that she saw all she wanted to see.

Smiling appreciative crowds applauded her everywhere she went, to demonstrate their gratitude for her work.

Accompanied by Madame Kislova of the Society for Cultural Relations with Foreign Countries, plus various other officials, Clementine journeyed first from Moscow to Leningrad. She saw motorways prepared by the Germans in readiness for their occupation of the city—so confident had they been of conquering it. She visited the hospital that called itself 'the factory for repairs of the human body'. It specialized in severe cases of head wounds, brain operations, shattered limbs, and plastic surgery.

With the help of Madame Kislova, who acted as interpreter, she talked to the men and women of Russia. She found them reluctant to volunteer information about their own sufferings, but 'burning with anger against the Germans'.

From Leningrad to Stalingrad an appalling scene of destruction met her.

'My first thought was, how like the centre of Coventry or the devastation around St. Paul's, except that there the havoc and obliteration seemed to spread out endlessly,' said Clementine.

'One building that caught my eye was a wreck that had been ingeniously patched and shored up. I learned that it was the building in whose cellar the Russians had captured von Paulus, the German commander. It was characteristic of them, I thought, to make every effort to preserve this ruin because of its symbolic value. It represented the final overthrow of the enemy after one of the most savage struggles in all human history. Stalingrad was the turning-point in the war, and that will be remembered by the Russians for centuries to come.

'In the middle of a big public square in Stalingrad, there was a huge common grave surmounted by an obelisk. This tomb, wherein lie so many of the brave defenders of the city, is called "The Brothers' Graves", a name that is moving, simple, and beautiful.'

The Germans left 60,000 dead when they were chased out of Stalingrad. The Russians buried them simply by dynamiting a giant valley out of the countryside and burying all the corpses together.

'Were you not afraid of some pestilence breaking out?' she asked officials in Stalingrad.

'We never thought of that until afterwards,' the Russians replied. Determined to see all she could, Clementine always sat in front with the driver whenever they travelled by car.

In Stalingrad her charm and sympathy lit up 'homes' that were no more than hovels in the ground. In front of one pile of rubble out of which a family had burrowed a shelter, Clementine stopped beside a placard displayed outside which read: 'A very fine shop is to open here soon.'

'What kind will it be?' Clementine asked the young Russian wife who stood respectfully beside the entrance to her 'home' to greet the wife of Winston Churchill.

'A barber's,' was the reply.

In the hospital wards, nurses enthusiastically and gratefully clapped her. In the streets, waving and applauding crowds trailed her. She found few Russians curious about British life or affairs, but their gratitude for the Aid to Russia Fund was obvious.

Few would talk of the days and nights of horror they had endured in the nightmare of German occupation. 'We do not even want to think about the Germans,' they would say.

Clementine confessed that she had never been more deeply moved in her life than by the spectacle of child victims of the siege of Stalingrad being cared for at a children's home.

The *Luftwaffe* had marked this hospital on their maps as a special target for their bombers.

As she toured the wards of the children's home, Clementine saw boys who had fought with partisans and were still suffering from wounds; children injured during the bombing of evacuation trains; children both of whose parents were at the front; and children whose parents would never return. She walked into one gymnastic class where the bodies of babies from eight months old were being repaired from the ravages of war, and watched a little boy of eight months perform astonishing physical feats while his woman instructor held him up by the heels. The little body firmly swayed to and fro like a trained gymnast. When Clementine expressed her amazement, the instructor said with a smile: 'Oh, any intelligent mother could do that if she chose to learn. If she loves her child, neither he nor she need ever have any fear.'

Language was no barrier between her and the children she met.

'When I was in a room with a group of them I would

sometimes feel a small hand put into mine. I would look down and find a two-year-old child with soft brown eyes who would pull me away to show me the bed where she slept or to give me a toy,' said Clementine.

Leningrad had a special surprise for her—the entire city, including the Lord Mayor, the Council, stars of stage, ballet, and opera, all turned out to greet her. And the Lord Mayor, Mr. Popkov, gave a great dinner in her honour. 'Would you like to dine first or hear a little music first?' he asked.

'I would like to hear the music,' she replied. As if by magic, chairs were brought in and the concert, which lasted for more than an hour, began.

But the guest of honour had a return surprise for her hosts. Towards the end of the evening she joined in the community singing of Russian folk songs.

When they began the 'Song of the Volga Boatmen', she sang that one too and surprised her hosts with her familiarity with their famous traditional song.

She found the despoiled towns of the Caucasus packed with Red Army convalescents. Sebastopol was 'a sight to wring one's heart', she said.

'Before the Nazis destroyed it in their blind rage, it must have been a dream of beauty, as lovely as a poem, with its many pillared and frescoed houses.'

Wherever she travelled, she brought to the people of Russia an understanding of the warm friendship felt by the people of Britain for them. She helped Russians to a better knowledge of their allies—a knowledge for which they had long thirsted. Her strenuous tour was of tremendous service.

In the Crimea she stayed at Vorontzov Palace where her husband had lived during the Crimea Conference. There she relaxed a while from the strain of the tour by visiting such shrines of literature as Chekov's house, where she was received by his sister Marian, then eighty-two years old.

One of the most vivid memories for her of the Russian journey was the visit to the Young Pioneers' Camp at Artec in the Crimea. Practically every child in Russia is a Young Pioneer, and Artec is their most famous camp. Every year thousands of children between the ages of seven and fourteen go there for a six weeks' stay. The voices of 600 children sang to her that day the haunting melody of 'The Song of Lenin'—a song of tragedy, a song of hope.

Then, in the city of Odessa, liberated after two and a half years of occupation, came two links with home—one happy, one tragic.

On arrival at Odessa she found a large number of British P.O.W.s waiting to be repatriated, and asked to be taken to see them immediately. A ship which was to transport them to Britain and home was in port. Clementine brought the men their first real touch of home as she moved and talked among them.

The next day she went to the dockside to wave them 'God Speed' as they sailed.

'It heightened for us the happy sense of liberation that filled the air,' she said.

'As war news poured in, it made the pulses beat faster to see our own men going home, free from the miseries of captivity, and knowing that soon they would be with their families again after the long and bitter separation.'

Also in Odessa was a camp of 1,000 French civilians deported by the Germans for forced labour, and most of them carried the tattoo identification marks of the slave labourer. Clementine stopped to speak to one of the women among them and asked her name.

The woman stared, faltered, and then murmured: 'I think I know it now, but up to a week ago I used to think of myself by my number only,' she said, looking at the terrible branded figures on her arm.

Clementine stood on street corners on Odessa watching the groups of marching men and women—freed slave labourers, freed P.O.W.s—of all nationalities. Then came another kind of tragedy. It was Friday, 13 April 1945, when a message brought news to her—President Roosevelt had died.

While the President was having his portrait painted, he complained of a 'terrific headache', then collapsed, and died a few hours later without regaining consciousness.

On his return from the Yalta Conference, Winston had shared with her his terrible fear for the President's health.

'I noticed that the President was ailing. His captivating smile, his gay and charming manner, had not deserted him, but his face had a transparency, an air of purification, and often there was a far away look in his eyes,' he said. 'When I took leave of him in Alexandria harbour, I must confess that I had an indefinable sense of fear that his health and strength were on the ebb.'

Clementine was travelling from Leningrad to Moscow, but was only due to stop briefly at Moscow Station, on her way elsewhere. As the train drew in, she saw Molotov and his wife waiting on the platform. They boarded the train, entered her compartment, and Molotov said: 'We come with bad news—President Roosevelt is dead.'

Clementine asked the Molotovs to join her in a two-minute silence in the carriage.

Although Winston had told her how terribly ill the President had looked at the Yalta Conference, the news nevertheless came as a tremendous shock. It was even more shattering because she knew that at such a moment Winston would need her, yet here she was thousands of miles away from him on a mission of mercy she had undertaken. She wanted to fly home but knew she couldn't. Instead she waited for the telephone call she was sure would come.

Clementine knew the shock would, in many ways, be even worse for him than the morning soon after Pearl Harbor when the telephone by his bedside had rung, and a voice said: 'Prime Minister, I have to report to you that the *Prince of Wales* and the *Repulse* have both been sunk by the Japanese. . . .'

With the destruction of these two warships, there were no American or British capital ships in the Pacific or Indian Oceans, except the American survivors of Pearl Harbor hurrying back to California, and the Japanese were supreme over the vast area.

'In all the war I never received a more direct shock,' Winston had said. But the President's death hurt deeply, and more personally.

Both she and Winston had been looking forward to welcoming President and Mrs. Roosevelt on a 'Thank you' visit to Britain which had been arranged for the month of May. The Roosevelts had already accepted the invitation from the King and Queen.

When Judge Samuel Rosenman had been a guest at Chequers, Winston had asked him to give the President a message: 'Will you tell him for me that he is going to get

282

from the British people the greatest reception ever accorded to any human being since Lord Nelson made his triumphant return to London?

'I want you to tell him that when he sees the reception he is going to get, he should realize that it is not an artificial or stimulated one. It will come genuinely and spontaneously from the hearts of the British people; they all love him for what he has done to save them from destruction by the Huns; they love him also for what he has done for the cause of peace in the world, for what he has done to relieve their fear that the horrors they have been through for five years might come upon them again in increased fury.'

As always, in times of emotional crises, Winston, whose incredible strength held the spirit of Britain high throughout the war years, turned to his Clemmie. She knew how terribly Winston would feel the loss, knew that with her thousands of miles away, the loneliness of the tragedy would be almost unbearable for him—he would have to have someone to talk to, to turn to.

At 3 a.m. the night bell in his personal detective's bedroom rang, and Detective Inspector Thompson hurried to discover the reason for the alarm. He found Winston pacing up and down his bedroom, his head sunk low, his eyes fixed on the floor.

'President Roosevelt has passed away,' he said, 'your friend and mine, Thompson. . . . We have to start all over again, and it is Friday the thirteenth. . . .'

He kept walking about the room, talking of Roosevelt, weeping, and talking. . . .

Winston had always told Clementine that without Roosevelt and the Americans behind him, Britain would surely have been lost. Winston and Clementine dearly cherished their friendship with Franklin and Eleanor Roosevelt. It was, as Winston said, 'a friendship which was forged in the fire of war'.

The telephone rang in Clementine's quarters in Russia. It was London, and Winston.

Together, over the telephone, they shared their loss. His first impulse, he told her, had been to fly to the funeral and he had ordered an aeroplane to stand by, but the pressures of Cabinet and Paliamentary arrangements made this impossible.

Winston sent Eleanor Roosevelt and her family a message of sympathy from Downing Street. Clementine sent her own from Russia.

When the all-too-short telephone call ended, he needed to go on talking—talking his heart and grief out—so he talked to members of his staff.

'No one realized what that man meant to the country, meant to the world. He was a great friend to us all. He gave us immeasurable help at a time when we most needed it,' he told his staff.

'He was loved by millions and hated too, as a wizard who gets things done. I'll be hated. But I'm composed about it. It requires no resignation on my part. I am sure it took none for Franklin.

'But at least he had the peace and the satisfaction to know his work was done. To see it done just before the end. His task was completed at Yalta. He died on the eve of victory, but he saw the wings of it. And he heard them.'

The following day Winston cabled a message to Stalin. It said:

I have been greatly distressed by the death of President Roosevelt, with whom I had in the last five-and-a-half years established very close personal ties of friendship. This sad event makes it all the more valuable that you and I are linked together by many pleasant courtesies and memories, even in the midst of all the perils and difficulties that we have surmounted.

I must take the occasion to thank you and Molotov for all the kindness with which you have received my wife during her visit to Moscow, and for all the care that is being taken of her on her journey through Russia. We regard it as a great honour that she should receive the Order of the Red Banner of Labour on account of the work she has done to mitigate the terrible sufferings of the wounded soldiers of the heroic Red Army. The amount of money she collected is perhaps not great, but it is a love offering not only of the rich, but mainly of the pennies of the poor, who have been proud to make their small weekly contribution. In the friendship of the masses of our peoples, in the comprehension of their Governments, and in the mutual respect of their armies the future of the world will reside.

Winston's tribute in Parliament to the President was printed in full by the Russian newspaper *Pravda*, and the report was translated in Moscow for Clementine.

In spite of her strong personal desire to return home at once, she continued the tour.

It was at the children's hospital at Kursk that she was confronted with one of the most terrible moments of the tour. The director of the hospital went over to a bed where a little girl was lying.

'Allow me to present to you the only living Jew in Kursk,' he said, grimly raising the child in her bed for Clementine to see. 'All the other Jews have been wiped out.' This little girl, the sole survivor, had been saved by hiding under a mattress. On her little arm was the infamous Nazi tattoo of shame.

Clementine became extremely friendly with Madame Molotov and, on returning to Moscow, she visited the school at which Madame Molotov's daughter Svetlana was a pupil, and watched an English lesson at the school conducted by a Russian woman who had spent only three years studying the English language, but who nevertheless had managed to achieve excellent pronunciation and intonation.

The lesson was conducted by question and answer.

'What colour is your tie?'

'The colour of my tie is red.'

It, apparently, was considered insufficient to say 'red'.

In Moscow, Clementine Churchill received two decorations. One was the Order of the Red Banner of Labour, the other the Distinguished Service Badge of the Russian Red Cross. She and Miss Johnson received their decorations at the Kremlin. Clementine was asked to extend her left hand, and a medallion was placed on the palm, while her services in organizing aid to the Soviet Red Cross and the peoples of the Soviet Union were cited.

Presentation of the Distinguished Service Badge of the Red Cross was made at a meeting of the Praesidium of the Red Cross. The ceremony lasted two hours, and Clementine, in reply, said that she felt there was no happiness before us or the world unless the great Soviet Union and the English-speaking world know each other, understand each other, and remain friends.

Speaking frankly to Madame Molotov, Clementine said:

'Unless the friendship that has been established between the Soviet Union and the English-speaking peoples during the war continues, increases and deepens, there will be very little happiness in the immediate future for the world, and by the immediate future I don't just mean the short span of our lives, but the lives of our children, grandchildren, and great-grandchildren.'

It was Clementine's wish as well as that of the Aid to Russia Committee that there should be some permanent memorial to commemorate the link forged between the peoples of the United Kingdom and the U.S.S.R., and at first it was thought it might take the form of erecting a hospital. Instead, the Soviet authorities undertook to provide the hospital buildings and suggested they should be equipped from the Aid to Russia Fund.

At Rostov on Don two hospitals—the Central City Hospital and the Clinical Hospital—had been almost destroyed. Clementine and her Committee promised to equip the Central 1,000-bed hospital, and the Scottish Central Council Branch of the British Red Cross undertook to do the same for the 500-bed Clinical Hospital, and equip it they did, down to such items as blotters, inkstands, and pen trays.

Plaques acknowledging the gifts were placed on the hospital buildings.

The snowball of victory began to grow, and the war in Europe approached its final phase. From the British Embassy in Moscow, Clementine received her own private news service of momentous events—Mussolini's capture and execution by anti-Fascists; three days later, the news of the death of Hitler; the Italian surrender to Field-Marshal Sir Harold Alexander; and then the mass surrender in Germany to Field-Marshal Sir Bernard Montgomery.

On 7 May, when she learnt that Admiral Doenitz had surrendered unconditionally on behalf of Germany, she longed to be with Winston in the hour of triumph, but she had promised to be present at a number of ceremonies in

286

her honour in Moscow and couldn't leave.

On that Monday in May everyone knew the war in Europe was over—though it was not to be officially over until the following day. The excitement of Moscow was electric. Crowds in the streets milled around, impatient for the news they knew would come any second.

Recalled Clementine: 'The memory of my last week in Moscow is unforgettable because of the affecting power of the emotions with which it was charged. It was 8 May—VE Day in Britain. In the Embassy I heard my husband's voice broadcasting from London the announcement for which the world had been waiting.'

Winston ended the broadcast with—'Advance Britannia! Long live the cause of freedom! God save the King!'

'Monsieur Edouard Herriot, the great French statesman, and his wife, who had been recently liberated after many hardships and discomforts from their German captivity, were with us in Moscow,' said Clementine.

'After the broadcast Monsieur Herriot said to me: "I am afraid you may think it unmanly of me to weep. But I have just heard Mr. Churchill's voice. The last time I heard his voice was on that day in Tours in 1940 when he implored the French Government to hold firm and continue the struggle. His noble words of leadership that day were unavailing. When I heard the French Government's answer, and knew that they meant to give up the fight, tears streamed down Mr. Churchill's face. So you will understand if I weep today."'

In London, Winston attended a Service of Thanksgiving at St. Margaret's, Westminster, while in Moscow, Clementine attended a similar service in the British Mission building. It was conducted by a Royal Naval Volunteer Reserve officer who was a Methodist minister, and an address was given by the 'Red Dean' of Canterbury, Dr. Hewlett Johnson, who had only arrived in Moscow the night before. 'Let's ask him to preach,' Clementine had suggested, and Dr. Hewlett Johnson's moving address took as its theme the death of President Roosevelt.

Clementine could not share Winston's historic, glorious day, when he left 10 Downing Street to make his Victory in Europe statement to the House of Commons. She could not be there to see the thousands in Parliament Square cheering and shouting 'Good old Winnie!', but she heard them over the radio and heard how the Prime Minister's car was almost pushed to Parliament by excited crowds. Nor was she able to be by his side when he appeared on the balcony of the Ministry of Health to greet the wildly cheering thousands. Each time he went inside they made him come out again.

It was a holiday in everyone's hearts, and Winston, always with the right words to say, told the happy faces below him: 'Why don't you take the day off tomorrow as well!' He began to sing the opening words of 'Land of Hope and Glory', and the thousands echoed it as one voice.

These were moments Clementine could not see, but in her heart she shared them just the same.

Then from husband to wife came the following message:

'It would be a good thing if you broadcast to the Russian people tomorrow, Wednesday, provided that were agreeable at the Kremlin. If so you might give them the following message from me, of which, of course, our Embassy would obtain approval:

'Prime Minister to Marshal Stalin, to the Red Army, and to the Russian people. From the British nation I send you heartfelt greetings on the splendid victories you have won in driving the invader from your soil and laying the Nazi tyrant low. It is my firm belief that on the friendship and understanding between the British and Russian peoples depends the future of mankind. Here in our island home, we are thinking today very often about you all, and we send you from the bottom of our hearts our wishes for your happiness and well-being, and that after all the sacrifices and sufferings of the dark valley through which we have marched together, we may also in loyal comradeship and sympathy walk in the sunshine of victorious peace. I have asked my wife to speak these few words of friendship and admiration to you all.

'Let me know what you will do. Much love, W.'

At a luncheon given by the Soviet Government in Clementine's honour two days before she left Moscow, Madame Molotov presented Clementine with a diamond ring.

'We ask you to accept this ring as a token of eternal friendship,' said Madame Molotov. 'May the relations between our two countries be as bright, as pure and as lasting as this stone.'

Thanking Madame Molotov, Clementine said she would in particular think of the ring as a symbol of Soviet womanhood whose achievements in the war and in the rebuilding of their country had won undying admiration. She added: 'I must also confess I take a very feminine pleasure in the beauty of the stone!'

Her last night in Moscow she spent seeing the *Swan Lake* ballet. At the fall of the curtain, the prima ballerina moved towards Clementine's box, applauding and smiling, and the whole company followed. The great, distinguished audience took up the applause to give a standing ovation to the woman who had done so much for their people.

Said Clementine: 'I pray as I turn to take my farewell look at Moscow, "may difficulties and misunderstandings pass, may friendship remain".'

On returning to London, the Fund's secretary, Miss Mabel Johnson, presented a report on their Russian journey to the British Red Cross, and Clementine supplemented this report with her own personal impressions of the experience. It is from this diary of the tour that I have taken her memories of the visit, and in this same record she wrote:

'It seems to me that the contact we have made is like a life-line which in her hour of peril and sorrow the British Red Cross threw to Soviet Russia. If things go well, as pray God they may, this life-line will be strengthened by other organizations representing the whole field of human intercourse. But if, alas, the relations between our two countries should go through dark hours, let us show that our life-line, though slender, is strong. What a wonderful thing it would be if the Red Cross were able to hold together a trembling and dissolving Europe!'

Months later, as the first chill of the Cold War began to be felt, she recalled:

'On Victory Day I remember being struck with astonishment that the Armistice was signed in Rheims and only it seemed as an afterthought in Berlin. This was rather incomprehensible to the Russians, and I confess that being rather cut off from home news, it was incomprehensible to me.

'I mention this because now that there are widening rifts and cooling feelings and dark suspicions, we must sometimes try to transport ourselves across the continent of Europe and imagine what a Russian would feel, isolated after the 1917 revolution for 25 long years, then drawn by terrible necessity into partnership and then, with the Nazi terror laid low, reverting to his loneliness.

'We do not want to be cut off from one another in the human race. However queer the Kremlin may behave, I am sure that the Russian people, if only we can get their human touch, want to be friends. The life-line which the British Red Cross threw to the Soviet Red Cross still holds fast. If it is to be severed the fault must not lie with us.

'During that memorable visit I learnt how different an event seemed when you view it in Moscow instead of London or Washington.'

On 14 May, Winston, accompanied by Field-Marshal Sir Philip Chetwode, was at the Northolt airfield of R.A.F. Transport Command waiting for Clementine's return from Russia. When the plane had taxied to a halt, the second the plane door opened, Clementine, wearing the uniform of the British Red Cross, almost burst out, to be greeted warmly by Winston.

They had been parted during historic days. They were to be together during still more momentous ones.

Clementine had much to tell him of her visit, and, in particular, of her conversation with Stalin.

'You hear people say, "You only see the things in Russia that they want you to see". That is a very foolish argument.

'These tremendous people are half-way through the most terrific experiment ever tried. All these years the Soviet Union has been quite happy to be left alone, but the war has made a tremendous difference.

'They are thrilled and astonished to find that all over the world their courage is acclaimed. We must not come to hasty conclusions until we know all the facts.

'I am certain that if we persevere now, friendship will increase.'

19

A WOMAN'S WORK

Winston was so overcome by his wife's Sovietization that he even asked ambassador to Britian, Ivan Maisky, if Clementine could be elected to the Soviet Parliament!

'She became completely Sovietized while organizing medical aid to your country,' he told ambassador Maisky. 'All she talks about is the Soviet Red Cross, the Soviet Army, and Mrs. Maisky.

'She is either writing to Mrs. Maisky, telephoning her, or taking part with her in demonstrations in support of Russia's war effort.

'I suggest that you make her a Soviet M.P. as a reward for her zeal.'

Winston talked repeatedly of her experiences in Russia. She had given him much to think about on the Soviet role in the future. Long after her return from Moscow, he would recall aspects of her visit—from the Moscow luncheon party for which all the Russian women invited had to be provided with dresses by the State, to the children of the country being instilled with the creed:

'I love Lenin,
Lenin was poor, therefore I love poverty,
Lenin went hungry, therefore I can go hungry.
Lenin was often cold, therefore I shall not ask for warmth.'

'Christianity with a tomahawk,' commented Winston.

Outside of Winston and her family, one of her greatest interests has always been her work for the Y.W.C.A. Whenever she has taken up a cause she has been prepared to walk into the limelight with poise, assurance, and a modest grandeur all her own.

Her personal success in public life is no mere reflected popularity. It is her own. Wherever she goes, whether she is making a speech at a political rally, visiting victims in a flood area, or walking over a pile of rubble which was a home before being bombed to dust, she is liked for herself, liked for the genuine smile which never degenerates into a fixed grin.

Few are aware of the time and effort she has devoted to causes.

Apart from the countless duties, both public and private, she had to perform during the Second World War, she made time for many causes, including getting more comfortable quarters for Service women.

'As the war goes on, women of my age are increasingly concerned about their daughters,' she said.

'They are doing splendidly but we do not want them in the monotony and hardness of their duties to forget the happiness and comforts and duties of home.'

Later, thinking of the thousands of girls living in hostels all over the country, girls who Clementine felt should have the chance to develop their own characters before undertaking responsibilities of raising their own families, she set a new target for the Y.W.C.A.—'For every girl a room of her own, with a lock on the door—a really cosy bed-sitter—that is my most ardent desire,' she declared.

'It is necessary—this room of her own—for the girls who have to leave home and their family to earn their own living.'

Clementine didn't just talk—she went to see, to plan for herself. Studying the problems of overcrowding in existing hostels, she made frequent unexpected visits to inspect hostels in their 'everyday clothes', and not wearing perhaps a party dress for her benefit.

After a visit to a hostel housing fifty girls, she said the place was only suitable for thirty-five girls.

'But where are the surplus fifteen to go to?' she asked.

'Some hostels have waiting lists as long as my arm,' she said.

'Also, by reducing the numbers, you incur a loss of income, which would have to be made up.' Clementine, economic and careful housekeeper, didn't forget that extra comfort must be paid for from somewhere.

Her answer was to compile a new 'Hostels Constitution'. With her committee she prepared and wrote a hostels handbook to which she devoted great time, thought, and effort.

She told the committee: 'It doesn't always follow that

girls are necessarily happiest in pale blue and white paint hostels. A warden who loves and understands her girls is the first essential. Wardens need to have so many qualities, and I formed a warm regard and admiration for them.

'They do a difficult and demanding and fatiguing job, and in addition, they have always imperative necessity of making both ends meet.

'All this is a great strain upon their temperament and character and, of course, not every warden is an angel any more than every nurse is a Florence Nightingale.'

Clementine's Y.W.C.A. committee handbook didn't speak dream language—it got down to basic essentials, basic necessities.

'An ablution block in every hostel with a ratio of not more than four girls to each washbasin, eight to each lavatory, and ten to each bath,' it demanded.

'The ablutions block, if possible, to be situated at the end of each floor. Each washbasin to have a cabin round it.' That final point was a typically considerate suggestion from a woman who loves and respects privacy.

'A laundry in every hostel, with space to dry clothes, and an airing cupboard; one electric iron to every six girls,' the handbook continued.

Clementine's lead—unknown to the public and to the mothers of the daughters for whose welfare she was so concerned—was taken up as the new aim of the world-wide Y.W.C.A. organization with its network of clubs, hostels, and cafeterias for women and girls in sixty-nine countries.

To help make her 'every girl her own room' desire a reality, Clementine pulled out all stops to raise funds. She even achieved a miracle in its cause by persuading Winston to sell one of his paintings.

It was the only picture he ever allowed to be publicly auctioned. The picture—the blue drawing-room at Trent Park—was knocked down to a Brazilian collector for 1,250 guineas. The money helped to build more of those Y.W.C.A. rooms.

Clementine was delighted with the result of the sale, but furious a little later when she heard that the Brazilian collector had admitted that he would have bid up to £13,000 for it if necessary.

'Her tremendous war-time work for the Forces—and, in

particular, for the girls in the Forces—led to her taking her great interest in hostels in later years,' said Miss Ruth Walder, National General Secretary of the Y.W.C.A.

'Many hostels were in a shocking state after the war, through being starved of funds—our consequent inability to remedy dilapidations, plus a terrifying shortage of domestic staff. It took a lot of money to reorganize everything, and getting us this money was Lady Churchill's major contribution to our work—in one year alone, during the war, she brought us £300,000. But her efforts on our behalf went far beyond the raising of money.

'After the war she was one of the few to recognize the great social and economic changes taking place, and the need for those social changes to be drastically applied to our entire organization and outlook.

'Because she firmly disagreed over future policy with some of our committee members, with typical Churchill spirit she started a war of her own to achieve what she fervently believed to be necessary and right. She launched her own offensive—a Battle of the Hostels—to improve standards of comfort for every girl who stays with us.

'As Chairman of the National Hostels Committee, she had visited many civilian hostels during the immediate postwar years and found that although an exceptional demand for accommodation was willingly met wherever possible, committees at old-established and newly opened hostels were being confronted with all kinds of difficulties as a result of changing conditions.

'She reported back to headquarters with devastating effect, saying that policy was increasingly dictated by finance, that everywhere buildings were suffering from unavoidable neglect, equipment was scarce and of poor quality.'

Realizing that a complete re-assessment of the work of the Y.W.C.A. was vital, she instituted the Hostels Self Study Survey, or how-to-put-your-house-in-order report.

'She revitalized our work,' continued Miss Walder, 'recognizing that looking after girls' spiritual welfare wasn't enough—she said we equally had to look after their beds, their food, their general comfort. She got quite frantic and very angry with certain committee members who couldn't appreciate that material comforts were as necessary as spiritual welfare, and that things needed to be put right fast.

She can be very forthright and very sharp with anyone she considers guilty of slackness or inefficiency.'

A hostels inspection tour took Clementine to Scotland, and she was appalled by conditions she found in one place she visited. The President of this particular hostel's committee happened to be a Duchess.

Clementine telephoned her then and there.

'Have you *seen* this hostel you are President of?' she asked the Duchess. She suggested the Duchess join her right away and take a good look with her. The Duchess came.

'Mrs. Churchill, as she then was, tore strips off the whole place, and started at once on plans to give it a new look and better management,' said Miss Walder.

When she visited the Y.W.C.A. hostel in Kingston, Jamaica, a grand reception was laid on for her. The Governor of Jamaica's wife, who was President of the hostel, was conducting her round the comfortable, nicely decorated ground floor club rooms, when Clementine pointed to a staircase and asked:

'What's up there?'

'Oh—that's nothing—it's just a little hostel,' replied the Governor's lady.

'Ah!' said Clementine, 'that's *just* what I'd like to see,' and was up the stairs like a shot.

'She was upset with what she saw, and said so most emphatically,' added Miss Walder, 'and that hostel has now been replaced. On her return to London, she related this incident to me with great satisfaction.

'She was the driving force of our reorganization. She has real dynamism—terrific nervous energy exudes from her. Some people are unnerved by it, but they have no reason to be provided they are doing their job. The general public have a picture of a cool, calm personality, but in fact, when she enters a committee room, it's as if an unexploded bomb has just walked in—mind you, a tremendously attractive bomb with scintillating wit—but nevertheless a bomb that is liable to go off at any time if it happens to land in the midst of complacency and bad organization.

'She could never be content to be President of anything and just be the name at the top of some nice headed notepaper—oh no!—she regularly attended monthly national committee meetings, as well as countless other meetings and always very definitely had her say.

'I witnessed an example of her loyalty to causes and people at one international Y.W.C.A. conference. The head of a delegation gave a number of points from America that clearly indicated they were very much out of touch with new thinking and trends. Several other delegates present sniggered and laughed at their out-dated attitude. Lady Churchill rose, white with anger, and proceeded to tear into the sniggerers with a tremendous speech that put great emphasis on how much we in Britain owed America. There wasn't a laugh felt after that. She cannot stand intolerance.

'At another conference which she attended as delegate, the mayor of the town gave us a reception. No alcoholic drinks were served, in deference to those members of our organization who don't agree with alcoholic refreshments, so the mayor very kindly provided a colourful-looking non-alcoholic cocktail. It looked gay, but tasted revolting.

'Lady Churchill came over to me with a glass of the stuff in her hand and said:

' "Miss Walder—what is this—Parrish's food?"

'She is terrifically expert on food and recipes. She is also, I think, a kind of frustrated architect—she is superbly good on plans. All blitzed hostels had, of course, to be rebuilt, and when we started the job she examined each plan in detail, and made a whole string of invaluable suggestions for improvements.

'She has a natural flair for this sort of thing; is very clever at interior decoration, and is consequently for ever changing her own homes round and adding new touches. She enjoys doing it.'

The 'architect' in Clementine had a field day as a result of the publication of a story in the *News Chronicle* criticizing the work of the Y.W.C.A. Mis-statements in the story were enough for her—she rose to the defence, and wrote to one of the newspaper's directors explaining that the story had caused considerable anxiety to the Y.W.C.A. in general, and herself in particular, as Chairman of their National Hostels Committee.

Clementine invited the paper's Editor to dine with her at the Dorchester Hotel. By the time dinner was through there was no longer any question of Clementine demanding a retraction of the damaging story in the newspaper—she had bargained for and got something better, something more practical—the Editor had promised that his newspaper, 'as an expression of its concern for the social welfare of women and girls', would foot the bill for an architect to design a Y.W.C.A. 'Hostel for Tomorrow'.

'The final design was the outcome of many months of study and discussion between Mrs. Churchill, a special Y.W.C.A. committee, and the architect,' said Miss Walder, 'and she made sure that all the most needed features for a modern hostel were included, with the emphasis on convenience, amenity, and friendliness—she wanted to make it home for each girl, the wardens, and the staff.

'When Mrs. Churchill received the model of the new hostel, she telephoned me to say she'd had a shock when it arrived because she hadn't thought it would be so small—"It's like one of these glass cases they keep ants in—like a little ants' house!"—she said.

'The original model was small enough to fold into a hand carrier. She asked them to enlarge it, and they did so, and also, at her suggestion, supplied water colour artists' impressions of the interior and exterior of the place so that when the model was displayed anywhere for fund raising purposes, the water colours helped to present a better dimension of the project.

'For some people the modern architecture of the new-style hostel took some getting used to, but as Mrs. Churchill said: "There is no going back, we must go forward all the time."'

Clementine would never condone or be associated with anything below standard as one market gardener discovered when he asked the Y.W.C.A. to take over administration of his private land girls' hostel. Instead of negotiating with one of the officials at Y.W.C.A. headquarters, he found himself dealing direct with Clementine, and she arrived in person to inspect his hostel.

A few days later, the farmer received a three-page, closely-typed letter that took his hostel apart and put it together again as it should be.

Her letter made it plain that neither she nor the Association would be connected with any establishment which was below 'minimum standard'. She added that she believed his hostel—'could be made into one of the most charming and

297

practical little hostels in the country. May I now say what I feel would make it so?'

And she said plenty. Her six-point reorganization plan raised every conceivable point, from a mirror and a chest of drawers for each girl, to criticism of the girls' washing having to hang up to dry over their heads, and of their dining-room being 'a very tight fit for eighteen girls'.

Clementine's inspection of the hostel hadn't missed a thing. Her letter concluded diplomatically:

> *I hope you will have read this very long letter to the end. I feel this is really all (practically all) and I hope it will not seem a great deal to you; but I feel that, as a business man, you would prefer that our requests be put before you in full at the beginning, rather than piecemeal.*
>
> *I am looking forward to seeing you one day here at Chartwell. Do ring up and propose yourself to luncheon. I have told Christopher Soames, my son-in-law, that you are coming to look at our market garden, and he is trembling with combined fright and pleasure.*
>
> *Yours sincerely,*
Clementine S. Churchill.

When she retired from the Chairmanship of the Y.W.C.A.'s national policy-making committee, Clementine continued to phone, or send by letter, devastating questions such as:

'If you don't have basins in all the bedrooms, where do the girls keep their sponges?'

Her fund raising activities were fantastic—nothing was too much trouble for her if it was to help a worthy cause. Her annual or biannual open days at Chartwell usually netted about £600 each. She held little luncheon get-togethers at home for people whose aid she wished to recruit for raising money for her pet charities. If Winston was around he would pop his head in to say 'Hello' to her guests, then vanish to let her get on with the task of finding ways and means of getting cash for new hostel improvements.

A wealthy Cuban named Giraudier had written to her some years before offering to make a donation to any charity she cared to nominate. She chose the Y.W.C.A.

298

Back came a dollar cheque, and Clementine wrote a note to their headquarters saying:

'I have received from Mr. Antonio Giraudier a Christmas present of one thousand pounds, and I would like to give it to the Special Hostels Fund. He knows about this, so I feel you would like to write to him. . . .'

A poor sugar crop made things difficult in Cuba the following year, but Mr. Giraudier still didn't forget. He wrote to Clementine:

'This year has been one of quite narrow earnings for Cuba and for all of us and it has put my heart, which is usually so large and generous, into a small restricted bag.

'But my thoughts and good wishes are always with my good friends—I do hope they will understand and forgive me for this temporary shrinkage of my donation purse.

'I am sending you herewith £500 as my Christmas gift to your charity purposes.

'It makes me happy to see that you and Sir Winston are in perfect health and he looks so strong and young! He has his secret about it, I am sure. . . .'

And a year later, a note from Clementine to the Y.W.C.A. announced:

'My Fairy Godfather Mr. Giraudier has again sent me a princely gift. . . .'

It was another cheque for £500, and he continued to send the same amount each year until Castro made it impossible.

'Lady Churchill frequently deflects to us money she is offered,' said Miss Walder. 'The most memorable example of this occurred in 1949 when an admirer of hers from Canada asked her whether she would accept a gift of a mink coat from him. Apart from owning a great newspaper, the admirer also happened to have interests in a firm of furriers and in mink farms.

'Mrs. Churchill told him that as much as she would love to have the coat, she would prefer its value in cash to give to charity.'

The admirer who bred minks was obviously a very generous sport—he sent a cheque, and Clementine wrote to the Y.W.C.A.:

'This cheque has just reached me from J. W. McConnell, the proprieter of the *Montreal Star*. I made his acquaintance towards the end of the war when I accompanied my husband to the second Quebec Conference. At that time I was President of the War-Time Appeal for the Y.W.C.A. and he very kindly gave me £1,000 for the fund.

'He was in London in October with Mrs. McConnell and they came to see me and offered to give me a mink coat! He is a very generous man and distributes them to his many acquaintances. (Among his many activities he is Chairman of a famous firm of furriers called Holt Renfrew.) I told him I would much rather have some money for the work I was trying to do for the Y.W.C.A. and I talked to him at some length about the hostels. He promised to send me a cheque, but nothing happened, and so I was afraid I had bored him. But now here comes Christmas and this wonderful gift....'

The cheque in lieu of the mink coat was for £10,000!

The receipt of the cheque was announced by Viscount Hampden, at a meeting of the Y.W.C.A. Finance Committee of which he is Chairman, and when Clementine heard him say that her 'gentleman admirer had sent her money instead of mink' she covered her face with her meeting agenda papers and screamed with laughter.

And that is how the Clementine Churchill Wing at the Association's headquarters in Baker Street, London, came to be built with a mink coat—and there was still £7,000 left over to pay towards rebuilding other hostels.

Apart from her extensive general work for the Y.W.C.A. she became the President of the War and National Service Fund of the organization from 1941 to 1946; Chairman of the Hostels Committee from 1948 to 1952.

In 1944, she launched the first of a series of special broadcasts to India. She said: 'For the first time in history women are no longer waiting at home for their menfolk. We are no longer called upon to listen for news, good or bad, of our husbands and sons who are fighting for us.

'We are, indeed, the chief target of the enemy.

'You in India can have no conception of the tyranny that would overtake you if the British were beaten.'

In addition to her Aid to Russia movement, and all her other efforts, she also became chairman of a maternity hospital—a duty she took very seriously. Each fresh task she undertook, she investigated thoroughly, studying requirements, planning solutions. She is meticulous in everything.

But, although a stickler for etiquette and certain formalities, she knows when and how to be informal.

A great mixer, she is always at ease, and puts everyone else at ease.

On a surprise visit to a hostel for girls working in munition factories, she walked into a factory dance. In no time at all she was dancing with one of the factory superintendents, thoroughly enjoying herself. Visiting a W.V.S. canteen, she found trade booming so she went behind the counter to lend a hand pouring tea. During her visit to a canteen for Servicemen, one of the canteen organizers commented: 'I watched her greet some of our sailors and airmen, and she approached each one as if he were the one person she had come to meet.'

Her preference for plain speaking was evident when she visited a hostel at Bristol. Delighted with its efficiency, she said: 'It would be a good idea to make a list of its assets and amenities and circulate it round the country to guide people who may be going to build a hostel or to rebuild an old one. There are luggage rooms on every floor so there is no need for girls to keep their suitcases under their bed, and a good laundry, not merely a tiny table and a hot iron.'

Her perceptive eye and inquiring mind makes a visit from her to any institution an unforgettable experience for everyone else.

In hostels, she would count the beds; feel mattresses; examine the quality of blankets and sheets; open cupboards; see whether beds in the dormitories were too close together; look into each pot on the kitchen stove.

Anyone presented to her was truly staggered at her knowledge of their personal background. The secret was her insistence on detailed briefing before each visit on everyone she might encounter.

For a Royal Air Force horticultural show at which she was to present the trophies, she arrived half-an hour before expected, to make a quiet advance examination of exhibits.

Putting on her glasses every few minutes to take a closer look, she turned to one of the officers to say: 'I cannot help reflecting—all this and flying too. I have never seen such vegetables in all my life—so beautifully grown and polished.'

Presiding at the Annual Court of Governors of the Royal

Free Hospital, in London, she called on supporters of the voluntary hospital system 'not to lie down with folded hands'.

'I urge you to accept what the Government is doing as a sort of groundwork on which the love and interest which you have shown for so many years may build a beautiful superstructure above the bare necessities provided by the State.'

If she considers anything wrong, she says so whether her opinion is unpopular or not. She was visiting Britain's first day nursery for spastic children when she spotted Press photographers taking pictures by flashlight of a five-year-old patient.

Clementine was furious. 'Children might easily be put back by that sort of thing,' she said angrily.

For the rest of the afternoon pictures were taken without flashlights. And the unfortunate children were left alone.

When flood disaster came to Norfolk, she was there—among housewives trying to repair the damage; visiting rest centres, clothing distribution centres and feeding centres; always with an understanding word of encouragement. She has the gift of seeming to smile confidence and strength back into people.

Her work has never been a token effort. For years, she has coped with a large daily postbag.

She personally reads every letter and dictates the reply to her secretary.

They can cover all manner of inquiries ranging from an old age pensioner asking her to intervene to get a rent reduction, to thanking a little girl for offering to make Winston a face cloth for his birthday and suggesting that he might prefer blue to pink edging.

She signs all her letters personally.

She also turned her attention to helping the millions of refugees throughout the world, and became the spirit behind the World Refugee Year which set out to raise millions to help the stateless.

Without the urgency of a war or a disaster visible to all, the task on behalf of the refugees was more difficult. Fifty influential people were invited by the Duchess of Marlborough to Londonderry House. The idea was to find an initial £35,000 for the fund. It was a tall opening target, and the chances of achieving it seemed, at first, remote. Clementine walked into the room. She spoke, and her words had the Churchillian ring about them:

'Remember there are no British refugees anywhere in the world,' she observed simply.

The case was won. The fifty left and the money was found in record time. But that was only the beginning.

She broadcast; addressed gatherings; talked to people in all walks of life urging them to help, and spoke the kind of words that made sense, words of sincerity. Her speeches were never 'ghosted'. What she said, she meant, and wrote herself.

Like Winston, to propel people into action, she didn't hesitate to make them face unpleasant facts, repeating again and again the story she had heard of a young refugee boy living in a camp in Austria who, with his father, was watching a camp being built in a nearby village.

'"Daddy," he asked. "What sort of people can live in houses?"

'I am glad I did not have to answer that boy's questions,' said Clementine.

'Let us face the fearful fact that if we had lost the war we might have been refugees.

'Some people will say "Charity begins at home". It may begin at home, but I believe it doesn't end there.

'We must not neglect those less fortunate than ourselves, however far they may be from us and how very easy it is to overlook them. They are our responsibility—a responsibility laid upon us 2,000 years ago by Our Lord. "Inasmuch as ye have done it unto one of the least of these my brethren, ye have done it unto me."'

In later years she could have justifiably taken things easily and given up most of her work. But for her, as with Winston, 'Living is working.'

Even on formal visits she prefers blunt talk to courteous chitchat, and has the knack of introducing the human touch.

At Middlesex School of Nursing, she told student nurses that the profession of nursing seemed to her personally to be not only one of the highest callings but one surrounded by an aura of glamour. 'Nurses,' she said, 'stand very high in the social hierarchy, but I have always longed to hear of any shortening of their working hours. To an onlooker, the working hours seem too long, and I wonder whether nurses have any time to use the beautiful restrooms provided for them in modern hospitals. The public would not like to feel that in restoring health, nurses have to give up their own health.'

As the distinguished writer Hannen Swaffer once said of her: 'She rose from obscurity to world prominence in which her inward grace shone resplendently beside the glory of her husband's triumphs.'

Presenting prizes at Berkhamsted School for Girls of which she is an old pupil, she gave 'one or two safe wrinkles gathered by making a great many mistakes myself over a long life'.

She said: 'If you find yourself in competition with men, never become aggressive in your rivalry. She who forces her point many well lose her advantage. You will gain far more by quietly holding to your convictions.

'But even this must be done with art, and above all with good humour. Never enlarge, except to a tried and trusted confidante, about your difficulties.'

Greeted by a crowd serenading her with 'Oh my darling Clementine!' she laughed and said she was neither 'lost', nor 'gone for ever'.

She can afford to laugh at the years because she has true beauty; and can afford to dispense with ceremony, because she has true dignity.

'I am no orator,' she once affirmed. 'If I say anything, I say what I like'—and that is a Churchill statement worthy of Winston himself.

Any woman with the temerity to describe that extraordinary man as being 'too chirpy' and to cope with his chirpiness is a force to be reckoned with. Little wonder that introducing her at a political meeting Lord Cottesloe declared:

'How she was able to do so much public work while at the same time looking after her man-eating tiger is one of the miracles of those war years.'

But even her 'man-eating tiger' of a husband was unaware of the extent of her work—she just didn't let him know, as Miss Edna Rowe, Hostels Adviser to the Y.W.C.A., witnessed for herself at Downing Street one day.

'We were both studying the plans of a hostel to be built at Cheltenham. The plans were all spread out on a table in her room, when Mr. Churchill marched in.

'Mrs. Churchill whipped round as the door opened, stood with her back to the table, and somehow managed to prevent him spotting the plans. Distracting his attention, she quickly answered the problem he had come to sort out, and practically shooed him out of the room without his even realizing it.

'She returned smiling, and this wonderful woman to whom so many people owe so much, said:

' "I didn't want him to see the plans. He mustn't know—he gets so cross if he thinks I'm doing too much." '

20

BITTER VICTORY

'WE are going to Paris!'—Winston announced to Clementine. His excitement at the prospect of visiting Paris for the first time since the Liberation was irrepressible.

Everything had been arranged. They were to go on 10 November; be present the following morning at a great Armistice Day military parade, and be seen by the largest possible number of people, without any previous announcement having been made.

Scotland Yard and the French police were worried. There were still large numbers of Germans in Paris and there was no doubt that an attempt might be made to assassinate Winston if he appeared in the streets.

Both he and the Cabinet were acquainted with the risk, and several members of the Cabinet pressed him not to go. He felt that he, as a symbol of Britain, should be there on the anniversary of Armistice Day, and that, in any case, there was danger in any large crowd.

He discussed the police warnings with Clementine, and explained his reasons for wanting to go. Unlike many of his well-intentioned Cabinet colleagues, she said nothing to dissuade him this time. She appreciated how great was his desire to share this day with millions of Parisians he had helped liberate, and realized how much sharing such a day of triumph meant to him. She started to pack for Winston, Mary, and herself.

In Paris, they found the entire first floor of the Quai d'Orsay at their disposal. But Winston's day was really made when Clementine, with a delighted grin, led him into the bathroom of their suite. What he saw there made him as happy as a schoolboy with a bag of sticky sweets. It was a golden bath. He was even more deliriously excited on being informed that she had discovered that the bath had been specially installed for Goering's personal use. And he was still more delighted on hearing that Anthony Eden's bath was only a silver one.

Next morning, Clementine, Winston, and Mary joined Madame and General de Gaulle for the drive to the Arc de Triomphe.

The welcome was overwhelming. Cheering, waving Parisians were everywhere—on the boulevards, hanging from windows, on every roof. From all sides they cried—'de Gaulle!—Churchill!'

At the Arc de Triomphe, they watched a march past lasting nearly an hour; then proceeded to the statue of Clemenceau to lay another wreath, and on to the tomb of Marshal Foch.

Following the Victory review seated beside Madame de Gaulle, Clementine watched Winston and the General as they drove, in open car, to the Arc de Triomphe to lay their wreath, and as together, defying any Nazi assassins who might have been left behind in the city, they walked half-a-mile down the Champs-Elysées to rejoin their wives.

After the ceremony, there was lunch at Rue St. Dominic —de Gaulle's headquarters. Once more, Clementine's cautionary warnings to keep on good terms with de Gaulle were heeded by Winston, and they hit it off well. Both were in excellent humour.

At the luncheon, Winston made a short speech in English. When they returned to their suite, Clementine suggested he make the next speech in French. She was sure the audience would love his fractured brand of French. He took her advice the next day, and French, as she is spoke by Winston, was a howling success.

Paris was crazy with joy. Winston and Clementine walked at every opportunity, and wherever they went in the city, thousands yelled themselves hoarse, trying to pass on to them some measure of their eternal gratitude.

*   *   *

Nazi Germany had been crushed, victory in Europe won, but Clementine knew better than anyone that, to Winston, the task was far from over.

For Winston, there were two victories yet to be achieved —the war with Japan and the reconstruction of Britain. But, with the coming of peace in Europe, he embarked on a nationwide election tour amid a delirium of welcome.

What neither he, nor Clementine, nor any of his entourage realized, was that the nation's new religion—Churchillism—was not reverence for a policy, but worship of a man.

The masses were still suspicious of the class he represented.

It is a notorious fact that the leader of a democracy usually suffers a steady decline in popularity during a war, and, as great as he was, Winston was not immune from the changing values of public opinion.

Even Lloyd George's popularity was at a low ebb in 1918.

Early in the war Winston had promised Clementine that he wouldn't commit the same mistake as Lloyd George had made in seeking to retain power once hostilities had ended. They both remembered only too well how, in the months that followed the First World War, Lloyd George's popularity and prestige vanished until he was finally dismissed from office.

Although preoccupied with the responsibilities of war, they were well aware of the wind of social change blowing through Britain, but neither doubted that the architect of victory would also be commissioned by the nation to build the peace. Both were confident that the people would continue to listen to the Churchill voice.

Winston had little time for internal affairs. Throughout the war, it was Clementine who kept him in touch with the masses. She began to caution him of the growing, and almost overwhelming desire of both working and middle classes for social reform. He accepted her advice but stressed his anxiety to avoid Party politics until the great task of reconstruction was well on its way. He wanted the great all-Party Coalition Cabinet to continue co-operation in solving the problems of the peace. 'At the very least, Clemmie,' he said, 'there should be no General Election until after the end of the war with Japan.'

Pressure within the Labour Party was too great—the Coalition Government was dissolved, and a Conservative 'caretaker' Government formed until such time as elections decided whom the people wished to rule.

Winston hated the idea of an election so soon when there was still so much to be done, in winning the peace. He was impatient with the election, irritated by it, and showed this

308

in many ways. As a result, much of the burden of his personal election arrangements fell on Clementine's shoulders. As always, she was ready to accept more than her share.

She knew that the war years had taken their toll of his strength and that, while in the past he had always treated an election as a good healthy British game, at this stage, he resented devoting precious time and energy to domestic front battles.

Together, they began the campaign in his own constituency of Woodford in Essex, where he was being opposed by a hopeful farmer. In spite of drizzling, miserable rain they had a tremendous welcome, and wherever he stopped to speak, Clementine held an umbrella over his head.

At unofficial halts he merely got out of the car, removed his famous square bowler hat, greeted constituents, and stepped back again into the car. In some places as they drove off, crowds sang 'For he's a jolly good fellow!' At Chigwell station they got out of the car and mounted into a grey open tourer from which he addressed the crowd.

It was then that he asked them to support his wife if he had to go away on 'international business'.

'We will, sir!' shouted the crowd.

He was in good form that day. 'You will all have to be quiet if my voice is to be heard; the young must have consideration for the old.'

And, taking off his bowler, he emphasized that his 'caretaker' Government consisted of 'the best brains he could find', by pointing at his own head. Realizing it might be taken personally, he said: 'I am of course, talking in general. I mean grey matter.'

Winston and Clementine perched themselves on the folded roof at the back of the car to acknowledge the cheers. At one stop, hat in hand and ignoring rain, he addressed the crowd saying: 'At my age, having already passed the allotted span, I might well have claimed relief from the burden which victory has not lightened. I feel, however, that my faculties and energies are as good as they have ever been. Therefore, unless relieved by the nation, I cannot shrink from the tasks which have devolved upon me.

'The war itself is not finished. The causes for which we drew the sword are not yet fully won—are not yet safe. I still hope to take my share in a peace which shall be both world wide and lasting, out of which will come victories and social progress not less than those in battle for which we are already well spoken of throughout the world.'

As he spoke, he ignored the rain, and avoided Clementine's offered umbrella protection until an old lady in the crowd called out: 'Please sir, do put on your hat. We don't want you to catch cold.'

Then, Winston and Clementine began a thousand-mile election tour of the cities and villages of Britain. But before the exhausting drive, they decided to spend a quiet week-end at Chequers. On the way, their car was diverted to Uxbridge, Beaconsfield, and Aylesbury, where whole populations turned out to greet them. At Uxbridge, they were almost torn from the car by over-enthusiastic crowds who had waited more than two hours.

People strained to touch their hands, and at one time, it was nearly impossible to proceed.

'Will you turn back?' Winston was asked. 'No, go on,' came the reply. And on the car went.

Standing up, he waved his bowler, while Clementine remained seated, waving and smiling to the crowd.

Suddenly the happy thousands roared and surged forward. Someone even tore the cigar from his fingers. Winston beamed ... they knew the answer of Uxbridge!

When the car stopped to enable him to speak a moment, he said: 'It was not by my desire that this election has come about, but we are bound from time to time to consult the people in this country.

'Irrespective of party, God bless you all.'

On went the car—on to High Wycombe where 15,000 waited outside the Red Lion Hotel—where Disraeli made his first political speech as a candidate for Wycombe in 1832.

Winston was puffing away at a new cigar. 'Where did Disraeli speak?' he inquired.

The spot was indicated to him. He entered the hotel, climbed briskly from a bedroom window, and crossed steps made of beer crates to position himself on the front of the platform beside the head of the large red lion where Disraeli had stood.

Clementine had cautioned Winston, with her unerring instinct, that with the war's end, the greatest desire of returning Service men and women, as well as civilians whose dearest possessions had been bombed, would be for homes. Remembering this, he told the crowd at High Wycombe: 'We must have the homes. There are half a million young men who want to marry, and half a million young women who want to have half a million young children as a first instalment. It will be a terrible thing if the British race ever fell behind its growth.

'I will do everything in human power, if I am charged with the responsibility for power, to get the maximum number of houses in the shortest possible time.'

'And if there are combines, rings, or monopolies, we will march through them and over them as our troops have marched over so many rivers and fortified lines.

'I am going shortly to Berlin to meet Mr. Truman and Marshal Stalin. Because the election was on—and I have no right to say I shall be returned, that I shall have the honour of representing the country—I said to my colleague Mr. Attlee: "Come along with me as a friend and counsellor" and he said "I will."

'I cannot conceive how we could differ. Now I hear with surprise that he may not be a free agent, that there may be forces behind him to tell him what to do.

'We must have good solid ground for speaking, and whoever speaks must speak in the name of this country.'

After the week-end's rest at Chequers, their thousand-mile tour began. It was an informal friendly pilgrimage. Wherever a crowd gathered, Winston and Clementine stopped for a 'chat'. Sarah also joined them on the tour.

They were already an hour behind their time-table when an eleven-year-old crippled boy hobbled out on crutches almost into the path of the car.

Clementine, seeing the child, ordered the car to stop. It came alongside the flushed and excited boy who with trembling hands thrust a bunch of red roses, poppies, white stocks, and blue pansies into her hands, then shyly asked whether the Prime Minister would give him his autograph. Winston drew his fountain-pen from his pocket and the boy, whose name was Roy Clarke, proudly produced a picture of himself. Winston took it on his knee and, on the leaf facing Roy's photograph, inscribed 'Winston S. Churchill'.

'Have you lost your foot in an accident?' inquired Clementine.

Roy replied that he had been paralysed from birth.

'That is a great misfortune,' replied Clementine.

'Is everything possible being done for him? Is he having the best medical attention?' she asked the boy's mother who now stood beside him.

Clementine smiled at Roy and said: 'You heard about President Roosevelt. He suffered from the same affliction as you, yet look how he triumphed over it. Whenever you feel downhearted about your trouble, always think of that great man.'

By this time a crowd of neighbours and friends had gathered round the car, but before Winston gave the order to continue, he asked Roy to stand on the running-board so they could have a photograph taken together.

The first day of the tour they drove through the Midlands —Rugby, Leamington, Warwick, Coventry, Birmingham— they made about fifteen stops every day and Winston, Clementine, and Sarah spoke to as many people as possible. The following day, they headed for Leeds, Halifax, Bradford, Preston, then on to Glasgow and Edinburgh.

A special train followed them from point to point throughout the tour. They slept in the train and in it Winston continued with official work. The tour imposed a great physical strain on him, for, in addition to the long road journeys and the speechmaking each day, he was constantly occupied with Government business until midnight or the early hours.

With each electioneering day that passed, Clementine observed Winston's impatience grow with what he felt to be an ill-timed interruption of the completion of the war.

Warned Winston in a message to electors: 'We have to put this land of ours on its feet again. On September 3rd, 1939, we began an heroic crusade for right and freedom. Our hard task is not yet finished.

'We have still to beat the Japanese, to work with our Allies, to ensure that victory leads to a durable peace, to put this land of ours on its feet again.

'Believing that these tasks call for continued national unity, I invited the leaders of the Labour and opposition Liberal parties to stay in the Government to help us to

312

finish the job. They refused.'

And then, in a radio broadcast, an angry Winston began to make personal attacks on Labour leaders who had served with him in the Coalition Government.

He warned that Socialism would result in a 'Gestapo'. His tactics began to boomerang, public opinion began to harden against him.

Addressing a number of women's meetings, Clementine sensed this changing opinion and warned Winston. She knew in her heart that these attacks of his were resentment at being forced, at this crucial stage, to engage in domestic warfare instead of international warfare. She knew he was fighting the election with little of his customary humour and tolerance.

Only Winston knew how enormous had been Clemmie's influence and contribution to his own career. He normally treasured and respected her advice, and would quickly heed a gentle admonition: 'Winston, I wouldn't say that.' Now, almost for the first time, her advice seemed to fall on deaf ears—ears that were only listening for the sound of final and certain victory in war.

People were saying—'Where is the Churchill of yester-year?' Many said: 'We can make allowances for him as the self-appointed hammer of the Socialists, but we remember when he had anti-Socialist virus in as violent a form as this, twenty years ago.' People began to wonder what had become of the gay, humorous, grinning Churchill who hither-to could always see the funny side even of higher states-manship.

Where was the man who could pause at the end of a great passage about fighting on the beaches, in the fields, etc., to add under his breath in the hearing of his colleagues who knew our defencelessness: 'and we'll hit them on the head with bottles. We have nothing else.' Or the man who had announced at so desperate a moment that we were all ready for the invader—'and so are the fishes'.

There was no glimpse of that Churchill in any of his election speeches. He had become harsh, humourless, with-out a quip—his campaign one unrelieved blistering of the Socialists. What had happened? What had clouded the happy side of his genius?

More than anyone Clementine had the answer, knew

how worried he was about future world security. Nevertheless, she was still convinced he would win—even the pessimists were certain he would get a majority of thirty seats. Overwhelming defeat was never seriously considered.

Said Winston: 'It is no use people saying you can vote for the Liberals and Labour and "the old man" will be in anyhow.

'It is no use people thinking I can continue to serve unless I have a great majority when I return to the House.'

Clementine made her own eve-of-poll tour of Winston's personal constituency at Woodford, addressing six mass meetings.

Speaking in the open air at Wanstead Park, she said: 'I would like my husband to have a very great majority, and a great demonstration of your confidence in him. I would like very much for him to know that when you vote for him you do it because you feel he has done a good job of work, and that he will serve the nation well in the future.'

Then she added: 'I deplore the fact that an election is being held before the termination of war with Japan.

'It is not the doing of my husband. He got on extremely well with all Parties.'

For years, she had given up platform speaking. She had returned to the platform for her son Randolph to help him fight a by-election, and that had been the first occasion Randolph heard his mother speak in public. She faced a stormy meeting and handled hecklers like a veteran.

When she made a political speech, she wasn't just voicing her husband's opinions. The opinions were her own. While Winston, in any election, busied himself in the main with national issues, she would personally lead the local fight in his own constituency of Woodford. Her speeches didn't echo round the world like Winston's utterances, but they deserved to.

So self-effacing has she always been, that when, on occasion, she spoke in public with skill, wit, and understanding, and an obvious gift of oratory, audiences were visibly surprised. It was no case of Winston's oratory rubbing off on her, for had she not, even in the earliest days of their marriage, proved herself a capable, confident, courageous speaker?

She had a reputation for shyness, but it was a deceptive

shyness, as electioneering crowds and guests who came to their home soon discovered.

When she felt she could be of value, she never hesitated to fight on political platforms for Winston, and for her son Randolph.

She was the power behind the throne—but in a completely different way. Her strength gave Winston even greater strength, but her strength was, above all, her ability to be a wife and a mother—her ability to be, there whenever he needed her.

Now, in this crucial 1945 Parliamentary battle, Winston needed all the help she could give.

As she made her election eve tour, she spoke from the back of a lorry. She climbed aboard and, smiling from beneath an umbrella, appealed to constituents—'give my husband a great solid magnificent vote.

'I would like you to put a cross against his name, firstly, to show that you think he and the Government have fought the war manfully and with skill, and secondly, to show you believe that he will be able to bring the resources of his brains, imagination, and driving power to the tasks of peace as he has brought them to the tasks of war.'

She paused, and added, with a hint of wistfulness: 'It would make me very happy if, at the end of my husband's life, he were to be associated with the great reforms which he proposed in his four-year plan issued two years ago.'

Clementine noted the growing public reaction to the bitter campaign he had been waging when he addressed an open air mass meeting at Walthamstow Stadium. It was Winston's own home ground—his own constituency area—yet hecklers from all sides started to shout him down. The opposition and interruptions were so bad that he could scarcely finish his speech.

Two days later, at Tooting, London, a firework was thrown at him. It hit him in the face, and exploded a few inches away. Miraculously, they were unhurt.

On 5 July, the people voted. It was a big day for Winston and Clementine.

They spent it together. First at the polling booth in Woodford.

Outside she made him put on his hat because of the biting wind. He looked tired, but she went on smiling. She was still smiling when Winston told his local party workers later: 'My dear wife has come to my aid and has taken a definite and recognizable part.' Clementine added to the helpers gathered around her: 'I am sure you will be prepared to give my husband your prayers and help.'

The poll was to remain sealed until the 26th of that month to enable the complete votes of the Forces overseas to be counted.

Meanwhile Clementine was invited to Oxford University to receive the honorary degree of Doctor of Civil Law.

The Chancellor, Lord Halifax, greeted her as 'The consort of our Jove the unconquerable, and one who watched over and sustained him while he sustained a tottering world.'

Winston, who accompanied her to the ceremony, was given a special seat in the Sheldonian Theatre so that immediately on receiving her degree, Clementine could obey the injunction of the Public Orator to: 'Let her assume the same silks as her husband and take her customary place— at his side.'

At the ceremony, the Public Orator of the University painted a word picture of the 'man about the Churchill house....'

'Preoccupied with problems of world government, he forgets there is a time for meals, or he'll look in for a meal unexpectedly, so that his wife must hoard her rations for him ounce by ounce.

'And all of a sudden he's out of the house and off for a conference anywhere and everywhere. What could a wife do? Either she goes with him or she fetches him home from Egypt more dead than alive, or, to get her own back drives off to Moscow herself.

'Besides, he's a perfect volcano, scattering cigar ash all over the house.'

She had seldom come in for personal honour, but Winston was present on this rare occasion when she did step forward in front of him for personal recognition.

She could have basked in her own limelight, but she chose to walk in his shadow.

In honouring her, she was described as a wife with a difference. When her husband came home from the office, the problem he brought with him was the fate of civiliza-

316

tion. When he was late for dinner or dropped ash on the carpet it was perhaps, because he was preoccupied with the worries of the world.

But Clementine followed her husband, forsaking much to find everything.

She had spent a lifetime learning how to keep one small corner of the world private and peaceful for him.

'A home,' she once said, 'should be happy, gay, and comfortable, where children can be brought up, and where true peace and contentment can be enjoyed.'

She made just such a home for Winston.

With her that day, receiving honorary Doctorates of Civil Law, were Admiral Lord Louis Mountbatten; Admiral King and Admiral Stark of the U.S. Navy; General Spaatz of the U.S. Air Force; Admiral of the Fleet Viscount Cunningham of Hyndhope; Admiral of the Fleet Sir James Somerville; General Crerar of the Canadian Army; Marshal of the R.A.F. Lord Portal of Hungerford; Air Chief Marshal Lord Dowding; Sir Ramaswami Mudaljr, Head of the Indian Delegation to the United Nations; and Lieutenant-Colonel Nawab Sir Malik Khizar Hayat Khan Tiwana, Premier of the Punjab.

*   *   *

The 1945 General Election results were still a question mark, and the Potsdam Conference was due to open in the latter half of July, so they decided to accept the offer of a brief holiday at a château in France owned by a retired industrialist. It was three miles from the Spanish frontier. With Clementine and Mary, Winston, who had badly needed this break, began to unwind a little, although one day at lunch he remarked: 'Soon we shall have to go back to London to see if they've thrown me in the gutter.'

When the time came to leave for Postsdam, Clementine needed to get back to London, so she sent Mary to Berlin to look after Winston.

Even Stalin was convinced Winston would be returned as Premier, asserting that all his information, from Communist and other sources, confirmed his belief that he would win by a majority of about eighty.

Winston preferred not to prophesy. He wouldn't even forecast the outcome to Clementine, because, he said, he was unsure how the Forces had voted. On 25 July, he arrived back at Northolt Airport. They dined alone that night.

The Conservative Party's Central Office was confident the Party would retain a substantial majority.

Winston's famous Map Room at the Ministry of Defence headquarters had been temporarily requisitioned to deal, this time, with a political battlefield.

On the night of 26 July—results night—by the time it was time to retire, the picture was still obscure. Winston kissed Clementine 'good-night', and went to bed in the belief that the people would wish him to continue his work. He hoped it would be possible to reconstitute the National Coalition Government in the proportions of the new House of Commons.

Just before dawn he awoke with a sharp stab of almost physical pain. A hitherto subconscious conviction that he had been beaten dominated his mind. He was suddenly sure that all the pressure of great events, on and against which he had for so long mentally maintained his 'flying speed', was about to cease; that he would fall, and that the power to shape the future would be denied him.

The knowledge and experience he had gathered, the authority and goodwill he had earned in so many countries would vanish. He fell asleep again, and didn't wake until nine o'clock.

Clementine and Winston entered the Map Room on that fateful 26 July. Results were streaming in.

In his siren suit, Winston sat in the Prime Minister's chair watching election results coming through and being chalked up on a giant scoreboard on the wall.

Clementine went with Mary to Woodford where a Northamptonshire farmer named Hancock, with no real political experience and no hope of toppling his opponent, was giving Winston a run in his own constituency.

As the votes were counted, she became increasingly alarmed at the size of the steadily mounting poll in favour of her husband's unknown rival. She was so shaken that she telephoned Winston, to hear equally staggering news of Socialist gains pouring in from all over.

She didn't wait for the Woodford result. She had to be with Winston.

318

She found him dazed, staring almost hypnotically at the white chalk figures on the wall charts opposite him.

As Duncan and Diana Sandys hurried in, he was pacing about the room. Repeatedly, Clementine went over to whisper something to him.

The warning trend she had telephoned from Woodford continued to be confirmed as result after result was recorded.

One of the staff brought the Woodford figures—his opponent had polled 10,488 votes! Even on his own home ground, people had turned so heavily on him, and politically smacked him in the face, after all his prodigious efforts on their behalf throughout the war years.

The votes took his constituency opponent nowhere near winning the seat, but there were, nevertheless, 10,488 hurtful stabs at Winston and Clementine's hearts.

The overall results were clear.

By noon defeat was a fact. To the astonishment of the whole world, he had been hounded from office!

Winston and Clementine lunched alone. There was little conversation. Looking at Winston she said: 'It may well be a blessing in disguise.' He replied: 'At the moment it seems quite effectively disguised.'

After the result, he left her to go to his room and write one of the most difficult messages of his life.

It was issued that night from Downing Street. It said:

'The decision of the British people has been recorded in the votes counted today.

'I have therefore laid down the charge which was placed upon me in darker times.

'I regret I have not been permitted to finish the work against Japan. For this, however, all plans and preparations have been made, and the results may come much quicker than we have hitherto been entitled to expect.

'Immense responsibilities abroad and at home fall upon the new Government and we must all hope that they will be successful in bearing them.

'It only remains for me to express to the British people, for whom I have acted in these perilous years, my profound gratitude for their unflinching, unswerving support which they have given me during my task, and for the many expressions of kindness which they have shown towards their servant.'

So confident had they been of victory that Clementine had even arranged a small family dinner-party to celebrate the results with a few friends. The dinner was held. Winston was almost silent throughout; stunned by his rejection. She feared the effect of the shock.

As much as he wanted to be present when Japan surrendered unconditionally, Winston's considerations of duty took, as always, precedence. Constitutionally he could have awaited the meeting of Parliament before taking his dismissal from the House of Commons. This would have enabled him to present, before resignation, Japan's surrender, but the need for Britian to be represented with proper authority at the Potsdam Conference made all delay contrary to the public interest. Moreover, 'The verdict of the electors had been so overwhelmingly expressed that I did not wish to remain even for an hour responsible for their affairs,' said Winston.

Therefore, having asked for an audience, he drove to Buckingham Palace to tender his resignation to the King.

Winston's four-year-old namesake grandson had to have things carefully explained to him when his grandfather was startlingly no longer Prime Minister.

Winston Junior listened to a long explanation from his grandmother of just what change of government means. Finally, asked if he understood he said, 'Yes, I see. I've got a new grandpa now.'

More than anything else it was the armies of freedom that Winston had led for so long, the young men and women of the Services, who had swung the vote towards Socialism. In their eyes Winston's stature had been temporarily diminished by his own insistence on the introduction of narrower animosities in the Party fight, thereby allowing greater national issues to slip into the background.

Clementine bore the terrible cruelty of the moment with him. She felt, just as deeply, this harsh snatching away of responsibility at the very climax of the war, with Japan still to be finished off, and the peace yet to be won. But, as a politician's wife, she knew gratitude belongs to history, not politics. Firmly, sympathetically, she emphasized to him that the crushing defeat inflicted upon his Party in no way brought into question his place in history, nor in the affection and gratitude of the people who had followed him, nor in national pride. The universal acclaim with which he had been received throughout their election travels had clearly shown that, she stressed.

Winston knew that in her was a spirit that equalled his own. In triumph she was gracious and proud, with a tinge of humility. In disaster, defeat, and disappointment, never disheartened.

She followed and fought for him and with him in the face of every kind of opposition and insult. There had been many moments in their lives when, more than anything else, he needed to be understood. She had given him that understanding; defended him against his enemies and against those who, in their ignorance and prejudice towards genius, would have cast him aside.

Throughout a career full of contrast and frequently punctuated with disasters that would have broken the strongest heart, she never wavered. Nor did her faith in him, or in the future, waver now.

Many of their friends urged him to leave Parliament and devote himself to writing the history of the war. Clementine absolutely disagreed, although she didn't really want him to be Premier again. He had served his country magnificently yet the people's 'thanks' had been vicious rejection. Nevertheless she said:

'For Winston to leave Parliament would be unthinkable —he is a child of the House of Commons.'

Nor would Winston retire from the leadership of the Opposition, she asserted. 'A little later,' he said, 'it would be easy for me to retire gracefully in an odour of civic freedoms, and the plan crossed my mind frequently. I feel now, however, that the situation is so serious and what may have to come so grave, that I am resolved towards carrying the flag so long as I have the necessary energy.'

As for resigning from Party leadership, he declared: 'my horse may not be a very good one, but at least it is better than being in the infantry.'

Winston and Clementine Churchill moved out of 10 Downing Street.

'We shall be coming back, Clemmie,' he said as the door shut behind them.

21

THE ORDER OF THE BOOT

THE big inquest began. Civilian and Service men and women gloried triumphantly in the Socialist victory, but, beneath it all, they were ashamed of what they had done to Winston.

They strove to clear their consciences by echoing the Labour Party's declaration that:

'He was not the man to correct the social ills of the past.'

Conservatives explained his defeat by saying that Britain's anti-capitalists had spent the war years undermining his abilities as a domestic politician with carefully sown propaganda. Others explained it as a desire of the people for a change after six years of war, adding that if Winston had not assumed leadership of the same Party that had been in power at the outbreak of war, he would have been returned as Prime Minister. People told themselves that they hadn't voted against him, but against the Party.

Winston was offered the Royal honour of the Order of the Bath. Declining, he said: 'How can I accept the Order of the Bath, Clemmie, when the people of England have just given me the order of the boot?'

The day he strode back into the House of Commons, no longer Prime Minister, but only Leader of the Opposition, Clementine sat watching from the Distinguished Strangers' Gallery in the House.

As he entered the Chamber, the bitterness of his defeat was made even more bitter, and her strength went out to him as he had to endure 'The Red Flag' being sung by some of the victorious Socialist M.P.'s in the place which, throughout his life, he had regarded as the temple of his faith.

He glared his contempt at the Government benches across the floor of the Chamber, and at this insult to Parliamentary tradition and glory.

In the midst of the war he had worked out a plan for peacetime development of Britain. He had believed he would see it through, with at least two Parliaments—ten years. Now the nation had spurned Winston the politician, although it still adored and respected Winston the man.

In the very moment of victory, Clementine had to witness the worst experience of Winston's political life, as the triumphant and crowded Socialist benches roared with laughter at one of his fiercest attacks on the Attlee Government.

The gusts of laughter stung him like a whiplash. He stared incredulously.

When she joined him outside the Chamber, he kept repeating, unbelievingly: 'They *laughed* at me ... they *laughed* at me!'

Astonishment turned to bitterness, and this time Clementine was too terribly wounded by his rejection herself to be able, in some way, to soften the terrible blow for him.

When, with great throngs massed ouside Buckingham Palace, the King received Winston at the war's end, he offered him any honour he would care to take—including a Dukedom. Winston reportedly replied: 'If your Majesty would allow me to decline—I have work to do yet.'

The King did not press him.

Winston had no intention of being kicked out of Downing Street, and then promoted out of the House of Commons—no matter how well meant the promotion offered.

At first his resentment goaded him into frequent ill-tempered, almost childish, outbursts in Parliament against his opponents. Before long, even many of their closest friends cautioned Clementine that in his desire to damage the Socialists Winston was doing and saying things that only damaged his own Party.

For the first time since he had taken the reins of supreme leadership, 'the Old Man' was being regarded by many prominent Tories as a liability, and blatant hints were dropped that he should retire from Party leadership.

Winston had other ideas. His favourite retort to those who suggested retirement was: 'Gladstone was Premier when he was eighty and *I am a youngster*!'

Then, as if to ram home his point, he stuck out his tongue in a schoolboy gesture of dişdain to Socialist Ministers seated on the Front Bench opposite him. His sense of rejection had even begun to swamp his sense of Parliamentary dignity.

It was then that Clementine decided to make him forsake the Parliamentary arena a while and take a well-earned rest and holiday.

'Man has only to conquer his last and worst enemy—himself,' her husband had once said. She knew he must either conquer this bitterness, or destroy himself.

He had always told her:

'Never give in! Never give in! Never, Never, Never, Never!—in nothing great or small, large or petty—never give in except to convictions of honour and good sense.'

She was determined not to let *his* spirit give in. Although in his seventies, he was still so vital, so versatile, so full of the future.

For good or ill, he had always looked vigorously ahead.

Then people whom she had never met, whose names she did not know, came to her aid. Winston became the man on the whole world's conscience—thousands of letters in every language and from every land poured into their home, with messages of sympathy at his repudiation after victory; gratitude for his years of leadership, encouragement for the future.

Clementine took the letters to him, made him read handfuls, read dozens of them to him herself.

The flow of 'thank you for freedom' gifts swelled into a flood. A man in Portugal sent him 116 gallons of old port wine; the Stockowners' Association of Australia sent him a kangaroo; Spain sent the stuffed head of a bull that had been born with a white V on its forehead; Jamaica sent enough cigars to keep him puffing happily for a year; people of New Zealand sent a generous gift of money which Clementine gave to St. Mary's Hospital in London—the hospital at which Sir Alexander Fleming had discovered that great life-saving secret weapon of war—Penicillin; an elderly woman living in London sent her precious Admiral de Ruyter chair, plus a beautiful dessert service for Clementine. From King Ibn Saud came a jewelled sword and dagger. From Switzerland came a perpetual motion clock, impossible to wind, but guaranteed to run for ever. A group of Maoris in New Zealand offered a male or female kiwi. Each day brought a fresh offering of gifts from the great and humble all over the world, to the greatest man of our time.

Clementine used them to breathe new fire, new fight, into a dispirited Winston.

Invitations came with almost every post from the United States. 'This is just the change you need,' said Clementine, so they travelled to the U.S., where he accepted honorary degrees from several American universities.

Finally, at Westminster College, in Fulton, Missouri, her wisdom in persuading him temporarily to leave the British political scene bore fruit—the great warning voice of Winston Churchill—the voice that had shouted to awaken the world of the thirties to the creeping menace of Fascism—startled the world again with a warning of the growing shadow of Communism.

Clementine knew that if Winston so frequently did not see eye to eye with his contemporaries, it was because he so often saw further ahead. When victory was in our grasp, he looked beyond it and saw that Soviet Russia had become a 'mortal danger to the free world', but the same peoples to whom his words had been lifebelts in the turbulence of war did not want to listen any more. As on so many other occasions throughout his career, conveniently deaf ears preferred not to hear his uncomfortable prophecies, while many who did denounced, derided, or ignored them. People wanted no more talk of war; they wanted to enjoy their newly restored normality. It took immense moral courage at such a time to cry aloud that danger again threatened, that preparedness was still necessary.

Clementine read the first draft of his historic Fulton speech, and realized it was certain to meet with harsh criticism. She was also just as certain that her husband would be, as he had been so many times before, vindicated by events. As she watched him rise to speak before the distinguished audience at Fulton, she could sense the unspoken question on everyone's lips: 'Had the great man lost his grip?'

She had already heard him rehearse before her in the privacy of their room the tremendous answer he was about to give them.

'Last time I saw it all coming and cried aloud to my own fellow countrymen and to the world, but no one paid any attention.... If the Western democracies stand together in strict adherence to the principles of the United Nations

325

Charter their influence for furthering those principles will be immense, and no one is likely to molest them. If however, they become divided or falter in their duty and if these all-important years are allowed to slip away—then indeed catastrophe may overwhelm us all....'

His call at Fulton gave birth to the North Atlantic Treaty Organization; to the Marshall Plan; it inspired the great airlift to Berlin; halted the march of Communism in Western Europe.

Once again his vision lit the way ahead, and his pulse had exploded like a cannon beat through fainter hearts.

At the very moment when the Stalin régime still appeared to be our ally, Winston could foresee the Cold War, and fearlessly said so in defiance of current popular belief.

'I have not always been wrong!' he added.

This was no more a dispirited, politically embittered Churchill. Here he was, again in the forefront, fighting for the things he cherished most—freedom, democracy.

But Clementine still considered it too soon to return to London and the Parliamentary fray.

She insisted on taking him on holiday.

Airport authorities fussed around him to see if they could be of service. Winston replied: 'You are very kind. I do not need anything, and you must remember that I am no longer a very important person.'

He still received full V.I.P. treatment, with flowers for Clementine and Customs officers apologizing for bothering them. They even changed the aircraft at his request and altered the lunch menus aboard the plane.

Then they became known as 'the Prisoners of the Château' in Switzerland.

At Château Choisi, on the shores of Lake Leman, scores of armed police patrolled the grounds, and police speedboats constantly manoeuvred within fifty yards of the shore.

Police built a nest in a high tree in the château's grounds from which a look-out man could survey surrounding territory and observe every movement. Miles of territory around the château were marked off as a no-man's land on which neither pedestrian nor car was permitted to loiter.

All this security was just too much for Clementine. She asked the police to relax some of the precautions, 'otherwise your over-zealousness will spoil the holiday', she said.

She supervised the refurnishing of the château with price-less Louis XV furniture obligingly loaned by local inhabitants. She had a bar built in one room and stocked it with an extensive range of wines, aperitifs, brandies, and champagnes.

An album, among their most treasured possessions, contains a record of this visit as seen through the eyes of school children.

When the schoolmaster of the little village of Emmenbrucke asked his pupils, as a drawing lesson, to illustrate Mr. Churchill's Swiss holiday, the well-known characteristics readily came to their pencils. There were drawings of Winston sunning himself, or striding down the street with his coat tails flapping, or sailing on the lake in a bow tie, shirt-sleeves and braces, or wearing various strange hats.

The album containing these drawings was presented to them by the schoolmaster of Emmenbrucke 'as a token of affection from the children of Switzerland'.

After Switzerland, Clemmie took Winston to other beauty spots where he could relax.

Unfortunately, privacy was a luxury they seldom got. On a typically 'strictly private' visit to Aix-en-Provence, within hours the first twelve 'See Churchill excursion' motor coaches arrived, some from two hundred miles away. By the afternoon their car was halted every few yards by cheering people as they drove round the town. By the evening, hundreds were clamouring to register at the same hotel, and masses of roses and gladioli were being delivered in almost endless stream to their suite from people who had somehow managed to discover Clementine's favourite flowers.

When, accompanied by Mary and her husband, they arrived to occupy what they thought was a small suite of rooms, they found instead a whole floor of the best hotel reserved for them, with each room containing valuable pictures and furniture lent by the townspeople who had got wind of their coming. And the town council, obligingly striving to ensure for them privacy and freedom of movement, supplied a dozen police on motor-cycles to follow them everywhere!

'Holiday rejoicing is necessary to human spirit,' said Winston, and Clementine Churchill knew how to cater for the holiday spirit in him.

She firmly believed in husband and wife holidaying together and seldom took a holiday alone. She liked to be around when Winston felt a desire to relax in the sun, for even on holiday he required everything about him to work with almost clockwork precision. His idea of a holiday was a mixture of work and play. Physically and mentally he was far too active to remain 'unemployed' for long in restful idleness.

When they took off on holiday, a staff, including a principal private secretary and masses of documents, also frequently took off with them. As far as Clementine was concerned preparations for a Churchill holiday virtually entailed the organization and launching of a combined operation of which she was the officer-in-charge.

Winston always expected everything, but everything, necessary for his personal comfort, convenience, and efficiency to be on hand, and Clementine's meticulous nature ensured that almost every possible eventuality was provided for. For one visit, when they and their staff occupied eighteen rooms in an hotel in Syracuse, she sent thirty-two trunks and suitcases ahead by rail.

On holiday she would decline all official invitations and see that he remained undisturbed in his room with every newspaper she could get for him until about 11 a.m. when he usually reappeared in his favourite large yellow straw hat.

Afternoons, they usually preferred to take a motor-boat or car ride, with easel and paint, to some quiet spot where he could indulge in his favourite pastime.

'Winston likes to eat, sleep, and enjoy the sun, and add to his large collection of paintings,' said Clementine.

'He says that trying to paint a picture is like trying to fight a battle. It is, if anything, more exciting than fighting it successfully; but the principle is the same. It is the same kind of problem as unfolding a long, sustained, intellectual argument.'

When Winston felt the urge to paint he was usually left alone in peace and quiet. Holidays he used for reading and revising proofs of his latest literary work. They also offered the opportunity for considering future strategy. Away from the detailed work of Westminster he could paint in the political scene with those broad imaginative strokes of which

328

he was master.

When the Churchills took a holiday, nothing was too much trouble for anyone to make it enjoyable.

The French air base at Marrakesh altered its routine because planes taking off at 7.30 a.m. woke up holiday-making Winston. Clementine, informing the French Air Force authorities of the disturbance, said: 'I do not know if you can help in any way.'

'At your service, Madam,' the Colonel at the training base replied, and issued the order: 'No planes to take off before 9 a.m. while he is here.'

The Marrakesh Hotel, Mamounia, also pulled out all stops—the hotel's French pastrycook produced a magnificent painting palette with a miniature easel, paintbrush, and a picture of Rabat on the easel. It was entirely made of coloured sugar, including the picture on the easel, and for Clementine there were some red sugar roses, of which there were also masses of real specimens in her rooms.

When they arrived at Marrakesh on holiday, a crowd of hundreds on the airfield shouted 'Vive Churchill!' as their plane came out of the sky; a French air force guard of honour was waiting; the British Ambassador motored 200 miles from Rabat to meet them; King Mohammed of Morocco sent a plane-load of V.I.P.'s to greet them, and the Governor of Marrakesh was on hand too.

They drove to the hotel along the sandy, palm-tree-lined road in the Governor's car flanked by uniformed Moroccan outriders. As they walked into the hotel, an American business man on holiday stepped from among the onlookers and pressed a cigar into Winston's hand.

Clementine had also packed something special for him. A case of his favourite champagne.

They had first visited Marrakesh in 1936, after Lloyd George had praised its beauty. Clementine and Winston particularly loved to visit the 'Square of Death' in Marrakesh—an incredible African market-place with the wares spread on the ground or on little stalls. All Africa seems to make for this famous square, which is like a scene from the *Arabian Nights* with its snake charmers, magicians, conjurers, story-tellers, and fire-eaters.

'I must paint it, Clemmie,' Winston said, as they walked one afternoon through the packed square. The question was how? The solution came after Clementine had conferred with a commercially minded shopkeeper in the square, who, appreciating her offered opportunity of making a profit without selling any of his wares, temporarily closed up to let Winston use his shop as a painter's vantage-point.

Another of their favourite holiday calls was Lord Beaverbrook's fifteen-room villa, at Cap d'Ail.

Surrounded by municipal counsellors and wearing his official tri-colour sash, M. Leon Gramaglia, Mayor of Cap d'Ail, always waited for the Churchills—Winston was honorary mayor of Cap d'Ail.

M. Gramaglia welcomed them in front of the Beaverbrook villa. Lord Beaverbrook usually contrived to be away when they came so that they could enjoy the run of the house to themselves.

A small motor-car with only a driving-seat and an armchair in the back, which Lord Beaverbrook used to go down to his private beach, was at their disposal there.

Picnicking and sightseeing together was one of their greatest delights. Clementine never forgot to pack his pet pair of brilliant red bathing trunks and the thermometer he used to test the Mediterranean's temperature before taking a dip.

At one time, when illness compelled Clementine to take a rest without Winston, she went to Ceylon. It was suggested that she be away for a couple of months but she felt three weeks would be long enough apart from him. Arriving in Colombo, she said she was 'looking forward to seeing a rogue elephant'—an elephant of savage temper living apart from the herd.

'But I will run and climb a tree if he tries to catch me,' she laughed.

Little is heard of Clementine's own state of health. The years of intense strain exacted one particular kind of toll on her—painful attacks of neuritis which often compelled her to cancel engagements for weeks.

On the whole her health had always been good, but from time to time, when she suffered bouts of neuritis, she wanted to be alone—to go to a nursing home, or to a spa; or suggested that Winston went away for a holiday. She preferred to suffer in silence, away from everyone else—including Winston.

Because of her neuritis she once had to decline an invitation to a Mansion House luncheon given in honour of the Queen, and her sixty-ninth birthday party had to be cancelled because of it.

Whenever a bout of neuritis prevented her from joining Winston on holiday, he would telephone every evening at 9.30 just to say 'goodnight, darling'.

During one of their holidays together they, and Sarah, made up a party with the Duke and Duchess of Windsor to celebrate New Year's Eve at Monte Carlo's Sporting Club.

At midnight everyone rose from the tables, linked hands, and sang 'Auld Lang Syne'. Suddenly the entire four hundred people present stood up, and turning towards Clementine and Winston, sang 'For they are jolly good fellows'. Winston rose to make his 'V' sign while Clementine and Sarah trapped large balloons from among hundreds released, and bust them over his head.

'Taking him away for a long time during that crucial period in his life, following his 1945 election defeat, was a deliberate policy on Clementine's part,' said their friend Sir Tom O'Brien, 'and it showed her political and personal judgement at its best. In her wisdom, she took him from the scene of his victory and of his defeat. Had she left him to wander all the time round the House of Commons, God knows what would have happened. Had she let him remain in Parliament during that period, his life would almost certainly have ended in tragedy because he was eating himself up with bitterness.

'He kept repeating over and over, "When I was turned out of office, I thought it was a very hard thing, after all I had done."

'Had he remained much longer in the House of Commons in the state of mind he was in, he might have destroyed his legend because his pain and feeling of ingratitude at being discarded in the election was making him lash out wildly and affecting his sense of statesmanship and diplomacy.

'There was no question that she saved his mind, saved his dignity. He certainly could not have concentrated on his historic books later had she not taken him away and helped him clear his mind and heart of the terrible bitterness that had taken possession of him. Had it not been for the en-

331

forced series of holidays she made him take from 1945 on; had he stayed in London, and rumbled through the House, he would undoubtedly have become a corroded force—the iron would have entered his soul, and he wouldn't have been the great post-war statesman he became when he was elected Prime Minister for the second time. In my view, all that is due to his wife. Her wisdom, her assessment of the situation, and her realization that her husband was growing bitterer and bitterer, made her decide and say: "This has got to stop"—and stopped it was.

'Wherever they travelled, during their first post-war round of holidays, they received the acclaim and blessings of peoples he helped to free from tyranny. The gratitude of these people helped Clementine breathe new life, new fight, back into Winston.'

Her 'let's-get-away-from-it-all' treatment after his terrible post-war General Election defeat worked, and soon he was ready for anything and anyone.

22

A MAN ABOUT THE HOUSE

IN October 1945 the Churchills moved into a town house, 28 Hyde Park Gate, a quiet cul-de-sac near Kensington Gardens and only about fifteen minutes by car from the Houses of Parliament. Using short cuts, the chauffeur could bring the journey down to seven minutes, which suited Winston very well, especially in the event of sudden calls to a Commons division.

Modest yet spacious, the house has the graceful high ceilings which Clementine and Winston liked. There are twelve rooms, which Clementine had decorated in soft shades of peach and cream. Most of the floors are of polished oak.

As you enter the hall you find yourself on a balcony, and you descend a staircase to the dining-room below. Twenty guests could be accommodated comfortably around its beautiful oak table.

From the dining-room, french windows open on to a walled garden where trees shade a grass plot surrounded by rockeries and ferns. Though it is fine for the dogs to play in, neither Winston nor Clementine ever devoted much time to the little garden—it was too cramped for their liking.

Clementine divided the house into eight bedrooms and three reception rooms, including the dining-room.

As in every Churchill house they installed a large library, and quarters for the secretaries. The main difference between Hyde Park Gate and her other homes was that Clementine introduced a note of modernity, and installed fitted furniture in many of the rooms.

She transformed an awkward little room in the house into a delightful intimate room, furnishing it with a long table and putting fitted seats behind it—the room was like a super Pullman railway carriage with an attraction all its own.

Clementine was having tea with a visitor in this room

one afternoon when in burst a jacketless Winston in his shirtsleeves calling—'Clemmie! Clemmie! Where are you?'

As he came in, Clementine sprang up to introduce a Winston slightly surprised at finding himself semi-dressed among company. 'This is my husband,' Clementine announced simply, as if anyone could mistake him. Winston gave a courteous little bow, got what he had come for—confirmation of the time of their evening appointment—and departed after another polite little bow.

You always knew when the Churchills were in residence, for as the front door opened the scent of incense reached you. Clementine lit the incense burner on the stairs as soon as they came home to Hyde Park Gate. It was a gentle, pleasant fragrance, which seemed to offend no one and which Winston loved, perhaps because it is an unusual perfume for a London house. He loved the unusual. A contradiction in himself, he was a champion of traditions, yet a lover of the unconventional, and not least in the matter of personal attire.

Clementine, meticulous about her own appearance, tried persistently to improve Winston's sartorial standards. She fussed around him, and he revelled in her attentions, but in the end he contrived to get his own way in his style of dress—as in so many other things.

Within their own home she made no protest about his often outrageous attire and the flamboyant dressing-gowns for which he had a predilection, but she strove her utmost to make him dress for public appearances in a manner more becoming a great statesman. Frequently she succeeded in modifying his dress, and he, in turn, delighted in modifying her modifications. The result was usually eye-compelling, irresistible.

Clementine could not resist accompanying him to the House of Commons on one of his 'better dressed' days to see for herself how the results were received. It was a warm July day. Together they walked into the St. Stephen's entrance of the House, and Clementine took her seat in the gallery to watch his entry into the Chamber.

Winston was a cool symphony in black and white. He wore no waistcoat, and below his bow tie an expanse of white shirt gleamed against the background of a well-cut

334

black jacket. His silver-grey trousers, wide in cut, impeccably creased, were a work of art.

But not for long did he remain cool.

Astonished, delighted Members gave him a tremendous welcome. There was a roar of cheers for his sartorial achievement. Winston blushed—and tripped over the walking-stick of a near neighbour on the front bench.

That minor mishap suddenly revealed, for all to see, Mr. Churchill's *chef-d'oeuvre*—black shoes with silver zip fasteners instead of laces.

The cheering swelled to even greater volume. Winston, now looking very warm, sat down. Then, with a broad grin across his cherubic face, he looked up at Clemmie in the gallery. Her smile was even wider than his.

Often the compromise which Clementine reached with her husband in her efforts to inject sanity into his clothes produced startling results.

One day in 1922, when he was leader of the Coalition Liberals in the House of Commons, Winston succumbed to her persuasion and, for the first time, turned up at Westminster wearing a silk hat. Mr. Austen Chamberlain, then Leader of the House, was the only other Member on the Treasury bench who wore a 'topper'.

At the last moment Winston decided to dodge his newfound splendour and walked hatless into the Chamber to answer questions; but looking up to the gallery and catching Clementine's cold frown he surrendered, left the Chamber, and returned a moment later to place the new silk hat boldly and jauntily upon the back of his head.

It is an infringement of order for a Member to wear a hat while speaking or moving to or from his place. Sitting, he may please himself though few Members elect to cover their heads.

Mr. Chamberlain arrived a minute or two later, and confronted by a silk-hatted Churchill, could not hide his laughing admiration of his rather self-conscious colleague.

Some months later, society was presented with an even more astonishing spectacle: Winston, as 'the noblest Roman of them all', dressed in a red-and-gold toga, sandals, head crowned with laurel wreath, and accompanied by Clementine as the Empress.

They dined in their Roman splendour at the House of the

Duchess of Roxburghe before going on to a Leap Year Eve ball given by the Duchess of Marlborough in Carlton House terrace.

The laurel wreath was symptomatic. Hardly a month went by without Winston finding some new sort of covering for his head. A hat was not a hat to him. It was a discovery, a challenge, a fresh expression of his personality.

At the historic battle of Sidney Street, Press photographs reveal, detectives and bystanders wore bowlers and caps. Winston alone considered a shiny silk hat *de rigueur* for anarchist-hunting.

When he took Stanley Baldwin for a ride in his new motor-car, both men wore trilbys—but Winston wore his back to front.

During a general election, when silk hats and smart bowlers were the rule for vote-seeking candidates, Winston, canvassing at Woodford, elected to wear a grey half-topper, a stunted creation which appeared to be cut off halfway up the crown.

After spring-cleaning Winston's wardrobe, Clementine once listed the following collection: three species of top hat, five kinds of trilby hat, one Sherlock Holmes deer-stalker, one cap, one cap with a peak, one 'Muller' (a square-topped hat which derived its name from Franz Muller, a German who in 1880 murdered a bank cashier in a train, threw the body into a tunnel near Bethnal Green, and was captured because his hat, with his name on the lining, fell on to the rails).

Clementine's list also included one naval cocked hat, two kinds of bowler, one cocked hat for Court dress, one Irishman's 'Paddy' hat (with clay), one 'Paddy' hat (without clay), one mortarboard, one St. Andrew's cap, one Army pillbox, one Hussar's busby, two kinds of Panama, one artist's beret, one military forage cap, one steel helmet, one railway engine-driver's cap, a rakish Mexican sombrero, and a green creation turned up all round, with a jaunty pocket effect on the left, which women might class as a kind of toque of rather uncertain origin.

Long ago, however, Winston himself had revealed the secret of why he became a noted collector of hats, why they interest him just as other men are interested in a collection of sticks or pipes, why he possesses practically every known type of twentieth-century headgear in his wardrobe, and why all have been worn at one time or another.

He said: 'One of the most necessary features of the equipment of a public man is some distinctive mark which everyone learns to look for and to recognize. Disraeli's fore-lock, Mr. Gladstone's collars, Lord Randolph Churchill's moustache, Mr. Joseph Chamberlain's eyeglass, Mr. Bald-win's pipes—these "properties" are of the greatest value.

'I have never indulged in any of them, so, to fill the need, cartoonists have invented the legend of my hats. This arose in the following way.

'I was at Southport during the General Election of 1910. I went for a walk with my wife along the sands. A very tiny felt hat—I do not know where it came from—had been packed with my luggage. It lay on the hall table, and with-out thinking I put it on. As we came back from our walk, there was the photographer! And he took this picture.

'Ever since the cartoonists and paragraphists have dwelt on my hats; how many there are; how strange and queer; and how I am always changing them, and what importance I attach to them, and so on. It is all rubbish, and it is all founded upon this photograph. Well, if it is a help to these worthy gentlemen in their hard work, why should I com-plain? Indeed, I think I will convert the legend into a real-ity by buying myself a new hat on purpose!'

Winston said that in 1931, and he continued buying and collecting new hats, like the famous astrakhan cap he acquired in 1945 at the Yalta Conference, ever after.

He preferred the easy comfort of old clothes. Detective Inspector Thompson related: 'When I first went to him in 1921, he had that mountain of a coat with the astrakhan collar. It was very heavy indeed. Years later, as I was help-ing him on with it one morning, he said to me: 'You know, Thompson, this is a good old coat. You know, it's really new. It's had a new inside, a new outside, a new astrakhan collar, and it's still a good coat."'

That Winston often appeared comparatively well dressed was due to the efforts of his wife and the watchful eye of his valet. His wardrobe contained few suits, and when finally convinced that he required new ones, it was Clementine who ordered them from an old-established firm of tailors in Savile Row, personally choosing the cloth.

It may be true that 'there is no substitute for wool'; but Winston was always partial to silk underwear of unchanging style, and Clementine would order twelve sets at a time.

Winston never entered shops. Clementine said: 'He doesn't need any money. He never does any shopping, and somebody else always buys his railway tickets for him.'

Nor was he a lover of personal jewellery. He liked plain cuff-links and studs. His gold watch and chain, and the gold signet ring bearing the Marlborough crest, which he wore on the third finger of his right hand, were gifts from his father. The stick which he usually carried was a long, plain cane with an unadorned gold knob. He once had another, of great sentimental value. How he came to part with it is in itself a story.

Both Winston and Clementine clung so fiercely to personal possessions that they might almost be termed hoarders. They hated to part with any article that had sentimental associations; but when the appeal was to their hearts, they weakened.

One of Winston's greatest loves was a beautiful gold-headed malacca cane. A gift from King Edward VII, it bore on its gold head the inscription: *Winston S. Churchill, Turf Club*. He took it with him wherever he travelled.

Then, some years before the last war, he suddenly discovered that he had lost it. The cane he was carrying—identical in every respect except for the inscription—was not his own.

He realized at once what had happened. He had picked up the wrong stick when leaving some function or other. But when? And where? It could have been at any of a hundred places on any of as many days.

Clementine organized the search in her efficient fashion. She went methodically through Winston's engagement book, making inquiries at every house, club, and business office which he had visited. Nobody could throw any light on the mystery; and Winston, who hated even to lose worn-out clothes, was in deepest misery.

As a last resort, Clementine inserted an advertisement in the personal column of *The Times*.

'LOST, probably on Friday, March 28th,' it ran, 'a gold-headed malacca cane, marked "Winston S. Churchill, Turf Club". Mr. Churchill has taken by mistake an almost identical cane, but since this has neither the name nor the address upon it he is unable to return it—2 Sussex Square, W.2.'

It worked. Just before noon on the day the advertisement appeared, Clementine received a telephone message from the Marlborough Club. It reported that the stick was 'safe and well' and in good hands, though—in Germany!

Years went by. One day they visited the Limbless Ex-Servicemen's Centre at Wellhampton. Winston, carrying his beloved cane, stopped to talk to an ex-soldier from Norfolk who had lost a leg in the First World War and was having an artificial limb fitted.

'You have a special limb and can walk without a stick?' Winston inquired.

'Yes,' said the disabled man, 'but I should like that stick of yours.'

Winston looked at Clementine, then turned to the old soldier and said: 'Here are my hand, my heart—and my stick. Look after it. It has been all over the world with me.'

There is one department in which he himself admitted that scope for nonconformity was lacking. Asked by a barber what style of haircut he would like, he smoothed the wisps on his pate and said: 'A man of my limited resources cannot presume to have a hair style. Get on and cut it.'

Unlike her husband, Clementine was always intensely interested in fashion and spent a great deal of time and money in keeping her wardrobe up to date.

Mrs. Thompson, the wife of Winston's former body-guard, who, as Miss Shearburn, was one of the Prime Minister's secretaries, said:

'Her dress sense was very, very good. She spent little time in shops; things were sent to her at Chequers or Chartwell or wherever she was staying. Once, during the summer before the war, she wanted a new nightdress. She wrote to the Irish linen place in Regent Street, and they sent six night-dresses for her to choose from. She liked them so much that she bought all six.

'While we were living at Admiralty House, she saw a snow leopard coat somewhere, and decided she would like one. She had two sent from different firms, and finally chose the one she preferred. It was perfectly wonderful, and she was like a child about it; but she said: "Don't say anything to Winston. I don't want him to know about it yet. He doesn't know it, but it's going to be his Easter egg to me."

'At times she would ignore the fact that you were a member of her husband's staff and treat you as an equal. She would say: "I want a cup of tea. Come in and have one with me." Then she would give you a cigarette and talk about clothes.'

Clementine has lovely feet and is correspondingly particular about her shoes. They must be beautiful, and of the finest quality. At Chartwell, dozens of pairs stand in long racks in the corridor outside her bedroom.

Like Winston, she never cared for jewellery, and would seldom be seen wearing anything more elaborate than a string of pearls and, occasionally, a brooch.

Her clothes are simple and elegant, and most are designed on flowing classical lines. For casual wear at Chartwell in the summer she favoured slacks and shirt of matching blue or tangerine linen. For visiting, or garden parties, she preferred tailored linen dresses to more elaborate attire. On warm evenings the choice was for one of a number of flowered chiffon dresses, rather full-skirted, with draped bodice, low neckline, and generally sleeveless. For dining in the winter, usually black, and invariably carrying a large chiffon or silk square in a pastel shade of green, pink, or blue.

A peculiarity of her shopping was that she usually bought her own birthday and Christmas presents (officially designated as 'from Winston'). Obsessed with his thoughts on matters of world import, or engrossed in writing a book, he often forgot such matters as his wife's birthday gift, a strange lapse, since he was so devoted to her that one intimate friend commented: 'He treats her like a piece of porcelain. She was, and is, the only woman in his life.'

Before meeting Clementine, Winston had shown little interest in women. He had been too busy trying to make himself financially independent and to establish his position in the world. Though he worshipped his mother, the knowledge that it was her money which was supporting him during his Army career never ceased to irk him, and his main objective was to put an end to that situation. Only when he had achieved his aim could he bring himself to think seriously of courtship and marriage. So it is true that the beautiful Clementine was the first and only woman in his life; and she it was who helped him to attain his ambitions.

Intolerant of criticism and opposition from others, he accepted both from her, because she alone knew how to handle him in the right manner.

One evening she was with Winston at a reception for about forty people. The gathering included M.P.'s and trade union leaders. Winston was discoursing in a light vein on a political topic of the day when Clementine intervened:

'Do make it clearer, do make it clearer for your audience,' she said. 'Let me say it for you.' And she did just that, explaining very simply things that Winston, with his relish for phrases, had been, perhaps, wrapping up a little too much.

He shrugged his shoulders, spread out his hands helplessly and good-humouredly, and said, 'What can I do?'

His audience—and Clementine—roared with laughter. But, in fact, she *did* make the topic clearer to everyone. But when she stepped into a conversation, she always did it in a way that couldn't possibly embarrass him.

Both Winston and Clementine could fly into sudden anger, but the loss of temper never lasted long; nor would they bear ill will against those who had offended them.

No one ever heard them arguing or quarrelling seriously with each other. Occasionally a good-humoured outburst was provoked by Clementine's love of expensive clothes, for though Winston delighted in seeing her dressed to perfection, the bills at times gave him, like so many husbands, some shocks.

'Do you realize how many articles *that* is going to cost me?' he would say with gentle reproof on hearing how much she had spent on a new gown. Clementine, an expert on economies in other directions, would promise to go easier with clothes expenditure in the future, but it was a promise she rarely found the willpower to keep.

On one pre-war occasion Winston advanced six pounds for the purchase of a new gown for their daughter Diana, warning that on no account must it cost more.

That evening Diana appeared in a gown which had plainly cost much more than the stipulated amount, and waited in some trepidation for the inevitable explosion.

Winston made her parade up and down the room, studying her from every angle, and even feeling the quality of the fabric in the new gown. He then pronounced judgement.

'I heartily approve,' he declared, and there was an audible sigh of relief from mother and daughter.

Winston's kindness wasn't confined to the women of his family. Mrs. Thompson, who, as his secretary, encountered him in his most difficult moods, testified: 'He was charming; charming in the way of saying the right thing which makes you respond. One evening down at Chartwell we had been working very late. Goodness! I was tired, and so was he. He said "Goodnight" to me as I was leaving, and then he suddenly called: "Are you tired, Miss Shearburn?"

'I said: "No," because of course I could not admit it.

'There was a little silence; then, not looking at me any more, he shook his head. "No," he said. "You wouldn't be. You are a soldier's daughter."

'Nothing would have made me admit I was tired. I would have gone on until I dropped. He always said the right thing, and she has a superb way with people too. A friend of the family once described her as a grand and sweet woman who hitched her wagon to a hurricane and has been more often in the driver's seat of this particular hurricane than is supposed. And the friend added that even with a hurricane, her hands are gentle and her sense of direction admirable.'

Winston and Clementine had a unique understanding. Although they shared many interests, others they pursued absolutely alone. She agreed with him that the cultivation of a hobby and of new forms of interest is a policy of first importance to a public man, and she would never selfishly deny him outlets essential to his well-being.

Their mutual code for living was: 'It is no use doing what you like. You have got to like what you do.'

Winston said: 'Broadly speaking, human beings may be divided into three classes: Those who are billed to death, those who are worried to death, and those who are bored to death.'

Said Clementine: 'A man can wear out a particular part of his mind by continually using it and tiring it, just as in the same way he can wear out the elbows of his coat. There is, however, this difference between the living cells of the brain and inanimate articles: one cannot mend the frayed elbows of a coat by rubbing the sleeve or shoulders; but the tired parts of the mind can be rested and strengthened not merely by rest but by using other parts.'

She never interrupted or interfered with Winston's hobbies. She recognized that he hated interruption, whether busy with a spade in the garden, a paintbrush in his studio, or pen in his library. He was a dynamic worker who, at times, could be so lazy that he would ring the bell for someone to hand him cigars lying just out of his reach.

Clementine and Winston loved reading. Although Winston could spare little time for this relaxation, he enjoyed the 'Hornblower' novels of C. S. Forester. She preferred the classics.

Both could become almost fanatically keen on a pursuit.

She maintained that those whose work is their pleasure are those who most need the means of banishing it at intervals from their minds. She always liked active sports, whereas Winston never took kindly to athletic exercise.

Clementine tried to interest him in golf. He replied that he was a great admirer of the game. He admired it so much that he liked to stand far away to see its finer points and niceties. He admired its influence on the health, character, and temper of those who took part in the game.

He had no doubt, he continued, that men who would face the game of golf were men upon whom the nation could confidently rely. Golf was the sport of kings—and of politicians. It was such a great stimulus to eloquence that some of his finest perorations had been achieved while he had been negotiating with his niblick a recalcitrant ball in a venomous bunker.

But, he concluded, he had never found anything like painting to take one's mind, for a spell, off grave matters.

'Golf is no use to me for this purpose,' he said. "I find myself thinking of serious business after a time.'

She would often take a picnic tea out to him and stay to talk about the progress of the current masterpiece. She said: 'He is difficult sometimes. Just when I have got his luncheon ready, he suddenly gets a huge plan of putting the world to rights and wanders into the garden to work it out.'

She frequently arranged visits to friends for 'painting weekends'. One Sunday at Lady Paget's house at Kingston

Hill, Winston and his friend, the late Sir John Lavery, were painting together, watched by Clementine, when a hearty voice behind them called: 'Hallo! Winston, when did you begin this game?'

Without turning, he replied: 'The day you kicked me out of the Admiralty, Lord Charles.'

The intruder, Lord Charles Beresford, retorted: 'Well, who knows? Perhaps I may have saved a great master.'

Clementine loved to arrange special surprises which she knew would particularly please him. That is how the little, unassuming Swiss paint-maker, Willy Sax, came to Chartwell.

Winston and Clementine had met him during a visit to Zürich in 1946. Winston had bought from him some special reds and blues, and ever since had been having paints made for him in the small factory founded by the Sax family almost ninety years ago.

Sax, accompanied by two of Switzerland's best-known painters, arrived at Chartwell for lunch at Clementine's secret invitation. The visit gave great happiness to everybody, and to Winston most of all.

Winston was so busy turning out paintings by the hundred that he seldom found time to title his works. He left that to Clementine.

The picture she called 'The Messenger' (it depicts a man walking through a snow-covered village) became a best-selling Christmas card. Winston painted Clementine's personal Christmas card every year. She chose the picture, but he insisted that the message be simple and sincere, and printed in clear, plain type. In the following year he would always dispose of the reproduction rights to a firm manufacturing cards for world distribution.

More than 20,000 copies of 'The Olive Trees'—Clementine's favourite of all her husband's pictures—have been sold. The original hangs in one of the living-rooms at Chartwell.

It has been estimated that Winston's collection of his own paintings would be worth something in the region of two and a half million pounds. His painting output was fantastic, but he hated parting with his work.

Sir Charles Wheeler, President of the Royal Academy, said that when he was arranging the Churchill Exhibition, he suggested: 'Altogether, you must have painted about four hundred pictures.'

'More like five hundred,' Winston replied.

All collectors would love to own a Churchill painting. El Glaoui, Pasha of Marrakesh, one of Winston and Clementine's oldest friends, told them that he would 'pay anything' to get one.

In North Africa, it is said, one genuine Churchill painting is valued at six wives.

'When I get to Heaven,' Winston said many years ago, 'I mean to spend a considerable portion of my first million years in painting, and so get to the bottom of the subject.' He was content to work in his studio at Chartwell, with his unframed pictures of Chartwell, Marrakesh, Cairo, Venice, and the Côte d'Azur stacked all around him.

Dominating the south wall of the studio is a portrait of the woman who had first handed him a paint-box—Clementine, gay-hatted and smiling, painted in a haze of blue.

A cable from Chartwell usually meant that top priority action was required for something of the utmost importance. Such a cable was received one day in San Giovanni in Italy. There was no doubt of its urgency. It concerned goldfish.

A few hours later, twenty-five *pesci rossi*, the world's most exotic goldfish, were on their way in special heated tanks to Chartwell.

The fish at the Churchill country home had been dying mysteriously, and Clementine, remembering the fish breeders of San Giovanni, who had sent him a gift of four rare varieties as 'a token of respect and admiration', was sure they would come to the rescue. They did; and, what is more, continued to send by air mail every week small cellophane packets of dried fleas to feed the *pesci rossi*.

Winston loved his fish. Whenever he and Clementine were in residence at Chartwell he never missed his daily visit to the pool to feed them and to squat down and tickle their under-bellies.

In his study Winston had four glass tanks containing about 120 tropical fish, including black mollies, zebras, and Siamese fighting fish. 'I find contemplation of the fish one of the greatest forms of relaxation I have ever known,' he said.

Two of the most important residents of Chartwell were Rufus, the poodle, and Mickey, the cat.

Whenever Winston and Clementine went away and Rufus had to be left behind, Clementine gave one of the maids express instructions on grooming, exercising, and feeding him. She knew how much Winston would worry if he were not properly cared for.

Rufus was, in fact, the second of his name. The original Rufus was run down by a car while out for a walk with one of the maids. The girl ran home, crying, to Clementine, who broke the news to Winston.

There was only one thing to do, and she wasted no time about it. She bought another poodle, choosing a dog exactly like the one they had lost.

Clementine's astuteness in the matter of raising funds for charity led to the opening of the Chartwell grounds to the public. She did not merely throw open the gates of her home for the benefit of charities, she personally acted hostess to the crowds, appreciating that it was the magic of the Churchill name that attracted visitors; that for the thousands who came, it was a form of pilgrimage.

She chatted to as many people as possible, pointing out their favourite spots and telling everybody to be sure to see her pet black swans with their cygnets.

When a visitor inquired if Winston would be coming, she replied gently: 'Not today, I'm afraid. He has one or two things on his mind.'

Someone else asked how Winston moved about the steep terraces to the lake and his black swans.

'He strolls downhill to feed the swans and goldfish, and the car picks him up at the bottom,' Clementine replied.

On every open day the crowds were amused by a notice in red-pencilled letters tied to Winston's basket chair near the diving-board at the swimming pool. It said, simply and effectively: 'No diving (not deep enough)—W.S.C.'

As far as Clementine was concerned, his worst domestic habit used to be 'climbing into the swimming pool at Chartwell, then suddenly remembering something important, getting out, paddling into the house without stopping to dry, and leaving large footprints on my polished floors'.

Not until publication of his war books had increased his fortune were Winston and Clementine able to gratify their ambition to own a string of racehorses. It was Mary's husband, Christopher Soames, who suggested they should become racehorse owners. They were delighted with the idea.

At a house-party in Warwick Castle, Winston had been discussing racing with the Aga Khan when Clementine remarked that he knew far more about racehorses than anybody realized. Winston promptly confirmed her claim by reciting, almost in one breath, the names of the past fifty Derby winners and their sires and dams. It was an extraordinary feat of memory.

The Churchill–Soames team had already walked away with honours as dairy farmers by winning first place in the national milk record competitions with the Chartwell herd of Jersey cows. Now, backed additionally by the expert judgement of Walter Nightingall, the Epsom trainer, they began to buy horses, beginning with a colt which was to become famous as Columnist II.

Carrying the chocolate and pink which had been the racing colours of Winston's father and grandfather, Columnist II, who cost only some £1,500, won thirteen of the twenty-four races in which he was entered and earned more than £22,000 in prize-money.

When circumstances prevented Winston and Clementine from seeing their horses run, they never failed to telephone Walter Nightingall to ask what the chances were for the race.

A West Essex Conservative party fête clashed with the appearance at Ascot of the Churchill horse le Prétendant. The race was due to begin at 3.40 p.m., and Winston and Clementine arrived at the fête at 3.35.

The Ascot meeting was being televised, so Clementine told the fête organizers: 'I think that if no one would mind, we should like to watch the TV first and postpone the speeches until immediately after the race.'

Into the TV room they went, and as their horse romped home the winner, Winston was bobbing up and down with excitement in an arm-chair, while his wife—hands clenched in front of her as though gripping reins—appeared to be riding le Prétendant past the post.

The only disadvantage they found in their racing was that any Churchill horse, irrespective of form, was usually backed down to odds-on favourite by the heavy betting of

347

thousands of loyal supporters who wagered from sentiment and superstition alone; but they both loved the sport, and often visited the lonely, empty Epsom Downs to watch their horses at trial gallops.

As they were leaving a race-course after a meeting at which Winston's luck had been in, a young boy pushed his way forward through the crowd.

'Oh! Sir Winston,' he said, 'weren't you thrilled to have a ticket on the winner?'

Clementine smiled as Winston replied in serious, deliberate tone: 'Well, young man, I *have* had bigger moments in my life.'

23

THE CHILDREN

THE red-headed girl bent over the passport application form and began to fill in the questionnaire.

Surname: Churchill.

Christian names: Sarah Millicent Hermione.

Father's occupation: Painter.

That is what she wrote, with a smile, and of course it was true—he was a painter—as well.

But behind Sarah's written jest lies something deeper.

Clementine's children have grown up and lived in the glow of their father's glory. They have also been handicapped by it. They are all rightly proud to be his children, but also recognize how fortunate they are to be Clementine's children.

Their father was devoted to them, and always snatched every possible moment he could to share with them, but those moments were few. It was Clementine who kept the family a family.

She bore the brunt of troubles caused by a family that inherited its father's independence of character.

They had four daughters and one son. Diana in 1909, Randolph in 1911, Sarah in 1914, Marigold in 1918, and Mary in 1922.

For years their mother tried to shield them even from the knowledge that their father was a famous public figure.

In the same way as she had always tried to keep a sense of normality about her home life, she was anxious to protect her children from the dangers of living in the public eye for as long as possible.

When the Germans started bombing London in the First World War, she evacuated Diana, Randolph, and Sarah to an old Kentish farmhouse run by a cousin of Winston's. Eight other little Churchills from other branches of the family joined them.

Diana and Randolph were almost inseparable, fighting constant battles in the fields. Sarah preferred to climb walls and trees alone, and her adventurousness was rewarded by a crop of scars many of which she still bears.

Clementine managed to keep the children out of the glare of limelight until Winston, in 1924, was appointed Chancellor of the Exchequer and the family moved into Downing Street, next door to the Prime Minister. She still played down their father's importance, so much so that Sarah and Mary used to be quite overwhelmed when the Prime Minister, Mr. Stanley Baldwin, used to pat their heads.

'When we moved to Downing Street my mother impressed on us that father's importance was not as great as that of the man next door—the Prime Minister, Mr. Baldwin,' says Sarah.

The children's first 'blooding' in politics had occurred a few years earlier when, on his way to speak for a friend who was fighting a Liverpool by-election, Winston drove with his family in an open car through the city's streets.

Supporters of the Opposition Party gave the Churchill children a taste of politics. They surrounded the car, shook fists at them, booed them, even threw things at them, and a brick narrowly missed Diana.

Clementine calmed them as the car slowly drove on, explaining:

'In your father's business such things sometimes happen.'

'Election campaigning was tremendously fascinating,' recalls Sarah. 'Diana and I, dressed alike, would accompany Father and Mother on tours forming a kind of family platform.

'We were involved in many free fights. Liverpool was particularly tough, but we became quite used to being booed and hissed and even pelted with bricks that sometimes landed in the car. It was a marvellous training for the stage. Neither boos nor bricks could disturb me now.

'As a little girl, I particularly remember one of my father's friends who was awfully good at games.' The friend was Mr. Lloyd George. 'We all loved Lloyd George,' said Sarah. 'He is the earliest friend I can remember, outside the immediate family circle.

'Politics were in the very air we breathed as children,' Sarah recalls.

But the most important of Clementine's children was Winston, so she had to have the help of nannies to bring up the others. Miss Whyte, 'Moppet', as she was known, was the best of these. Miss Whyte was Clementine's cousin. When she was with the family, Clementine was able to devote as much time and attention as was necessary to Winston.

As the only son, Randolph more than any of them felt the effects of the shadow of his father's image.

Clementine strove to give Randolph some of the stability and roots she had given Winston.

Winston himself had struggled for years to overcome the handicap of being the son of a famous father, and Clementine well realized how much help Randolph would need to fight the same fight.

Even Randolph's schooling was affected by his father's shadow, for, although they had wanted the boy to attend Harrow School, he finally went to Eton for a rather unusual reason. When Winston went to Harrow to put his son's name down for the school, on stepping out of his cab he found himself being hissed at by some of the boys—perhaps as a result of some of his unpopular political views. He immediately got in the cab again and drove straight to Eton.

Randolph was only eighteen when he stepped into the political arena. Clementine and Winston went to a little village meeting in Essex to hear their son give his first political speech and help his father in an election battle.

She had listened to Randolph rehearse the speech at home, had given him advice on intonation, expression, and on platform speaking in general.

Now the moment of trial had come. Dressed in a new suit, his thick mop of hair smartly combed to one side, young Randolph stepped forwards to address the meeting after a smile of confident encouragement from his mother— the same smile that Winston always sought before making so many of his speeches.

In a firm, clear voice Randolph said his piece. It finished to a roar of applause. The obviously proud father moved to his feet and said: 'I have not had the pleasure of hearing him before and from what I have heard I think I can say that after having fought and contested elections now for

351

thirty years—this being my fourteenth—I can see at no great distance a moment when I shall be able to sit at home in comfortable retirement and feel that the torch which falls from my exhausted hands will be carried boldly forward by another.

'But that is not going to happen immediately. At any rate, not until after this election has been fought.'

There were now two politicians in the Churchill family. Clementine left the hall that night with her own two favourite politicians on either side of her.

Three years later came another great night in their family life—Randolph's twenty-first birthday party.

Clementine decided to organize a very special kind of party. There would be a dinner at Claridge's, she would receive all the guests, then disappear and leave the celebration to the men.

She chose the guest list. It finally totalled more than seventy—all men—many of them, like their host, distinguished fathers accompanying promising sons.

Clementine, the only woman present, welcomed her guests to the great Claridge's dining-room. Radiantly, she greeted famous fathers and sons.

Viscount Hailsham and his son Mr. Quintin Hogg arrived. Lord Beaverbrook and his son the Hon. Max Aitken; Viscount Rothermere with the Hon. Esmond Harmsworth; Lord Camrose with the Hon. Seymour Berry. From the peerage, politics, and the Services, they came—the Marquis of Reading, the Marquis of Salisbury, Admiral of the Fleet Lord Beatty, Sir Archibald Sinclair, Admiral of the Fleet Sir Roger Keyes, Mr. Bryan Guinness, Sir John Lavery, Mr. Robert Boothby, Major G. Lloyd George, were announced. The night of 16 June 1932 was to be a night that neither Randolph, Winston, nor Clementine would ever forget.

She assembled her guests round the oval dinner table. To the right of Winston, who sat at the centre, she placed the Marquis of Salisbury, opposite him, the Duke of Marlborough. Randolph she sat beside Lord Reading.

Then, as soon as she was satisfied that all her guests were comfortably and correctly seated, she diplomatically slipped away.

The young Lord Birkenhead stood up, and, leaning forward with studied nonchalance like his famous father, proposed the health of Randolph. He showed that he was already a master of humorous invective. In cultivated tones and language he sketched Randolph Churchill's (according to him) rather graceless career at school and indifference to discipline at Oxford. Thereafter, he depicted his rise to fame as a public figure.

Amid loud laughter, Lord Birkenhead described his inability to force a way into Winston's office owing to the crowd of retainers and a number of income-tax collectors who came to take toll of the youngest payer of super tax in the kingdom.

Then Randolph himself got up, and, with grace and modesty, captured everyone. He chided Lord Birkenhead for harping upon youthful indiscretions, and bade him remember how lucky it was for his career that a veil of oblivion was allowed to fall over it.

But his final remark brought down the house, when he said he hoped the younger generation would copy their elders and produce sons as competent as the proposer of the toast and himself.

Sir Austen Chamberlain rose next to propose the health of the Younger Generation, and recall the party at which he, his father, and young Winston had been present. He was ten years older than Winston and had come prepared to dislike a political upstart. His father, the famous Joe Chamberlain, on returning from the party had, however, assured him that he wished that some of the elder statesmen there had been half as stimulating as Lord Randolph's son.

It was the turn of the young men to reply in the persons of Mr. Quintin Hogg, Mr. Seymour Berry, and the Duke of Marlborough.

Then came Winston's moment. He spoke of how the generation of fathers to which he belonged had witnessed the extension of an enormous empire, and had made it secure during the war. He could not believe that the younger generation was not equal to the task of consolidation or would prove faithless in patriotic purpose.

Lord Hugh Cecil followed to describe with gusto the idealism of the early Winston, admitting that anyone who came to know Winston succumbed to one common emotion

—love and affection.

Lord Beaverbrook, Lord Hailsham, and Mr. Esmond Harmsworth added their words of wisdom and advice to young Randolph, and it was long past midnight when the celebration broke up. Clementine was waiting at home for the two men of her family. She had stayed up to hear whether everything she had planned had gone well, and to give them both a 'goodnight' kiss on a great day in their lives.

Already, at the age of twenty-one, Randolph was saying: 'The sky should be the limit of youth's ambition. My two main ambitions are to make an immense fortune and to be Prime Minister. In twenty years' time, however, when I shall probably have fought four or five unsuccessful elections and have been bankrupt more than once, I do not see then why I should regret my youthful ambition however laughable this may appear in more experienced eyes.'

The previous year, when he had been invited to make a lecture tour of the United States, his mother had encouraged him to go. With an engaging cocksureness, he informed the people of America how the British Empire should be run, and criticized the 'invertebrates', as he called them, who were then running it.

Audiences were amused. They liked the youth with the Churchill touch; the Churchill rhetoric; and the Churchill manner. There was no mistaking the uncanny resemblance between son and father.

There is a close parallel between Winston's admiration for his mother, and the Churchill children's admiration for Clementine. As soon as Randolph was interested in a girl he used to say: 'Why don't you do your hair like my mother does?' or 'You know, my mother could really show you how to dress.'

From his early twenties, Randolph started hitting the headlines ... being washed overboard on a yacht with the fabulous June, Lady Inverclyde ... interviewing the Kaiser ... dressing up as a woman for a Cecil Beaton party....

For a time his efforts to get into Parliament were frustrated by the independent line he took. Like all the Churchills, he couldn't run easily in Party harness.

Fighting colourfully, but unsuccessfully, three by-elections in two years, he went off to Hollywood to appear as an extra in a House of Commons scene in the film *Parnell*.

Not until 1940, when Winston became Prime Minister, did Randolph finally enter Westminster as unopposed Conservative member for the Lancashire constituency of Preston.

Winston acted as one of his son's sponsors when he was introduced to the House of Commons and smiled broadly at Clementine seated in the gallery when Randolph, in his maiden speech, appealed for indulgence because of embarrassment caused by 'paternal propinquity'.

There was no doubt about his brilliance, no doubts of his courage, both moral and physical, but he was, nevertheless, a young man with a handicap—his father. But even his enemies couldn't ignore his war record.

He appeared on the staff of G.H.Q. Middle East as a military spokesman; disappeared into the western desert on long-range desert Commando raids; arrived in South Africa to consult with General Smuts, and then, in New York, predicted the end of the war in 1943 or 1944. He parachuted into Jugoslavia to meet Tito; joined his father for the Teheran talks with Roosevelt and Stalin; went with him again to Athens during the violent days of the Greek Communist uprising.

When German airborne troops raided Marshal Tito's H.Q., Randolph succeeded in escaping to the mountains with the Marshal.

Winston always had the greatest possible affection and regard for Randolph, but it was Clementine who understood Randolph best.

Father and son argued frequently, and Randolph, if he thought he was right, seldom budged his opinion an inch, no matter how much his father told him off.

Their temperaments, so alike, were usually apt to clash in flaming political arguments. Clementine had to keep the peace between them.

In spite of their frequent arguments, Randolph asserted:

'Unquestionably, the man I most admire in the world is my father. My admiration for him is not necessarily due to the belief that he is the greatest and the best man in the world, but I have naturally had more opportunities to cultivate admiration for him than I have for anyone else. Perhaps it is for this reason that so many people admire their fathers more than anyone else.

'I admire him for his courage and for his love of adventure, for his complete sincerity, for his tolerance, and for his immense capacity for hard work and concentration. Curiously enough my admiration for him is in no way diminished by the fact that he has always been extremely kind to me.'

And the woman Randolph most admires in the world is his mother.

Randolph married in 1939, and had a son called Winston Churchill. The marriage was dissolved in 1945. Three years later he married again.

One Sunday, reading the newspapers in bed, Clementine marked a passage in an article published in the *Observer*, and sent it to Winston's bedroom.

The passage read: 'No one can set the adrenalin flowing simply by the rumour of his approach like Randolph Churchill. At the news that he has arrived at a party, at a press conference, at a railway station, hearts pump more madly, temperatures rise, lips tighten, voices sharpen. It is like the day war was declared over again.'

Another newspaper clipping she kept for Winston was a defence of Randolph by Malcolm Muggeridge in which he declared:

'Hostesses on both sides of the Atlantic may grow pale at the prospect of one of his visitations, but they know that, as a topic of conversation, he is inexhaustibly diverting. As a conversationalist himself he is often as devastating as one of those hurricanes which sweep away whole towns in their train; as a stimulant, *in absentia*, of other conversationalists, he is in the very top class.

'For myself, I would not have him otherwise. Like the sirens in the blitz, his arrival at any social gathering sends everyone scampering for cover; produces that slight shiver and tautening of the nerves which presages danger and excitement. When the "all clear" sounds and he departs there is a corresponding sense of relief, but the intervening experience (as long as one has not been personally involved in the explosion) is exhilarating or at any rate memorable.'

Perhaps one of the greatest, yet lesser-known qualities of Clementine and Winston was their love of children. Children instinctively sense someone who truly loves them, and even strange children, meeting Clementine or Winston for the first time, took to them immediately.

As a boy, Winston was starved of fatherly affection. His father, Lord Randolph, was too busy to spare him much time. Winston consequently endeavoured never to be 'too busy' for his own children, but whatever he was unable to give them, Clementine more than made up for. Together, they completely complemented each other in the love and affection they gave their family.

Diana, their eldest daughter, was always very close to her mother, and like her in many ways.

Lucky wedding favours of white heather, taken from silver baskets with white satin pin-cushions hanging from their handles were distributed to eight hundred guests when Diana married John Milner Bailey, eldest son of South African millionaire, Sir Abe Bailey.

The ceremony took place at St. Margaret's, Westminster, and, in an incident reminiscent of her parents' own wedding, many of the congregation stood on the seats as the wedding march pealed out.

Clementine did her daughter proud with a magnificent reception at the Duke of Marlborough's house in Carlton House Terrace, and Mary and Sarah were among the six bridesmaids.

But the lucky wedding favours of white heather did not bring good fortune to the bride and groom. Within months of the ceremony, the marriage was virtually over. It ended in divorce. Diana found happiness elusive. Like her parents, she too was an emphatic personality. As a little girl, she went on one occasion to see a theatrical performance with her parents. She was dressed in bright green, which toned perfectly with her red hair and fair complexion:

'I am Miss Diana Churchill,' she informed someone.

One onlooker, who did not know who the mischievous-looking child in green was, whispered to his neighbour: 'I've seen that little girl before,' he said. 'She had a row with one of my kids at the seaside.'

'They say that girls inherit their father's qualities,' remarked someone else.

After her first marriage ended in divorce, Diana wed Duncan Sandys—already at that time a rising politician. Both Clementine and Winston agreed he would go a long way, but Diana and Duncan separated; were later divorced, and she announced that she would revert to the name of Diana Churchill.

Of all her children, it was Diana with whom Clementine was closest although she never showed favourites among her family. In later years Mary became very close, mainly because, for so long, she lived on the Chartwell estate, which her husband managed, and because her children were forever making Chartwell Manor their own and running in to kiss grandma and grandpa.

Diana was the eldest, and an intelligent sophisticated young woman with whom her mother could enjoy companionship.

As soon as she was in her teens, Clementine treated her as an equal.

Like her mother, Diana served others, quietly, unobtrusively. Early in 1962, she began voluntary work as a 'Mrs. Spencer', for the Samaritans—an organization to help those tempted to suicide or despair.

Five days a week, from early morning to night, she sat at an office desk with a telephone that was a life-line for thousands of desperate people. It was her job to take calls from men and women who had no one else to turn to.

The Samaritans became her main and all-consuming interest. She frequently admitted that she lived for the Samaritans. Then, one week-end in October 1963, Diana arranged to visit her mother who was in hospital for a rest at the time. She also intended to have dinner with her father. She kept neither appointment.

She was found dead at her home. The cause of death was barbiturate poisoning.

PART II. THIRD GIRL FROM THE LEFT...

In poise, style, and looks it is Sarah who completely takes after her mother. In most other respects, Sarah has her father's character.

Whereas Diana was the intellectual dreamer among the Churchill girls, Sarah is the complete individualist.

Even as a child she was highly imaginative, and forever busy with her own thoughts and dreams.

'Sarah is an oyster, she will not tell us her secrets,' her

father would chide, and she was constantly teased about her tendency to stay silent.

'Come on Sarah, say something,' the others would press, but she seldom did.

Winston liked the children to join in family discussions, but would not tolerate mumbling.

'Say what you have to say, say it clearly, or don't say it at all,' their mother counselled.

Recalls Sarah:

'To a certain extent, I lived in a secret life of my own, apart from the happy one I shared with my brother and sisters.

'My father's memory was, of course, one of the most incredible things, and we as children were taught to memorize as much as we could. Great lashings of poetry were stashed away inside us.'

Facially, Sarah has her mother's fine bone structure, her serious expression, and her smile. But her red hair is an inheritance from her father.

Clementine's nickname for Sarah is 'Mule'.

Counters Sarah: 'Stubbornness can also be called firmness in certain circumstances.'

But pet names have always been the custom in the Churchills' home.

Winston would often lean across the dining-table and affectionately squeeze Clementine's hand and purr: 'Dear cat!' To which she would affectionately reply: 'Dear pig.'

Mary was known among the family as 'Mary the Chimp', and every member of the family has an affectionate noise reserved for them. When they were living at Admiralty House in the early part of the last war, Winston would return to their apartment for a meal and 'Meow!' at the door; an answering 'Meow!' would come from Clementine.

It was at Admiralty House that Sarah was born during the First World War, on 7 October 1914.

When she was very little, her mother arranged for her to be given roller-skating lessons. She was getting on well when suddenly she went down with a wallop.

'Well, we've had a great many falls, haven't we?' said her instructor as the lesson ended.

'I don't know why *you* fell down,' answered Sarah with a very emphatic expression in her little green eyes, 'but *I* fell down because I wished to.'

Admission of defeat doesn't come easily to a Churchill—not even a small one.

Understanding Sarah's desire to be alone with her thoughts, Clementine asked Winston to build her a treetop Wendy house at Chartwell. Years later Sarah was to fly to one just like the house that Winston built when she played the role of Peter Pan on the stage.

She was in her teens when artist William Nicholson, visiting Chartwell frequently to paint a conversation piece of Clementine and Winston, suggested Sarah might like to join his grand-daughter in having dancing lessons.

'I think he noticed this lumbering teenager clumping about the house and sensed I needed something to do,' said Sarah. That was the beginning of Sarah's theatrical ambitions.

'Any opposition the family made—and it was only mild —was because of the fact that I was such a clumsy child.

'My entire early life was punctuated by sudden and noisy tumbles. Once I cut my head open and almost bled to death when I tangled with a barbed wire fence while racing across a field with Randolph. I also fell off a fifteen-foot wall.

'Whenever there was a loud crash the family would look at each other and exclaim: "That's Sarah!" so the very idea of my wanting to be a dancer when I could scarcely keep my feet at ordinary activities amused them.'

But she was stage struck and had made up her mind to become a dancer and an actress. Winston didn't like the idea. It was Clementine who persuaded him to let her go on with her career. She had long been prepared for Sarah to break out on her own in some way, and when she saw that Sarah had made up her mind to succeed in a career of her own choosing, she backed her ambitions all the way.

Confided Sarah to her mother: 'I don't want my parentage to make any difference either to my career or to my friendship with other girls.

'My parentage has nothing to do with it one way or the other. I want a stage career. I mean to stand or fall on my own merit.' Years later shy, independent Sarah admitted: 'I didn't become an actress to find myself. To lose myself was what I wanted.'

Her still anxious father said to Sarah: 'What about your

scars? You can't even keep on your feet when you are *not* dancing.' And then added: 'It's for you to decide. But if you are going to be an actress take it seriously.'

Some weeks later, Clementine and Winston sat in the audience at London's Adelphi Theatre, watching the revue *Follow the Sun*, and the third girl from the left in the chorus was a 'Miss Smith'. 'Miss Smith' was Sarah.

Society was shocked, so were many of the Churchills' friends. Clementine simply said: 'Bless you Sarah'—and went to see the show four times.

She was proud that Sarah had insisted: 'I won't be billed as the daughter of anybody. I stand on my own feet.'

Clementine had already been to the out-of-town opening of the show in Manchester on one of the foggiest nights of the year. She saw it three times in Manchester, then went again with Winston when it came to London.

It was during the run of *Follow the Sun* that Sarah became friendly with its star comedian from America, Viennese-born Vic Oliver.

One morning Sarah handed a letter to her friend Jenny Nicholson, daughter of Robert Graves, the poet, and said: 'Please be sure to give this letter to my mother.' With that, she took the boat-train for the New York-bound liner *Bremen*.

Jenny Nicholson put the letter on a train to Westerham. A few hours later, Clementine opened it at Chartwell.

In the letter, Sarah told her mother that she had eloped to marry Vic Oliver.

Clementine broke the news to Winston and the rest of the family.

When Sarah's letter arrived at Chartwell, Randolph left immediately for New York.

On arrival, he went straight to her hotel to find that she was being chaperoned by Lady Astor.

For hours brother and sister talked. He was not there as an instrument of parental opposition, but as brother and a confidant.

When the storm of publicity broke, Sarah and Vic Oliver dined with Bernard Baruch.

'Well, children,' he said, 'tell me the whole story.' Sarah explained her concern over what her parents would think of the situation.

Mr. Baruch allayed their fears like a guardian uncle. 'I'll talk to the family,' he promised, and did.

On Christmas Day, 1936, twenty-two-year-old Sarah married thirty-eight-year-old Vic Oliver.

Clementine cabled: 'Best wishes and a Happy Christmas.'

The marriage was happy for two years, then rifts appeared.

On 3 September 1941, Sarah joined the Women's Auxiliary Air Force, a month after her younger sister Mary had joined the A.T.S. She abandoned her successful stage and radio career to do more direct work for the nation. She also told Vic Oliver that their marriage had been a mistake.

With her father completely absorbed in fighting the war, it was to her mother Sarah turned. Clementine advised that work was the best answer, and saw to it that, apart from her duties in the W.A.A.F., Sarah acted as her father's aide on some of his war-time travels.

Sarah became another Churchill at war, and wrote a little poem echoing the hour, which she showed to her parents one week-end at Chequers. It read:

> *Arise, oh countrymen, arise*
> *And with defiance face the darkening skies.*
> *Turn on the tyrant and say*
> *The black night is yours but we will have the day.*
> *Dreams, hopes, faiths may yet dissolve;*
> *You may break our hearts, but never our resolve.*

She became a photographic officer. One of her fellow officers—Constance Babington Smith, who wrote the history of photographic intelligence in the Second World War —said: 'Sarah was definitely an asset on the station for, apart from the good job she did, when the station was shared by Americans, she was especially good at getting along with them. Having an American grandmother, I think, helped her to see their point of view.'

Miss Babington Smith also remembers one particular forty-eight-hour leave week-end at Chequers. At the time, preparations were in hand for the North African landings known as 'Operation Torch'.

It was nearly 1 a.m. Sarah was curled up in a big chair

362

near the fire and Winston was pacing up and down. The clock struck.

'At this very minute,' announced Winston with measured gravity, 'at this very minute, under cover of darkness, the 643 ships that are carrying our troops on a great enterprise are approaching the shores of Africa.'

'644,' said Sarah's voice from the armchair.

'What's that?'—questioned Winston.

'I've been working on Torch for months,' said Sarah.

'Why didn't you tell me?'

'I was told not to mention it to anyone,' she replied.

Winston grinned. 'Suppose you thought I didn't know,' he added.

In March 1945, Sarah was divorced from Vic Oliver following a petition presented by him on the grounds of her desertion.

At the end of the year, demobilized from the W.A.A.F., she returned to the stage at a little theatre at Henley-on-Thames, and the Churchill family turned up almost in full strength, led by her mother, who was accompanied by Randolph, Mary, son-in-law Duncan Sandys, and the American Ambassador, Mr. John Winant.

Winston was busy that night, so Clementine brought him a few nights later.

Then, in the spring of 1948, Sarah brought a guest to 'meet the family' at Chartwell. His name was Anthony Beauchamp—a distinguished society photographer whom Sarah had known for some time.

Tony Beauchamp loved to recall that nerve-racking first meeting with the Churchills.

'It was terrifying,' he said, 'but in the nicest possible way.

'When we reached Chartwell, Sarah ran up the path ahead of me and vanished behind a bush. Then I heard a tremendous "Wow!"—it literally exploded across the quiet countryside. I later learnt that this was the traditional Churchill family greeting for each other adopted from the call of Sir Winston's famous Australian black swans. The "Wow!" had become part of the family special vocabulary of expression.

'Sarah reappeared from behind the bush with her arm round her father. I was suddenly scared stiff, aware that no less "suitable" prospective husband for his daughter could exist.

'I was still very nervous when we walked into the house to meet her mother. Suddenly, I felt more at ease. She had a wonderful knack of making you feel immediately at home and more comfortable. Although I knew I was being "inspected", she somehow made me feel she was as much on my side as on Sarah's.

'The whole family was there for lunch, and I was able to enjoy the meal, mainly thanks to the charm and soothing influence of her mother.'

Clementine and Winston made their new prospective son-in-law feel at home. Some months later he was invited to join them for a week when they were staying in Monte Carlo with Sarah. Sarah was very much in love with Tony, and her mother, more than anyone else, knew this. She felt that although he was a complete stranger to their world, this could be a much better match than Sarah's first marriage.

One afternoon, sitting in the Riviera sun alone with Clementine, Tony discussed gambling. They, in fact, discussed most things—except Sarah—although this was the subject uppermost in both their minds.

'Winston likes to pay an occasional visit to the Casino,' Clementine remarked. 'He likes to try his luck now and again.'

Tony mentioned that a friend of his had told him of a roulette system that always worked the first time. 'After that, you can lose a fortune with it, as I did,' added the friend.

'Tell Winston about this system,' advised Clementine, 'he will be very interested.'

Tony took her advice and, on the last night of his Monte Carlo stay, joined Winston at the Casino.

Tony decided to try out the system—and won, and won again.

Winston watched his run of luck, and started to place his own bets the same way. Chips began to pile up in front of him too, and he beamed with pleasure. It turned out to be the best night Winston had ever had at roulette. Said Tony: 'He began to take a more benevolent view of me after that evening. Her shrewd advice to me worked out very well.'

364

When Winston returned to the hostel with his winnings, he happily described Tony to Clementine and Sarah as a— 'Very clever young man indeed.'

Sarah accepted a theatrical tour of the U.S. starring in the Philip Barry play, *Philadelphia Story*. She scored a tremendous hit. Tony was unable to join her for several months because of his own work commitments. Then, as he was about to leave for America, Clementine asked him down to Chartwell.

She was a mother concerned over a daughter who had already had one unfortunate marriage.

Beside Winston's beloved fishponds where he kept his golden carp, the prospective father-in-law and prospective son-in-law discussed the future. A little later, when Winston was out of the room for a while, Clementine also talked about Sarah and of her concern for her happiness. Clementine was obviously still considering the prospects of a marriage between Sarah and Tony, but one thing was sure —she knew her daughter was in love.

On 7 October 1949, at a private house at Sea Island, Georgia, before an improvised altar banked high with masses of chrysanthemums, dahlias, magnolia, and ivy, Sarah and Tony were married.

There were no preparations for a formal wedding, they wanted it quiet. It didn't stay quiet for long.

After the ceremony they drove to a secluded honeymoon bungalow on the island. Located on the moonlit ocean side, it was a dream setting for the first night of a marriage. Suddenly, in their secret hideaway, the telephone rang. Sarah answered. It was a call from England.

Clementine was speaking from Chartwell. She was upset. 'Why didn't you let us know you were getting married?' she asked Sarah. 'Our first knowledge of it was through reading the papers.'

Sarah explained that she had in fact sent them a cable the day before but had sent it to their London home, which was obviously why they hadn't received it as yet.

Tony and Sarah continued their independent careers— Sarah went to Hollywood to star with Fred Astaire in *Wedding Bells*—Tony concentrated on photography and producing television series such as *Fabian of the Yard*.

Clementine saw Sarah and Tony spending almost half of

each year apart; rarely being in the same place at the same time. She herself had seldom been apart from Winston, and now she was anxious again for Sarah, appreciating that constant separations make shaky foundations for a sound marriage.

As Sarah later admitted: 'I lived for years in travelling trunks and hotels and on B.O.A.C. and T.W.A., and never properly unpacked once.'

Clementine and Winston were proud of her achievements as an actress, but they were concerned about her.

The end was tragedy. When they were 6,000 miles apart, Anthony Beauchamp, overworked and ill, was found dead from an overdose of sleeping drugs in his London apartment.

In April 1962, Sarah married Lord Audley in Gibraltar. Fourteen months later, he died.

Sarah tried to lose herself in her love of the theatre, as she had done on her return to England after being a top salary star for nine years in America. Then, she had begun all over again on the stage of the tiny Connaught theatre in Worthing, Sussex, with a local repertory company in which the average wage of the cast was £6 a week.

In the audience, the night of her comeback, sat her mother and father.

'Of what I know of children of famous people, if they have been brought up happily and properly, they are entirely unconscious of their parents' fame,' said Sarah. 'They expect to compete fairly in the career they have chosen.'

During the months that followed, she spent as much time as she could with her mother and father, but especially with her mother.

To help ease her tension, Clementine suggested she follow her father's example, and take up painting.

'Daddy encouraged me,' said Sarah.

'He said it was a great way of relaxing—he didn't start until he was forty.'

The months back with her family were just what Sarah needed.

Then, at Christmas, Clementine organized a fifteen-strong family party to visit the Scala Theatre, London. The party included Winston and four of their grandchildren. The occasion was Sarah's debut as Peter Pan.

366

Clementine led eleven of the party down to the front row of the stalls, while Winston sat with his grandchildren and hundreds of other children around him, in the front row of the circle where there were fewer stairs for him to climb.

Sarah, in coffee-coloured tights, flew through the air with the greatest of ease.

'I made ninety-six scheduled flights a week in this play. I felt like British European Airways,' said Sarah afterwards.

And, of the daughter who had gone her own way and lived her own life, Winston said at the end of the performance: 'I am very proud of her. I think she is wonderful.'

'And so do I,' added her mother.

PART III. HOW TO LOOK AFTER FATHER

ONE of Winston's greatest strengths was the family life Clementine wove around him. In everything, this was the mainspring of his existence. Clementine employed all her resourcefulness to free his mind from personal worries, reassuring him, supporting him with her confident cheerfulness.

And whenever domestic or other duties, or her own health prevented her from joining him on journeys, she made sure all her daughters were well briefed on 'How to look after father'.

Lloyd George said that she had once told him that if she should die she would leave behind written instructions to her successor on how to manage Winston.

'Chief item? His food,' said Clementine.

'First and most important is to feed him well. You must give him a good dinner. His dinner is a very important item in his daily routine,' she stressed.

Knowing that, at some time during most of his travels he would feel like indulging in his delight in picnicking, she issued standing instructions to her daughters and member of his staff, on the preparation of his picnic sandwiches.

'The sandwiches should be solid and substantial. Get hold of a large loaf and don't cut the slices too thin—or too thick, either. Trim the crusts off the edges and put plenty of butter on the bread. Be sure there's enough beef for him to know it's a beef sandwich.

'Be sure that the beef comes clear to the edge of the

bread. He doesn't like to bite twice into a sandwhich before he can tell what's inside it.

'He likes fish. He insists on meat being roasted because in roasting none of the juices and none of the flavour is lost.'

Winston enjoyed a perfectly done lamb chop, considered soups 'a good culinary institution'; was a firm believer in salads, and preferred to prepare the dressing himself. His preparation of a dressing was a ritual in itself. He had a special weakness for all kinds of cheese, which he liked to eat with his salad.

In her instructions Clementine would add: 'Don't forget the bowl of fruit in rooms.' A well-filled bowl was kept in his rooms as he loved to bite into a peach or an apple at odd times of the day or night.

'He likes anything—as long as it's the best,' said Clementine.

As a mother, she never allowed herself to become dependent on her children for companionship, and has never been lost without them. The family's greatest interest, of course, was always Winston. She encouraged her daughters to take over from her, from time to time, even in the undertaking of civic and political duties in their father's constituency, and all the children took a keen interest in the Chartwell estate.

Mary was the daughter who, when she was invited anywhere, always used to say: 'I'd love to, but I must ask Mummy first.'

She possessed the Churchill spirit even as a child. Wandering away from her mother for a few moments during an election campaign at Epping, Mary, aged six-and-a-half, did some canvassing of her own.

'Well, *are* you going to be Conservative or *aren't* you?' said Mary, holding her pencil poised over a piece of paper, 'because if you are not, I shall cross your name off, and whenever I pass you in the street I shall say "Shame! Shame!"'

'You must not be Liberal,' she said with determined emphasis. 'I despise them. Nobody ought to vote for Mr. Sharp (her father's Liberal opponent). Mr. Sharp said that my papa broke his promises, and I said "Pooh! pooh!" to him. My papa has never broken a promise.

'You must make up your mind quickly what you are going to be. If you do not decide to be Conservative I shall never come to see you and I shall take a house twenty miles away from you so that you can't come and see me.'

'But I might have a fast car,' said one person under fire from little Mary.

'Then I shall go and live in France so as not to see you.'

'But I could go and live in Paris,' came the reply.

'Then I should go to Australia and have a pet kangaroo and a bush baby and a ring opossum.'

When the object of one of her arguments said he wasn't convinced and was going to vote Socialist, Mary, grey eyes blazing, reared as if about to attack him physically, then, controlling herself, said: 'You are *disgusting*!'

Then, remembering her mother's discipline on how a lady should behave in public, and with a touch of Churchill diplomacy, she added, as her mother reappeared on the scene: 'If you change your mind, let me know. Don't forget.'

Clementine was expecting Mary when she went to Frinton for the seaside holiday with her cousin, Miss Whyte. They stayed at a house called Marylands.

'The baby will surely arrive here, Clemmie,' said Miss Whyte, 'and you'll have to call it Mary after the name of the house.'

And they did call it Mary.

At the age of fifteen, Mary still only looked about ten or twelve and would think nothing of walking barefoot into her father's office at night with a dirty old mackintosh over her pyjamas.

She loved to gossip, and read poetry she'd written to her father, mother, and members of the household staff—and it was very good poetry.

Mary loved her horse, and used to do a lot of riding at Chartwell, but had to leave the horse behind when the family left Chartwell for Admiralty House at the beginning of the war. She cried for days at being parted from the horse.

But for the war, Mary, the only one of the Churchills to inherit the beautiful dark brows of her grandmother, Lady Randolph Churchill, would have been *the* debutante of 1940. Not just because she was Winston Churchill's youngest child, but because of her own charm and beauty. But the war stopped the Courts, so Mary could not make the traditional curtsy to the King and Queen, and enjoy acclamation as the 'Season's loveliest deb'.

Instead, her mother arranged for her to 'come out' on Leap Year night at a great charity ball held in aid of Queen Charlotte's Hospital.

Clementine chose a white dress for her to set off her youthful freshness, adding a wreath of white flowers to her hair, and giving her a Victorian posy basket to carry. But there is no picture of Mary Churchill in her coming-out dress—her mother forbade it to be taken.

Mary had never posed for a studio portrait in her life, and she just wouldn't be photographed—even at the proud age of seventeen-and-a-half.

When photographers asked Mary to pose in her coming-out gown, Clementine answered: 'Thank you, it is very kind, but Mary would rather not.'

Knowing her daughter to be a sweet seventeen who preferred riding, country walks and looking after the pets at Chartwell, Clementine was determined to protect her as much as she could from the dangers of too much limelight too soon.

It was in 1941, at the age of eighteen, that Mary, who had been working as an assistant librarian in a hospital, stepped out on her own to become Private Mary Churchill A.T.S.

'Mummy and Daddy were delighted that I should keep the army in the family,' said Mary. Winston had, of course, served in the previous war with the rank of Lieutenant-Colonel.

Private Mary Churchill passed her preliminary selection test for anti-aircraft work and was posted to a mixed battery. Her mother introduced only one careful parental note into Mary's choice of war-time career—she arranged for Mary's friend, Judy Montagu, daughter of her own cousin, to be in the same unit.

Clementine also saw to it that she was treated as just an ordinary girl. Mary slept in a hut with twenty girls, made her own bed, cleaned the hut in her turn, and sometimes served in the officers' mess.

And Mary enjoyed herself as an ordinary girl too—even to the point of getting spanked in public by an ordinary soldier.

Mary, by now Sergeant Mary Churchill, was dancing with an American sergeant at a local hop near her unit.

The sergeant, all six-foot-one of him, towered over her, and his outsize feet trod all over her. Finally she could take it no longer, and made some remarks about his standard of dancing. He wasn't going to be dressed down by a woman and, without hesitation, laid Mary across his knees and gave her a good spanking in front of everyone.

His big hand pumped up and down, dishing out punishment, while Mary yelled the roof off.

When someone told him he had just tanned the behind of Winston Churchill's daughter, he simply said:

'Well, whaddaya know!'

Mary—brave campaigner that she was—stayed until the last waltz, although she couldn't sit out any more dances for the rest of the evening.

In 1947, Clementine added an eighteenth-century touch to the reception she organized for eight hundred guests at the Dorchester Hotel, London, to celebrate the wedding of Mary to Captain Christopher Soames, at St. Margaret's, Westminster.

With her typical flair for showmanship and taste, she arranged for twenty-four candelabra to be used to supplement the hotel's lighting in the ballroom, so that the bride and groom could walk out of the dancing shadows to the platform where they cut the three-tier cake made for them by Mr. Frank Boreham, the baker who had supplied the Churchill family at Chartwell for twenty-four years.

Mary's husband became Winston and Clementine's new son, taking over Chartwell farm and transforming it into a thriving business. He also supervised Winston's string of racehorses; and became an M.P., his father-in-law's Parliamentary Private Secretary, and a Government Minister.

When he became a Minister, Mary began to take on similar social and political duties that her mother had fulfilled nearly forty years before, and Clementine began to teach her to understand and how to undertake the kind of responsibilities with which she herself had had to contend as a young wife. Mary was to be the one who, more than her other daughters, was to follow in her footsteps.

Mary had very special 'how-to-look-after-father' guidance from her mother when she deputized for Clementine during part of Winston's convalescence after his stroke in 1953.

She and her husband Christopher Soames were with the

Prime Minister when he went to Lord Beaverbrook's house at Cap d'Ail, for some recuperation in the French Riviera's sunshine.

Learning that Winston's friend, Sir Tom O'Brien, was also holidaying close by, Christopher Soames telephoned to invite him to lunch with his father-in-law.

'I went there for lunch, and it was the first time that anyone from Britain had seen the Prime Minister since his stroke, and few seemed to know how he was really progressing,' said Sir Tom. 'I fully expected to see him in bed, laid up hard. Instead of that, he was in the lounge reading his newspaper, and got up to greet me as I walked in. We went out into the garden; had a drink there with Mary and Christopher, and it was almost impossible to realize he had just gone through such a serious illness ordeal.

'Thinking that Clementine was there, I said to Mary, "Is your mother upstairs?—I would like to see her."

' "My mother," said Mary, "is a great woman as well as a great wife. My mother feels that the later she comes to see my father, the better it will be for him."

'I asked what she meant, and she replied: "Well, he is recovering remarkably, and whatever irritations he has, he's got to have them with himself, so she's keeping well out of the way. My mother is a wise woman."

'That is a tribute from her child to her mother's knowledge and patience. It was a human family thing. We spent the afternoon talking about every conceivable subject, and although Clementine wasn't there in person, there was the feeling that she was nevertheless present somehow.

'I think Mary is closest of all the daughters to her mother's disposition. Sweet, understanding—with that domestic warmth—that love of family that her mother has.

'Lady Churchill has always been a wonderful mother. She has had difficult times with her children, as have millions of other parents, but the children of a public man have their troubles blazoned across the world, they can't be suppressed, can't be hidden. Their mother has acquitted herself with great dignity through various domestic crises in the family. Few women can do that. They would, in some way, betray lack of trust in their children or would publicly indicate some rebuke, but not Clementine. Whatever her domestic difficulties, she behaved with that tact and understanding that had made her such a remarkable woman.'

Again following in her mother's footsteps, Mary kept some of her work for good causes secret from her father. But she also kept it secret from her mother for a very long time. Mary plays a very active part in the organizing and reorganizing of Church Army hostels.

Clementine admitted to a friend: 'I only discovered this quite by chance. She didn't even tell me.'

The rest of Clementine and Winston's family consists of their grandchildren, Julian, Edwina, and Celia—the children of Mr. and Mrs. Duncan Sandys; and Winston Churchill Junior, and Arabella—Randolph's son and daughter.

Mary gave them five grandchildren, including a Winston Soames, and a Clementine Soames.

Mary also gave her mother and father something else— her very birth brought them consolation at a time of great personal tragedy.

The night of 23 August 1921 was a never-to-be-forgotten night in the lives of Clementine and Winston.

Marigold Frances Churchill was their fourth child.

Marigold had her father's gingery red hair, and her mother's engaging smile. Already, at the age of three, she was a miniature ball of fire delighting in reciting nursery rhymes to everyone in sight, and running races with servants round the dining-table.

She was a 'Mummy's girl', shadowing her mother almost everywhere. Marigold clung much more to her mother than shy Sarah.

During the summer of 1921, Clementine sent Marigold and her nanny, Miss Whyte, away for some sea air at Broadstairs, Kent. Marigold was having a wonderful time on the beach when she was suddenly taken ill.

Clementine hurried down. Marigold was too ill to be moved, and doctors were unable to diagnose the nature of the illness.

Winston couldn't get down to Broadstairs until the weekend and then had to return to London on the Sunday night because of urgent Ministry business.

Clementine and Miss Whyte hardly left Marigold's bedside, taking it in turns to watch over her day and night.

The instant Winston was able to free himself of his ministerial duties, he hurried down there again to be by his wife

373

and child, but was compelled to return again to Whitehall.

One morning, a message from Clementine sent him rushing back to Broadstairs.

For a time, he sat with Clementine beside Marigold's bed. In the early evening he went out into the grounds of the house on South Cliff Parade, and just walked up and down, tears streaming down his face. He spoke to no one. Clementine remained inside with Marigold.

His wife's voice called him, and he hurried in.

Within moments, he reappeared in the garden. For the first time in hours, he turned to one of his staff and spoke.

'I know you were very fond of her,' he said. 'I'm sure you'd like to see her.'

Winston was like a man lost, and could not stop his tears. Clementine joined him, but there were no tears from her. The rigid self-discipline, now so much a part of her make-up, seemed to grip the emotions within her.

She didn't cry, nor did she speak. She had just lost her child. Now her one concern was to comfort her husband in his grief.

Clementine's discipline of herself seldom allowed her to lower the barrier she kept permanently in front of her innermost feelings.

She steeled herself against personal tragedy in her own way, and looked at the other side of death.

She treasured the memory of her dead sister with a photograph of her lying in her coffin. She had the photograph taken because her sister had looked so beautiful even in death.

When her mother died at Dieppe, Clementine and Winston went across together. Again she restrained her tears.

Only to their friend Professor Lindemann did she, years later, give a revealing insight into her emotions when, in a letter of condolence to the Professor at the death of his mother, she wrote:

'The loss of one's mother is a sad milestone in one's life. After that one is nobody's child and it is a lonely feeling.'

Joy and laughter she will let everyone see. Sorrow she would share with no one, except her husband.

Clementine talked of her mother, talked of her sister, but never of Marigold.

24

THE DISTINGUISHED STRANGER

ON 8 June 1946, Winston and Clementine took their places on the great V.I.P. grandstand erected for that day of days —the Victory Parade. There, with the Royal Family, Mr. and Mrs. Clement Attlee, and finally joined by the King, they witnessed the great march and drive past of representatives from every branch of the fighting services, and of the civilians who had fought equally well in the Home Front line.

When the massive parade was over, they all went to Downing Street for lunch, and in the evening, to the House of Commons to watch the victory firework display over the Thames. There they found the King, the Queen, Queen Mary, Princess Elizabeth and Princess Margaret, the Dutchess of Kent, the Crown Prince of Norway, the Athlones, and the Attlee family. It was a gathering of gatherings, a night of nights, a day and night of emotions for them that no words could possibly capture.

Winston was his fighting self again and Clementine was back in her customary seat in the Distinguished Strangers' Gallery of the House of Commons watching him in action.

He was attacking Socialist expenditure when one of the members on the Labour benches of the House cried: 'Why don't you sell your horse?'—a reference to his racehorse Columnist II, which had already run several races and become a popular favourite.

Winston rounded on the interrupter: 'Well, that at least is a piece of property which has increased its value since it came under my control,' he countered.

'As a matter of fact, I was strongly tempted to sell the horse; but I am doing my best to fight against a profit motive.'

He looked up at Clementine with a boyish, impish grin as he heard her laugh above the roar of amusement on the floor of the House.

It was in 1946 that a group of their friends bought

Chartwell Manor for the National Trust. Some years before the war, their personal finances were hard hit—Winston had never been a rich man—and, at one time, it seemed they would be forced to sell the house they cherished so much. Preliminary plans were even made for its sale. Then friends evolved a financial arrangement whereby the Churchills could live at Chartwell tax free for the rest of their lives, after which it would go to the National Trust as a memorial of his services to the Commonwealth.

With his wife's moral support, affection, and understanding, Winston recovered from the wounds which the election defeat had inflicted upon him. He became Leader of the Opposition with a capital 'O'. He fought the Socialists ferociously; moved votes of censure regularly; battled Herbert Morrison every Thursday over such small things as the business for the following week.

It was a fighting example to the Tory Party, bewildered by its downfall after years of power. On world problems he was still the world's greatest statesman, and, time after time, Clementine was there in the gallery of the House of Commons, smiling down her encouragement.

Whenever he made an important speech in Parliament, as he rose to speak, he never failed to look to the gallery where Clementine sat, and she would acknowledge his gaze with a little encouraging wave.

Then, when he had finished, and before resuming his seat, he would look again to her for the smile of approval.

* * *

The wounds had completely healed by the 1950 General Election. Clementine was confident they would be returning to 10 Downing Street.

She was not really keen on his returning to Downing Street, but recognizing that, at that time, the fortunes of the Conservative Party vitally needed him to resume the Premiership for at least two years, she did not press him to quit the leadership of the Party.

Without her—his 'devoted aide', as he himself called her —it is doubtful whether he would have come so robustly and so magnificently through life. Marriage to a genius requires in itself a measure of genius. Little wonder that Lord Riddell, describing her, said she was: 'A queen of wives', and 'manages Winston very well'.

But Winston's own eloquent testimony to her is better than anyone else could hope to give.

After General Lord Ismay had proposed a toast to them both at a private party, Winston, in replying, said: 'I could never have succeeded without her.'

And at Strasbourg, his eyes brimming with tears, he declared:

'It would not be possible for any public man to get through what I have gone through without the devoted assistance of what we call in England one's "better half".'

It was not the only public tribute he paid to her. He once wrote: 'My marriage was much the most fortunate and joyous event which happened to me in the whole of my life, for what can be more glorious than to be united in one's walk through life with a being incapable of an ignoble thought.'

'My most brilliant achievement was my ability to be able to persuade my wife to marry me,' he once remarked.

How different might have been his career, and the history of the world if she had chosen otherwise for herself?

On polling day, 1950, she was the first member of the Churchill family to vote in London. She drove from their home in Hyde Park Gate early in the morning and gave the V sign to the canvassers.

Winston arrived at the same polling station a little later. As he went in to vote, Winston removed his hat, put on his glasses, and studied the candidates' list. He then entered a booth, and stayed for a minute and a half.

'He is thinking it over,' someone cracked. Winston emerged, shook hands, and they were greeted all the way down the street by other cars, honking V in Morse code chorus. They drove to Woodford, where hundreds lined the streets for them.

Leaving Woodford Memorial Hall after a meeting in the constituency, they found themselves surrounded by members of the local Labour Party League of Youth. Young Socialists offered them handfuls of the Labour Party leaflets.

'No,' exclaimed Clementine, 'I daren't take them. They might convert me.'

Election night they spent together at their Hyde Park

377

Gate home. When it was over, Winston beamed at Clementine: 'I like the look of this house much better than the old one,' he said.

On 31 October 1950, 275 Conservative Peers and M.P.s gave a dinner to mark the fiftieth anniversary of Winston's first return to Parliament. This was one great milestone Clementine had to forgo. She had promised to attend an important engagement in Edinburgh on the night of the banquet and so missed an occasion granted to few Parliamentarians in any age. Even so, Clementine was still, in certain respects, represented at the dinner. Each course traced his Parliamentary life from election at Oldham in 1900.

Sherries, turtle soup, and appetizers were named after two of his constituencies. Fillets of sole were named after the Cinque Ports of Dover, Hastings, Sandwich, New Romney, and Hythe of which he had been Warden since 1941. Mushrooms from his constituents of Epping Forest followed.

Partridge on toast with English sauce became 'les perdreaux rôtis sur canapés Clementine', and in this sense Clementine was there in the flesh.

Dinner was topped off with coffee, 'hot and strong à la Winston Spencer Churchill'.

Presented by a Conservative group with a medallion of the unscupulous ill-tempered Sarah, first Duchess of Marlborough, Clementine responded to the gift with: 'I am very grateful indeed, and to show my gratitude I shall do my best to develop as few as possible of Sarah's qualities.'

Vivacious, quick-witted, ever the perfect helpmeet, she walked by Winston's side while continuing to keep out of the limelight, preferring it to be directed on him. But perhaps her greatest talent was her own genius for helping a dynamo husband to relax. Her cheerfulness, even in times of crisis, her gay conversation and knack of making people feel brighter, all helped to restore Winston to his former self. He was right back on form.

At the opening of the Festival of Britain, organized to mark the centenary of the Great Exhibition in Hyde Park of 1851, and to display the British contribution to civilization, past, present, and future, in science, the arts, and industrial design, Winston and Clementine were among the many distinguished guests at the royal opening day. The King and Queen, Queen Mary, and all the members of the Royal Family were there, but suddenly Winston was absent. Clementine had to go hunting for him—she found him riding up and down, and down and up, over and over again, on an escalator—he had never been on one before.

*   *   *

The spirit of victory was in the air once more in their home. The voters were about to go to the polls in the 1951 General Election.

Clementine felt an overwhelming certainty that Winston would be back in Parliament as Prime Minister. She was sure that after fifty-two years of political life, he was about to become Prime Minister of a peace-time Britain, with a strong and workable majority.

She joined him in fighting the election on the high cost of living at home, and the fall in British prestige abroad.

This time the Socialists made the big campaign blunder—they branded him 'a warmonger'. Furious at this attack, Clementine denounced it as 'cruel, ungrateful and the opposite of the truth. Bursting as he does with the sense of justice and fair play which inspires the British people, Winston is sure these taunts and insults will recoil upon the heads of those that make them.'

Once again she gave him her arm, her charm, and her strength on a nation-wide electioneering tour. It was a prodigious feat of stamina on both their parts.

No two cities were treated to the same speech; each was composed and typed out an hour or so before it was delivered. Clementine was always there doing her utmost to lessen the fatigue of the journeying, supervising staff—domestic, and innumerable political arrangements, ensuring everything was as Winston liked it to be—the baggage on the trains, the wardrobe, the arsenal of cigars and papers of reference, including the famous black dispatch boxes that he had kept from his tenure of various Crown offices.

Always on the cushions of his special railway coach were two or three of these boxes, including those of the Ministry of Munitions from the First World War, and another with the dulled gold lettering of the 'Chancellor of the Exchequer'. Clementine carried on the important morning

379

routine of carefully scrutinizing all the newspapers, looking for items that might be necessary or valuable ammunition for Winston to consider and use.

And she made sure that every afternoon he took his very necessary after-lunch nap and rest with a comforting cigar in his hand.

Voices continued to accuse Winston of being 'not interested' in the problems of peace, and concerned only with war. While the war was on, that was in fact true, and Clementine had told friends: 'Winston says that unless we win the war, we need not plan for the peace, for there will be none!'

While the cries of 'Warmonger!' grew in volume, Winston dreamed of, and worked for, his now famous Four Year Plan with its visionary schemes for fuller employment and trade, and for social welfare. The mind that had invented labour exchanges to offer men work was very much concerned with the problems of peace.

Only Clementine completely understood his intolerance of the election, his complicated character, his irascibility, and his gentleness, with its deep understanding of the difficulties of others. She went alone to his constituency at Woodford, and five hundred people heard her deliver a full-scale attack on the Government's foreign policy and, in particular, its treatment of the Palestine problem. She condemned what she called 'an instance of the most appalling bungling which committed all the arms being used by the Arabs against the Jews to be provided by Britain, and allowed British officers to command the Arab legions'.

Clementine knew how to handle crowds, knew how to handle people. She could also address a conference, and bring it to its feet with admiration for her oratory. She too has mastery of words.

At a women's conference at Central Hall, Westminster, she said the right things in the right way when she proclaimed: 'In the next election the Conservatives will be returned to power. Then will come their opportunity: they will have to be very brave, very wise, and very patient. It might not be possible to unpick everything the Socialists have done, and they would have to consider very carefully what might be unpicked, what must be rearranged, and what they could do.'

At another meeting she shrewdly aimed at election targets with an accuracy women particularly appreciated. She brought home the housing shortage. 'The Labour Government is putting up houses all over the country at the rate of 500 a day. But before the war the Conservatives turned them out, like shelling peas, at 1,000 a day,' she declared.

She knew how to hit home on domestic issues, and never lost touch with the mass of women.

The last speech of the campaign had been arranged for Plymouth, where their son Randolph was campaigning at near-by Devonport. Before they left for Plymouth they listened to the radio election address of the then Prime Minister, Clement Attlee. When Attlee finished, Winston said nothing for the moment, then Clementine, with that political shrewdness seldom seen by the public and equal to that of her husband, said: 'Winston, I think that is a very good speech—but it is a recessional speech.'

'Very well put, Clemmie, that's exactly the right word for it,' said Winston with an appreciative smile.

The air of defeatism in the Attlee broadcast made them even more certain of victory.

Accompanied by Sarah, their son-in-law photographer Anthony Beauchamp, and Randolph's son, young Winston, they left by train to appear before a crowd of 10,000 at Plymouth Argyle football ground.

After attacking the Socialist warmonger charges, Winston added the kind of human note that endeared him to the crowd when he said: 'I am always glad to come to the West Country, and here we have the candidates for Totnes, Tavistock, Bodmin and Sutton, and,' he said, glancing at Randolph, 'as you will understand, last but not least to me, Devonport.'

That night they dined with Lord and Lady Astor at their house on Plymouth Hoe. Thousands who knew they were inside milled around outside, hoping to catch a glimpse of them.

'Don't disappoint them, Winston,' said Clemmie. 'Speak to them,' she advised. He took her advice, and from the balcony of the Astor home made an informal speech that was unreported. It was impromptu, and straight from the heart.

'Whichever way you vote,' he told the crowd, 'whether it

is for us or for the Socialists at least you must give us a good working majority. It will be far better to return the Socialists to power once again than to send us back with a majority so small that it would be impossible to govern.'

As he said this, there were a few boos from the crowd, to which he replied: 'I must say I like to hear some boos. After all, if you have a right to have cheers, you have a right to have boos.'

Then, speaking slowly and with emphasis, he went on: 'I would rather have a Socialist Government for four or five years——' There were cheers and boos.

Turning to the booing section of the crowd, he observed: 'Don't do them in the wrong place,' and continued—

'—than to have a continuance of this present indeterminate miserable situation.'

Winston went on: 'Don't you think it is time there should be a new eye on the sea, a new hand on the tiller, a new approach to our foreign and our home problems?' There was an overwhelming 'Yes!' Winston, turning to Clementine, remarked: 'I think the majority is with me.'

Jacob Astor got his Socialist opponent out at Plymouth but Randolph, though succeeding in greatly reducing the Socialist majority at Devonport, failed to win the seat.

Winston and Clementine returned to Hyde Park Gate for election day, and attended the Conservative election party at the Savoy Hotel given by Lord Camrose of the *Daily Telegraph*. By the time they went home, the Socialists and Conservatives seemed to be running level. Winston and Clementine remained confident.

In the early hours of the morning, when key constituencies had clearly indicated the result, Clementine crossed the room to Winston and kissed him, he kissed her, and neither spoke a word.

For both of them this triumph softened the bitterness of the 1945 defeat.

In the middle of that night a crowd gathered outside their home, and voices started calling 'Winnie!'

Exhausted by the strenuous campaign, he little felt like answering their calls—he just wanted to go to bed. Clementine, wearing the two red roses on her black dress he had given her to mark the occasion, had retired to her room too, but the crowd refused to go.

Finally, in their dressing-gowns, they appeared at the window to give a happy victory wave. Satisfied, the crowd gave a last cheer and quietly left to give 'the old man' a well-deserved night's sleep.

'I have the reins of the country in my hands again, Clementine,' he said. She kissed him 'goodnight' and went to her room.

The famous poured into Chartwell to confer with Winston before the formation of the new Government. Life was hectic and exciting, and Clementine had her hands full acting as hostess to the ceaseless stream of notabilities.

She had her own post-election comment:

'To those who wonder why my husband continued to bear in public affairs a burden that would crush many a younger man, the answer is that Winston thinks things are being managed so badly!'

It was with a new kind of confidence, not a confidence founded on the past, but one based on the future, that they returned to No. 10 Downing Street.

25

THAT WAS NO LADY

THE discovery of an entirely new eavesdropping device planted by the Russians in the U.S. Embassy in Moscow started a security scare that hit every Government office in London, including 10, Downing Street.

The Russians had secreted a mini microphone in a model of the Great Seal of the United States thereby inviting themselves to all the discussions in the American Ambassador's study.

10 Downing Street was consequently almost taken apart, and when the searchers were horrified to discover a microphone hidden, in of all places, the Prime Minister's chair in the Cabinet Room, there was, of course, an immediate alarm. But when told about it, Winston confessed, with some embarrassment:

'It was not the work of a spy. I had it installed there myself. It was Clementine's idea, and a very good one.'

He had been getting rather deaf, so Clementine tactfully arranged for his armchair to be 'bugged' with a secret microphone to enable him to hear his Ministers without resorting to an obvious deaf aid.

She always saw to his comforts while he took care of the nation.

In December 1952, they sailed to America again and Mary and her husband Christopher Soames, were with them in mid-Atlantic when they joined passengers in the main lounge to welcome in the New Year.

As they appeared in the lounge, dancing stopped and everyone crowded round.

Champagne was poured, and, as midnight struck, bells and hooters sounded throughout the ship. Winston rose, took Clementine's hand on one side, and Mary's on the other, and joined in 'Auld Lang Syne'. Then he kissed Clementine as they went to their table. On the stage a bearded figure pronounced the death of 1952, followed by a young girl representing 1953. The purser welcomed the

New Year, 'and our distinguished guests, Mr. and Mrs. Churchill'.

'Some of you,' he said, 'may think that I have gone off the stage with the old year.'

'Never!' came a deafening shout from everyone.

He smiled. 'You have given me a mandate to progress into the future,' he declared, and sat down as cheers ran round the ballroom, and guests stood with glasses raised to toast the Churchills.

Fifteen minutes later they were back in their suite—and he was back at work.

Visiting Canada, Winston, in an interview, was asked: 'Mr. Churchill, why am I not calling you Sir Winston?'

'Why what?' exclaimed Winston.

'Why are you not knighted?' persisted the interviewer.

Winston looked thoughtful, then at Clementine, and they both laughed. Suddenly, he became serious and said: 'I don't want to make merry over "sirs",' he explained with complete gravity, 'but you know, titles are all matters of taste—and I don't believe I've got the taste. My own unadorned name will have to do me, I'm afraid.'

Later, at the Coronation of Queen Elizabeth II in June 1953, leading the magnificent procession of Commonwealth Prime Ministers in Westminster Abbey came a resplendent Sir Winston in the plumes and dazzling robes of a Knight of the Garter—the honour he had refused after his political defeat in the 1945 election.

When Winston accepted the Order of the Garter from Queen Elizabeth, Clementine said: 'Now we will have to have our visiting cards changed.'

Winston remembered this remark when they were on their way to Windsor Castle for the investiture ceremony of the Garter.

As their car drove past a village railway station, Winston, observing the word 'Ladies', pointed to the notice and said to Clementine: 'As from tomorrow you will be entitled to go in there!'

Winston had refused an offer of the Garter in 1945, immediately after his defeat in the post-war election. An official announcement said 'he begged his Majesty (George VI) that, in present circumstances, he might be allowed to decline'.

385

At that time, recommendations to the order were made by the Prime Minister of the day—then Mr. Clement Attlee.

The procedure was changed, and it became for the Sovereign alone to decide who should be admitted.

So Winston, who throughout his fifty-three years in public life had steadfastly refused a title, assumed one—by personal wish of the Queen.

With Clementine he drove to Windsor from Downing Street, and the ceremony took place before dinner, in one of the drawing-rooms.

Watched by his wife, the seventy-eight-year-old Prime Minister knelt before his young Queen to receive his knighthood. The Queen did, in fact, offer him a Dukedom. Years later she explained:

'I thought that when he resigned as Prime Minister, and would no longer play an active role in party politics, I might honour his wholly exceptional achievements by offering him a dukedom. No such distinction had been proposed for nearly a century.

'But he wanted to spend his last years where he had passed almost all his adult life—in the House of Commons —and indeed he had no need for distinction greater than the name of Winston Churchill.'

Clementine had herself been created Dame Grand Cross of the Order of the British Empire for her war-time services but she always disliked her official title of Dame Clementine Churchill, and used it rarely, preferring to be known as Mrs. Churchill. She was delighted in fact when, in accordance with custom, she was able to lose the designation of Dame as soon as Winston was created a Knight.

Clementine tackled every task with supreme confidence. Only once was she visibly shaken and really nervous, and that was when she went to accept the Nobel Prize on his behalf.

It was December 1953, and Winston was busy meeting world statesmen across the other side of the Atlantic.

If the Nobel Prize winner is unable to receive the reward in person it is customary for his country's ambassador to do so, but, acknowledging the tremendous part Clementine had played in her husband's life and career, the Swedes invited her to receive it in his place.

The Swedes recognized her as an outstanding personality

on her own merit.

They also realized that no one who could imagine what it must be like to look after a husband who is at times a volcano and at times a whirlwind could possibly cease to marvel at her management of Winston.

To one woman who complimented her on being married to such a great man, she replied, with a laugh: 'Oh! Do you think it is amusing all the time, every day? If you do, you are very wrong. Not so long ago I said to Winston that if I had to be born a second time and was asked if I would be willing to marry a man of genius, I am not quite sure that I would answer "Yes"!'

But she *had* married a genius, and here she was, excited and very nervous at the thought of representing him at the great, historic, Nobel Prize ceremony.

On many occasions she had stepped in when he had been unable to make a public appearance and then, and only then, had she used his words, his speech.

One evening, when he was suffering from a severe bronchial cold, she had taken his place at a political dinner and read his speech on the Suez Canal crisis.

Another time she stood in for him at the launching of the Cunard liner *Saxonia*, on the Clydeside. The ship was the largest to be built to go up the St. Lawrence River to Montreal.

But before reading Winston's message at the launching, she added a personal note. She said: 'I asked Sir Winston for a message; he spoke very quickly and I had to grab a piece of paper to scribble it down. Then I pinched his arm and said "Now pay attention while I read it back."

'He did, and here is the message....'

Now here she was going to Stockholm to deliver another kind of message from him.

With Mary to support her morale, she crossed to Stockholm to be the guest of King Gustav.

In the privacy of her suite in the royal palace she practised the speech she was to make at the Nobel Prize banquet.

'I must rehearse and make sure I have it right—the speech isn't very long, but I have never had to read a message from him on such an important occasion before,' she said to Mary. And, for the first time, cool, calm, composed

Clementine admitted she was having a mild attack of 'stomach butterflies'.

'It is not the place, but *The Speech* that is upsetting me. I'm just a tiny bit nervous about reading Winston's speech at the banquet.'

Sensing how she would feel, Winston began to bombard her with a series of cables from distant Bermuda.

Said the first: 'I will keep my fingers crossed while you read my speech.'

Said the second, with painful memories of his New York car accident: 'Be careful in the Stockholm traffic. It still keeps left like ours but may soon change to right.'

And the third, which arrived on her breakfast tray on the morning of the banquet, said: 'Good luck and all my love, Winnie.'

'A trip round the world would be a good way to spend the prize-money,' (£12,000) commented Clementine.

'That is something I've always wished to do, and I may have made the trip if the money had been awarded to me.'

She confided to Mary: 'As it is a short speech if I talk quickly it will be over in less than five minutes.'

Winston had written the 500-word message before flying to Bermuda.

Clementine and Mary shook Stockholm by wearing exactly the same shaped hats. Clementine's was a turquoise blue with a veil, and Mary's white, without a veil.

King Gustav Adolf and Queen Louise personally conducted them on a tour round the Summer Palace at Drottingholm, then came the great day and the frightening moment for Clementine.

She arrived for the presentation looking every inch, as she is, a queen among women. She had dressed in a steel-grey evening dress with pale blue tulle stole and a diamond tiara and white gloves.

Mary wore a pearl-peaked coronet.

Two thousand people, representing science, art, and fashion, stood as she curtsied to the King in Stockholm's magnificent concert hall.

She had listened in the past to hundreds of speeches, from the great and the lowly, praising Winston, but she had never heard greater tributes to him than were paid that day in Stockholm.

388

'The Grand Old Man' of Swedish literature, Dr. Sigfried Siwertz, painted a glowing word-picture of the life, personality, and achievements of the first statesman ever to receive the Nobel Prize award. Then Dr. Siwertz bowed low to Clementine sitting with Mary a little to the left of the six members of the Swedish Royal Family.

Speaking in English, he said: 'The Swedish Academy express joy at your presence and asks you to convey our respects to Sir Winston. The Nobel Prize for Literature is meant to give lustre to the author. In this case the author gives lustre to the prize.'

Clementine walked a few paces to where King Gustav Adolf stood, and curtsied. The King grasped her hand which he held for almost a minute as he spoke in a low voice to her. Then he handed her the Nobel book and medal while a triumphal fanfare sounded.

Applause for her was prolonged and loud, contrasting with the restrained handclapping that normally greeted other prizewinners. But it was still not yet time for Clementine to carry out her duty. Her reply was to be reserved for the banquet to be held later in the lakeside Town Hall.

Immediately after the ceremony, most of the guests scrambled for taxis or walked through the streets to the Town Hall for the banquet.

Attended by 950 guests, the banquet was held in a large hall with 1,000 candles burning in candelabra. It was a magnificent setting for a magnificent occasion.

The hall was decorated with Byzantine mosaics in tens of thousands of tiny, gilded pieces; Romans staring glassy-eyed, and ancient Swedish heroes wielding swords and battle-axes.

Men were in their evening dress covered in colourful Swedish orders, and elegant women wore elegant gowns.

Then, in a clear, firm voice, Clementine stood to read Winston's words—a typical Churchillian speech full of that rolling rhetoric which, as much as his writings, had gained him the Nobel Prize.

On his behalf Clementine declared: 'The Nobel Prize for Literature is an honour for me alike unique and unexpected and I grieve that my duties have not allowed me to receive it myself here in Stockholm from the hands of his Majesty your beloved and justly respected sovereign. I am grateful that I am allowed to confide this task to my wife.

'The roll on which my name has been inscribed represents much that is outstanding in the world's literature of the 20th Century. I am proud but also I must admit awestruck at your decision to include me. I do hope you are right.

'I feel that we are both running a considerable risk that I do not deserve it. But I shall have no misgivings if you have none.'

The great banqueting room roared with laughter, and Clementine paused, smiling happily at the reception of her husband's humour.

She continued: 'Sir Alfred Nobel died in 1896. We have entered an age of storm and tragedy. The power of man has grown in every sphere except over himself.

'Never in the field of action have events seemed so harshly to dwarf personalities. Rarely in history have brutal facts so dominated thought, or had such a widespread individual virtue found so dim a collective focus.

'The fearful question confronts us: Have our problems got beyond our control? Undoubtedly we are passing through a phase where this may be so. Well may we humble ourselves and seek for guidance and mercy.

'We in Europe and the Western world who have planned for health and social security, who have marvelled at the triumphs of medicine and science and who have aimed at justice and freedom for all, have nevertheless been witnesses of famine, misery, cruelty and destruction before which pale the deeds of Attila and Genghis Khan.

'And we who, first in the League of Nations and now in the United Nations, have attempted to give an abiding foundation to the peace of which men have dreamed so long, have lived to see a world marred by cleavages and threatened by discords even greater and more violent than those which convulsed Europe after the fall of the Roman Empire.

'It is upon this dark background that we can appreciate the majesty and hope which inspired the conception of Alfred Nobel. He has left behind him a bright and enduring beam of culture of purpose and inspiration to a generation which stands in sore need.

'This world-famous institution points a truth path for us to follow. Let us therefore confront the clatter and rigidity we see around us with tolerance, variety and calm.

'The world looks with admiration and, indeed, with comfort to Scandinavia, where three countries, without sacrificing their sovereignty live united in their thought, in their practice, and in their healthy way of life. From such fountains new and brighter opportunities may come to all mankind.

'These are, I believe, the sentiments which may animate those whom the Nobel foundation elects to honour, in the sure knowledge that they will thus be respecting the ideals and wishes of its illustrious founder.'

Clementine sat down to a tremendous ovation. The most frightening minutes of her life were over.

She was wearing the same evening dress she had worn at the prizegiving but with the addition of her sash as a Dame of the Order of the British Empire, and her medals.

Following the banquet came the great ball, attended by 550 students, with dancing in the splendid brick-walled lower hall.

Clementine and Mary watched the dancers from a balcony overlooking the hall. She was seated beside the King and Queen. Here she was in the place of honour in the gallery of the Town Hall, and below were students and their girl-friends celebrating the event.

Suddenly, some of the students started to sing, and everyone on the floor took up the words and melody of the song. It was 'Oh my darling, Oh my darling, Oh my darling, Clementine!'—and they sang it in English.

It was a rare, unforgettable moment in more ways than one. Clementine, who seldom reveals her emotions before others, this time could not hide her tears. She stood up, waved, and smiled as the students below clapped and cheered.

The Nobel Prize she had accepted the previous day had been to honour her husband. This demonstration by the great crowd of Swedish students was to honour her.

26

THE SHADOW M.P.

Clementine Churchill's main career in life was to give
the greatest statesman of our age the stability without
which his finest qualities might never have come to fruition,
but, had she wished, she could have been an M.P. in her
own right. She had the ability, the experience, and the right
sense of leadership for it.

She was, in fact, a diplomat, a statesman without office,
without public recognition, and there were many significant
moments when her influence and opinion were urgently
sought by other statesmen.

Ending the Cold War with Russia increasingly absorbed
Winston's thoughts in 1953, and his obsession with this
subject became greater after Stalin's death. Impatient with
British and American opposition to his idea for direct talks
with the new Soviet leaders, he angrily made the issue one
of confidence, warning his Cabinet that if they vetoed him
visiting Moscow, it would mean their losing his Premiership.

But his wasn't the only Cabinet resignation threat. Two
Ministers who disagreed with him, also said they would
quit. In desperation, Harold Macmillan went to Clementine. He told her the Cabinet was about to fall apart on the
issue, unless she could persuade Winston to be patient and
allow time for deeper, more cautious preliminary soundings
of the new Kremlin clique.

She promised to talk to Winston and counsel him to hold
his hand awhile. But only days later, events overtook the
crisis when the Russians themselves requested a meeting,
not of Churchill and Malenkov, but of 32 powers to discuss
a European Security Plan.

'Foreign Secretaries of the World unite; you have nothing
to lose but your jobs,' commented Winston.

Clementine, the unofficial politician, once defined the
duties of an M.P. thus: 'First is to do what in his faithful
and disinterested judgement he believes right and necessary

for the honour and safety of our beloved country. The second duty is to his constituents, of whom he is the representative but not the delegate. It is only in the third place that a man's duty to the party organization or programme takes rank. There is no doubt of the order in which they stand in any healthy manifestation of democracy.

'Latitude and tolerance ought to be allowed to members of a party. Leaders should prove their capacity to cope in the House of Commons, and on the platform, with personal opponents, however misguided or ambitious they might happen to be.'

Every M.P., she told her election workers at Woodford, must use Parliament as the place where 'true statements can be brought before the people'. She believed it useless to send members to the House of Commons just to say the popular things of the moment, merely endeavouring to give satisfaction to the Government whips by cheering loudly every Ministerial platitude, and walking through the lobbies oblivious to the criticisms they hear.

Like Winston, she maintained: 'People talk about our Parliamentary institutions and Parliamentary democracy. If these are to survive, it will not be because the constituencies return tame, docile, subservient members and try to stamp out every form of independent judgement.'

And 'Winston,' she said, 'considered that in politics, if you have something good to give, give a little at a time, but, if you have something bad to get rid of, give it altogether and brace the recipient to receive it.'

When Winston took over at Woodford she was with him, working very hard, constantly beside him when he spoke, and herself often addressing meetings in all parts of the constituency.

Winston became Member for Woodford when his old constituency, the Epping division of Essex, was split in 1945 into two divisions.

Said Mr. Rowland Arnison, when he was Chairman of the Woodford Conservative Association: 'It is wrong to assume that Sir Winston's eminence as a world statesman made his parliamentary election automatic. We never took his victory for granted. That is why his wife's work during election time was a tower of strength to her husband—as at all other times.

'No man knew more about fighting an election than Winston, for there was no man living who had been a candidate more often. Since he first stood for Oldham in a by-election in 1899 and was defeated, he fought every general election and several by-elections.

'His wife was of tremendous importance to him as a candidate. Though as President of the Woodford Conservative Association she naturally took a close interest in all constituency matters, her most important role was at election time when she played a personal part in every phase of the campaign.

'Whenever Winston travelled the country to speak in support of other candidates, during his absence on these tours, his wife held the fort here.

'Many of our divisional meetings ended with a call of "Three cheers for Churchill!" Whereupon he would come forward and, with his broadest smile, call for another three —for his wife.'

In any election campaign Winston was a firm believer in a thorough house-to-house canvass. Once satisfied that the organization was running smoothly, he left details of the subsequent stages of the campaign to Clementine and her efficient team of workers.

During campaigns he and Clementine toured together in an open car from which he could address meetings. On polling day they were invariably excited and restless, even though canvass returns predicted a substantial majority.

After the election Winston and Clementine personally answered the thousands of letter which they had received during the campaign from well-wishers; and, in particular, their letters of thanks to the campaign workers were far from mere formal acknowledgements of services rendered.

Some Woodford Tories referred affectionately to Clementine as 'Our Shadow M.P.' This implied no lack of loyalty to Winston. It was an acknowledgement of the immense amount of work she put into the constituency.

Clementine earned her honourable title of 'Shadow M.P.' because, in order to spare Winston's strength, she shouldered most of the constituency duties, particularly on the important social side, which would be carried normally by the sitting Member.

Clementine became expert at protecting him from much

misplaced enthusiasm. Unobtrusively but very firmly, she managed always to be between Winston and the thrusting well-wisher. Says one who has watched her in action: 'She seemed to flutter in front of him. You might say she bore the brunt of the attack to see that he wasn't surrounded.'

Although President of the Woodford Conservative Association since 1945, Clementine had no personal political ambitions.

When, in 1952, Winston suffered his first stroke, there was considerable concern in the constituency as to whether he would be able to carry on as its Member.

'It was quite on the cards at that time,' Colonel Barlow Wheeler, their constituency agent, admitted, 'that Lady Churchill might have been asked to stand in his place, but I don't think she would have done so. She was never a political figure; yet over the years I have noticed that she had vast knowledge and was a biting political speaker.

'She wasn't merely an echo of her husband. She knew her stuff very well indeed. She had a strong will, and a very strong grasp of situations and of people. Her audiences were ever conscious that they wouldn't get very far by heckling her. She had superb command, and reacted swiftly to attack.

'In any audience there is always somebody who is a bit of a nuisance, but it was remarkable how she could "freeze" such people. The heckler suddenly realized that it was no use going on with the argument he thought he was going to enjoy. She could be positively icy; but more generally, was known and loved for her warmth and sympathy.'

Before going into the constituency to deal with any particular problem, Clementine made sure she was properly briefed. Her research was methodical, meticulous. When, by telephone, she had acquired all the necessary background, she composed her speech. When she had polished it to her own satisfaction, she often telephoned Colonel Barlow Wheeler, read it over to him, and asked: 'Now, is there anything in that which is going to offend anybody?' She took tremendous care.

When Winston had a second stroke at the age of seventy-eight, she realized she would have to carry more of his political responsibilities. He was the last of the aged giants, but you can only stay at the top of the greasy political pole as long as you are physically strong and mentally vigorous.

For fourteen months, the issue that dominated the Government of the time was When Would The Old Man Go?

The Cabinet wanted him out because he was too old. Clementine, and his friends, advised him to let go, but his prestige was so great that they could not bring themselves to insist on it. And, occasionally, he could still spark on all cylinders.

Nobody is ever again likely to stay in power long enough to achieve such eminence.

As long as the ailing Winston wanted to keep hold of the political reins, Clementine knew she would have to take more of the strain.

At election time she would virtually assume the role of commander-in-chief of the campaign. During the crucial election of 1955 she made three tours of the entire constituency, visiting committee rooms, conferring with the Association executives, cheering on the voluntary helpers, making each one feel that it was on him or her alone that success depended. Her unfailing good humour, her apparently inexhaustible energy, her genius for being in the right spot at the right time, inspired her little army much as Monty inspired his Desert Rats. And when Winston came down to address a meeting of his supporters, she would always be on the platform.

Always eagerly awaited by the Woodford Conservatives were Clementine's invitations to visit Chartwell.

Said Mrs. Doris Moss, the present Chairman of the Woodford Conservatives, who made several of the excursions: 'She was very clever about it. Unobtrusively, she kept everybody moving so that people never clustered about him and got in his way. Before you could say "nines", everybody had shaken hands with him and been led smartly away without realizing it to another part of the grounds to see the flowers. Then Winston could toddle off and do whatever he liked without worrying about the visitors at all.'

Colonel Barlow Wheeler has vivid memories of one of his first meetings with the Churchills. He had just been selected as Woodford's Conservative Party agent, but his appointment was subject to Winston's personal approval. Accordingly, with the chairman of the Association and a few other local notabilities, he was invited to lunch at No. 10 Downing Street.

Winston was at a Cabinet meeting, so Clementine received her guests in the drawing-room. After they had drunk a glass of sherry, she said: 'I don't think there's any point in waiting for my husband. I don't know how long he's going to be. It might be another hour or it might be five minutes.' And in they went to lunch—about eight people in all, sitting at a round table. Clementine kept the conversation general.

'Then,' the Colonel remembers, 'Winston came in, looking as black as thunder. I suppose he hadn't made his mind up about some situation or other. He just sort of grunted: "Good afternoon", sat down, and got on with his soup. I had been placed on his left.

'After a while, his face cleared. Obviously he had made a decision about his problem and dismissed it from his mind. He began to take an interest in the luncheon party, and said a few words to my companion (he knew them all except me). Then he turned right round—he does not usually bend his neck—and looking straight at me, demanded: "Who are *you*?" It shook me to the core.

'I said nervously: "My name is Barlow Wheeler."

' "Well, what are you doing here?"

'I was terrified. After all, he was the Prime Minister and my potential boss. I thought: "Oh! My God. This is frightful."

'Lady Churchill intervened at once. "Don't be rude, Winston!" she said.

'He looked at her impishly. "I thought it was a very frank question," he retorted.

'I summoned enough nerve to explain, and after that everything was all right. He said he was very glad to see me, and by the time we returned to the drawing-room I knew I need not worry about my appointment.'

The Colonel is inclined to agree that he was asked not only a frank but a fair question.

There was to be another slightly embarrassing moment for Colonel Barlow Wheeler when he was invited to a cocktail party at No. 10, to meet some newly elected Tory members.

He recalled: 'My wife and I were looking at one of the

pictures when Churchill came up, shook hands, and said "Good evening." He stared, puzzled, and then inquired: "It's Barlow Wheeler, isn't it?" I said "Yes," and he went away.

'About ten minutes later, walking into another room, he found us looking at another picture. Again he shook hands, stared at me, and said: "Barlow Wheeler, isn't it?" Once more I agreed.

'A quarter of an hour went by. We were examining a piece of sculpture depicting Winston painting at Marrakesh when, behind my back, I heard the familiar, gruff "Good evening". I turned, and there he was, with hand outstretched. But just as I was about to take it, he grinned and said: "Oh, no! You're not going to catch me again."

'He never made a similar mistake. If he saw me at even the most crowded affair, he would come across the room to chat with me.

'He was delighted to recognize anybody. I think he tended to look at perfect strangers with an uneasy feeling that he *ought* to recognize them. I suppose it happens to most men of his eminence, meeting so many people every day.'

Here, again, Clementine was a great help to Winston. At every function she remained on the alert. Suddenly she would whisper something to him, and he'd turn and beam at a guest he had failed to notice. Nobody had a chance to feel slighted or overlooked with Clementine around.

Still another memorable evening for his agent came during the 1955 election. There were some accounts which had to be signed, and the Colonel rang Winston to say that he would bring them to London.

'I arrived at Hyde Park Gate at about half past six,' he said, 'and told my wife, who had come with me for the drive: "I'll just nip in and get these things signed; then we'll have a spot of dinner somewhere."

'Sir Winston, wearing a red velvet siren suit, received me in the upstairs drawing-room. "Have a drink?" he asked.

' "I'd like to, very much," I said, "but my wife is waiting outside in the car."

' "Well, don't leave her out there," he said. "Bring her in." He stumped through the hall, opened the door, and said: "Come in, my dear. Come in."

'We had a glass of sherry, and then he suggested: "Why don't you stay for dinner? Wait a minute, though. I'd better check up with the cook."

. 'With that he put his head through the door and gave a sort of bellow. There were hurried footsteps outside, a few muttered words; then Churchill said: "Oh! *He* won't know, anyhow. I'll see to it myself." He stumped down to the kitchen and returned with the report that the cook could make the meal stretch to two more people. The only other guest expected was their daughter, Diana.

'At this point Lady Churchill, who had been dressing, came into the room, and Sir Winston told her proudly: "I've fixed it. They're staying to dinner. The cook says he has enough."

'"That's very nice," said Lady Churchill. "I'm glad to hear that." But as he went off to attend to some other matter, she sighed and told us: "I *do* wish he'd leave it to me, you know. I do it so much better."

'We sat down to dinner, not in the dining-room but in a tiny room at the front of the house. The butler handed round the carrots in a saucepan, and Sir Winston growled: "Is that the best you can do?"

'"Yes, sir," the butler replied. "We haven't got the crockery out yet."

'And Lady Churchill cut in: "Don't interfere, Winston. You're only making things worse."

'They had only moved into Hyde Park Gate a couple of days previously, and the place was still at sixes and sevens. It was all delightful—just like having a family picnic.'

Conversation during dinner naturally turned to the coming election, and Winston asked: 'Do you think I could be unopposed?'

'No,' the Colonel replied. 'The Socialist will stand. He is only a youngster, and it will be rather an honour to be able to say he stood against Winston Churchill.'

'Well, it's a bit of a waste of time,' Winston commented.

'Of course,' their guest agreed. 'But casting your mind back to the age of twenty-seven or twenty-eight, given the chance of opposing the Prime Minister at the time, wouldn't you have taken it?'

'It never arose,' Winston said. 'I took good care to be on the same side as the Prime Minister!'

The house at Hyde Park Gate was the repository of John Napper's little-known portrait of Clementine. It was presented to Winston at a meeting of his constituents in the Girls' County High School at Woodford to mark his eightieth birthday. The painting depicts Clementine dressed in a lavender lace evening gown, with a triple row of pearls about her neck. Those who have seen it say it is a delightful likeness.

Let Colonel Barlow Wheeler recall the presentation in his inimitable fashion:

'Sir Winston was not supposed to know anything about it,' he says, 'but I am darned sure he did. The meeting was public, and he made a political speech. It was at the time when the newspapers got excited because he claimed to have told Montgomery to keep the German arms carefully because he might have to reissue them to stop the Russians getting into Berlin.

'When the speech ended, the cunningly concealed portrait was turned round and presented to him.

'After thanking everybody and saying what a good likeness he thought it was, he said: "I think the only possible thing on an occasion like this is to salute the sitter as I do the portrait." And with that, he went across and kissed her in public. Everyone was delighted. They thought that was just the stuff. It was quite unaffected.'

Clementine was obviously as happy as Winston with the gift, and they inspected the portrait hand in hand.

Their genuine affection for each other impressed the Colonel. He said: 'I noticed time and again at social gatherings that if he spoke, she looked at him, taking in every word he said. And when she spoke, he looked at her, taking in every word. They could almost have been a young, newly married couple, completely absorbed in each other.'

A story of another presentation relates to Clementine's visit to Epping in 1954 to accept an eightieth birthday present from the Epping Division Conservative Association. It was a seat made of teak recovered from H.M.S. *Ajax*, which took part in the battle of the River Plate. The seat had been inscribed with a quotation from a speech which Winston made shortly after he had been elected Member for Epping in 1924.

The inscription reads: 'I have now found a resting place

in the glades of Epping Forest.'

Clementine told the Association: 'When we sit on it we shall remember you.

'In 1924 you accepted my husband as your representative and he was determined to fight for his seat and gain it on his own merits. He wanted to be accepted as he was. Later, he joined "the Old Firm".

'It is a fact that you gave him his chance to re-enter politics. From 1904 he had been in Parliament without a break and, in 1922, when he lost his Dundee seat, it was a great shock to us.

'Through everything, you in Epping have pinned your confidence on him.

'We had wonderful times in the old days. When my husband first came here, he was new and strange. He says that one of the greatest compliments that he has ever been paid was that a strong Conservative seat should accept a non-Party man. When he came here he was intending to rejoin the Conservative Party, but, before he did so, he was determined to fight the seat on his merits. When he was approached he was asked to stand as a Conservative, but he said he could not accept a gift like that.

'He was a lonely little boat floating in the political sea, and it was only some time after he won his seat that he rejoined the old firm.'

The wooden garden seat now has its own resting place in the peaceful glades of Chartwell.

27

HAPPY BIRTHDAY!

THE great, historic Westminster Hall was a scene of bustling preparation. Chairs were being set out, flowers arranged, carpets unrolled, for the following morning Winston was to receive gifts from, and the acclaim of, both Houses of Parliament on his eightieth birthday.

Westminster Hall is a chilly place, so a thoughtful Ministry of Works official ordered electric pads to be fitted to the backs of the chairs to be occupied by Winston and Clementine.

There were to be two birthday cakes weighing ninety pounds each before icing—one for cutting after the ceremony in the hall, the other for the private luncheon party to be held at Downing Street. Iced in pale amber, the first cake had eight giant candles, and coloured badges depicting milestones in the Prime Minister's career—Harrow, Sandhurst, the Order of the Garter, the Nobel Prize medal, the crest of Bristol University, and the Churchill racing stable colours of pink and brown with a jockey cap.

The cake also carried a picture of St. Margaret's, Westminster, and a wreath of orange blossom.

In words of gold set in a circle was the phrase, adapted from one of Winston's famous war-time quotations: 'A thousand years hence free people will say this was our finest man.'

On the eve of the celebration Clementine went along to a special exhibition of manuscripts and books being held in honour of his birthday, and came home with her personal present for him—a large and heavy volume, *Divi Britannici*, published in 1675, and written by another Sir Winston Churchill—the fervent seventeenth-century Royalist. When someone expressed the opinion that it was a very dull book, Clementine punning the old Latin pronunciation commented: 'I can't wait to dive into it.'

She hurried back to Downing Street from the exhibition to complete arrangements. They were giving a dinner for

Members of the Government and the House of Commons, together with the Speaker of the House and two Back Benchers chosen for the honour of moving and seconding the address in reply to the Queen's speech at the following morning's opening of the new Parliamentary session.

Even with five absentees, over seventy sat down to dinner with Winston and Clementine that evening.

In the morning, the sun streamed through the windows of the ancient Westminster Hall on to the 2,500 people gathered to honour him as well as the woman at his side.

He wore morning dress, and Clementine a fur coat and green feather hat.

As they were received at the St. Stephen's entrance, a bouquet of orchids was presented to her, then to shouts of 'Happy Birthday!' they entered the hall.

To slow drum-beats they walked forward to receive the welcome of the reception committee of M.P.s and their wives. Winston and Clementine shook hands with each one of them.

The portrait of himself painted by Graham Sutherland, and a commemorative book of the occasion signed by nearly every M.P., were presented.

When the ceremonies were over, they returned to Downing Street for her family-only birthday lunch. The birthday cake at this party weighed ninety pounds before being iced, and measured a yard across—three inches less than the door of No. 10.

Sugared in pink and white with white roses raised above the pink, it also had a round centre posy with the quotation: 'He is a man, take him for all in all, we shall not look upon his like again '

This cake had eighty candles.

Each year Winston's cake was Clementine's secret, shared only with the staff of the bakery which made it. Every year the design, decided by Clementine, remained a last-minute surprise.

Clementine's own birthday cakes stayed secret from her too. One year, to depict her interest in gardening and croquet, the top of her cake was a representation of a green lawn, with croquet hoops and mallets. And, within a border of flowers, was the verse:

You stand mayhap in the shadow of the man.
Who with your undoubted help our history has made.
You stand demurely and becomingly
And dignify that very shade.

April 1955 brought Clementine's seventieth birthday. She had just recovered from a severe neuritis attack, but was back in top form, busily completing the preparations for her celebration.

It was to be a small dinner party for the family at No. 10, to be followed by an evening for friends.

Her birthday cake arrived from Soho; it was a thirty-pound fruit cake, and again because of her love of gardens, the top had been fashioned into a garden of grass with flowers made of icing, and a big chocolate Easter egg in the centre. The baker had taken the idea of this touch from the continental custom of hiding Easter eggs in the garden for the children to find.

Around the sides of the cake and on its platform were four more Easter eggs, representing one for each of their children. There were also nine smaller eggs for her grandchildren, and, to complete the family scene, a sugar cigar cut into a fireside slipper.

It was a wonderful evening, and, although there was a houseful of politicians in the premier political home of the country, there was no talk of politics, yet there was one unspoken political question uppermost in the mind of every one of the guests that night.

For days, newspapers throughout the world had been speculating—'Will he, or won't he?'—in a great guessing game about Winston's possible retirement. There had been no hint from him, yet everywhere people were preparing themselves for the event.

M.P.s were even making unprecedented applications for tickets for the public galleries of the House of Commons for the following Tuesday, believing it to be the day of his final appearance in Parliament as Prime Minister.

Asked on one occasion whether he would give an assurance that he was not on a slippery slope to 'another place', he replied: 'provided the term "another place" is used in a strictly Parliamentary sense, I will gladly give the assurance required.' Beyond that he would not go. The secret remained secret from even their closest friends.

Two months earlier she and Winston had made one of their rare visits to a House of Commons evening reception. She seldom attended such occasions.

As they walked that night through the corridors of the House, they met Sir Tom O'Brien and stopped to speak to him. Rumours of Winston's retirement were strong even then, and Sir Tom said:

'Well, Prime Minister, how long are we to address you as Prime Minister?'

'I'll answer that—later on,' Clementine replied.

'And she wasn't, of course, referring to later that evening,' said Sir Tom.

By the first week-end in April 1955 the rumours were making world headlines, and expectant crowds started to watch in Downing Street—waiting tensely for something to happen.

People filled the length of Downing Street pavement, even stretching into Whitehall itself. Among them could be heard speculation and discussion of the retirement reports with a clear reluctance to believe them.

On Monday 4 April, a little before eight o'clock, the Foreign Office floodlights were switched on, transforming the frontage of No. 10 into a theatrical setting. The stage was set for an evening without precedence in Downing Street. The Queen was coming to honour a Prime Minister and his lady and be their guest at dinner.

Other guests were to include members of the Churchill family, and past and present statesmen associated intimately with Winston and Clementine's lives and achievements.

First to arrive were Captain Christopher Soames, M.P., the Prime Minister's Parliamentary Private Secretary and son-in-law, with their daughter Mary. By this time the crowd had swelled to about 2,000.

A long black limousine glided to a halt outside and from it stepped Sir Anthony and Lady Eden, to be greeted with applause and cheers.

Just before 8.30 the door opened, and two figures emerged almost on to the pavement. Clementine looked magnificent and regal in a white evening gown; Winston wore Court dress, and both of them were resplendent in the brilliant sashes of Royal Orders. This was the moment for which everyone had been waiting. Their welcome was affectionate and unrestrained. Within seconds the Royal car arrived.

The Queen had come with the Duke of Edinburgh, and an excited crowd watched as Her Majesty, in silver-beaded white crinoline dress, and the Duke, in Court dress, stepped from their car to be received by their host and hostess.

As the Queen, wearing a glittering tiara and drop pearl ear-rings, alighted, Winston and Clementine stepped forward.

Clementine was also wearing a tiara and drop pearl ear-rings.

Winston held the Queen's hand an instant, and bowed low over it, silent, and clearly moved. The Queen then turned to Clementine.

In a moment, the pavement reception was over and the door of No. 10 closed behind its host and hostess and their distinguished guests.

It started to rain, but the crowd remained.

The dinner, of which Clementine had supervised every detail, was held in No. 10's State dining-room on the first floor. She had arranged pink carnations in silver bowls in the oak-panelled room, and spring flowers massed along the approaches to it—she had personally chosen some of the flowers she had nursed herself at Chartwell.

Guests included forty-six statesmen and their wives, as well as distinguished officials and their wives. The evening somehow had the atmosphere of a farewell party for close political friends of past years, as well as Winston's fighting team represented by the Earl and Countess Alexander of Tunis, and Field-Marshal Viscount Montgomery of Alamein.

There was also one special guest. Mrs. Neville Chamberlain, widow of the last of the five Prime Ministers under whom Winston had held office, had been invited by Clementine.

In proposing the health of Her Majesty and the Duke of Edinburgh, Winston proclaimed: 'I have the honour of proposing a toast which I used to enjoy drinking during the years when I was a cavalry subaltern in the reign of Your Majesty's great-great-grandmother, Queen Victoria.'

The Queen rose and said she wished to do something which probably few of her predecessors had had an opportunity of doing, and that was to propose the health of her Prime Minister.

At the end of the brilliant function, Winston and Clementine saw their Royal guests to the door. Winston bowed deeply: Clementine curtsied gracefully, and they stood together on the doorstep of No. 10 watching the Queen's car until it disappeared at the end of the street.

Not until the following afternoon did rumour resolve into certainty. The door of No. 10 opened to reveal Winston in black frock-coat, shiny top hat, gold-headed cane, zippered shoes, and cigar in mouth.

Behind him in the doorway was the ever-present, smiling Clementine, plainly proud of his unusually smart attire.

He waved his hat to acknowledge the cheers, signalled to a car, and got in. Clementine waved to him as it moved off almost surrounded by people eager to catch a glimpse of the great man with his jutting cigar and jaunty smile, and his lovely wife; eager to remember him as they had known him throughout the war.

For everyone there was a feeling that a chapter of British history was about to close.

At 4.22, a cluster of sightseers outside Buckingham Palace saw the Queen arrive, followed ten minutes later by Winston.

During his thirty-five-minute audience with Her Majesty, a Royal Navy helicopter, bringing the Duke of Edinburgh from Chatham dockyard, hovered down in the grounds overlooked by the room in which the audience was taking place.

At 5.12, Winston's car drove out. People outside were strangely silent, then, suddenly, they went mad. He was no longer Prime Minister, but he was still their Winston. Hundreds surged forward cheering and singing 'For he's a jolly good fellow,' and shouting 'good luck!'

When his car arrived back at Downing Street, he looked flushed and excited. He hurried from the limousine to reach Clementine waiting to meet him on the doorstep.

After giving the V sign, and taking a final public puff of his cigar, they vanished inside the shadow of the doorway.

At 5.21, the official announcement of his resignation was

issued from Buckingham Palace, and at 5.30, Ministers arrived at No. 10 for the final farewell.

The crowds still wouldn't go. Even after eleven o'clock, they stood outside calling and singing.

When, eventually, Winston and Clementine appeared at a first-floor window, they roared appreciation.

The following afternoon, they said 'Goodbye' at No. 10 to a hundred of the staff—private secretaries, typists, telephonists, cleaners, messengers, drivers, cooks, maids, Forces personnel, kitchen staff—all who had served them at No. 10 and at Chequers.

Clementine had arranged a tea party for them during Winston's last hour at No. 10.

In the first floor dining-room—the same State room in which the Queen had dined—they both received each of the guests. The servants were waited on with ham sandwiches, cakes, pink and white ice cream, and laughed at the jokes in Winston's speech in which he also thanked them for the service and loyalty they had given both him and Clementine.

Then came the departure. Two cars were drawn up at the door. In a cage on the floor of the first car was Winston's pet budgerigar, Toby, while his poodle, Rufus, sat alone on the front seat of the second car. In the hall, their office staffs lined up, and as they moved towards the front door, the whole staff began to sing, cheer, and applaud. The cheers were taken up by the crowd of a thousand outside as the door opened.

Clementine didn't join Winston in the car, nor did she come out, as she usually did, to see him off. She had to remain another day in their house of memories to attend to many things and prepare No. 10 to receive its new master and mistress—Sir Anthony and Lady Eden. Winston drove alone to Chartwell.

At Chartwell the sun burst through the skies as his car hurried through the lanes, and the sadness of his leaving Downing Street gave way to the simple warmth of a country homecoming.

To the little group of thirty people, most of whom had waited from noon to greet him, he laughed and shouted: 'Come in the grounds, all of you, and see my goldfish.'

Asked whether he had any last message as Prime Minister, he smiled, hesitated, then said: 'Yes—it is always nice to come home.'

Weeks later, he made it publicly plain that he hadn't been 'pushed out'.

'I gave up my office because I thought it was my duty. Whatever one's feelings, one must not think only of one's self, especially after a long life such as I have lived.

'I thought I would go in such a way as would be right and proper for me, to leave my successor to choose for himself the moment of election and the programme for which he would be responsible.

'Don't you think it was the right thing to do? I have no doubt about it.'

When their old friend Sir Will Lawther, ex-President of the Miners' Union, asked Winston why he hadn't retired at the end of the war in all his greatness and glory, Winston replied: 'You should know, because, like me, you were born into mischief, and, like me, you believe you'll be in it to the end.'

'It was his wife who largely influenced his retirement decision,' said Sir Tom O'Brien. 'She could see that he wasn't doing the job any longer to his *own* satisfaction, and that this worried him. His hearing was affected, and he was not answering questions in Parliament properly—particularly Supplementary questions—because he couldn't quite hear what he was being asked. So she persuaded him to retire because she knew he had become physically unable to do his job in accordance with the fullness with which he himself wanted to do it. She realized that if he was allowed to become more and more dissatisfied with the manner and efficiency in which he was carrying out his duties as Prime Minister, this growing dissatisfaction with himself would have created a terrific psychological reaction both in him, and in her. She knew that if he carried on much longer in this way, he would blunt his past. It was for those considerations, rather than any feeling that he had done all he could do, that made her decide to press him to resign.'

'What will he do?' Clementine asked as his retirement began.

'Well,' suggested one of her friends, 'he will be able to paint to his heart's content; he will be able to travel; he will be presented with the freedom of a large number of towns and cities and many university degrees both here and abroad—wherever he goes he will be received with great honour.'

'Yes,' answered Clementine, 'I can see all that, but that still does not tell me what he is going to *do*.'

She need not have worried. A few months later, M.P.s crowding the entrance to the Chamber of the House of Commons, stood aside to permit a familiar figure to stride through. The man paused at the traditional Bar of the House; gave a dignified bow to the Speaker of the House, and returned the many smiles of recognition and welcome.

There was a hasty movement on the Government Front Bench below the gangway, and a first seat was vacated. Winston made for the vacated seat, lowered himself into it, and then M.P.s and people in the galleries stood as one and cheered themselves hoarse.

Winston blushed and wiped a happy tear from his eyes.

He was back in Parliament for the first time since his resignation as Prime Minister. But this was one outstanding moment in his career that Clementine missed. She had fallen down the stairs in their Hyde Park Gate home that day, and broken her left wrist.

28

ROSES, ROSES ALL THE WAY

'WHERE does the family start? It starts with a young man falling in love with a girl—no superior alternative has yet been found'—was Winston's comment on the secret of domestic bliss.

He added: 'Many things in life are settled by the two-staged method. For instance, a man is not prevented from saying "Will you marry me, darling?" because he has not got the marriage contract drawn up by the family solicitors in his pocket.... It is hard, if not impossible, to snub a beautiful woman—they remain beautiful and the rebuke recoils....'

As for what the role of women should be in the future, he asserts: 'The same, I trust, as it has been since the days of Adam and Eve....'

Closer to home was his comment on Clementine:

'She has been the companion and prop of all my life in so many ups and downs and stresses, long and hard.'

On 12 September 1958, the sun shone on the French Riviera for a golden day. Seated in the shade of the patio of Lord Beaverbrook's brownstone villa perched on the rich red hillside of Cap d'Ail, Winston sat working on a canvas, spending a little of their golden wedding-day on the pastime he loved most.

Inside the villa Clementine was opening hundreds of messages of congratulation. She wanted to open every parcel, telegram, and letter herself.

Never before had the tiny post office in the local village had such a flood of mail to handle. The little post office staff had to be augmented for the occasion from neighbouring villages. All the world wanted to wish them well. Messages and gifts continued to arrive, and by mid-afternoon they had not been counted, let alone opened.

Red roses came from the people of Cap d'Ail, and when Winston came downstairs his eight-year-old granddaughter, Arabella, welcomed him with a special greeting for the occasion by reciting most of a classical Greek poem, with a rose garden as its theme.

. Clementine and Winston listened as flaxen-haired Arabella managed without stumbling, thirty of the fifty lines of 'The Garland of Meleager'. Knowing roses had always been Clementine's favourite flower, admirers, known and unknown, sent them to her this day. Hour after hour, more and more roses were delivered.

First of the huge pile of telegrams Clementine opened, was one from the Queen and Prince Philip, and Winston and Clementine's first pleasurable duty of the morning was to send their thanks to Buckingham Palace.

There were telegrams too from Prime Minister Harold Macmillan and his Cabinet; from France's President Coty; from General de Gaulle; the King of Norway; and a special one, from Mr. and Mrs. Eisenhower, was brought by hand by the American Consul from Nice.

Randolph, who with his little daughter Arabella, were the only members of the Churchill family present, gave his parents the family's golden-wedding present. He told them their gift was to be an avenue of golden roses, and that the avenue was to be planted the following month in the grounds of Chartwell.

There were to be 146 standards and bushes in 29 varieties of gold and yellow.

And, because the avenue could not bloom until the following June, they had prepared a souvenir book giving details of the avenue and embellished with paintings of the twenty-nine roses.

Randolph presented them with the beautiful vellum book.

Together, Winston and Clementine sat turning the pages of the magnificent volume which had been produced in only five weeks. All the roses in the book had been painted by noted British artists, among them Augustus John, Cecil Beaton, Sir Matthew Smith, Paul Maze, Duncan Grant, and Mr. R. A. Butler, the Home Secreary—Winston's amateur painter 'pupil'.

The box holding the book had been embossed in gold: 'Sir Winston and Lady Churchill, 1908 to 1958', and the book itself titled: 'The Golden Rose Avenue at Chartwell'.

Randolph, Diana, Sarah, and Mary spared no effort to make the book perfection. All the script and illumination in it had been carried out by Denzil Reeves, of the Colchester College of Art, and inside, it contained a simple dedication in raised gold lettering on a page decorated by Sir Winston's artist nephew, John Spencer Churchill. The verse, by the poet Paul Jennings read: 'Once golden words transmuted leaden gloom and fired all England to a golden age; now golden roses for you two shall bloom whose golden peace turns one more private page.'

Beneath it was a water colour of a single rose on a tree with Toby, Winston's budgerigar, perched on a branch.

The inside of the cover and the front of the first page of the heavy handmade parchment-like paper with deckled edges, had been backed with green watered silk, and the pages bordered with roses tooled in gold, symbolic of the avenue to be erected at Chartwell.

A miniature Blue Garter Sash, with the initials 'W.S.C.' and the motto 'Honi soit qui mal y pense' embroidered on it—a gift from the Garter King-of-Arms, Sir George Bellew —was the bookmark.

By now the volume of gifts had grown so great that members of the staff were stacking them in the corridors of the villa. There was a chocolate cigar weighing 25 lb. from a Swedish Countess, a 5-litre bottle of cognac 119 years old, from the restaurant on the Riviera where Winston and Clementine often dined; there were pictures from many amateur painters, dozens of bottles of champagne of the best vintage from champagne companies, and a box of cigars brought to the villa by an old French tramp who had walked 1,500 kilometres to give Winston his golden-wedding gift.

The tramp, Henri Marchand, had been one of thousands of soldiers standing around when Winston arrived in France after the war.

'Suddenly there was Churchill, and he thrust one of those great cigars into my hand,' said Henri Marchand, recalling the day. 'Now I have walked all this way to give him cigars for his golden wedding. I begged the money for them.'

While the world's congratulations poured in, excitement at the villa was deliberately restrained for eighty-three-year-old Winston and seventy-three-year-old Clementine

The celebration lunch was held on the vine-covered first-floor terrace of the villa. Winston sipped a little champagne

413

and Clementine sat opposite him. Their sole guests were Randolph; Arabella; Mr. Montague-Browne, Winston's personal secretary; and two women secretaries. Clementine, who had arranged all the masses of flowers around the villa, also specially chose a celebration menu of some of Winston's best-loved dishes.

After lunch, on being told fifty photographers were waiting outside hoping to take a golden-wedding photograph, Winston and Clementine opened the gates to them.

'Come in, come in,' they called. Photographers crowded round to photograph them as they sat side by side in armchairs on the villa's sunlit terrace.

He politely refused to walk across the terrace for newsreel cameramen saying: 'No, I'm too old for that,' adding, 'Go and have a glass of champagne instead.'

Winston, Clementine, and little Arabella served the champagne. Arabella, copying her grandmother, behaved like an experienced hostess.

Winston turned a golden-wedding smile on Clementine when she put a very feminine foot down and said in French and English, to the cameramen: 'Don't come too close. I don't mind if there are fifty of you, but I don't want any close-ups. Don't forget, I'm not so young now.'

As an additional tribute, the Mayor and citizens of Cap d'Ail spent £5,000 to have the road that passes the villa where Winston and Clementine stayed so often, widened and renamed 'Avenue Winston Churchill'. Commented Winston's secretary, Mr. Anthony Montague-Browne: 'They spent a quiet and happy day, profoundly touched by the kindness shown.'

Later, on the villa's terrace, Winston and Clementine sat together in the glow of a rose-tinted sunset.

The day must have brought back memories of their fifty years—half a century unparalleled in a man's history. But their over-riding thoughts must have been for the deep and abiding love that helped each of them through.

Despite his many human public tributes to her, no one will ever know just how much she sustained him throughout the spectacular triumphs and failures of the long political career which led to the pinnacle of greatness.

Mr. John Napper, who painted her portrait, said: 'There was a greatness radiating from Lady Churchill as well as from Sir Winston. I would call it a partnership in greatness. This is a case of seeing a great man and looking at his wife who is partly the cause of it.'

Sympathetic, understanding, co-operative, encouraging, possessed of freshness and charm, 'spoiling' Winston but never allowing him to spoil their grandchildren too much. There were many times when the changing emotions and moods of her husband made her feel like counting him among her children.

An example of her motherly care of him was witnessed during the 1945 election campaign by Mrs. Doris Moss, who was then one of their Woodford constituency committee-room helpers. Said Mrs. Moss:

'They had been on a non-stop tour of committee rooms in the constituency and our place was the last stop. When they came into the room, he looked exhausted—he wasn't a young man then, and although he had remarkable powers of relaxation, he took so much out of himself. As soon as they walked in, Mrs. Churchill came over to us and said, "You know, Winston's tired. Do you think he could have a real rest for a few minutes?'

'She made him comfortable in a large easy chair; he closed his eyes, and was asleep in a few minutes—being able to go off like that was a gift he had. She went on chatting to us, keeping everything around her going in the extraordinary way she always did while, at the same time, diverting attention from him awhile.

'After about ten minutes she went over to him, and it was just like a mother waking a baby. She roused him gently and said softly—"Winston—time to go now." He opened his eyes, and the smile that passed between them was something to see.'

As Chairman of the Woodford Conservatives, Mrs. Moss presided over the last big public meeting Winston addressed.

'We were a little worried about him,' said Mrs. Moss, 'because he hadn't done any public speaking for some time, and Lady Churchill was also obviously worried lest he should let his own high standards down in some way.

'I was seated on the platform next to her, and, as he began to speak, I could see her sitting tense; tying herself in knots. Knowing her well, I was very conscious of what she

415

must have been feeling at that moment.

'He rose and moved to the high box on which he always rests his papers. He took a pair of glasses from his pocket, put them on, and Lady Churchill gasped: "Oh!—he's got the wrong glasses!—He must have put the wrong glasses in his pocket!'

'We breathlessly watched him peering through the strange glasses, then he removed them as they were obviously useless, and suddenly a great beam spread across his face.

'"I can *read without my glasses*," he announced to everyone.

'As the speech continued, I could see the knots untying, and gradually her nervous hands rested and relaxed peacefully in her lap—she could see he was going to be all right. Then, when he had finished, she leant right across the platform behind him, and, unseen to the audience he was still facing, got hold of his hand and *squeezed* it in the way that young lovers would.

'When we met again some weeks later, and I asked about his glasses, she announced with delight: "Oh, he's still not using them!"

'Invariably, she would always ask him before a speech, "Have you got your speech glasses?" and he would pat his pocket and grin.

'She would never allow anyone to talk with him when he was about to make a speech. He insisted on a period of concentration before he faced the microphone or stepped on the platform, and she made certain his concentration remained strictly uninterrupted.'

Good-humouredly, Clementine always managed to cope, always managed to inject a little discipline whenever necessary. At the Royal Garden Party at Buckingham Palace she noticed Winston reaching for one too many cream cakes. She caught his eye, and he took his hand away again.

She delighted in his successes, was downcast when things went wrong for him, but never showed her disappointment in public. Whatever happened, she, a soldier's daughter, remembered when she was 'on parade'.

Her own antidote for the poison of worry is:

'Whenever you are vaguely oppressed by you don't know what, write down all the things you can think of as possible annoyances. Once they are down on paper, you can deal with them. This one won't happen for six months ... I know the answer to this one ... this—the only real and immediate difficulty—crying for an answer—you deal with.

'You make it all manageable the moment you break it into precise and concrete issues. The one thing the human mind can't stand up against is mystery.'

Her counsel and opinions were important to him. Whenever unavoidably parted, he had longed for her to be with him. She was always at hand when he needed her in a crisis.

It had been to her that this man—this tower of strength among men—in fact turned in so many decisive moments of his life. In moments of world tragedy, and in personal political defeat, he had literally run to his Clemmie calling for her, seeking solace in her smile, and in her words.

It was to Clemmie he ran with tears streaming down his face on hearing the early morning announcement of the death of King George VI. It was to Clemmie he ran, bewildered and wounded, when his political enemies branded him 'warmonger' on the eve of the 1951 election. She alone had breathed strength and spirit into him, renewing his will to go on.

In those moments they had stood alone, but together.

Wrote *The Times*: 'He has been sustained through the ups and downs of his eventful career by great domestic happiness. In sickness and in health, in and out of office, through triumph and disaster at Chartwell, Chequers, and Downing Street, Mrs. Churchill has been his gay and understanding partner through all these exacting years.'

One morning a telegram was delivered at their Hyde Park Gate home. It came from delegates attending a great political conference in London. It offered 'greetings and thanks for your incomparable service rendered to the nation and Empire'.

It was addressed to: 'Mr. and Mrs. Churchill'.

Back came the modest answer: 'We are so glad you think our services were of use.' The reply was signed Winston and Clementine.

They had shared everything—glory and heartache, and continued to share great moments and little things like holding hands in public at a Buckingham Palace garden party.

Little things like Winston ever being proud to tell people how much he loved his Clemmie.

'When he was in hospital in 1962, following his leg accident, I had to see Lady Churchill at Hyde Park Gate,' said Mrs. Doris Moss. 'We lunched and discussed all sorts of constituency matters. I asked how Sir Winston was, and she replied:

' "Would you like to go and see him?"

'I said I would love to, but thought I'd better wait until he came home.

' "Well, I'm going this afternoon; how about coming with me?' she said.

'Sir Winston's personal assistant, Anthony Montague-Browne, was lunching with us, and suddenly there was a domestic crisis in the kitchen.

' "I'm afraid this will mean, Doris, that I will be unable to come with you to the hospital," she told me, and turning to Anthony Montague-Browne, added: "You take Doris, and I'll come along later."

'When we got to the hospital we had to wait quite a time because Sir Winston was doing his exercises, and that went on and on, and, as you know, what he wanted he usually got. Anyone who thought the famous will wasn't what it was didn't know what they were talking about. As a result of his sudden enthusiasm for exercises we had to wait about twenty minutes. Finally we went in. He looked very well—it was only a few days before he left hospital. We had been there fifteen minutes, and I thought I'd better not outstay my welcome. I was about to leave when Lady Churchill came in.

'She was visiting him twice most days, and had already seen him that morning, but you would have thought they hadn't met for years. One felt almost embarrassed being there. She had eyes for nobody else, nor he for anyone else from the moment she walked through the door. She went to him, took his hand, and never let go.

'Few people realize the terribly worrying time she had during the later years.

'I asked her one day on the telephone: "Why don't you have a holiday? You haven't had a real holiday for ages." She replied: "Oh, but I couldn't go away! You see,

Winston needs me.'

'She wouldn't go. She had to be there when she was needed. It had been the same, I know, from the beginning of their marriage.

'When she and Lady Reading spoke at a function in Woodford during the year that my husband was Mayor, they were both replendent in the colourful sashes of a Dame Grand Cross of the Order of the British Empire, and in her speech Lady Reading said: "You may have noticed that we are both wearing the same decoration. Now mine was given to me for doing what hundreds and thousands of women have done, but Lady Churchill's was given to her for what she is, and has done." '

Lady Reading, a close friend since 1931, had this to say of her:

'I have the deepest personal regard and respect for Lady Churchill, especially as I think she has been able to do what is rarely done—kept herself quietly in the background, and always been the support, rather than the somebody that's always getting limelight recognition of what she's doing.

'She has a forceful strength; she never misses a single thing; she stimulates where necessary but never interferes. In other words, she lets people get the kudos for what they're doing and gives recognition to everyone rather than ever snatching it for herself.

'I honestly think she was the ideal wife. If a wife loves a husband enough to sink herself completely in him, in what interests him, and in his work, ignoring her own advancement except through him—that is the perfect relationship of husband and wife.

'As a woman she is ideal. By saying that, I mean she is practical; wouldn't obtrude her views at awkward moments, has poise and diplomacy, and knows how to do things.

'You expect a man or woman who has had background advantages to be able to do many things, but it is another matter as to whether they manage successfully to exert to the best advantage all the different strengths, all the contributory powers that have taken years of discipline to generate. It is a question of discipline, of observing what is necessary, and tailoring yourself to do it. This, I think, Clementine Churchill has done because she has known that

419

it was a strength. After all, she has gone through all Winston's difficulties with him, gone through all the political upheavals, all the disappointments, all the elations.

'A husband with a flibbety-gibbet wife very seldom reaches the zenith. Interference in continuity of thinking, and irritation, can do an awful lot of harm—you have only got to look at a machine to see what it does, and it does a great deal more to a human being.

'Clemmie Churchill's contribution to her husband was a very great one.

'She and her husband were absolutely devoted. She automatically felt she should give him everything, and did. She also did this in the finest possible way because lots of people who give are very blatant in the giving. She has never been blatant in the giving. Her devotion to her husband showed the depth of true feeling.

'She was there when she was wanted, yet arranged to do things she had to do on her own. She has always been faithful to her friends. Those who were her friends in childhood are still her closest friends, and that is a wonderful thing to be able to say.

'She hasn't a wide circle of friends, but they are very close. It isn't a matter of loyalty, it is real friendship, and that is quite a different thing. Loyalty is something you command through discipline of your mind. Friendship is companionship—a natural thing. Her complete companionship is what I think is so wonderful in her. It's the greatest thing one can have.

'Her husband was always the most important thing in her life.

'I have been dealing with women for a very long time now, and in large, large numbers, and when I express my really deep and sincere admiration of a person, it is not a light thing. It's a considered, a balanced thing, and I think that any person who aimed to have the perfect daughter would want her to be able to behave as Clemmie Churchill behaves. You can't say any more than that. It is the height of one's admiration for her.

'For any woman—especially a good-looking woman—to be selfless is a tremendous thing. She is a very good-looking woman, and always looks right. Even when feeling ill, she always mirrored whatever was needed to back her husband.

'She didn't obliterate herself—she was simply, naturally there—where it was necessary for her to be.

'My admiration for her is so great that it knows no bounds at all. The reticence in her behaviour is the quality that everyone admires. Discipline, reticence, not unselfishness—selflessness; courage to meet every sort of adversity —and she's had plenty—this is Clemmie Churchill.'

The lasting quality of her thoughtfulness and friendship is something Sir Tom O'Brien has good reason to appreciate. He was attending an official reception connected with the War Office in 1962, when Clementine arrived escorted by Randolph.

She saw Sir Tom O'Brien looking at some paintings on the walls of great soldiers of the past. He thought she was about to speak to someone else, but she went over to him instead.

'They can wait,' she said, 'I want to talk to you. Don't think that because we don't see each other so often nowadays, and because I am no longer so much in the public eye, that I ever forget your great loyalty to Winston on that horrible New Year's Eve when he went, a sick man, to Bermuda, and you sent him that wonderful good-luck telegram. Nor do either of us forget that you were battered about because of it. We still remember that, as well as your many other kindnesses.'

She was referring to the year that Sir Tom had been President of the T.U.C., which was also the year Winston was re-elected Prime Minister for the first time after the war. He had just taken office again, Eisenhower had been elected President, Stalin was still around, and there was great agitation for Summit talks between the three former war comrades to sort out the urgent problems in Germany and elsewhere.

'Winston was going to Bermuda for a fortnight's rest, and had decided to call on Ike as well,' said Sir Tom. 'On the night of his departure from London, there was a terrible blizzard. It was shocking flying weather. Clementine was very concerned, but blizzard or not, he was going.

'The night before, I had sent him a telegram saying that he would carry the goodwill of everyone with him, and that we hoped he would be able to bring back to Britain a glimmer of light—things were bad at the time and people feared the danger of yet another war.

'One of Winston's secretaries phoned my office to say the Prime Minister was delighted with my message and asked whether I objected if he made the telegram public. I said "No." He released it to the Press. The following morning every newspaper carried it, and hell was let loose. One or two of the Communist branches started to send letters of protest to the T.U.C. I was censured, kicked upon, spat upon, my resignation was demanded, the agitation went on for months.

'As soon as Winston returned, Christopher Soames saw me at the House of Commons and asked me over to Downing Street for a drink. Both Winston and Clementine were there. She said: "I do hope you are not going to get into too much trouble because of the telegram." The trouble was only just starting then.

'I said: "Don't worry about that."

'That evening they invited me over again. We sat in his room, and he said: "I've been reading the cuttings about what these people are trying to do to you, but it doesn't matter—they're only scratches and mauls—they can't *eat* you—just a few scratches, that's all!"

'Both Winston and Clementine were genuinely worried that all the hullaballoo would do me harm, which it finally didn't, as sensible people in the trade union movement knew my telegram had solely been a gesture of goodwill. Winston and Clementine offered me true friendship during that difficult period, and their friendship remained. With them, the description "friend" wasn't just a word. It was something of deep value.'

While Winston will go down to posterity as the most dynamic and impulsive of all our Premiers, Clementine will be known as the most gracious hostess 10 Downing Street ever knew.

In the years of their marriage Clementine accustomed herself to an extraordinary way of life, but of one thing she never could complain—she could never say her husband didn't appreciate her. Winston made no secret of the fact that he had adored her from the beginning.

His dependence on her, his adoration of her had always been something to be seen. He loved to select a rosebud from one of the bushes in their golden-wedding avenue of roses at Chartwell, and personally nurse it day after day until it was beautiful enough to present to her.

Their golden wedding gave great pleasure to people all over the world. This was one occasion when a successful marriage made front-page news.

Said the *Sunday Times*:

'It has cynically been said that happy marriages are not news; it is those that have failed that make the headlines but here, to confound the cynic, is a marriage the success of which has never been in doubt which has always been news; for all the civilized world has known that for 50 long years beside the fighting, turbulent personality that has evolved into the much-loved figure of today has been the serene and strengthening companionship of his wife, comforting and supporting him in good days and in bad.

'It is a tremendous tribute to Lady Churchill that, never seeking the limelight of public life herself, though always engaged in good works, she should have so impressed herself on the public mind by her perfect share in one of the most felicitous partnerships of our time.'

Today, in the garden of Chartwell, a living and loving tribute to Winston and Clementine's golden years together stands for all to see. And, among the twenty-nine varieties of roses making up the golden avenue, is that favourite of thousands of gardeners all over Britain—'Peace'.

A sundial standing halfway down the avenue is encircled by ten standards of the magnificent rose 'Peace', a yellow rose with strong shadings of cerise-pink on the edges of the petals. Outside this circle is another one planted with twenty trees of the bright yellow fragrant rose 'Lydia'. All the famous rose-producing countries are represented, and the avenue in full bloom is a breathtaking vista of golden beauty.

On the occasion of a previous milestone in their marriage—their twenty-fifth wedding anniversary—their friend, Lady Desborough, organized the presentation of a 'signed letter' to them, and asked another of their dearest friends, Eddie Marsh, to compose the message. He wrote:

You are not among those who are happy in having no history, but from all the vicissitudes of your two distinguished lives, in which Fortune has shown you

423

both her faces, you have emerged with unshaken dignity and courage breathing united force with fixed thought and have given your countrymen an illustration of faith and happiness in marriage.'

29

WITH LOVING CARE

HER role in the last years of his life was, in many ways, her greatest contribution to his memory. It was also the most exciting.

The truth about his health had largely been kept secret from the public for many years. So many times—unknown to everyone except his family and his doctors—he had suffered temporary paralysis, and had lived in fear of a day when words might suddenly fail him in the middle of a speech.

'I might rise to speak, and no words would come, Clemmie. That would be the end,' he said. 'I'd have to pull out.'

At times his speech would slur, and his left hand and arm and left leg also become affected. His leg would drag as he walked; he was unable to walk without two people helping him, and was compelled to use a wheel-chair to propel himself about the house.

He hadn't wanted to retire, but, as he said to Clementine, 'I must do what is best for the country.'

'I don't mind dying in harness,' he added, 'but I don't think I shall, although I am not sure the effect of giving up everything all at once would be very good for me.

'Everything depends on whether I can appear in public. How I appear in public is what matters. I have nothing to gain from hanging on.'

She knew that the inevitable outcome of his remaining in public life would be an earlier death. His health could no longer bear the strain.

'I am not afraid of death,' he told her. 'At least I don't think I am. But I want to be buried like a soldier.'

'You shall be buried like a soldier,' she reassured him.

He sometimes regretted his retirement decision. 'Supposing some world event happened and I wanted to take a hand in it? I might be very sorry I'd pulled out. It might well be a course of events which I could have directed and perhaps guided the country safely through.'

But she had fought constantly to decrease his public life —the danger signals of his health were all too clear. Their friends, Lord Beaverbrook and Lord Camrose, as well as Lord Moran, had been her main allies in bringing pressure on Winston to slow down. They were afraid he would collapse in the House of Commons, or make some blunder in public when a bout of illness dulled his mind. They were anxious to safeguard his reputation.

'I know you want me to get out, Clemmie,' he said. 'I have had a good life, so I don't mind if I die.'

She was worried to distraction by his health. Whenever his speech slurred, or he was frighteningly unable to speak at all, she dreaded a further stroke. The cause of the attacks, she was informed, was the blockage of small arteries. This cut off circulation to his speech centre.

After one of these bouts he insisted on keeping a date to address a public meeting in his constituency.

'His voice was so feeble that much of his speech couldn't be heard,' said Clementine, 'and once he stumbled and I was terrified he was going to break down.'

She could see he was ageing, and, guarding his reputation, wanted him to quit politics altogether before, in some off-colour moment, he damaged his magnificent image. She watched, helplessly, the increasing paralysis of his faculties.

'When he is not well, he would begin a sentence, then forget what he wanted to say,' she explained.

She was his greatest ally in his secret battle—his fight to work on in some way for as long as he possibly could.

'I am not only thinking whether I can do anything to help,' he told her, 'not what will be the effect on me. I may still have an influence on what I care about above all else— the building of a sure and lasting peace.'

Whenever he was engulfed in terrible apathy, appearing to lose heart and the will to live or think, she strove to change his mood by prodding his mind and challenging it in some way.

Never, in his more vigorous days, when he lived and made history, did he visualize himself feeble and infirm. In the final years, he even fought Time, struggling to conquer from within himself reserves of stamina, for, as he told his Clemmie—'There is still so much to do. . . .'

She was determined not only to sustain his public image,

but to make him feel that the world, which owned him so much, wasn't casually filing him away in its folder of elder statesmen who had served their usefulness. Such brutal indifference would have killed him years ago—of a broken heart.

She saw to it that the great and the influential still came to inform him, and be informed of his opinions. He could no longer stride the political stage, but she wanted him to remain at the pivot of world events and to feel he could still light torches of thought. This was the breath of life to him.

Understanding the loneliness of advancing years, she increasingly encouraged close and cherished friends to visit frequently. They had few truly intimate friends, few acquaintances unconnected with his career, and she had restricted her social life to devote herself to him.

She arranged that their guests should be mainly old acquaintances.

'You know, Winston doesn't really like to meet new people,' she explained.

She insisted on his wearing his hearing aid constantly, and laughed appreciatively when on occasions, as if his deafness and inattention had been an act, he would raise his head and the old wit and wisdom would startlingly burst forth again almost repudiating his frailty.

Dining with their friend, Lord Beaverbrook, he suddenly asked: 'Beaverbrook—have you ever been to Moscow?'

'Of course,' a puzzled Beaverbrook answered. 'You ordered me to go there in 1941.'

'That may be. That may be,' he chuckled. 'But did you actually go there?'

Winston plainly enjoyed this piece of mischief.

When conversation focused on old age, they recalled the words of Wilfrid Scawen Blunt, their friend of early years, who once wrote: 'In youth, feeling, in manhood battle, in old age meditation, this is the perfect life.'

Said Clementine:

'Winston admitted he was grateful for having been given the chance to rest for the few years left to him, although he felt strange when finally the great affairs of state were no longer brought to him. But he always insisted that he had no regrets. "I leave my name to history," he said. "I feel that history will give me a fair reading."'

Visitors to their table still tasted illuminating, brilliant samples of Churchillian wit and wisdom, although it is true that between bouts of incredible lucidity that revived the famous fire, their host was either completely intent on his food, or not really with them at all.

Clementine would never stand any nonense from him, and always spoke her mind. At dinner one evening she criticized Volume 3 of his Memoirs. 'It is too full of minutes and memos, and is all rather dull,' she said.

Winston blushed with anger, and barked his irritation at her. The atmosphere became tense and strained.

'Now, Winston dear, you really can't talk to me that way,' she countered, and with humorous pretence at anger, threw her large dinner-napkin across the table at him. Everyone roared with laughter—Winston loudest of all— and Clementine, like the wise general she was, immediately took advantage of the move to marshal the ladies around her and sweep from the room.

'I don't argue with Winston,' she explained, 'because he so often shouts me down. If I have anything really important to say, I write a note to him.'

To make things more comfortable for their guests, and Winston, she installed a special additional hearing aid for him—she had the dining room at Hyde Park Gate wired like the House of Commons. When the system was ready for testing, she brought him into the room and spoke softly. He heard every word and was delighted with the innovation.

Lord Montgomery, who visited them as often as he could, reflected:

'I suppose that during the years after the end of the Second World War, I was as close to Winston Churchill as anybody else—possibly closer than most. When he resigned as Prime Minister and retired finally to private life, I visited him regularly: it seemed to me at that time that he needed his friends to rally round him, to help keep up his spirits in the evening of his life.

'When he became a private citizen, all the old "fire" disappeared. He became very gentle in his old age. At first it seemed to me that he found some difficulty in adjusting himself to the changed conditions. But gradually he developed a new daily routine.

'We would sit together for long periods, sometimes in his bedroom before he got up in the morning, and often in the garden in the summertime. There were occasions when I stayed up talking with him until two o'clock in the morning. One just could not go to bed—he was too interesting.

'I valued those quiet talks. His thoughts now often took him to the past, and he was more interested in talking about that than of the present.

'Few men can have been blessed with a more loving and devoted wife than Winston Churchill. Clemmie—as she is known to all her friends—is a most gifted and cultured lady, with great wisdom and a sound judgement. She watched over Winston with great care, and was always— and is—a most gracious hostess. And Winston was always the first to admit all these things about his wife.'

She had to ask the policeman on duty outside to help carry him to bed the night he fell and chipped his spine.

It was November 1960. The accident happened two weeks before his eighty-sixth birthday.

He was in great pain after the fall. Trying to reassure everyone even though she was seriously concerned, she smiled and said, 'Don't worry. But isn't it terribly sad?'

When she asked Winston how he felt he replied, 'Bloody awful,' but he said it with a grin.

Although confined to bed, he didn't want to miss his birthday celebration and was determined to go downstairs for the party. Clementine wouldn't allow it. Instead, she organized a small party in her own room.

Three months later, his recovery was complete.

Aristotle Onassis offered his yacht for a convalescent cruise.

The combination of Churchill and Onassis puzzled many. It was an unexpected friendship, but a strong one. Winston and Clementine enjoyed the company of the Greek shipping millionaire, and away-from-it-all weeks they spent aboard his yacht, *Christina*, were among their happiest. They revelled in the sunshine, the sea, good living, and scintillating conversation. There were lovely women—Maria Callas, Margot Fonteyn, Greta Garbo—and Winston still had an appreciative eye for beauty, and life. Afloat offered welcome relaxation, especially with a host who plainly showed his affection and respect for them both.

Onassis absolutely worshipped Winston and fussed around him like a doting parent.

'Winston likes to be surrounded by people petting him and doing things for him,' said Clementine.

Onassis would brush Winston's clothes if there were specks on them; would tuck blankets around him when he rested on deck, and, one evening at dinner, even fed him teaspoonfuls of caviare as if feeding a baby.

And he ordered his captain to experiment with different speeds to find the one that Winston found most comfortable—the one producing least vibration.

Winston affectionately called him 'Ari' instead of Aristotle, and Onassis was rewarded and honoured when his distinguished guest declared: 'I like living on your ship.'

Seated cross-legged on the deck, Onassis would listen for hours as Winston held forth on a variety of subjects.

Discussing the sea, Winston commented: 'I ask myself, why is it that a ship beats the waves, and they are so many, and the ship is one?

'The reason is that the ship has a purpose, and the waves have none.

'They just flock around, innumerable, tireless, but ineffective. The ship with a purpose takes us where we want to go.

'Our lives are what we choose to make them.'

On their first cruise aboard the yacht, the ship struck heavy seas in the Mediterranean. One by one the guests were seasick. Not wishing to mar her husband's fun, Clementine remained in her cabin so that he shouldn't observe how ill she felt.

Winston didn't miss a meal.

During another cruise, he rang at one o'clock in the morning for his personal valet, Fritz Schmied.

'Awaken the Captain!' he instructed. 'The engines are too noisy. I can't get to sleep.'

An explanation that the engines were not noisier than usual didn't placate him and he summoned his private secretary, Anthony Montague-Browne.

'Get me the Captain,' he demanded. 'Those blasted engines are keeping me awake.'

Montague-Browne replied: 'If you act like this we will have to break up the crews or get another captain—and that won't make the engines any quieter.'

In the morning, Clementine stepped into the situation. She explained the trouble to their host then gave Winston a talking to. She was always the only one who knew how to bring him to order. The complaint stopped.

Winston liked his own way, and on the rare occasions he failed to get it, he was testy and unhappy. But when others found it difficult or impossible to settle a problem with him, it was left to her to change his mind, for he had a disconcerting way of failing to accept objections to his own point of view—unless he wanted to.

The antics of Toby, the pet budgerigar presented to him by Christopher Soames, were a comforting diversion on some of the voyages.

Toby was a V.I.P. (Very Important Pet) in the Churchill homes, and was even permitted to strut about the dining table when they entertained guests. Toby loved pecking salt from the cruet, but this made him very thirsty and he invariably quenched the thirst with some wine from a guest's glass. Winston and Clementine were constantly having to sweep him away from the salt cruet, but whenever Toby managed to help himself he would politely say, 'Thank you, Sir Winston. Thank you.'

When they journeyed abroad, Toby went too. They were guests aboard the yacht of Aristotle Onassis, when, deciding that he needed cooling off, Toby dived into Clementine's glass of water, spilling it over the table. As he was carried off to be dried, he politely apologized: 'Sorry, Sir Winston. Sorry.'

One day Toby flew out of a hotel window at Monte Carlo and never returned.

Clementine and Winston were terribly upset. They organized a widespread search, but the budgie was never found.

'Freedom is the birthright of all God's creatures,' declared Winston sadly.

Onassis would do anything for the Churchills. He even broke his no-gambling rule to join Winston at trente-et-quarante at the Monte Carlo Casino. Gambling has never amused Onassis, who was not seen at the tables—except with the Churchills. Winston loved to gamble, and Clementine constantly worried that he would lose more money at the gaming tables than the family exchequer could stand.

Onassis learnt bezique just to be able to play with Winston. They played bezique or baccarat for hours—and Winston usually won.

They cruised the Canary Islands, the Adriatic, and the Greek isles. Margot Fonteyn and her husband, Dr. Roberto Arias, joined the vessel at Venice for one cruise.

When the *Christina* anchored off Yugoslavia, Marshal Tito and his wife boarded to pay their respects to the Churchills.

Clementine loved watching Fonteyn chattering happily to Winston about anything and everything. He insisted on staying up late every night to watch a film in the saloon, and liked Clementine on one side of him, and Margot Fonteyn on the other—and he held hands with both of them in the dark.

He even persuaded guests to join him in after-dinner sing-songs—usually devoted to melodies from his younger days, such as 'Tipperary', 'Daisy, Daisy', and 'Tarara boom-de-ay'.

'He was in splendid form,' said Margot Fonteyn.

'He didn't miss a single sightseeing trip. Even in Athens, where the heat was broiling, he spent the whole day looking at the ruins.

'He would sit soaking up the sun all day while I cooled off swimming at the side of the yacht.'

But, at times, he preferred to skip some sightseeing trips and let Clementine go off with other members of the party.

The day that she was keen to visit the ruins at Corinth, Winston and Onassis chose to stay on the beach. When she returned, they had vanished. She went looking for them and her search ended in a little bar near the beach where she discovered them drinking whisky and eating fried fish from a communal bowl.

Trouble and Winston were seldom long apart, as Clementine had good reason to know.

The telephone rang at Hyde Park Gate. The call was for Lady Churchill—from Monaco. It was the summer of 1962, and Winston was staying in a penthouse suite at the Hotel de Paris. Clementine wasn't expecting a call from him at the time. Instinctively she knew something was wrong.

It had happened at about six o'clock that morning as he got out of bed unaided. He had stumbled against a table,

432

fallen heavily to the floor, and fractured a leg.

Dr. David Roberts, the British doctor in Monaco, who had long been a friend of the family, was called in and immediately moved the patient to the Princess Grace Clinic.

Clementine was advised that an X-ray revealed the femur, or thigh-bone, to be broken. An emergency operation was necessary to set it. It was simple surgery, but Winston was eighty-seven, and the danger to an elderly person after an accident such as this is through prolonged confinement, when fluid is liable to accumulate in the lungs and cause 'hypostatic' pneumonia which doesn't respond to antibiotics.

Professor Charles Chatelin, head surgeon of the Clinic, who carried out the operation, was at Winston's bedside as he emerged from the anaesthetic. As Winston became aware of the doctors' faces around him, he strained to raise himself and roared: 'You monsters! You monsters! Leave me alone. Get out of here, all of you!'

He had suddenly realized that his left leg had been encased in plaster from the waist to ankle, and he was furious —even with his good friend Dr. Roberts. A further phone message to Hyde Park Gate advised that he was 'quite comfortable, but a bit crotchety'. His resistance was described as 'remarkable—positively Churchillian', and Clementine was even more relieved when she heard that immediately after his fall he had eaten a breakfast of bacon and eggs. He was showing his customary resistance to disaster.

The Queen and Prince Philip sent a message to her asking to be kept informed of his progress.

She decided it would be wise to bring him close to home where he could see more familiar faces, and where she could handle him in the event of his impatiently deciding to give doctors and nurses a rough time.

A room was reserved in the private wing of the Middlesex Hospital, London, and she accepted the offer and an R.A.F. aero-medical Comet.

Anxious to avoid discomfort or strain during the flight, she discussed details, including cabin pressure and flying altitude, with the R.A.F. department concerned. It was agreed that to spare him any acceleration stresses from the jet engines, gentle use should be made of engine controls when the aircraft taxied and took off, and that it fly at

28,000 ft., instead of the normal 40,000 ft. for this route. At 28,000 ft. pressure could be maintained as at 3,000 ft. inside the cabin. Cabin pressure is usually equal to over twice this height when flying at 40,000 ft. This would allow Winston to breathe more easily.

She contacted the Middlesex Hospital to check arrangements for his reception. She appreciated that the staff would do their best, but knew how much of a handful he could be, and how much comfort, food, and atmosphere could contribute to his full and speedy recovery.

The room she chose with the matron overlooked a peaceful inner garden square with birch and cherry trees. The bed was moved to enable him to look on to the goldfish flashing in the waters of an ornamental pond, and see the lawn patrolled by three important-looking pigeons. Winston would enjoy that. The room was spick and span enough to meet the demands of even the strictest regimental sergeant-major. Clementine tactfully mentioned to the hospital dietician that it would be advisable to allow him a little of his favourite foods—and drink. She knew her Winston.

She was at London Airport when he arrived in the R.A.F. Comet, and for hours after his arrival at hospital, she waited in a room close by while doctors examined him. When they declared themselves satisfied with his general condition and told her an operation would be necessary, she left. Turning to a friend, she said simply, 'He's all right.'

The operation took place soon afterwards. Steel pins were run through the fractured ends of the bone to hold them together. The hour-long operation enables a patient to get up early. She returned to the hospital as soon as the surgery was over, and remained there forty minutes. He had not yet recovered consciousness.

Regular bulletins declared he was making satisfactory progress and a smiling Clementine repeatedly told newspapermen: 'He is quite cheerful.' She told no one except the immediate family the complete truth—that he was more seriously ill than had been generally admitted.

He developed bronchitis which brought on pneumonia. The very morning pneumonia was diagnosed he was propped up in bed smoking a cigar, and refused to remove the cigar from his mouth even during a medical check-over.

A week later, he had thrombosis, and a week after that,

jaundice. When he didn't feel like it, no power—except Clementine's—could persuade him to have an injection. It was frequently left to her to convert an adamant 'no' into a reluctant 'yes'. She warned him that it was essential he get back on his feet quickly to prevent the hip and the knee stiffening, as they so easily do in old people.

'Sir Winston needed little urging—he had quite made up his mind he was going to walk again,' said Miss Margery Simpson, who was in charge of the hospital's orthopaedic unit.

Clementine visited morning and afternoon. Happily, the day came when, helped by two nurses, he walked up and down the thirty-yard corridor outside his room. The event was celebrated with champagne.

Clementine had known he was well on the way to recovery by studying his daily diet at the hospital. A man's state of health and spirits cannot usually be diagnosed by simply waving a couple of menus, but you could do this with Winston, and she smiled when she noted his menus for the previous day:

LUNCH

Asparagus Soup

Fricassée of Chicken

Coffee

Brandy

DINNER

Cream of Chicken Soup

Plain Omelette

Strawberries

Ice cream

Coffee

Brandy

Champagne

In preparation for his homecoming, she ordered alterations to their London home and reorganized several rooms on the ground floor into a complete suite for him to save him the stairs.

She arranged a bedroom, bathroom, and a room for a nurse. She had a special low-design bath installed to minimize the effort of getting in and out, as well as the risk of

435

falling. She also ordered special handles for the bath sides to assist him.

After fifty-four days in hospital, he was fit enough to go home. With Clementine walking beside him, he was borne in a legless carrying chair to an ambulance as a crowd of some two thousand people cheered 'Good old Winnie!'

When he was comfortably settled in the ambulance, she drove on ahead to greet him at the door of their home.

Thereapy continued to restore strength to his limbs. He was, as ever, interested in the details of his own state of health, but was like a mother hen whenever Clementine visibly showed the strain of his convalescence.

Almost a year later, the House of Commons, which in the circumstances could have concluded that it might never again see the great man in his familiar corner seat, was electrified by his return.

Clementine appreciatively witnessed the scene as he entered the Chamber for the first time since the accident. Until that moment, Parliamentary debate had been devoted during Question Time to whether pillar boxes should have larger slots, and the possible effect of a new communications tower on the behaviour of homing pigeons. Suddenly the Commons Chamber was enveloped by a strange atmosphere that meant one thing——

'Winston is here!'

The words inflamed the House which, though often slow to show tender emotions, behaved in unprecedented style.

As the doors swung open and, minus the expected wheelchair, he appeared with his son-in-law, Christopher Soames, supporting his left arm, and Mr. Dudley Williams, M.P., assisting on his right, the House rose almost as one man, cheering and waving Order papers as the little procession slowly proceeded to Winston's seat.

He made his way to the Bar, bowed, and moved on smiling and nodding his thanks for the tremendous welcome. He paused a moment, beamed about him, then sat down.

There is no Parliamentary order that permits a Prime Minister to break into the regular business of the House with a speech of welcome, but Prime Minister Harold Macmillan decided this was an occasion for convention-breaking.

'At the risk of being out of order'—said Mr. Macmillan,

and rose to greet 'our most distinguished member'.

The leaders of the Opposition and Liberal parties added their welcome, and Winston's face showed his delight. Parliament's love for him was equalled only by his love for it.

He beamed pleasure to all sides of the House—and so did Clementine as many of the Members below gazed up at her.

But it wasn't long before he was being written off again. Around the places known as 'political circles' and 'well-informed quarters' they were saying he was about to announce his retirement from Parliament. And, when it became known that Winston as the Member, and Clementine as the President of the Woodford Conservatives, had invited their constituency Party Executive to a surprise meeting 'for a talk and a drink' at Kensington Palace Hotel, close to their Hyde Park Gate home, speculation ran even wilder.

His constituency agent, Colonel Barlow Wheeler, admitted to Clementine: 'I don't know why the rumours have become so strong, but everybody is asking "Does he plan to announce that he will resign his seat at the next election?"'

She assured him that the topic had not engaged Winston's thoughts for a long time. He had, in fact, made up his mind to fight the next election—the twenty-second Parliamentary election of his career.

The total had never been equalled.

On the evening of 6 January 1959, Winston in evening dress, accompanied by Clementine, and their daughter Mary, arrived at the hotel to meet the local Party Executive in a private suite. In a fifteen-minute speech—one of his rare public utterances since resigning as Premier in 1955—he killed the rumours. He intended to contest the next election, whenever it came, and promised to address a large constituency meeting in April.

They kept the date with six hundred of their constituents.

'I shall do my utmost to serve you so long as my breath holds out,' Winston told them, and there were tears in his eyes as he said it. The audience serenaded him and his wife with 'For they are jolly good fellows.'

Clementine agreed with friends that at eighty-four, a man might reasonably feel the time had come to close his chapter of public service. But, she explained, in seeking re-election, Winston felt he was doing what his fellow countrymen would wish him to do.

Inevitably, a large measure of the weight of the election fell on her. Working ceaselessly with his agent, Colonel Barlow Wheeler, and the local Party Chairman, Mrs. Doris Moss, she personally supervised every aspect of the electioneering. These days, Winston tired easily, and she realized he would need all her strength, as well as his own, for the campaign.

No one expected him to undertake a house-to-house canvass at the age of eighty-four, but when it was suggested that they have an armchair election ride, both he and Clementine reacted typically. They might not be able to walk vigorously, but they could still tour by car.

Clementine saw to it that he was well protected by a warm overcoat and muffler to guard against October winds, then set off with him on their first open car tour of the campaign. Many among the waving crowds sensed they were witnessing something historic, something they were unlikely to see again.

At times, when he rose to speak, it seemed as if the strain of the battle was telling on him, and Clementine hovered around with obvious concern. But usually, after the first few moments of a speech, the familiar voice would regain strength and its old magic, and he was once more confidently re-wording prepared speeches as he went along. All the old tricks of oratory revealed their mastery again, compelling attention.

'Some Socialists look at private enterprise as a predatory tiger to be shot,' he growled. 'Others look on it as a cow to be milked. Only a handful of Socialists see private enterprise for what it really is—the strong and willing horse that pulls the whole cart along.'

Whenever he got into his stride like this, Clementine, behind him on the platform, visibly relaxed and smiled. He was in form.

Parliament reassembled and he resumed his seat, this time as the new Father of the House. The last Father of the House hadn't stood in the election.

Although Winston's record as a Member of Parliament went back to 1900, to become Father a Member must have served in the Commons without a break. Therefore only his years since he began to represent Epping in 1924, and latterly Woodford, counted.

So the commencement of this Parliament in 1961 was particularly significant for Winston and Clementine. It was to become significant for another reason. It was to be his last term as an M.P.

When Mrs. Doris Moss opened the familiar envelope that she knew had come from Hyde Park Gate, she expected to find a letter from Lady Churchill regarding some local constituency matter, but it was from Sir Winston. It read:

'I write to tell you that I shall not be able to present myself as a candidate for the next General Election.

'This is because the accident which I suffered last year has greatly decreased my mobility and it has become difficult for me to attend the House of Commons as I would wish.

'I hope that the time that will elapse before the next election will enable the association to find a candidate who will have the opportunity of becoming well known in the constituency and himself getting to know you all.

'I need not tell you with what sadness I feel constrained to take this step. I have now had the honour and privilege of sitting in the House of Commons for more than sixty years: for thirty-nine of these I have represented Epping and Woodford.

'It is against the background of the unswerving support of the people of southwest Essex that the most important phases of my political life have unfolded. I shall never forget your loyalty and kindness to my wife and myself over these momentous years.'

Winston Churchill, Member of Parliament since 1900, apart from two short breaks in his parliamentary career, had finally decided to retire. The news broke at the beginning of May 1963.

The decision had taken months to reach.

Lord Moran had warned Clementine of the great physical strain entailed by Winston's continued attendances at the House of Commons. But their wise old doctor and friend realized that although his patient would accept the significance of his advice, he would nevertheless continue to do as he pleased. The only peson to whom he would really

439

listen regarding such matters was, as always, his wife.

Too often she had witnessed great men, their powers diminished, their faculties impaired, their bodies ailing, still striving to cling to power and limelight.

She discussed the future with Winston, and together they decided the time had come for his retirement from Parliament. She was determined that he should show it was possible for a great, aged man to retire with dignity.

She knew he would be content to let his past speak for itself, and leave the stage to the men who had succeeded him in the positions of power.

He could occupy himself in retirement by painting and completing his history of the English-speaking people. Although she was aware of his sustained interest in public affairs, she felt his public appearances should become fewer. With shrewd insight, she was determined to avoid the example of other famous statesmen—Chatham and Disraeli —whose continued activity in old age simply pointed the painful contrast between the years of achievement and the years of decline.

Although his genius remained, they both felt it would be better expressed with a serenity and dignity befitting his age.

On 27 July 1964, they shared the sorrow and glory of his last attendance at the House of Commons.

Before leaving home, she carefully inspected his attire to be certain that his socks matched, that he was wearing the correct black jacket and striped trousers, and that across his waistcoat was the customary watch-chain made of large gold links. She also made certain there was plenty of white shirt-cuff showing. He liked that. He had taken to slitting the sleeves of his shirt at the top so that he could show more cuff, and she so often had to remember to warn him in no circumstances to remove his coat when he was out! He kept six shirts cut this way.

It was a sparsely attended House and could have been an ordinary Monday when, at exactly five minutes past three, the Member for Woodford appeared.

Slowly, leaning heavily on his stick, guided by Sir Rolf Dudley Williams and Captain Laurence Orr, he moved with faltering steps to the corner seat below the gangway which had been his for so many years.

There was no visible change in the mood of the House; no sudden excitement. Yet, in the Visitors' Gallery, crammed with a holiday crowd, there was a stir, and a hundred necks craned forward.

Winston was out of view to most, but visitors sensed something.

He sat slumped in his seat, head sunk into his shoulders, his face wearing the dogged expression the world knew so well. He was home in what he fondly called 'the best club in London'.

He listened to the routine parliamentary business of Question Time, occasionally turning to Captain Orr beside him for clarification of various points. Because of his deafness, Captain Orr had to answer in a loud whisper which the microphones and amplifiers broadcast around the House.

The sadness and emotion of those final moments, in the arena in which Clementine had watched him fight his most heroic battles, was somehow more profound than any words he had ever uttered in the House. But, on this day, he did not speak.

At 3.48 he rose, unaided, to his feet, but did not resist when his self-appointed guardians helped support him as he moved with an old man's jerkiness from the Chamber.

At the door, he turned, and stood for some half-minute facing the speaker. Then, with a brief last glance at the scene of his triumphs and struggles, he shuffled from the place he loved and had commanded for so long, to the wheelchair that would return him to Clementine and home.

Outside, the hands of Big Ben stood at ten to four. A moment of history.

The following day, the Commons bestowed an honour it had only previously approved one hundred and fifty years before, when it had honoured the Duke of Wellington. It unanimously assented to a formal motion recording the nation's admiration and gratitude to Winston Churchill.

The emotion of that Parliamentary day has had no equal. For forty minutes M.P.s paid tribute, but neither Winston nor Clementine was there to hear it all. His Front Bench seat was conspicuously empty. It was, in fact, the only empty seat in the House.

As the curtain descended on the greatest of all Parlia-

mentary careers, Winston and Clementine remained together at home.

Harold Macmillan, Sir Alec Douglas-Home, Harold Wilson, Jo Grimond—the leaders of the House, paid tribute.
Then Sir Thomas Moore, who, after Winston, was the
longest-serving M.P., summed up:

'The House will seem strangely empty. And I think the
country will feel sort of empty.'

Political rivals spoke movingly, in similar terms of personal affection, admiration, and awe, from the depths of
their hearts.

A car took six men from the House to Hyde Park Gate.
Out stepped Sir Alec Douglas-Home, Harold Wilson, Jo
Grimond, Selwyn Lloyd, Leader of the House, Sir Thomas
Moore, and Emanuel Shinwell—the most venerable back
benchers of the Tory and Labour parties. As they entered
No. 28, a young man stepped forward and shouted: 'Winston Churchill is a traitor! The betrayer of the British
people. The greatest war criminal unhung.' No one took
much notice, and police quietly led him away.

Clementine received the delegation and took them to
Winston. They had brought a Commons' motion printed on
vellum, expressing the admiration and gratitude of all the
nation's elected politicians. They had come to honour the
great man leaving them in his ninetieth year, and to pay
their respects to the woman who had done so much to
make that greatness possible.

She had always shown an amused awareness of her importance to him. When she spoke for him during one of his
last election campaigns, a heckler handed up a newspaper
cutting which quoted a fierce criticism of Conservative
policy made by Winston in 1908.

She glanced at it, read it aloud to the crowd then added:
'I have been married to my husband forty-one years. This
statement was made forty-two years ago—before I got control of him.'

For longer than most people knew, she had applied her
years of experience with him to the responsibilites of helping to maintain efficient Parliamentary liaison with thousands of constituents who could no longer turn to him for
active help, even though he still represented them in Parliament. She reported all her work in the constituency to him,

letting him continue to feel completely in the picture.

'Of course, his health and spirits varied, as you would expect in someone his age,' said a friend, 'but even to the day he retired from the House of Commons, he would return from the Commons and delight everyone with his commentary on the speeches and personalities. His views still had all the old fluency and pungency.

'It was a pleasure to hear that voice crackle out with something like the old sparkle.'

On one of his final visits to the Commons, an M.P. made the error of patronizing him. Thinking to be kind to the old warrior, the M.P. called out: 'And what are you going to do this evening?'

Winston slowly shifted his cigar. 'I shall go home, have dinner, then a bath, read the newspapers, and have some conversation with my wife,' he told the astonished Member. 'Not a bad programme, I think.'

'HE'S getting a bit too old for all the publicity,' Clementine concluded, and did something about it.

Gently, she instituted stricter control on his public appearances, and instructed that he was not to be bothered with affairs other than those of which she knew he would wish to be informed.

In public, when photographers were around, she would steady him, see that he was neatly attired, then step backwards and to the side to leave him alone in the limelight. And, whenever photographers asked her to stay beside him, she appeared as flattered as any young girl.

Although suffering frequently from acute attacks of lumbago, she never failed in the prodigious responsibility of caring for her aged husband. He could be the old bulldog with others, but with her he was gentle and docile. She knew how to win a smile from him and change his mood when it needed to be changed.

He now wrote little, finding it difficult to concentrate for lengthy periods.

He worked on his books, but admitted he had begun to find thinking and composing difficult.

'He got confused at times,' said Clementine.

He took to writing his name over and over on scraps of paper to check the steadiness of his hand, for his hands often seemed to become uncontrolled and he would suddenly drop his cigar or a cup.

'Lots of people want to see me, but I am not always fit to see them,' he confessed, and Clementine confided to a friend: 'He is often depressed. The days are long and dull for him. It was never like this in the past. He found a hundred things to do and was always so busy with his own plans that he had little time for reading. Now he reads a lot but doesn't really enjoy what he reads.'

Said Lord Beaverbrook: 'His moods of exultation seemed to alternate with moods of depression. One moment he would talk as if he were Prime Minister, and the next as if he were no longer anyone at all.'

Winston would point to his head and say: 'I had a busy scheming brain once, and now it's empty. Bed, cards, and work—that is my life now, and I don't mind when it stops. One can't go on for ever.'

Arrangements for his funeral were already in hand. He discussed them with Clementine and told her he had changed his mind—he didn't want to be buried at Chartwell as he had originally planned, but at Woodstock, with his father.

Sometimes he spoke of death, and once remarked: 'I look forward to dying. Sleep, endless, wonderful sleep—on a purple, velvety cushion. Every so often, I will wake up, turn over, and go to sleep again.'

On another occasion, he said: 'I have no fear of death and of judgement. When I reach the Holy Gates I am confident that St. Peter will be glad to see me. It might be said that perhaps I have sometimes eaten and drunk too well, but on balance I think I shall qualify for entry.'

He enjoyed being reminded of his own great speeches and phrases. In later years, he was frequently guilty of misquoting himself, and was delighted whenever Clementine or one of their guests corrected his misquotation. He liked his words to be remembered.

She encouraged him to exercise his memory by asking him to recite long extracts from Longfellow, Pope, or the *Decline and Fall*. His illnesses hadn't, on the whole, hurt his remarkable memory, and he enjoyed testing it.

He would often close his eyes in front of guests and go to sleep, not because he was uninterested in their discussions, but simply because he suddenly felt in need of rest. He might only sleep for a few moments, but as soon as he awoke, his interest in the conversation revived and he was obviously rejuvenated by the brief relaxation.

Whenever he dozed, Clementine made certain he remained undisturbed. Winston might be sleeping, or brooding on a problem, but, whatever the reason for closing his eyes, she knew it was not rudeness and that it was essential not to interrupt him at such times. He was often in no mood for conversation, and preferred to seek the solitude of his own thoughts though surrounded by people.

He was devoted to his grandchildren, so she saw to it that he enjoyed their company at every opportunity. They awakened his interest. He was like a little boy with them, and whenever they brought new toys to show him, he delighted in trying them out.

He still loved to play bezique with her or with friends, although he found it increasingly difficult to concentrate on the two decks of cards in the game. He disliked losing at cards, but never begrudged losses. He would either note the debts and send a cheque by the next post with a slip of paper bearing the words, 'With the compliments of Winston S. Churchill', or Clementine would settle them for him, in which case he would carefully note that too, and give her an IOU.

Painting, which had brought him so much pleasure, was now impossible. He could no longer control a brush. In later years, he seldom painted an English scene, and had taken to beginning paintings whenever abroad, then finishing them when he got home.

One of the few portraits he ever painted was one of Clementine which he decided to attempt in later years because she felt she had never been painted properly. He never fancied himself as a portrait painter, but wanted to try and do his Clemmie justice on canvas. But there were no live sittings—he worked from an old newspaper photograph of her.

'I have had a wonderful life, full of many achievements. Every ambition I've ever had has been fulfilled—save one,' he announced one day.

'Oh, dear me, what is that?' Clementine asked.

'I am not a *great* painter,' he replied.

As he could no longer indulge in his hobbies she had to occupy him with other things. She managed to keep him keenly interested in his many business ventures—television series; speech recordings; his fantastic output of books—and in feature films being prepared on his life.

He urged writer-producer Carl Foreman to hurry the film production to be based on his book *My Early Life*.

'I want to be at the premiére,' said Winston, and was irritated when informed that it was likely to take two or three years to complete.

'We mounted the Second Front quicker than that,' he

446

grumbled.

'You had more money than I have,' said Foreman.

Winston chuckled. 'Well,' he said, 'be sure you have an Englishman playing me.'

In spite of the mounting strain of looking after his creature comforts, Clementine continued with her largely unpublicized personal work, for the Y.W.C.A., world refugees, and innumerable other social welfare causes.

He was an intense hoarder of his own art work, but she persuaded him to put one of his paintings into a Sotheby's sale and donate the proceeds to world refugee work. Nor did she let him select the picture—she chose one of the best herself.

He enjoyed their small garden at Hyde Park Gate, so she saw to it that he spent much of his time there. She guarded against the unpredictable chills of London weather by arranging that he made his well-heated library his headquarters.

He hated being mollycoddled—except by her. Even in later years, he could be as pugnacious as ever. There was the afternoon at Chartwell when he insisted on staying out in the rain. 'I won't melt,' he said, and refused to move. Then, when certain he was alone, he heaved himself from the chair and slowly shuffled back to the house, soaked.

At Chartwell, when he was no longer able to walk any distance, he was pushed in his basket chair—with whisky and soda on a special table—across the lawns he loved to the lakes and fish-pond, where, with Clementine, he would throw bread to his black swans. There he was—the great hunched figure in the chair; the smell of a cigar; and the slim, silver-haired woman beside him.

He startled her one morning by announcing that he wanted to go to a theatre. This sudden interest was unlike him, and she knew his deafness would prevent him hearing the players. He nevertheless insisted he would be able to follow the play, and the unusual request worried her. She knew instinctively that he was dwelling on death again, and that he felt this would be his last visit to a theatre.

She knew he no longer found any real enjoyment in life. He could no longer read, and found it increasingly difficult to converse with anyone. He couldn't keep track of a conversation for any length of time.

'I'm waiting for death, but it won't come,' he said. 'There is nothing to do now...'

She arranged for the first day of his ninetieth year to pass quietly, with a smaller family celebration dinner party than usual, although she made certain that he had his customary giant birthday cake. She chose as the theme for the cake his honorary citizenship of the United States. Attached to the white iced sides of the cake were replicas of his honorary citizenship document and President Kennedy's proclamation when it was conferred, with the inscription on a plaque:

'Never in the fields of human endeavor has so much been owed by all mankind to one Man.'

His ninetieth birthday was a day when the world paused for nostalgia. A day when the world came to his front door to offer congratulations and gratitude.

The Queen sent greetings and a bouquet of lilies. The Pope, President Johnson, General de Gaulle, and other world leaders cabled congratulations. The not-so-great came, too. A fifty-six-year-old German cycled all the way from Nuremberg to deliver a box of cakes. A sixty-eight-year-old war-time Dutch underground leader came 'because Churchill is the greatest man in the world, and he saved my country and all Europe. I am old, too, and I walk with a stick. And I remember,' explained the Dutchman.

The day before the birthday was a Sunday. Hundreds stood in damp, dreary drizzle outside 28 Hyde Park Gate. Clementine couldn't allow their gesture to remain unanswered. Curtains were pulled back, and Winston appeared for the crowd in his dark-green velvet siren-suit. She kept out of sight, but Winston could be seen rebuking with some testiness a disembodied arm that attempted to support him. After waving for a few moments, he finally leant precariously out of the open window, and the curtains were drawn again.

The crowd shouted for more, but Clementine opened the window to announce that he would not be appearing again. 'Thank you all for coming,' she said, 'we're saving him up for tomorrow.'

That night they watched the B.B.C. TV tribute *90 Years On*, featuring Winston's favourite songs which Clementine had personally helped list for the producer. They listened to a dramatized radio version of his only novel, *Savrola*, published sixty-four years earlier, and to a radio play entitled *Loyal Servant*, about his famous ancestor, John Churchill, the first Duke of Marlborough. And they viewed a private showing in their home of a television film, *The Other World of Winston Churchill*, which studied his career as an amateur artist and was based on his book *Painting as a Pastime*.

After the birthday luncheon, Clementine welcomed Prime Minister Harold Wilson who arrived to drink Winston's health and bring birthday greetings from the Cabinet and the country. Opposition Leader Sir Alec Douglas-Home also called, and the front door didn't stay shut for more than a few minutes at a time.

When Winston awoke from his afternoon rest, she brought him more greetings, then prepared the family birthday party.

At dusk, rain fell, but the crowd outside didn't budge. Four girl music students with two flutes, a bassoon, and a clarinet, played *Happy Birthday, Land of Hope and Glory*, Harrow School songs, and the theme music from *The Valiant Years*—the television tribute to Winston.

Dinner party guests started to arrive. Randolph and his daughter Arabella; Christopher Soames and his wife Mary; Sarah, Lady Audley; Celia and Julian Sandys; Winston Churchill Junior and his wife, and others.

Winston appeared with Clementine at a window to acknowledge the crowd, the curtains were drawn, and the party began.

Winston was in great form. Randolph toasted his father, and Winston Churchill Junior toasted his grandmother.

For dinner, Clementine had chosen oysters, watercress soup, partridge, cheese, and ice cream, with of course, champagne and brandy. Winston handed cigars to all the men, and when the get-together broke up just before midnight he was still up, smoking and sipping brandy as the guests left.

The remains of the birthday cake bore a scroll with the words: 'In War—Resolution. In Defeat—Defiance. In Victory—Magnanimity. In Peace—Good Will.'

Sir David Llewellyn, who served in a post-war Winston government, added his own comment on that memorable birthday: 'Why has he not worn himself out, as have other men, with so much doing? The answer must lie in his indomitable spirit. Once a friend was bold enough to ask him when he was going to retire as Prime Minister. He replied: "I was always brought up on the principle never to leave the pub till closing time."

'But the answer to his long life is not only in himself. Certainly his wonderful wife has sustained him through all the changing fortunes of his life, in victory and defeat, in joy and despair, for better for worse, for richer for poorer, in sickness and in health.

'There is the key to his ripe old age, to his and her happiness and to their long life together.

'May God bless them as they have blessed each other and their lives have blessed us all.'

Added their friend, Sir Tom O'Brien: 'I am sure he never really wanted to end his magnificence as an old man tottering through long bouts of enforced inactivity and boredom with merely occasional good days to recall something of past brilliance and glories.

'His wife worked ceaselessly, striving to sustain his interest in living, and that was far from easy—especially with a man who was never easy to handle, to say the least, at the best of times.

'Asked his thoughts on reaching his ninety-first year, he replied, simply: "All I can say for it is that it is a great age."

'Somehow, I don't think he meant "great" in the sense with which it was always applied to him.'

To those who questioned how a man, after such an active life, could survive to the age of ninety, his wife offered a simple answer: 'If you tell Winston he ought to do something, he will not listen. But if you can convince him that it is to his advantage, he will always listen.'

Of that period, Sarah Churchill remembers:

'Apart from the physical factor of the effort it cost him to speak in the last years—and it was physical—his mind was clear. I think his increasing silence was largely because he felt that he had said all that he could say, written all he could write, done all he could do, and was only waiting with increasing patience and courtesy for the end. It must have been very hard for him.

'Sometimes when I used to sit with him in the long afternoons he would repeatedly ask the time. I would tell him.

He would sigh deeply. About an hour later he would ask again. "What is the time now?" I would tell him. "Oh Lor'," he would say. My heart would ache for him.'

Day after day, in the winter months of his last year, he sat for hours gazing blankly into the fire, and Clementine fussed around him babying him more than ever.

Added Sarah Churchill:

'In my mother he found an undiminishing star. "Mule," he would nudge me (using his private nickname for me), "at her best no one can beat her."'

His last battle began with a cold. Then, on 15 January 1965, Lord Moran announced: 'He has developed a circulatory weakness, and there has been a cerebral thrombosis.'

In chilling wind and rain people gathered quietly outside 28 Hyde Park Gate. Telegrams and flowers arrived by the thousand from the humble and the great.

At first, Clementine wanted the news of the illness kept secret. So many times in his life he had rallied and beaten a health crisis, but the world soon knew Winston was ill.

Said Randolph: 'At his age every illness must be regarded as a serious one. This is a cold, however, and so far as I know, it is nothing more.'

But the condition worsened.

Clementine called Sarah home from Rome, and consoled other members of the family as they arrived. She supervised the two nurses, greeted old friends when they called, and kept the Queen constantly informed of the situation.

Silent crowds outside often glimpsed her through the windows, and a happier throng remembered how, only a few weeks past on Winston's ninetieth birthday, she supported him at the window as he was seen for the last time in public, wearing one of his famous velvet siren-suits.

All through the wet Sunday afternoon, the crowd grew, and callers continued—Lady Audley, Miss Celia Sandys, Lady Monckton, Mrs. Sylvia Henley, Mrs. Christopher Soames, and an anonymous little girl carrying a large bunch of white flowers.

Clementine received them all, but most of the time she walked about the house in a daze.

The grandchildren came, then the Apostolic Delegate, Archbishop Cardinale, arrived at the side door with a personal message for Clementine from the Pope. The Queen and her family led the nation in special prayers.

Somewhere below consciousness, the powerful old will held on, in keeping with its reputation.

Clementine ventured for a brief drive. She walked with Mary in Hyde Park. The day was dark and dim, but Clementine had known many shining days. It seemed impossible he should die. But then his life and achievements never would. They had shared so much.

The end developed from drowsiness to deep coma, and on Sunday, 24 January, shortly after eight a.m., he died.

Randolph and his sisters were with their mother when the last bulletin was issued. A voice in the crowd outside cried: 'God bless Lady Churchill.'

A statement from the house simply asked: 'Lady Churchill requests that no flowers should be sent.'

The Queen sent a message to Hyde Park Gate: 'The news of Sir Winston's death caused inexpressible grief to me and my husband. We send our deepest sympathy to you and your family.

'The whole world is poorer by the loss of his many-sided genius, while the survival of this country and the sister nations of a Commonwealth in the face of the greatest danger that has ever threatened them will be a perpetual memorial to his leadership, his vision, and his indomitable courage.'

The Queen Mother also wrote to her, as did other members of the Royal Family.

Amid the thoughts of tribute and grief, many at 28 Hyde Park Gate recalled words Winston had broadcast to the people of defeated France in 1940:

'Good night then; sleep to gather strength for the morning. For the morning will come. Brightly will it shine on the brave and true, kindly upon all who suffer for the cause, glorious upon the tombs of heroes. Thus will shine the dawn.'

He was to be buried in the shadow of a cypress tree in the village churchyard of Bladon, a mile from Blenheim Palace, where he was born. At one time both he and Clementine had arranged to be buried at Chartwell, near their poodles, Rufus I and Rufus II, until one day, while visiting Blenheim, he decided he should finally rest with his beloved parents and brother Jack.

He was to lie in state on a catafalque in Westminster Hall—the Hall of Kings—on the Wednesday, Thursday, and Friday, and the Queen requested that he be given a State Funeral.

The Speaker took the Chair in a crowded House of Commons, with one single empty seat to which all thoughts were directed. Parliament agreed to be silent for a week in tribute to its greatest orator.

Looking down from the Gallery were Sarah and Mary.

Said the Prime Minister:

'We meet today in this moment of tribute, of spontaneous sympathy this House feels for Lady Churchill and all the members of his family; we are conscious only that the tempestuous years are over, the years of appraisal are yet to come; a moment for the heartful tribute this House, of all places, desires to pay in an atmosphere of quiet.'

Sir Alec Douglas-Home added:

'To Lady Churchill who has stood by him all his life and was with him at the end, we would like to join with the Prime Minister in sending our admiration and our affection as we stand in homage with the nation.'

As thousands queued to see him lie in state, she stood against a wall with Mary facing the catafalque bearing his coffin. People filing through didn't recognize the two bareheaded, black-coated women, who stood hands clasped, heads bowed.

The night before the funeral, she visited the Hall for the third time as the public continued to file past at the rate of over 6,000 an hour. She stayed half an hour, then, leaning heavily on the arm of her son-in-law, Christopher Soames, she walked down the side of the Hall, alongside the procession of mourners, before leaving.

Sir Alec Douglas-Home sent her a letter on behalf of the Shadow Cabinet. It said:

Dear Lady Churchill:

The Shadow Cabinet have asked me to convey to you and to your family their profoundest and warmest sympathy on your personal loss and their great grief at the loss which the nation has proclaimed in the death of Sir Winston Churchill.

They are deeply conscious of the debt which Parlia-

ment and our country owe to the greatest Englishman of our time.

His courage, his humanity and his unshakable belief in our free institutions have been an inspiration to all who work in Parliament, for whatever party.

Sir Winston's illustrious career now passes into the history he so largely created, and will remain for all time a glorious example and inspiration to all who may be called upon to defend the cause of freedom wherever it may be challenged.

Yours sincerely,
Alec Douglas-Home

As the doors of Westminster Hall closed at six o'clock in the morning on the last of the 321,360 people to pass the catafalque, crowds had already gathered in the icy dawn to await the greatest State Funeral, apart from those of monarchs, since the Duke of Wellington was buried in St. Paul's Cathedral in 1852.

As Big Ben struck a quarter to ten—before being silenced until midnight—Clementine, head bowed beneath a black veil, entered the first mourners' carriage in New Palace Yard outside Westminster Hall.

The scarlet-coated coachmen replaced their black silk hats, the chiefs of staff took up their position at the gate to lead the gun-carriage into Parliament Square, and the order to move off was given. At the head of the procession, the R.A.F. band broke into Beethoven's solemn Third Funeral March, and from St. James's Park and the Tower of London, the first of ninety rounds of gunfire—one a minute for each of Winston's ninety years—boomed across London.

Behind the gun-carriage walked the men of the Churchill family. The women and girls followed in five carriages, each drawn by two bays. The scarlet coachmen's cloaks vividly contrasted with the mourners' clothes.

It was a day of intense sorrow, yet, in many ways, it was not a sad one. How could it be when death had come only after a life so long, so rich, so full of achievement?

Winston would have revelled in the pageantry, the music, the historic magnificence of it all.

'This,' said one of Clementine's friends, 'is just how he would have loved it to be.'

454

Kings and princes, heads of State, men and women of eminence from all over the world, filled St. Paul's to pay their respects. Sunlight seemed to bathe the cathedral. The great West Door opened and the procession moved slowly up the nave. Clementine and the family followed the coffin, which was placed on a bier.

The funeral service began. The music of valiant hymns swelled and the congregation of three thousand joined in. High in the cathedral the silver trumpet of a lone bugler gleamed over the edge of the Whispering Gallery to echo the Last Post under the dome. A momentary silence followed and then a single trumpeter answered with Reveille.

Guardsmen shouldered the coffin and carried it back down the aisle, and Clementine, on the arm of Randolph, with her two daughters and her grandchildren, followed. As they reached the West Door, the bells rang in honour.

When the coffin was once more on the gun-carriage, the procession moved towards the Tower of London, to the river, and the waiting launches for the last part of the State Funeral.

The coffin was placed on a bier on the deck of a launch. With twelve of the family mourners aboard, the vessel headed upriver to the sound of pipers playing the lament, *Flowers of the Forest*, and the first boom of the nineteen-gun salute from the Tower of London sent gulls winging across the Thames.

At Waterloo Station, Clementine and her family boarded the funeral train for the last seventy-eight miles of Winston's journey home. She had asked the public to respect her wishes for this part of the funeral and ceremony to be private, in order that the solemn last moments should be quietly and properly observed. There were no television cameras, no photographers, no reporters at Bladon village churchyard.

As the committal service ended, the bearer party moved off leaving the family to walk past the grave before it was filled with soil and covered with fresh turf.

She was the last to leave the graveside. Her wreath said:

'To my darling Winston, Clemmie.'

Speaking his thoughts on the day, Sir Robert Menzies, Prime Minister of Australia said:

'On this great day, we thank him, and we thank God for him.

'There are two other things I want to say to you on a day which neither you nor I will ever willingly forget. One is that Winston Churchill was not an institution, but a man; a man of wit, and chuckling humour, and penetrating understanding, not a man who spoke to us as from the mountain tops, but one who expressed the simple and enduring feelings of ordinary men and women. It was because he was a great Englishman that he was able to speak for the English people. It was because he was a great Commonwealth statesman that he was able to warm hearts and inspire courage right round the seven seas. It was because he was a great human being that, in our darkest days, he lit the lamps of hope at many firesides and released so many from the chains of despair. There has been nobody like him in our lifetime. We must, and do, thank God for him, and strive to be worthy of his good example.

'The second thing that I will never forget is this. Winston Churchill's wife; a great and gracious lady in her own right. She has suffered an irreparable personal loss but she has proud and enduring memories. Happy memories, I venture to say. We share her sorrow, but I know that she would wish us to share with her those rich remembrances which the thought of the great man evokes.'

On September 19, 1965, as the bells rang out across the country, and the skies echoed with the thunder of R.A.F. fly-pasts to honour Battle of Britain Day, a thanksgiving service was held in Westminster Abbey at which the Queen unveiled a commemorative stone to Winston, whose words about The Few had become an immortal epitaph. At noon a Spitfire and a Hurricane flew low, saluting the grave of their war-time captain in Bladon churchyard.

Into Westminster Abbey came representatives of all the ranks of the Air Force, past colours of famous squadrons, air crews who had fought the Battle, and members of the families of many of those killed. There were the nostalgic uniforms of air-raid wardens, of the Women's Voluntary Services, and the Royal Observer Corps, while from London's East End had come a contingent of those who had borne the brunt of the blitz.

The Prime Minister, politicians, Service Chiefs, and a

456

large party of former Air Ministers joined the congregation, and beneath the pulpit sat a group of more than forty members of various branches of the Churchill family.

The entire congregation rose as Clementine came down the aisle with Randolph to join her family.

The Queen and the Duke of Edinburgh entered escorted by a squadron of the chaplains of the Services, followed by the Royal Air Force ensign accompanied by twenty officers and non-commissioned officers who had flown in the Battle. The Duke of Edinburgh read the lesson from St. Luke about the man who built a house and digged deep, and laid the foundation on a rock.

As the moment came for the Queen and the Churchill family to move in procession to the great West Door, a march of homage to Winston, composed by Sir Arthur Bliss, a massive sombre piece of music, echoed through the Abbey.

The Churchill Stone, in the middle of the aisle immediately west of the Unknown Warrior's Stone, was unveiled by the Queen. It had been covered by two Union Jacks. The grained and spotted grey-green marble inscribed 'Remember Winston Churchill', records that it was placed there according to the wishes of the Queen and Parliament, on the twenty-fifth anniversary of the Battle of Britain.

At the close of the final hymn, Clementine was presented to the Queen, while outside in the sunshine, sixteen fighter planes saluted overhead.

The following month, No. 28 Hyde Park Gate came under the auctioneer's hammer. The home had always offered gracious living at its best. Everything seemed to move with a quiet flow from the moment you entered. Clementine had organized it into two distinct houses—a private house and a business house—and the atmosphere in each was always completely different. The instant Winston had stepped from the business to the private house, he visibly relaxed. The place was, in fact, two houses—No. 27 Hyde Park Gate had been added to provide more accommodation for Winston's office staff.

The fourteen-page catalogue contained twelve photographs of the inside and outside of No. 28, but neither Winston's bedroom, nor the one in which he died, was illustrated. Clementine was adamant that these rooms should not be photographed.

She had found herself a new home—a small apartment near Hyde Park Gate—and was already busy arranging for Chartwell to be opened to the public in accordance with the terms of the agreement made in 1946, when the house was bought from Winston by a group of his friends so that it could be preserved as a memorial to him. It was handed over to the National Trust and leased back to Winston and Clementine.

She selected personal possessions she wanted retained in the place to preserve its atmosphere.

'I want to keep Chartwell looking as it did when we lived there,' she said.

Their Chartwell lease expired in March 1965, but she could still be near whenever she wished, as she had kept a cottage for herself in the area.

A few weeks before her eightieth birthday, she decided to seek sunshine and rest in Jamaica. On the day of her departure, the Prime Minister brought her a leather-bound book of the tributes to her husband made in both Houses of Parliament.

Her birthday was a day Winston never cared to miss, however great the affairs of State. Her eightieth birthday could have been a sad occasion without him at her side, but the family set out to make it a very special one for her. A celebration luncheon was arranged at the Cafe Royal, London, and the evening before, Randolph was busy until midnight completing details to ensure perfection for his mother's party.

The family gathered first in the Derby and Queensberry room of the famous cafe in which Winston had been guest of honour on so many occasions, and everyone brought a gift and flowers.

The superb menu ended with Winston's favourite dessert —strawberries and cream, and there was hock, claret, and the finest brandy—a Churchillian meal Winston himself could not have faulted.

A month later came another memorable day. Clementine was made a Life Peer.

It was the third time she had been mentioned in Honours Lists. The first was at the end of the First World War when she received a C.B.E. for her work as organizer of canteens

458

for munitions workers. In 1946 she was awarded a G.B.E. (Dame Grand Cross) of the British Empire Order, for her many Second World War activities as the Prime Minister's wife. Now she was to be a Peer in her own right and sit in the House of Lords.

Two weeks later, the London Gazette announced she had chosen her new title—Baroness Spencer-Churchill of Chartwell in the County of Kent.

She had returned to the original family name, Spencer-Churchill. Winston dropped the hyphen. She also selected two of his most devoted associates and friends as sponsors for her introduction into the Lords—Lord Ismay, his wartime Chief of Staff, and Lord Normanbrook, who had been Secretary to his Cabinet.

The Lords had seldom seen such a crush. Every gallery was full on the day she took her seat. Watching from the south-east gallery were the family: Sarah, Mary, and Randolph, with their children. On the right sat Sir Robert Menzies, Australia's Prime Minister, and his wife Dame Pattie. Gaily dressed women in stylish hats gave the galleries an Ascot look.

With poise, dignity, and grace, Clementine made it a splendid occasion. Not for her the hired second-hand robes that so many Life Peers acquire for the day. She ordered her scarlet, gold, and ermine robes from a dress designer, and her black tricorn hat had also been specially fashioned.

Every eye followed as she began the walk to the Table, and its dispatch box—the same that Winston used to hammer when he was Leader of the Opposition after the war, and the Commons was waiting for its blitzed Chamber to be rebuilt. Across her chest she wore the great gold chain of Dame Grand Cross of the British Empire.

The Lord Chancellor, in full-bottomed wig and tricorn hat, sat upon the Woolsack, and Peers on either side watched her pace slow-motion the length of the Chamber. She walked erect, without falter, to the various positions where, in accordance with custom, the House must be acknowledged with bows and the doffing of caps by the new Peer's sponsors.

She knelt to the Lord Chancellor, and when it came to the moment for taking the oath, her voice rang loud and clear:

'I, Clementine, Baroness Spencer-Churchill do swear by Almighty God that I will be faithful and bear true allegiance to Her Majesty Queen Elizabeth, her heirs and successors, according to law. So help me, God.'

There was the final handshake with the Lord Chancellor and the ceremony ended with a tremendous roar of approval from all Peers present, including Winston's war-time colleagues, Field-Marshal Viscount Montgomery, Earl Attlee, and the Marquis of Salisbury.

'I think it went off very well,' concluded the new Baroness Spencer-Churchill of Chartwell.

She was determined to be no rubber-stamp Peer and constantly made her emphatic views on a wide range of subjects very much felt. She also deeply involved herself in various aspects of the literary research for Winston's biography which Randolph was writing. In June 1968, Randolph died. His work had to go on, so Clementine personally supervised reorganization of the mammoth compilation and publication of Winston's historical papers.

She was 87 when, in 1972, she fell and broke her hip. Emergency surgery was necessary, and, for a time, her condition gave rise to considerable anxiety, but, like Winston, she was resilient to disaster. Only weeks after the accident, walking with a stick, she led 29 members of her family into a cinema for the world premiere of 'Young Winston', the film of his early life.

Sir Noel Coward greeted her. 'We are both going to cry,' he said. The film brought back so many memories and much heart searching, but she shortly afterwards experienced another kind of heart searching—over the proposed site for a statue in Parliament Square, Westminster. She objected, until Lord Eccles reminded her that the northeast corner of Parliament Square was Winston's own choice.

Lord Eccles explained to her: 'As Minister of Works I had to propose to him a site for the statue of General Smuts. I guessed he wanted the best place kept for himself, so to have a little fun, I suggested Smuts should occupy the north-east corner.

' "Oh! not there, that position should be reserved," he said, but to tease him I persisted, remarking that the corner did need something. Chuckling at the game he knew I was

460

playing, he replied: "No, No. An appropriate occasion will present itself. Now tell me where do you propose to put Smuts."'

Clementine constantly added to her personal photographic records of memorials, plaques, and other commemorative symbols and signs, including six statues of Winston in Britain; one in Brussels, as well as others at home and abroad. One, flown to America by the R.A.F., stands outside the Churchill Memorial and Library at Westminster College, Fulton, Missouri, but she was particularly delighted when a sculptured Winston was put in the company of Nelson, Wellington, Chatham and Pitt—who also preserved freedom—in London's ancient Guildhall, at the heart of the nation's world trade and commerce.

Leaning heavily on two sticks she appeared with Sir Robert Menzies for the unveiling of a bronze of Winston on the village green of Westerham, close to their beloved Chartwell and Biggin Hill fighter aerodrome, of equally immortal renown. The plinth on which the statue rests was a gift from President Tito of Yugoslavia.

Said Sir Robert:

'Winston was lucky to be married to one of the greatest women of our time. It was to her he could always turn.'

She went to Dover to see the great Churchill statue presiding over the white cliffs which he guarded against invasion, and, nearer home, unveiled a bust of him at Conservative Party headquarters in London. After the ceremony, Edward Heath, then Leader of the Opposition, confessed to her:

'In 1951, the Chief Whip suggested to Mr. Churchill in Opposition, that I should become a Whip. I shall never forget what he said to me: "It will be hard work" (and it was). "It will not be remunerative" (and it wasn't). "But so long as I am your leader, it will never go unthanked".'

Winston once remarked: 'I am a child of the House of Commons, its servant. All I am I owe to the House of Commons.' It was therefore inevitable that a bronze, belligerent, cherubic statue of him should be unveiled by his widow showing him standing at the Churchill Arch entrance to the Chamber of the Commons. After paying tribute to Winston's love of Parliament, Dr. Horace King, the Speaker of the House, added:

461

'No great man had a greater wife than had Sir Winston. Through a long life she shared the lean years—years of disaster and defeat. But she also had the supreme joy of sharing golden years.

'In welcoming Lady Spencer-Churchill on this historic day, we thank her for her own splendid services to Britain as well as for those she rendered with her husband.'

When invited to unveil the Parliament Square statue of Winston in November 1973, the Queen, declining, explained: 'For more than fifty eventful years, Lady Churchill was his deeply loved companion, and I think it would be right, therefore, for her to unveil the statue of her husband.'

There is a lesser known Churchill sculpture at Chartwell, and it is a very special one because it was done at Winston's express wish. It is of Winston and Clementine together.

Sculptor Oscar Nemon, renowned for his works of Winston at the Guildhall, the House of Commons, and Westerham, started to fashion the statuette of Clementine at Winston's request when he found him one day struggling to paint Clementine from memory. Recalled Oscar Nemon: 'He was trying to capture the amused expression he loved so much, but seemed to sense he never could portray it, so he asked me. I tried to bring out her extraordinary graciousness and elegance and combine it with that amused relaxed expression. She was always rather shy of posing, but finally consented because she knew Sir Winston wanted it so much.'

So at Chartwell, visitors can see the figurines of Winston and Clementine seated at home together—the most famous couple of the century.

During recent years, her particular interest was the Winston Churchill Memorial Trust and its award of fellowships to men and women in all parts of the Commonwealth and America.

'Winston knew of the fellowships plan and liked it very much,' said Clementine.

Fellowship winners, called 'Churchill Fellows', are chosen for qualities of character, intellect and responsible leadership, as well as for skills or academic qualifications. The travelling fellowships enable winners to further their knowledge, experience and education.

But the year 1974—centenary of Winston's birth—brought an especially busy time for Clementine. On April 1, her 89th birthday, surrounded by Government Ministers, Peers, M.P.s of all parties, and ex-colleagues and admirers of her husband, she launched her campaign to raise a pound each from a million people to support two Churchill projects—the Memorial- Trust and Churchill College, Cambridge.

The College, which he saw begin in his lifetime, was originally endowed by British industry and commerce, and is dedicated to science and technology. Clementine agreed that an Archive Centre be established there to hold all of Winston's papers, works, and personal documents, thereby creating a unique fountain source for historical research. She offered every letter and record she could find to the Archive Centre.

She always wants Churchill College to remain a living and fruitful symbol of Winston's dual nationality—citizen of the United States as well as British subject—because, as she says, 'Winston was a fervent believer in the cross-fertilization of English-speaking peoples.' To the College, through the Winston Churchill Foundation of the United States, come twenty men and women a year to further their knowledge. Seven have already won Nobel Prizes, five after studying at Churchill College.

Apart from fund raising for the Memorial Trust and the College, Clementine was also deeply occupied with the vast Churchilliana exhibition, open from May to October, 1974, in the fine rooms at London's Somerset House in the Strand. Not since the Royal Academy of Arts moved from Somerset House in 1837, have the splendid rooms the Academy used to occupy been opened to the public.

Clementine and the Churchill Centenary Committee organized the unique exhibition, and everything in it was subject to her approval. She lent many of his and her possessions; selected exhibits from Blenheim Palace; from Government departments; private collectors and donors.

One room she devoted to his ancestors, including the Duke of Marlborough, Lord Randolph Churchill, and his mother, Jenny Jerome, and Clementine permitted many of their personal possessions to be displayed for the first time.

But five of the breathtaking rooms were for Winston and his work alone. She refused to allow anything that might seem morbid. It had to be a great tribute to a great career.

Many of the smaller mementoes she rediscovered in a basement storage room at Chartwell which the family called the 'Muniment Room'. For years, the room had stayed locked. When it was re-opened, and Clementine looked again at its contents, the years came flooding back.

Inside, on tables and shelves, were long-forgotten family heirlooms and albums, personal papers, awards, including cups, tureens, medallions, batons, ceremonial trowels, daggers, cigarette boxes, cigar humidors, a silver miniature of an infantry tank which Winston sponsored in World War I, and ... an American Indian costume. Each item recalled for her a moment of history, a memory.

On what would have been his hundredth birthday, a sheaf of chrysantheums was placed on his grave at Bladon churchyard. The flowers came from the gardens at Blenheim Palace at Woodstock, where he was born.

The message on the card with the chrysanthemums read:

'From Clemmie.'

'Without Clemmie, the history of Winston Churchill, and of the world, would have been a very different story,' said Lord Ismay, one of their closest friends for many years.

'Without her restraining influence, he would have spent himself long ago. Winston was the kind of man who attracted trouble, but she didn't care—she only cared about Winston.

'His stoicism and unswerving confidence were not only due to his inherent physical qualities. Her complete confidence in him was his most important mainstay.

'Her sense of loyalty to him was unfailing.

'They both had the courage to be individual, and that can be a very lonely thing, but they lived steadfastly according to their convictions, regardless of the consequences.

'Winston took strength from Clemmie. She was a full partner in his incomparable career. His life was her career from the day she married him. She sustained and shared his glory.

'She was his right hand, and for her contribution to his greatness, the world will forever be in her debt.'

But it is appropriate that Winston's own words to his wife should sum up this book—this tribute to his darling Clementine:

It gives me so much joy when I feel that with all my shortcomings, absorption, and sunlessness, you can still find in me the pith and nourishment for which your soul seeks in this vale.

The courage and good sense you have shown all through these strange times are wonderful.

There is no doubt that it is around the family and the home that all the greatest virtues, the most dominating virtues of human society, are created, strengthened, and maintained.

What you have done for me, Clemmie, no one can measure.'

On July 17, 1915, before he left to fight in France, he wrote a letter and sealed it in an envelope marked—'To be sent to Mrs. Churchill in the event of my death.' It was many years before Clementine opened that letter. In it, Winston listed his assets at the time, including stocks, shares and insurance policies, as well as debts requiring settlement. After detailing the financial provision made for her he ended . . .

Do not grieve for me too much. Death is only an incident, and not the most important which happens to us in this state of being. On the whole, especially since I met you my darling one, I have been happy, and you have taught me how noble a woman's heart can be.

If there is anywhere else I shall be on the look out for you. Meanwhile look forward, feel free, rejoice in life, cherish the children, guard my memory. God bless you.

Goodbye
W.

BIBLIOGRAPHY

ARNOLD, GENERAL H. H.: *Global Mission* (Hutchinson)

ASQUITH, MARGOT, COUNTESS OF OXFORD AND ASQUITH:
More Memories (Cassell)

BABINGTON SMITH, CONSTANCE: *Evidence in Camera*
(Chatto & Windus)

BARRYMORE, ETHEL: *Memories* (Hulton Press)

BARUCH, BERNARD M.: *The Public Years* (Odhams)

BEAVERBROOK, LORD: *Politicians and the War* (Hutchinson)

BEVERIDGE, LORD: *Power and Influence* (Hodder & Stoughton)

BIRKENHEAD, THE EARL OF: *The Prof in Two Worlds* (Collins)

BLUNT, WILFRED SCAWEN: *My Diaries* (Martin Secker & Warburg)

BRITISH RED CROSS AND ST. JOHN: *Official War History*
(1939–47)

BROAD, LEWIS: *Winston Churchill* (Hutchinson)

BRYANT, ARTHUR: *Triumph in the West* (Collins)
The Turn of the Tide (Collins)

CHURCHILL, JOHN SPENCER: *Crowded Canvas* (Odhams)

CHURCHILL, SARAH: *A Thread In The Tapestry*
(Andre Deutsch)

CHURCHILL, WINSTON SPENCER: *My Early Life* (Odhams)
Thoughts and Adventures (Odhams)
The Second World War (Cassell)

CLARK, GENERAL MARK: *Calculated Risk* (Harrap)

COLVILLE, JOHN: *Action This Day* (Macmillan)

COOPER, LADY DIANA: *Trumpets from the Steep* (Rupert Hart-Davis)

COWLES, VIRGINIA: *Winston Churchill* (Hamish Hamilton)

CRIPPS, COLONEL THE HON. F. H.: *Life's a Gamble* (Odhams)

EDEN, GUY: *Portrait of Churchill* (Hutchinson)

EISENHOWER, DWIGHT D.: *Crusade in Europe* (Heinemann)

ELLIS, JENNIFER (edited and arranged by): *Thatched with Gold*
(Hutchinson)

ESHER, VISCOUNT: *Journals and Letters* (Ivor Nicholson & Watson)

GILBERT, MARTIN: *Winston S. Churchill, Companion Volume
III, Parts 1 & 2* (Heinemann)

GRAEBNER, WALTER: *My Dear Mr. Churchill* (Michael Joseph)

GRIGGS, G. P. (edited by): *Sailor's Soliloquy* (Hutchinson)

466

HALIFAX, THE EARL OF: *Fulness of Days* (Collins)

HASSALL, CHRISTOPHER: *Edward March* (Longmans, Green)

HOLLIS, GENERAL SIR LESLIE (with JAMES LEASOR):
War at the Top (Michael Joseph)

HORROCKS, LIEUTENANT-GENERAL SIR BRIAN: *A Full Life*
(Collins)

HYDE, H. MONTGOMERY: *Carson* (Heinemann)

ISMAY, GENERAL LORD: *Memoirs* (Heinemann)

KENNEDY, MAJOR-GENERAL SIR JOHN: *The Business of War*
(Hutchinson)

MARCHANT, SIR JAMES (edited by): *Winston Spencer Churchill:
A Tribute* (Cassell)

MARSH, SIR EDWARD: *A Number of People* (Heinemann)

MASTERMAN, C. F. G.: *Lucy Masterman* (Ivor Nicholson &
Watson)

MCGOWAN, NORMAN: *My Years with Churchill* (Souvenir Press)

MONTGOMERY OF ALAMEIN, FIELD-MARSHAL VISCOUNT: *Memoirs*
(Collins)

MOSLEY, LEONARD: *Gideon Goes to War* (Arthur Barker)

NEL, ELIZABETH: *Mr Churchill's Secretary* (Hodder &
Stoughton)

NORWICH, LORD: *Old Men Forget* (Rupert Hart-Davis)

OLIVER, VIC: *Mr. Showbusiness* (Harrap)

PAWLE, GERALD: *The War and Colonel Warden* (Harrap)

PICKERSGILL, J. W.: *The Mackenzie King Record*
(University of Toronto Press)

RIDDELL, LORD: *War Diary* (Ivor Nicholson & Watson)
More Pages from My Diary (Country Life)

ROOSEVELT, ELEANOR: *The Autobiography of Eleanor
Roosevelt* (Hutchinson)

ROOSEVELT, ELLIOT (edited by): *The Roosevelt Letters* (Vol. 3)
(Harrap)

ROSENMAN, SAMUEL I.: *Working with Roosevelt* (Harper &
Brothers)

SHERWOOD, ROBERT E.: *The White House Papers of Harry L.
Hopkins* (Eyre & Spottiswoode)

SMALLEY, GEORGE: *Anglo-American Memories* (Duckworth)

STEINBERG, ALFRED: *Mrs. R.* (Putman)

TABORI, PAUL: *Alex Korda* (Oldbourne)

THOMPSON, WALTER H.: *I Was Churchill's Shadow*
(Christopher Johnson) *Assignment Churchill* (Farrar, Straus
& Cudahy)

WEBB, BEATRICE: *Our Partnership* (Longmans, Green)

WIART, SIR A. CARTON DE: *Happy Odyssey* (Jonathan Cape)

WINANT, JOHN G.: *A Letter from Grosvenor Square*
(Hodder & Stoughton)

INDEX

472

473

474

Moran, Lord, 181, 183–4, 186, 192–3, 194, 195, 196, 198, 202, 204, 244, 261, 426, 439, 451
Morgenthau, Henry, Junior, 175
Morrison of Lambeth, Lord, 376
Moss, Mrs. Doris, 396, 415–16, 418, 438–9
Mountbatten of Burma, Admiral Lord Louis, 173, 317
Mudaljr, Sir Ramaswami, 317
Muggeridge, Malcolm, 356

Napper, John, 400, 414–15
Nemon, Oscar, 462
Nicholson, Jenny, 361
Nicholson, Sir William, 360
Nightingall, Walter, 347
Normanbrook, Lord, 459
Norwich, Viscount, *see* Cooper, Duff

O'Brien, Sir Tom, 208, 260–1, 331–2, 372, 405, 409, 421–2, 450
Oliver, Vic, 133, 236, 361, 362
Olivier, Sir Laurence, 212–13
Onassis, Aristotle, 430–2
Orr, Captain Laurence, 440
Oxford and Asquith, Countess of, *see* Asquith, Margot

Paget, Lady, 343
Pankhurst, Sylvia, 43
Pickhardt, Dr. Otto, 103
Pile, General Sir Frederick, 145–7, 158–9, 226–7, 241
Popkov, Lord Mayor, 280
Portal of Hungerford, Marshal of the R.A.F. Lord, 226, 237, 317
Pulvertaft, Lieutenant-Colonel R. J. V., R.A.M.C., 181

Queen Elizabeth, The Queen Mother, 142, 167, 172, 331, 375, 379, 452